Marion,

BECOMING A
MASTER MANAGER

A COMPETENCY
FRAMEWORK

BECOMING A MASTER MANAGER

A COMPETENCY FRAMEWORK

SECOND EDITION

Robert E. Quinn
University of Michigan

Sue R. Faerman
State University of New York at Albany

Michael P. Thompson
Brigham Young University

Michael R. McGrath
Personnel Decisions International

JOHN WILEY & SONS, INC.

New York • Chichester • Brisbane • Toronto • Singapore

Acquisitions Editor: Petra Sellers
Marketing Manager: Leslie Hines
Senior Production Editor: Jeanine Furino
Assistant Editor: Ellen Ford
Designer: Harry Nolan
Manufacturing Manager: Mark Cirillo
Illustration: Christine Rae—Wiley Canada

This book was set in Berthold Garamond by Christine Rae and printed and bound by R.R. Donnelley & Sons, Inc. The cover was printed by New England Book Components.

Recognizing the importance of preserving what has been written, it is a policy of John Wiley & Sons, Inc. to have books of enduring value published in the United States on acid-free paper, and we exert our best efforts to that end.

Library of Congress Cataloging in Publication Data:

Becoming a master manager: a competency framework / Robert E. Quinn
 . . . [et al.].—2nd ed.
     p.   cm.
     Includes bibliographical references and index.
     ISBN 0-471-00744-7 (alk. paper)
     1. Leadership. 2. Executive ability. 3. Management.
     4. Organizational behavior. I. Quinn, Robert E.
     HD57.7.B43   1996   95-36769
     658.4—dc20   CIP

L.C. Call no.   Dewey Classification No.   L.C. Card No.
ISBN: 0-471-00744-7 (pbk)

Printed in the United States of America

10   9   8   7   6   5   4   3   2   1

PREFACE

A CHANGING WORLD

When we wrote the first edition of this book, the preface talked about a "changing world." This changing world was characterized by two interrelated changes that were occurring in the late 1980s—one within the world of work, and the second within schools of management themselves. In the world of work, the emergence of the global economy was affecting organizations in both the public and private sectors, leading them to question what had previously been well-accepted approaches to organization and management. Directly related to this first change was an emerging change in the educational practices of schools of management. While the organizations that hire the graduates of management schools were beginning to raise uncomfortable questions about the education process—questioning whether management schools were really "close to the customer," whether they were providing an education that merely prepared students to be technically proficient or one that developed students to be future organizational leaders—the management schools themselves were beginning to experiment with new approaches to teaching management. There is no doubt that one of the greatest forces for change within schools of management was the AACSB-sponsored Porter and McKibbon report, *Management Education and Development: Drift or Thrust into the 21st Century?*, which called for a greater emphasis on leadership skill development in the business school curriculum.

Six years later, the world is still changing. As we complete this second edition of *Becoming a Master Manager*, the global economy continues to be one of the strongest forces pushing organizations to rethink how they do business. In addition, developments in the field of computing and telecommunications technology have also forced organizations to rethink how they do business, providing great opportunities as well as challenges. Interestingly, these changes have only increased the need to create leaders, at all levels of the organization. Some of these leaders bear the organizational title of manager; others are called team leaders; still others are members of autonomous work teams where everyone is called upon to play leadership roles. Regardless of title, more and more, organizations are calling for employees at all levels to take on responsibilities that were previously reserved only for upper-level managers, and this has in turn changed the nature of managerial work.

Within schools of management, curricula also continue to change, as do modes of delivery. More and more, schools of management are offering courses and other educational experiences that are designed to enhance students' managerial leadership capacities; and leadership is being more broadly defined, recognizing that managers need to be both technically and interpersonally competent. In addition, computing and telecommunications technology have allowed for an increasing number of courses to be conducted outside the traditional classroom setting.

It should be noted that in the late 1980s, many of these changes were seen as revolutionary. They reflected a tremendous rethinking about the very nature of university education. Faculty engaged in heated debates over whether schools of management should be concerned with job-specific relevance of course material, or should focus solely on providing broad concepts and knowledge that students could later determine how to apply to their work settings. But like many of the issues you will see discussed in this book, we do not believe that this is an either/or question. Management schools do not need to choose between job-relevancy and cognitive concepts. Rather, both can—and should—be taught together, in the same classroom wherever possible. As we indicated in the first edition, although universities have in the past been organized to inform, the new demands call for us to transform our students. To inform is to give the student additional information. To transform is to help the student discover and become a new self, to be more capable of understanding and leading change. Shifting from the values of informing to both informing and transforming is not easy, but it is necessary. Perhaps more importantly, we need to shift our thinking away from either/or approaches which have underlying assumptions that lead us to believe that we must choose between opposites, and begin to recognize the need to use paradoxical thinking to create both/and approaches.

This text is built around a framework of leadership competency, the Competing Values Model, that is grounded in such paradoxical thinking. It is a framework that forces one to think about the competing tensions and demands that are placed on managers in new ways. The model has been used now in management education and in management and executive development programs across the nation, as well as in a number of international settings, with impressive results.

OVERVIEW

Chapter 1 of the book explains the Competing Values Model. This theoretical framework integrates four contrasting perspectives on organizing. The four perspectives require managerial leaders to perform eight different managerial roles. To accomplish the productive functions that are necessary in any organization, a managerial leader must play both a director and a producer role, focusing on setting the organization's direction and encouraging productivity and efficiency. On the other hand, to accomplish the human relations functions that are necessary, a managerial leader must play both a mentor and a facilitator role, helping organizational members to grow and develop as individuals, as well as to work together in teams. Although these two sets of roles are highly contrasting, there is another set of contrasts. To accomplish the organizing or stabilizing function that is necessary in any organization, a managerial leader must play both a coordinator and a monitor role, ensuring that work flow is not unnecessarily interrupted and that people have the information they need to do their jobs. In contrast, to accomplish the adaptive function, one must play both an innovator and a broker role, suggesting changes that allow the organization to grow and change and acquire new resources. The framework clarifies the complex nature of managerial work. It also makes clear the bias that most people have for or against the values, assumptions, and theories that are associated with each of the above areas. It makes clear the need to appreciate competing values and the need to master and then to balance and blend competencies from each area. The evolution of the model is traced and developed in Chapter 1.

Chapters 2 to 9 of the book are each dedicated to one of the eight roles. Each chapter is broken into three sections, with each section dedicated to a particular competency associated with the role. In the chapter on the mentor role, for example, the three sections respectively cover understanding self and others, communicating effectively, and developing subordinates. Each section or competency is presented around a five-step learning model: Assessment, Learning, Analysis, Practice, and Application. These steps will be explained further in the first chapter.

In the first edition of this book, we presented the roles in the historical order suggested in Chapter 1. Based on feedback from colleagues, as well as our own experience, we have changed the order of the roles. While we believe that all the roles are important to effective managerial leadership, we also believe that knowing yourself and communicating effectively are two of the most basic skills one needs in order to develop as a leader. We therefore moved the mentor role, which includes these competencies, to the beginning of the book. While there are many reasons why an instructor might desire to present the roles in a different order, we see the mentor role as a good place to start. In the Instructional Guide, a number of alternatives are explored.

We have also changed a number of the competencies from the first edition of this book, as well as updated much of the material within the remaining competencies. As noted above, this is a changing world where the nature of managerial work has evolved along with changes in many organizations' external and internal environments. In the paragraphs above we call for greater use of paradoxical thinking. One example of this thinking is the notion that the framework can be simultaneously consistent and changing. That is, while the eight roles remain consistently relevant, and indeed have been shown to be relevant for managers at all levels of the organizational hierarchy, it is sometimes necessary to reevaluate which competencies are most important for managers in the current organizational environment. We have chosen these competencies based on our understanding of current trends in organizations. As with the order of the chapters, different instructors may very well see other competencies as more important and will decide to focus on different competencies within any one of the roles.

As in the first edition, we have included an integration following each set of two roles. The integration reviews the two roles in a given quadrant (perspective of organizing) in the Competing Values Model and helps the student to put the roles in the more general perspective. It helps them to see the forest for the trees and to value the trees within the forest.

The final chapter of the book returns to the overall model. It provides an integrative perspective and helps the student to consider the process of lifelong learning and development. It reminds students that becoming a master manager is a process that will continue as long as they open themselves up to new growth experiences.

This particular approach has grown out of over 15 years of research and instructional experimentation. All four authors of this text have been involved in doing research that has helped to shape the meta-theory. We have worked with these materials in our university classrooms with undergraduate and graduate students, as well as in management and executive development programs. We have also helped major organizations in both the public and private sectors design large-scale programs to improve the competencies of professional managers. Several thousand professional managers have completed programs that have used the Competing Values Framework as an underlying foundation and integrating theme. The results have been gratifying and instructive—gratifying because our students were transformed. We hope that the use of this textbook will lead to similar outcomes for you.

HOW TO USE THIS BOOK

This book may be used in several ways. It can be employed alone as the main text in a course specifically designed to develop competencies, or it can be used with a more traditional text to accomplish the same objective. It can accompany more traditional texts in either an organizational behavior or a management principles course. The Instructional Guide includes several papers written by colleagues in these fields that propose alternative uses of this book. The prospective user may find them to be stimulating in considering new approaches. We would like to thank the contributors to the Instructional Guide who responded to our request for alternative teaching methods with creativity and enthusiasm: Dan Denison, University of Michigan; Bill Metheny, North Texas State University; Larry Michaelsen, The University of Oklahoma; Deborah L. Wells, Creighton University.

Developed along with the book is a pre-and post-course self-assessment for the student, available in software or hard-copy form. The assessment instrument is based directly on the material in this volume and creates two profiles. The first is a general profile across the eight roles. This allows the student to examine more general changes in the eight managerial leadership roles that may occur during the course. The second is a more specific profile focusing on the 24 competencies. Because of the one-to-one relationship between the assessment and the text material, the student should find this tool to be especially helpful. Note that if the instructor focuses on different competencies, or only focuses on one or two of the competencies in each role, students will need to adjust their scores accordingly.

APPRECIATION

Many of the ideas for this book were originally developed in 1983, and elaborated in 1985, in conjunction with two professional development programs designed for New York State. Funding for those programs and for the first edition of this book was provided by the negotiated agreements between the state of New York and the Civil Service Employees Association, Inc., and the Public Employees Federation, AFL-CIO, and made available through New York State's Governor's Office of Employee Relations, Program Planning and Employee Development Division (now Division for Development Services). We particularly thank Don Giek, former Director of the Division for Development Services. Don truly is a master manager, and we respect and appreciate the enormous efforts he made for us and for so many people in and outside of New York State.

We would also like to thank Laurie Newman DiPadova who co-authored the innovator chapter and is the author of the Instructional Guide. We are most appreciative of her efforts.

We would also like to express sincere thanks to Ellen Ford, our editor at John Wiley. To say that Ellen did not know what she was getting herself into, working with four different authors in four different parts of the country, is perhaps an understatement. Ellen has been a joy to work with. She understands the value of paradox, and has been both patient and demanding. Moreover, she has kept her eye on the big picture issues, while paying careful attention to detail. Perhaps most importantly, she has provided us with many good insights and has maintained her good sense of humor through it all. We thank her for sticking with us!

A number of people were asked to review this book. They are Meg G. Birdseye, University of Alabama; David E. Blevins, University of Mississippi; Kent D. Carter, University of Maine at Orono; Paul D. Collins, Purdue University; Daniel Denison, University of Michigan; Dennis L. Dossett, University of Missouri-St. Louis; Stuart C. Freedman, University of Lowell; Ester E. Hamilton, Pepperdine University; Marcia Kassner, University of North Dakota; William E. McClane, Loyola College; Edward J Morrison, University of Colorado at Boulder; Paula C. Morrow, Iowa State University; Ralph F. Mullin, Central Missouri State University; William E. Stratton, Idaho State University; Charles N. Toftoy, Golden State University; Mark Wellman, Bowling Green State University; Barry L. Wisdom, Southwest Missouri State University; Joseph Weiss, Bentley College; David Szczerbacki, Alfred University; Joseph Petrick, Wright State University; Fred Tesch, Western Connecticut State University; Richard A. Grover, University of Southern Maine; Kimberlee M. Keef, Alfred University; John D. Bigelow, Boise State University; Gerald D. Klein, Rider University; David M. Leuser, Plymouth State College; Steve Iman, California State Polytechnic University; Richard B. Ives, Tarrant County Junior College; Gregory Stephens, Texas Christian University, and Gerald Schoenfeld, James Madison University. We appreciate their many helpful comments and insights.

Many others also contributed to the work of this and/or the first edition, and we would like to thank Debbi Berg, Bill Bywater, Bill LaFleur, Chris Dammer, Bruce Hamm, Steven Simons, Onnolee Smith, Chuck Klaer, Warren Ilchman,

Tom Kinney, Kary Jablonka, Norma Riccucci, David McCaffrey, Ted Peters, Rachel Ebert, and Eugene Thompson. All contributed significantly and we are grateful. Finally we thank our families for their continuous support.

Robert E. Quinn
Sue R. Faerman
Michael P. Thompson
Michael R. McGrath

BRIEF CONTENTS

CONTENTS

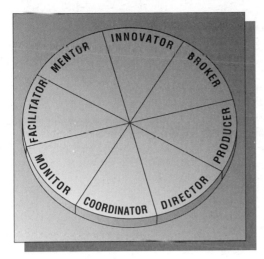

THE EVOLUTION OF MANAGEMENT MODELS

1

A New Approach

We all have beliefs and we all make assumptions about the right way of doing things. This is certainly true when it comes to managerial leadership. Although our beliefs and assumptions can make us effective, they can sometimes make us ineffective (House and Podsakoff, 1994). When they do make us ineffective it is hard to understand why. We are not usually very experienced at examining our basic beliefs and assumptions. Nor are we very experienced at adopting new assumptions or learning skills and competencies that are associated with those new assumptions. Often it takes a crisis to stimulate such change. Consider the following case.

I have always seen myself as a man who gets things done. After 17 years with a major pharmaceutical company, I was promoted to general manager in the international division. I was put in charge of all Southeast Asian operations. The unit seemed pretty sloppy to me. From the beginning I established myself as a tough, no-nonsense leader. If someone came in with a problem, he or she knew to have the facts straight or risk real trouble. After three months I began to feel like I was working myself to exhaustion, yet I could point to few real improvements. After six months or so, I felt very uneasy but was not sure why.

One night I went home and my wife greeted me. She said, "I want a divorce." I was shocked and caught off balance. To make a long story short, we ended up in counseling.

1

Our counselor taught me how to listen and practice empathy. The results were revolutionary. I learned that communication happens at many levels and that it's a two-way process. My marriage became richer than I had ever imagined possible.

I tried to apply what I was learning to what was going on at work. I began to realize that there was a lot going on that I didn't know about. People couldn't tell me the truth because I would chop their heads off. I told everyone to come to me with any problem so that we could solve it together. Naturally no one believed me. But after a year of proving myself, I am now known as one of the most approachable people in the entire organization. The impact on my division's operation has been impressive.

MODELS OF MANAGEMENT

The man in the preceding story had a problem of real significance. The lives of many people, including subordinates, superiors, customers, and even his family members, were being affected by his actions. He was less successful than he might have been because of his beliefs about what a leader is supposed to do. For him, good management meant tight, well-organized operations run by tough-minded, aggressive leaders. His model was not at all wrong—but it was inadequate. It limited his awareness of important alternatives and, thus, kept him from performing as effectively as he might have.

It turns out that nearly everyone has beliefs or viewpoints about what a manager should do. In the study of management, these beliefs are sometimes referred to as **models**. There are many different kinds of models. Although some are formally written or otherwise explicit, others, like the assumptions of the general manager, are informal. Because models affect what happens in organizations, we need to consider them in some depth.

Models are representations of a more complex reality. A model airplane, for example, is a physical representation of a real airplane. Models help us to represent, communicate ideas about, and better understand more complex phenomena in the real world.

In the social world a model often represents a set of assumptions for, or a general way of thinking about or seeing, some phenomenon. It provides a particular perspective about the more complex reality. Although models can help us to see some aspects of a phenomenon, they can also blind us to other aspects. The general manager mentioned before, for example, had such strongly held beliefs about order, authority, and direction that he was unable to see some important aspects of the reality that surrounded him.

Unfortunately, our models of management are often so tied to our identity and emotions that we find it, as in the preceding case, very difficult to learn about and appreciate different models. Because of the complexity of life, we often need to call upon more than one model; thus we can see and evaluate more alternatives. Our degree of choice and our potential effectiveness can be increased (Senge, 1990).

The models held by individuals often reflect models held by society at large. During the twentieth century a number of management models have emerged.

Understanding these models and their origins can lead managers to a broader understanding and a wider array of choices.

AN EVOLUTIONARY PERSPECTIVE

Our models and definitions of management keep evolving. As societal values change, existing viewpoints alter and new models of management emerge. These new models are not driven simply by the writings of academic or popular writers; or by managers who introduce an effective new practice; or by the technical, social, or political forces of the time. These models emerge from a complex interaction among all these factors. In this section, we will look at four major management models and how they evolved from the conditions in each of the first three quarters of the twentieth century. In doing this we draw upon the historical work of Mirvis (1985). Keep in mind as you read that the emergence of each new model did not mean that old models were swept away. Rather, many people held onto the beliefs and assumptions they had developed under the old model and continued to make decisions based on the old models. Note also that the choice of 25-year periods is arbitrary; we use them to simplify the discussion.

1900 –1925: THE EMERGENCE OF THE RATIONAL GOAL MODEL AND THE INTERNAL PROCESS MODEL

The first 25 years of this century were a time of exciting growth and progress that ended in the high prosperity of the roaring twenties. As the period began, the economy was characterized by rich resources, cheap labor, and *laissez-faire* policies. In 1901, oil was discovered in Beaumont, Texas. The age of coal became the age of oil, and soon after, the age of inexpensive energy. Technologically, it was a time of invention and innovation as tremendous advances occurred in both agriculture and industry. The work force was heavily influenced by immigrants from all over the world and by people leaving the shrinking world of agriculture. The average level of education for these people was 8.2 years. Most were confronted by serious financial needs. There was little, at the outset of this period, in terms of unionism or government policy to protect workers from the demanding and primitive conditions they often faced in the factories.

One general orientation of the period was social Darwinism: the belief in "survival of the fittest." Given this orientation, it is not surprising that *Acres of Diamonds,* by Russell Conwell, was a very popular book of the time. The book's thesis was that it was every man's Christian duty to be rich. The author amassed a personal fortune from royalties and speaking fees.

These years saw the rise of the great individual industrial leaders. Henry Ford, for example, not only implemented his vision of inexpensive transportation for everyone by producing the Model T, but he also applied the principles of Frederick Taylor to the production process. Taylor was the father of **scientific management** (see Theoretical Perspective 1.1). He introduced a variety of techniques for "rationalizing" work and making it as efficient as possible. Using Taylor's ideas, Henry Ford, in 1914, introduced the assembly line and reduced car assembly time from 728 hours to 93 minutes. In six years Ford's market share went from just under 10% to just under 50%. The wealth generated by the inventions, production methods, and organizations themselves was an entirely new phenomenon.

Rational Goal Model.   It was in this historical context that the first two models of management began to emerge. The first is the **rational goal model**. The symbol that best represents this model is the dollar sign because the ultimate criteria of organization effectiveness are productivity and profit. The basic means-ends assumption in this approach is the belief that clear direction leads to productive outcomes. Hence there is a continuing emphasis on processes such as goal clarification, rational analysis, and action taking. The organizational climate is rational economic and all decisions are driven by considerations of "the bottom line." If an employee of 20 years is only producing at 80% efficiency, the appropriate decision is clear: Replace the employee with a person who will contribute at 100% efficiency. In the rational goal model the ultimate value is achievement and profit maximization. The manager's job is to be a decisive director and a task-oriented producer.

Stories abound about the harsh treatment that supervisors and managers inflicted on employees during this time. In one manufacturing company, for example, they still talk today about the toilet that was once located in the center of the shop floor and was surrounded by glass windows so that the supervisor could see who was inside and how long the person stayed.

Internal Process Model.   The second model is called the **internal process model**. While its most basic hierarchical arrangements had been in use for centuries, during the first quarter of the twentieth century, it rapidly evolved into what would become known as the "professional bureaucracy." The basic notions of this model would not be fully codified, however, until the writings of Max Weber and Henri Fayol were translated in the middle of the next quarter

THEORETICAL PERSPECTIVE 1.1

TAYLOR'S FOUR PRINCIPLES OF MANAGEMENT

1. Develop a science for every job, which replaces the old rule-of-thumb method.

2. Systematically select workers so that they fit the job, and train them effectively.

3. Offer incentives so that workers behave in accordance with the principles of the science that has been developed.

4. Support workers by carefully planning their work and smoothing the way as they do their jobs.

Adapted from: Frederick W. Taylor, *The Principles of Scientific Management* (New York: Harper and Brothers, 1911), p. 44.

century. This model is highly complementary to the rational goal model. Here the symbol is a pyramid, and the criteria of effectiveness are stability and continuity. The means-ends assumption is based on the belief that routinization leads to stability. The emphasis is on processes such as definition of responsibilities, measurement, documentation, and record keeping. The organizational climate is hierarchical, and all decisions are colored by the existing rules, structures, and traditions. If an employee's efficiency falls, control is increased through the application of various policies and procedures. In this model the ultimate value is efficient work flow, and the manager's job is to be a technically expert monitor and dependable coordinator.

1926–1950: THE EMERGENCE OF THE HUMAN RELATIONS MODEL

The second quarter of the century brought two events of enormous proportions. The stock market crash of 1929 and World War II would affect the lives and outlook of generations to come. During this period the economy would boom, crash, recover with the war, and then, once again, offer bright hopes. Technological advances would continue in all areas, but particularly in agriculture, transportation, and consumer goods. The rational goal model continued to flourish. With the writings of Henri Fayol, Max Weber, and others, the internal process model (see Theoretical Perspectives 1.2 and 1.3) would be more clearly articulated. Yet, even while this was being accomplished, it started to become clear that the rational goal and internal process models were not entirely appropriate to the demands of the times.

Some fundamental changes began to appear in the fabric of society during the second quarter of the century. Unions, now a significant force, adhered to an economic agenda that brought an ever larger paycheck into the home of the American worker. Industry placed a heavy emphasis on the production of consumer goods. By the end of this period, new labor-saving machines were beginning to appear in homes. There was a sense of prosperity and a concern with recreation as well as survival. Factory workers were not as eager as their parents had been to accept the opportunity to work overtime. Neither were they as likely to give unquestioning obedience to authority. Hence, managers were finding that the rational goal and internal process models were no longer as effective as they once were.

Given the shortcomings of the first two models, it is not surprising that one of the most popular books written during this period was Dale Carnegie's *How to Win Friends and Influence People*. It provided some much desired advice on how to relate effectively to others. In the academic world, Chester Barnard pointed to the significance of informal organization and the fact that informal relationships, if managed properly, could be powerful tools for the manager. Also during this period Elton Mayo and Fritz Roethlisberger carried out their work in the famous Hawthorne studies. One well-known experiment carried out by these two researchers concerned level of lighting. Each time they increased the level of lighting, employee productivity went up. However, when they decreased the lighting, productivity also went up. They eventually concluded that what was really stimulating the workers was the attention being shown by the researchers. The results of these studies were also interpreted as evidence of a need for an increased focus on the power of relationships and informal processes in the performance of human groups.

THEORETICAL PERSPECTIVE 1.2

FAYOL'S GENERAL PRINCIPLES OF MANAGEMENT

1. *Division of work.* The object of division of work is to produce more and better work with the same effort. It is accomplished through reduction in the number of tasks to which attention and effort must be directed.

2. *Authority and responsibility.* Authority is the right to give orders, and responsibility is its essential counterpart. Whenever authority is exercised, responsibility arises.

3. *Discipline.* Discipline implies obedience and respect for the agreements between the firm and its employees. These agreements are arrived at by discussion between an owner or group of owners and workers associations. The establishment of such agreements should remain one of the chief preoccupations of industrial heads. Discipline also involves sanctions judiciously applied.

4. *Unity of command.* An employee should receive orders from one superior only.

5. *Unity of direction.* Each group of activities having one objective should be unified by having one plan and one head.

6. *Subordination of individual interest to general interest.* The interest of one employee or group of employees should not prevail over that of the company or broader organization.

7. *Remuneration of personnel.* To maintain their loyalty and support, employees must receive a fair wage for services rendered.

8. *Centralization.* Like division of work, centralization belongs to the natural order of things. The appropriate degree of centralization, however, will vary with a particular concern, so it becomes a question of the proper proportion. It is a problem of finding the measure that will give the best overall yield.

9. *Scalar chain.* The scalar chain is the chain of superiors ranging from the ultimate authority to the lowest ranks. It is an error to depart needlessly from the line of authority, but it is an even greater one to keep it when detriment to the business could ensue.

10. *Order.* A place for everything, and everything in its place.

11. *Equity.* Equity is a combination of kindliness and justice.

12. *Stability of tenure of personnel.* High turnover increases inefficiency. A mediocre manager who stays is infinitely preferable to an outstanding manager who comes and goes.

13. *Initiative.* Initiative involves thinking out a plan and ensuring its success. This gives zeal and energy to an organization.

14. *Esprit de corps.* Union is strength, and it comes from the harmony of the personnel.

Abridged from: Henri Fayol, *General and Industrial Administration* (New York: Pitman, 1949), pp. 20-41.

THEORETICAL PERSPECTIVE 1.3

CHARACTERISTICS OF WEBERIAN BUREAUCRACY

Elements of Bureaucracy:

1. There is a division of labor with responsibilities that are clearly defined.

2. Positions are organized in a hierarchy of authority.

3. All personnel are objectively selected and promoted based on technical abilities.

4. Administrative decisions are recorded in writing and records are maintained over time.

5. There are career managers working for a salary.

6. There are standard rules and procedures which are uniformly applied to all.

Adapted from: A.M. Henderson and Talcott Parsons (eds.), and Max Weber (trans.), *The Theory of Social and Economic Organizations* (New York: Free Press, 1947), pp. 328-337.

Human Relations Model. By the end of the second quarter of the century, the emerging orientation was the **human relations model**. In this model, the key emphasis is on commitment, cohesion, and morale. The means-ends assumption is that involvement results in commitment, and the key values are participation, conflict resolution, and consensus building. Because of an emphasis on equality and openness, the appropriate symbol for this model is a circle. The organization takes on a clanlike, team-oriented climate in which decision making is characterized by deep involvement. Here, if an employee's efficiency declines, managers take a developmental perspective and look at a complex set of motivational factors. They may choose to alter the person's degree of participation or opt for a host of other social psychological variables. The manager's job is to be an empathetic mentor and a process-oriented facilitator.

In 1949, this model was far from crystallized, and it ran counter to the assumptions in the rational goal and internal process models. Hence it was difficult to understand and certainly difficult to practice. Attempts often resulted in a kind of authoritarian benevolence. It would take well into the next quarter century for research and popular writings to explore this orientation, and for managerial experiments to result in meaningful outcomes in large organizations.

1951–1975: THE EMERGENCE OF THE OPEN SYSTEMS MODEL

The period 1951 to 1975 began with the United States as the unquestioned leader of the capitalist world. It ended with the leadership of the USA in serious question. During this period the economy experienced the shock of the oil embargo. Suddenly assumptions about cheap energy, and all the life patterns upon which they were based, were in danger. By the late seventies the economy was staggering under the weight of stagflation and huge government debt. At the beginning of this period, "made in Japan" meant cheap, low-quality goods of little significance to Americans. By the end, Japanese quality could not be matched, and Japan was making rapid inroads into sectors of the economy thought to be the sacred domain of American companies. Even such traditionally American manufacturing areas as automobile production were dramatically affected. There was also a marked shift from a clear product economy to the beginnings of a service economy.

Technological advances began to occur at an ever-increasing rate. At the outset of the third quarter of the century, the television was a strange device. By the end of this period, television was the primary source of information, and the computer was entering the life of every American. At the beginning of the 1960s NASA worked to accomplish the impossible dream of putting a man on the moon, but then Americans became bored with the seemingly commonplace accomplishments of the space program.

Societal values also shifted dramatically. The fifties were a time of conventional values. Driven by the Vietnam War, the sixties were a time of cynicism and upheaval. Authority and institutions were everywhere in question. By the seventies the difficulty of bringing social change was fully understood. A more individualistic and conservative orientation began to take root.

In the work force, average education jumped from the 8.2 years at the beginning of the century to 12.6 years. Spurred by considerable prosperity, workers in the United States were now concerned not only with money and recreation, but also with self-fulfillment. Women began to move into professions that had been closed to them previously. The agenda of labor expanded to include social and political issues. Organizations became knowledge intense, and it was no longer possible to expect the boss to know more than every person he or she supervised.

By now the first two models were firmly in place, and management vocabulary was filled with rational management terms, such as management by objectives (MBO) and management information system (MIS). The human relations model, however, was also now familiar. Many books about human relations became popular during this period, further sensitizing the world to the complexities of motivation and leadership. Experiments in group dynamics, organizational development, sociotechnical systems, and participative management flourished.

In the mid-sixties, spurred by the ever-increasing rate of change and the need to understand how to manage in a fast-changing, knowledge-intense world, a variety of academics began to write about still another model. People such as Katz and Kahn at the University of Michigan, Lawrence and Lorsch at Harvard, as well as a host of others, began to develop the open systems model of organization. This model was more dynamic than others. The manager was no longer seen as a rational decision maker controlling a machinelike organization. The research of Mintzberg, for example, showed that in contrast to the highly systematic pictures portrayed in the principles of administration (see Theoretical Perspective 1.2), managers live in highly unpredictable environments and have little time to organize and plan. They are, instead, bombarded by constant stimuli and forced to make rapid decisions. Such observations were consistent with the movement to develop contingency theories (see Theoretical Perspective 1.4). These theories recognized the simplicity of earlier approaches.

Open Systems Model. In the **open systems model,** the organization is faced with a need to compete in an ambiguous as well as competitive environment. The key criteria of organizational effectiveness are adaptability and external support. Because of the emphasis on organizational flexibility and responsiveness, the symbol here is the amoeba. The amoeba is a very responsive, fast-changing organism that is able to respond to its environment. The means-ends assumption is that continual adaptation and innovation lead to the acquisition and maintenance of external resources. Key processes are political adaptation, creative problem solving, innovation, and the management of change. The organization has an innovative climate and is more of an "adhocracy" than a bureaucracy. Risk is high and decisions are made quickly. In this situation common vision and shared values are very important. Here, if an employee's efficiency declines, it may be seen as a result of long periods of intense work, an overload of stress, and perhaps a case of burnout. The manager is expected to be a creative innovator and a politically astute broker (someone who uses power and influence in the organization).

1976–THE PRESENT: THE EMERGENCE OF "BOTH=AND" ASSUMPTIONS

In the first part of this quarter of the century, it became fully apparent that American organizations were in deep trouble. Innovation, quality, and productivity all slumped badly. Japanese products made astounding advances as talk of U.S. trade deficits became commonplace. Reaganomics and conservative social and economic values fully replaced the visions of the Great Society. In the labor force, knowledge work became commonplace and physical labor rare. Labor unions experienced major setbacks as organizations struggled to downsize their staffs and increase quality at the same time. The issue of job security became increasingly frequent in labor negotiations. Organizations faced new issues, such as takeover and downsizing. One middle manager struggled to do the job previously done by two or three. Burnout and stress became hot topics.

Peters and Waterman published a book that would have extraordinary popularity. *In Search of Excellence* attempted to chronicle the story of those few organizations that were seemingly doing it right. It was really the first attempt to provide advice on how to revitalize a stagnant organization and move it into a congruent relationship with an environment turned upside down. Like Carnegie's book, long before, it addressed and, in so doing, made clear the most salient unmet need of the time: how to manage in a world where nothing is stable.

As the decade of the nineties approached the midpoint, the rate of change moved to new heights. Longstanding political and business institutions began to crumble. The Berlin Wall came tumbling down. A short time later the USSR itself disintegrated. In the United States some of the most powerful and admired corporations seemed strong one day and in deep difficulty the next. In the new global

THEORETICAL PERSPECTIVE 1.4

CONTINGENCY THEORY

Appropriateness of Managerial Actions Vary with Key Variables:

1. *Size.* Problems of coordination increase as the size of the organization increases. Appropriate coordination procedures for a large organization will not be efficient in a small organization, and vice versa.

2. *Technology.* The technology used to produce outputs varies. It may be very routine or very customized. The appropriateness of organizational structures, leadership styles, and control systems will vary with the type of technology.

3. *Environment.* Organizations exist within larger environments. These may be uncertain and turbulent or predictable and unchanging. Organizational structures, leadership styles, and control systems will vary accordingly.

4. *Individuals.* People are not the same. They have very different needs. Managers must adjust their styles accordingly.

economy nothing seemed predictable. In the management vocabulary the new buzz words were *innovation, organizational learning, flexibility, speed to market, empowerment, positive urgency, reengineering, process improvement, vision, quality, benchmarking, rightsizing,* and *paradigm change.* These seemingly very different notions actually all reflected a single organizational need, the capacity of the organization to deal with paradox and conflicting values and to successfully change.

In such a complex and fast changing world, simple solutions became suspect. None of the four models, summarized in Table 1.1, offered a sufficient answer. Even the more complex open systems approach was not sufficient. Sometimes we needed stability, sometimes we needed change. The key was to stop assuming that it was an "either-or" decision, to stop thinking about choosing between the two (Quinn, Kahn and Mandl, 1994). More and more we needed to learn about "both-and" assumptions, where both could be needed at the same time. By the mid-nineties it became clear that no one model was sufficient to guide a manager and it was in fact necessary to see each of the four models as elements of a larger model. It is around this notion of a larger, integrated model that this book is organized.

TABLE 1.1   Characteristics of the Four Management Models

	Rational Goal	*Internal Process*	*Human Relations*	*Open Systems*
Symbol	$	△	○	✾
Criteria of effectiveness	Productivity, profit	Stability, continuity	Commitment, cohesion, morale	Adaptability, external support

TABLE 1.1   Characteristics of the Four Management Models (continued)

	Rational Goal	*Internal Process*	*Human Relations*	*Open Systems*
Symbol	$	△	◯	✿
Means-ends theory	Clear direction leads to productive outcomes	Routinization leads to stability	Involvement results in commitment	Continual adaptation and innovation lead to acquiring and maintaining external resources
Emphasis	Goal clarification, rational analysis, and action taking	Defining responsibility, measurement, documentation	Participation, conflict resolution, and consensus building	Political adaptation, creative problem solving, innovation, change management
Climate	Rational economic: "the bottom line"	Hierarchical	Team oriented	Innovative, flexible
Role of manager	Director and producer	Monitor and coordinator	Mentor and facilitator	Innovator and broker

THE FOUR MODELS IN A SINGLE FRAMEWORK

A SINGLE FRAMEWORK

At first, the models discussed seem to be four entirely different perspectives or domains. However, they can be viewed as closely related and interwoven. They are four important subdomains of a larger construct: organizational effectiveness. Each model within the construct of organizational effectiveness is related. Depending on the models and combinations of models we choose to use, we can see organizational effectiveness as simple and logical, as dynamic and synergistic, or as complex and paradoxical. Taken alone, no one of the models allows us the range of perspectives and the increased choice and potential effectiveness provided by considering them all as part of a larger framework. As we'll explain soon, we call this larger framework the **competing values framework.**

The relationships among the models can be seen in terms of two axes. In Figure 1.1 the vertical axis ranges from flexibility at the top to control at the bottom. The horizontal axis ranges from an internal organization focus at the left to an external organization focus at the right. Each model fits in one of the four quadrants.

The human relations model, for example, stresses the criteria shown in the upper-left quadrant: participation, openness, commitment, and morale. The open systems model stresses the criteria shown in the upper-right quadrant: innovation, adaptation, growth, and resource acquisition. The rational goal model stresses the criteria shown in the lower-right quadrant: direction and goal clarity, and productivity and accomplishment. The internal process model, in the lower-left quadrant, stresses documentation, information management, stability, and control.

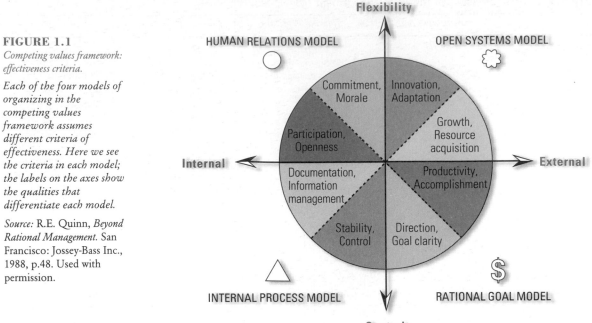

FIGURE 1.1

Competing values framework: effectiveness criteria.

Each of the four models of organizing in the competing values framework assumes different criteria of effectiveness. Here we see the criteria in each model; the labels on the axes show the qualities that differentiate each model.

Source: R.E. Quinn, *Beyond Rational Management.* San Francisco: Jossey-Bass Inc., 1988, p.48. Used with permission.

As can be seen in Figure 1.2, some general values are also reflected in the framework. These appear on the outer perimeter. Expansion and change are in the upper-right corner and contrast with consolidation and continuity in the lower left. On the other hand, they complement the neighboring values focusing on decentralization and differentiation at the top and achieving a competitive position of the overall system to the right. Each general value statement can be seen in the same way.

Each model has a perceptual opposite. The human relations model, defined by flexibility and internal focus, stands in stark contrast to the rational goal model, which is defined by control and external focus. In the first, for example, people are inherently valued. In the second, people are of value only if they contribute greatly to goal attainment. The open systems model, defined by flexibility and external focus, runs counter to the internal process model, which is defined by control and internal focus. While the open systems model is concerned with adapting to the continuous change in the environment, the internal process model is concerned with maintaining stability and continuity inside the system.

Parallels among the models are also important. The human relations and open systems models share an emphasis on flexibility. The open systems and rational goal models share an emphasis on external focus. The rational goal and internal process models emphasize control. And the internal process and human relations models share an emphasis on internal focus.

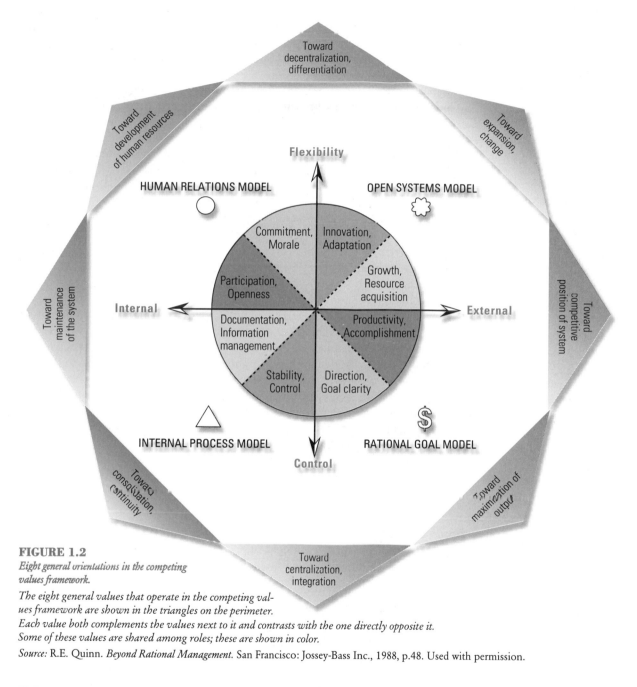

FIGURE 1.2
Eight general orientations in the competing values framework.

The eight general values that operate in the competing values framework are shown in the triangles on the perimeter.
Each value both complements the values next to it and contrasts with the one directly opposite it.
Some of these values are shared among roles; these are shown in color.

Source: R.E. Quinn. *Beyond Rational Management.* San Francisco: Jossey-Bass Inc., 1988, p.48. Used with permission.

THE USE OF OPPOSING MODELS

We will use this framework of the four opposing models throughout the book as our management model. We call this framework the **competing values framework** because the criteria within the four models seem at first to carry a conflicting message. We want our organizations to be adaptable and flexible, but we also want them to be stable and controlled. We want growth, resource acquisition, and external support, but we also want tight information management and formal communication. We want an emphasis on the value of human resources, but we also want an emphasis on planning and goal setting. In any real organization all of these are, to some extent, necessary.

The framework does not suggest that these oppositions cannot mutually exist in a real system. It does suggest, however, that these criteria, values, and assumptions are at opposites in our minds. We tend to think about them as mutually exclusive; that is, we assume we cannot have two opposites at the same time. Moreover, in valuing one over the other we tend to devalue or discount its opposite. As we shall see, however, it is possible, in fact, desirable, to perform effectively in the four opposing models simultaneously.

The four models in the framework represent the unseen values over which people, programs, policies, and organizations live and die. Like the pharmaceutical executive at the outset of this chapter, we often blindly pursue values in one of the models without considering the values in the others. As a result, our choices and our potential effectiveness are reduced.

For managers the world keeps changing. It changes from hour to hour, day to day, and week to week. The strategies that are effective in one situation are not necessarily effective in another. Even worse, the strategies that were effective yesterday may not be effective in the same situation today. Managers tend to become trapped in their own style and in the organization's cultural values. They tend to employ very similar strategies in a wide variety of situations. The overall framework, consisting of the four models described here, can increase effectiveness. Each model in the framework suggests value in different, even opposite, strategies. The framework reflects the complexity confronted by people in real organizations. It therefore provides a tool to broaden thinking and to increase choice and effectiveness. This, however, can only happen as three challenges are met.

Challenge 1   To appreciate both the values and the weaknesses of each of the four models.

Challenge 2   To acquire and use the competencies associated with each model.

Challenge 3   To dynamically integrate the competencies from each of the models with the managerial situations that we encounter.

BEHAVIORAL COMPLEXITY AND THE EFFECTIVENESS OF MANAGERIAL LEADERS

When a person meets Challenge 1 and comes to understand and appreciate each of the four models, it suggests he or she has learned something at the conceptual level, and increased his or her cognitive complexity as it relates to managerial leadership. A person with high cognitive complexity toward a given phenomenon is a person who can see that phenomenon from many perspectives. The person is able to think about the phenomenon in sophisticated rather than simple ways.

Increased complexity at the conceptual level is the primary objective in most traditional management courses. Meeting Challenge 1, however, does not mean someone has the ability to be an effective managerial leader. Knowledge is not enough.

To increase effectiveness, a managerial leader must meet Challenges 2 and 3. Meeting these challenges leads to an increase in behavioral complexity. The term *behavioral complexity* was coined by Hooijberg and Quinn (1992) to reflect the capacity to draw upon and use competencies and behaviors from the different models. "Behavioral complexity includes cognitive complexity and is the ability to act out a cognitively complex strategy by playing multiple, even competing, roles in a highly integrated and complementary way" (Quinn, Spreitzer and Hart, 1992).

Several studies suggest a link between behavioral complexity and effective performance. In a study of 916 CEOs, Hart and Quinn (1993) found that the ability to play the multiple and competing roles produced better firm performance. The CEOs with high behavioral complexity saw themselves as focusing on broad visions for the future (open systems model), while also providing critical evaluation of present plans (internal process model). They also saw themselves tending to relational issues (human relations model) while simultaneously emphasizing the accomplishment of tasks (rational goal model). The firms with CEOs having higher behavioral complexity produced the best firm performance, "particularly with respect to business performance (growth and innovation) and organizational effectiveness." The relationships held regardless of firm size or variations in the nature of the organizational environment.

In a study of middle managers in a Fortune 100 company Denison, Hooijberg and Quinn (1995) found behavioral complexity, as assessed by the superior of the middle manager, to be related to overall managerial effectiveness of the manager, as assessed by the subordinates. In a similar study, behavioral complexity was related to managerial performance, charisma, and the likelihood to make process improvements in the organization (Quinn, Spreitzer and Hart, 1992).

BECOMING A MANAGER:
THE NEED FOR NEW COMPETENCIES

The competing values framework integrates opposites. It is not easy to think about opposites. The failure to understand them, however, can hinder the development you need as a managerial leader. We will therefore begin by describing the competing roles managers play in their organization. We will then turn to the specific **competencies** that are embedded in each role. Finally we will describe a process for developing each of the competencies at the behavioral level.

EIGHT ROLES

The competing values framework is helpful in pointing out some of the values and criteria of effectiveness by which work units and organizations are judged. It is also useful in thinking about the conflicting roles that are played by managers

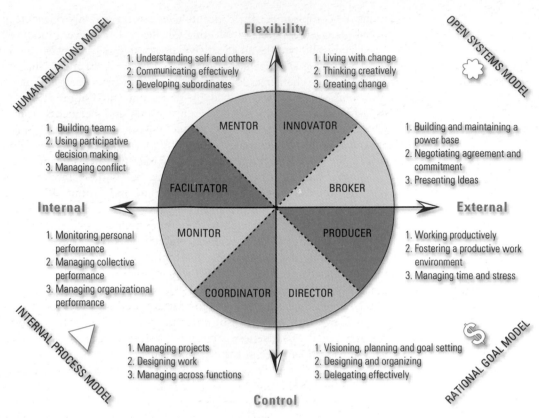

HUMAN RELATIONS MODEL

OPEN SYSTEMS MODEL

Flexibility

1. Understanding self and others
2. Communicating effectively
3. Developing subordinates

1. Living with change
2. Thinking creatively
3. Creating change

1. Building teams
2. Using participative decision making
3. Managing conflict

1. Building and maintaining a power base
2. Negotiating agreement and commitment
3. Presenting Ideas

MENTOR   INNOVATOR

FACILITATOR   BROKER

Internal   **External**

MONITOR   PRODUCER

1. Monitoring personal performance
2. Managing collective performance
3. Managing organizational performance

1. Working productively
2. Fostering a productive work environment
3. Managing time and stress

COORDINATOR   DIRECTOR

INTERNAL PROCESS MODEL

RATIONAL GOAL MODEL

1. Managing projects
2. Designing work
3. Managing across functions

1. Visioning, planning and goal setting
2. Designing and organizing
3. Delegating effectively

Control

FIGURE 1.3

The competencies and the leadership roles in the competing values framework.

Each of the eight leadership roles in the competing values framework contains three competencies.
They, like the values, both complement the ones next to them and contrast with those opposite to them.

Source: R.E. Quinn. *Beyond Rational Management.* San Francisco: Jossey-Bass Inc., 1988, p.48. Used with permission.

(Quinn, 1984, 1988). Figure 1.3 shows a second version of the competing values framework. The structure of Figure 1.3 is very similar to the structure of Figure 1.1, but this time the figure focuses on *leadership* effectiveness, rather than organizational or work-unit effectiveness. This framework specifies competing roles or expectations that might be experienced by a manager.

Rational Goal Model: The Director and Producer Roles. In the lower-right quadrant are the director and the producer roles. As a **director**, a manager is expected to clarify expectations through processes, such as planning and goal setting, to be a decisive initiator who defines problems, selects alternatives, establishes objectives, defines roles and tasks, generates rules and policies, and gives instructions.

When someone is playing the director role, there is no question about who is in charge. Consider, for example, the following statement made about a particularly directive manager:

She is everywhere. It seems as if she never goes home. But it is not just her energy; she is constantly reminding us why we are here. I have worked in a lot of organizations, but I have never been so clear about purpose. I know what I have to do to satisfy her and what the unit has to do. In some units around here, the employees really don't care; she has caused people to care about getting the job done.

When people think about the director role, they often think of a hard-driving person known for a no-nonsense, take-charge attitude. An excellent example is provided by the opening scene of the movie *Patton.* When George C. Scott, portraying General Patton, addresses his soldiers prior to entering battle, they absolutely know what the objective is and how they are to obtain it. People who excel at the director role are often highly competitive, swift-acting decision makers, who make their expectations clear. People walk away knowing exactly what they are to do. These people often argue that there are times when people simply must be kicked around or even removed from their jobs. In such situations directors tend to act decisively.

Patton, and others like him, also tend to serve as excellent examples of the producer role. **Producers** are expected to be task oriented and work focused and to have high interest, motivation, energy, and personal drive. They are supposed to accept responsibility, complete assignments, and maintain high personal productivity. This usually involves motivating members to increase production and to accomplish stated goals. Stereotypes of this role often have a fanatic desire to accomplish some objective. Like Captain Ahab in the novel *Moby Dick,* they drive themselves and their crews unrelentingly toward a stated objective.

Internal Process Model: Monitor and Coordinator Roles. In the bottom-left quadrant are the monitor and coordinator roles. As a **monitor** a manager is expected to know what is going on in the unit, to see if people are complying with the rules, and to see if the unit is meeting its quotas. The monitor knows all the facts and details and is good at analysis. Characteristic to this role is a zeal for handling data and forms, reviewing and responding to routine information, conducting inspections and tours, and authoring reviews of reports and other documents.

Consider, for example, this description of a manager:

She has been here for years. Everyone checks with her before doing anything. She is a walking computer. She remembers every detail, and she tracks every transaction that occurs. From agreements made eight years ago, she knows which unit owes equipment to which other unit. Nothing gets past her. She has a sixth sense for when people are trying to hide something.

The monitor role suggests a care for details, control, and analysis. Here we think of Robert Crandall, a CEO in the airline industry. This man loved to study every alternative in the finest detail. Indeed, some argued that he had an obsession for detail which was reflected in the constant probing questions that he unleashed on everyone around him. In meeting with managers from even the smallest cities, he would hold nonstop, eight-hour meetings going over every line in the manager's budget. In staff meetings he dominated each session, demanding facts from everyone present. He knew every aspect of what was going on in his organization. He did not let anything slip by unnoticed.

As a **coordinator**, a manager is expected to maintain the structure and flow of the system. The person in this role is expected to be dependable and reliable. Behavioral traits include various forms of work facilitation such as scheduling, organizing, and coordinating staff efforts; crisis handling; and attending to technological, logistical, and housekeeping issues. Here we think of Jim Manzi who was the CEO of Lotus Development Corporation. He took over the company when it was growing with enormous speed. The obvious need was to control the growth in a positive way. This CEO popularized the quotation from Edward Abey: "Growth for growth's sake is the ideology of the cancer cell." Always looking for applications of computer technology, he regularly had people experiment with new ways to communicate and coordinate efforts within the company. His overall coordinating efforts held the fast-growing company together.

Human Relations Model: The Facilitator and Mentor Roles. The **facilitator** is expected to foster collective effort, build cohesion and teamwork, and manage interpersonal conflict. In this role the manager is process oriented. Expected behaviors include intervening in interpersonal disputes, using conflict-reduction techniques, developing cohesion and morale, obtaining input and participation, and facilitating group problem solving.

Consider, for example, this description of a public manager:

> *It is like any company. The finance people and the operations people are always at war. He brings people like that into a room, hardly says a word, and walks out with support from both sides. Same with subordinates, he brings us together, asks lots of questions, and we leave committed to get the job done. He has a gift for getting people to see the bigger picture, to trust each other, and to cooperate.*

A particularly outstanding example of the facilitator role is Suzanne de Passe, who served as president of Motown Productions. A highly energetic manager, she was recognized as having many skills, yet the one that stands out the most is her incredible ability for team building. With her, no subject was taboo. Her staff felt free and safe in raising any issue, including the shortcomings of the boss, herself. She refused to let any conflict stay hidden. All issues were raised and worked on until there was a resolution and consensus. Her people had a sense of involvement and influence. The level of openness and cohesiveness astounded most newcomers. Many commented that the organization was the only one they had ever seen where the truth was always told and potentially divisive political issues were immediately confronted and resolved. The sense of openness and cohesiveness created an exciting and productive organizational context.

A **mentor** is engaged in the development of people through a caring, empathetic orientation. This might be called the concerned human role. In this role the manager is helpful, considerate, sensitive, approachable, open, and fair. In acting out this role, the manager listens, supports legitimate requests, conveys appreciation, and gives compliments and credit. People are resources to be developed. The manager helps with skill building, provides training opportunities, and plans for their individual development. Here we think about a man who was the head of finance in a Fortune 100 company. He was known as a master of this role. He would carefully select graduates from the best business schools, bring them into the company, train them, and then watch over every aspect of their career development. To be one of his protégés was to be on the sure track to success.

Open Systems Model: The Innovator and Broker Roles. The innovator and broker roles, in the upper-right quadrant of the framework, reflect the values of the open systems model. As an **innovator**, a manager is expected to facilitate adaptation and change. The innovator pays attention to the changing environment, identifies important trends, conceptualizes and projects needed changes, and tolerates uncertainty and risk. In this role, managers must rely on induction, ideas, and intuitive insights. These managers are expected to be creative, clever dreamers who see the future, envision innovations, package them in inviting ways, and convince others that they are necessary and desirable.

Consider, for example, this description:

> *In a big organization like this, most folks do not want to rock the boat. She is always asking why, looking for new ways to do things. We used to be in an old, run-down wing. Everyone accepted it as a given. It took her two years, but she got us moved. She had a vision, and she sold it up the system. She is always open, and if a change or a new idea makes sense, she will go for it.*

Innovators are usually people with vision. They see a need and a way to fulfill the need. They are willing to take risks in pursuing their vision. An example of an innovator is Sandra Hale, who is commissioner of the Department of Administration in Minnesota State Government. In the middle of the state bureaucracy she has instituted programs that stimulate innovation. Employees join with people from outside the agency to insure the pursuit of customer needs, participation, accountability, information sharing, and productivity improvement. Hale brings concepts like "marketplace activities" from outside government and asserts them onto various segments of her own organization. These "outside" models force people to ask new questions and consider new activities. Change follows.

The **broker** is particularly concerned with maintaining external legitimacy and obtaining external resources. Image, appearance, and reputation are important. Managers as brokers are expected to be politically astute, persuasive, influential, and powerful. They meet with people from outside the unit to represent, negotiate, and to acquire resources; they market, and act as a liaison and spokesperson.

THE EIGHT ROLES AT DIFFERENT ORGANIZATION LEVELS

As you think about the eight managerial leadership roles described above, you may notice that these descriptions are as applicable to first-level supervisors as they are to executive-level managers of large organizations, and that the descriptions of the eight roles represent general descriptions of managerial behaviors that are not necessarily tied to a particular level of organizational hierarchy. Indeed, researchers and consultants have used the *competing values framework* to structure management education, development, and training programs for first-, middle-, and upper-level managers in a wide variety of public, private, and not-for-profit organizations in the United States as well as internationally (Ban and Faerman, 1988; Faerman, Quinn and Thompson, 1987; Giek and Lees, 1993; Quinn, Sendelbach and Spreitzer, 1991; Sendelbach, 1993).

Managerial responsibilities do, however, vary across levels of organizational hierarchy. Common sense will tell you that the specific job tasks and responsibilities associated with the first-level manager in the broker role, for example, will likely be starkly different from those of the upper-level manager performing in this role. In some cases, however, while the specific job tasks and responsibilities vary across levels of organizational hierarchy, some of the required competencies for performing in the various roles will remain the same. For example, all managers need to have good interpersonal skills and to have a high level of self-awareness (Kiechel, 1994). Similarly, all managers need to be able to develop plans and to adapt those plans when circumstances change. In this latter case, however, the scope and time frame of planning will likely differ as will the steps of the planning process. Thus managers may need to learn different competencies to plan at different levels of the organization. As managers are promoted from one level of the organization to the next they need to identify which behaviors associated with the various role competencies will generally remain the same, as well as which new behaviors need to be learned and which must be unlearned (Faerman and Peters, 1991). They must also understand how the means to balance the various roles and perform in behaviorally complex ways may change from one managerial position to another. Similarly, human resources managers and those who are mentoring managers as they are promoted need to understand what are the similarities and differences in managerial jobs across levels of organizational hierarchy so that they can help these individuals to grow and develop as they make these transitions (DiPadova and Faerman, 1993).

THE NEGATIVE ZONE

Learning to perform well as a managerial leader requires a different approach than does learning to perform well in any one of the leadership roles. In the same way that none of the models discussed above provides the sole answer to organizational effectiveness, no one of the managerial leadership roles provides the sole answer to managerial leadership performance. While a person may become very strong in a given role, and this strength may carry him or her a long way in his or her career, this does not necessarily mean that he or she will be an effective managerial leader. Effective managerial leaders are behaviorally complex and are able to integrate opposite roles. Sometimes a person becomes so committed to the behavior in one role that he or she loses touch with the opposite. This can make a normally effective person ineffective. General George Patton was, as indicated earlier, an effective

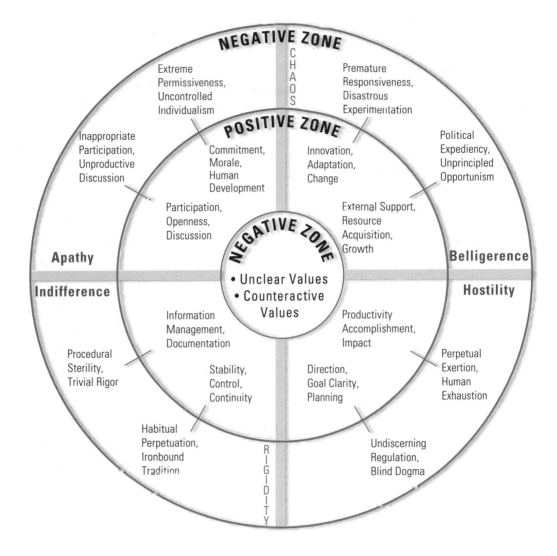

FIGURE 1.4

Negative zone in organizational effectiveness.

Source: R.E. Quinn. The University of Michigan. Used with permission.

director and producer, but he sometimes lost sight of facilitator, mentor, and broker roles and this led to some major setbacks in his career.

Without behavioral complexity one's strengths can become the source of one's failure. Low behavioral complexity on the part of a manager can lead to unfortunate organizational outcomes. To illustrate this, Faerman and Quinn (1985) developed the concept of the "negative zone." It can be seen in Figures 1.4 and 1.5. The first reflects organizational effectiveness. The second reflects leader effectiveness. In

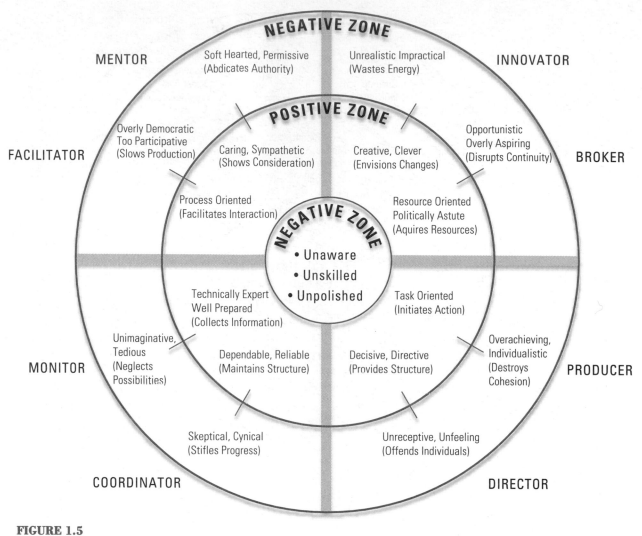

FIGURE 1.5
Negative zone in leader effectiveness.

Source: R.E. Quinn. The University of Michigan. Used with permission.

each of the two figures three circles are divided into four quadrants. In the middle circle are the positively stated values from the competing values framework. The inner and outer circles are considered negative zones. The inner circle is well understood and represents a lack of ability to perform in a given role. The most interesting circle, however, is the outer circle. Here each set of positive values is "pushed" until it becomes negative. In the upper-right quadrant of Figure 1.4, for example, innovation, adaptation, and change become premature responsiveness and disastrous experimentation. External support, resource acquisition, and growth become political expediency and unprincipled opportunism. Here an organization intending to be a responsive adhocracy becomes a tumultuous anarchy. In each quadrant of the outer circle the reader can see what happens if a set of positive values is inflated by ignoring or negating the opposite set of positive values.

IDENTIFYING THE CORE COMPETENCIES

The eight roles help us to organize our thoughts about what is expected of a person holding a position of leadership. Although the eight roles are a useful organizing structure, we have not as yet specified what competencies are necessary in order to perform effectively in each of the eight roles. It is to that issue that we now turn.

Several years ago a group of experts, consisting of 11 nationally recognized scholars and 11 prominent administrators and union representatives, were brought together to identify key competencies associated with each role in the competing values framework (Faerman, Quinn and Thompson, 1987). Participants were chosen based on their experience and expertise as practitioners or scholars in the field of management. Over 250 competencies were identified and given to this group. Their task was to identify the most important competencies in each of the eight roles. Based on the results of this exercise, a framework was developed. This framework was used in the instruction of thousands of people and modified by their feedback. Based on their feedback, the model was improved and this book is organized around the important competencies in each role. These are shown in Table 1.2.

TABLE 1.2 The Eight Managerial Leadership Roles and Their Key Competencies

Mentor Role	1. Understanding self and others 2. Communicating effectively 3. Developing subordinates
Facilitator Role	1. Building teams 2. Using participative decision making 3. Managing conflict
Monitor Role	1. Monitoring individual performance 2. Managing collective performance 3. Managing organizational performance
Coordinator Role	1. Managing projects 2. Designing work 3. Managing across functions
Director Role	1. Visioning, planning, and goal setting 2. Designing and organizing 3. Delegating effectively

Producer Role	1. Working productively
	2. Fostering a productive work environment
	3. Managing time and stress
Broker Role	1. Building and maintaining a power base
	2. Negotiating agreement and commitment
	3. Presenting ideas
Innovator Role	1. Living with change
	2. Thinking creatively
	3. Creating change

Each of the chapters is divided into three sections, and each section is organized around one of the three competencies in the role. Thus the next eight chapters cover 24 key competencies. The competencies are highly consistent with the existing literature (Ghiselli, 1963, Livingston, 1971, Miner, 1973, Katz, 1974, Mintzberg, 1975, Flanders, 1981, Yukl, 1981, Boyatzis, 1982, Luthans and Lockwood, 1984, Bigelow, 1991, Hart and Quinn, 1993, Whetten and Cameron, 1994). Completion of the next eight chapters is likely to greatly broaden your skills and increase your capacities. As you work through the chapters, however, keep in mind that this is only one of the eight roles and that the ultimate goal is for you to find the appropriate balance across the competencies that will allow you to operate well in a world of competing values.

ORGANIZING THE LEARNING PROCESS

A competency suggests both the possession of knowledge and the behavioral capacity to act appropriately. To develop competencies you must be both introduced to knowledge and have the opportunity to practice your skills. Many textbooks and classroom lecture methods provide the knowledge but not the opportunity to develop behavioral skills.

In this book, we will provide you with both. The structure we will use is based on a five-step model developed by Whetten and Cameron (1994), which takes learning from an instructional approach (an expert giving a lecture) to an instructional-developmental approach (an expert giving a lecture plus students experimenting with new behaviors). We have modified the labels for one of the components in the five-step model and call it the ALAPA model. The components are as follows.

Step 1: Assessment	Helps you discover your present level of ability in and awareness of the competency. Any number of tools, such as questionnaires, role plays, or group discussions, might be used.

Step 2: Learning   Involves reading and presenting information about the topic using traditional tools, such as lectures and printed material. Here we present information from relevant research and suggest guidelines for practice.

Step 3: Analysis   Explores appropriate and inappropriate behaviors by examining how others behave in a given situation. We will use cases, role plays, or other examples of behavior. Your professor may also provide examples from popular movies, television shows, or novels for you to analyze.

Step 4: Practice   Allows you to apply the competency to a worklike situation while in the classroom. It is an opportunity for experimentation and feedback. Again, exercises, simulations, and role plays will be used.

Step 5: Application   Gives you the opportunity to transfer the process to real-life situations. Usually assignments are made to facilitate short- and long-term experimentation.

In working with the model, we discovered that the five components, and the methods normally associated with each component, need not be mutually exclusive. A lecture, for example, does not need to follow an assessment exercise and precede an analysis exercise; a lecture might be appropriately combined with a role play in some other step. The methods can be varied and even combined in the effective teaching and learning of a given competency. In the following chapters, the presentation of each of the 24 competencies will be organized according to the ALAPA model.

Each of the eight roles are presented and illustrated using the competing values model. Chapters 2 through 9 are each organized around one of the eight roles. In each role there are many competencies. The three sections in each chapter are organized around what we consider to be the three most important competencies in each role. In turn, each competency is presented using the ALAPA model.

CONCLUSIONS

People use models that sensitize them to some things and blind them to others. When acting as a managerial leader in an organizational unit, our models greatly affect our level of effectiveness. In this chapter we have traced the evolution of four basic models in management thinking: rational goal, internal process, human relations, and open systems. Each model is based on assumptions that lead to different sensitivities, decisions, and behaviors.

In recent years, world conditions have made it increasingly obvious that there is a need for "both-and" thinking. As we increase the number of models that we can use to assess a situation, we increase our array of choices, and we increase both our cognitive and behavioral complexity.

In this chapter we considered the competing values model. It suggests that the four basic models of organizational effectiveness can be integrated into a comprehensive whole. The model is called the "competing values" model because we tend to see the oppositions as conflicts. They are not, however, mutually exclusive. In fact, they need to be complementary. We can use the model to get out of a single mindset and to increase choice. In becoming a master manager, we seek to use, simultaneously, two or more seemingly opposite approaches. Think, for example, of the leader who practices "tough love." This person is effectively integrating or making complementary domains that we normally keep separate.

The competing values model suggests three challenges: to use multiple mindsets in viewing the organizational world; to learn to use competencies associated with all four models; and finally, to integrate the diverse competencies in confronting the world of action. People who meet these three challenges are behaviorally complex and are the most effective managerial leaders.

We use the ALAPA model in presenting these competencies. Although the book allows the instructor to follow traditional instruction methods, it also allows a second phenomenon to occur. It allows you to develop, grow, and internalize new competencies. The emphasis, then, is not on learning traditional social science theory, but on learning how to apply certain aspects of this literature to learning to perform more effectively as a managerial leader.

ASSIGNMENT: Course Preassessment

There is an instrument that will allow you to do a preassessment of yourself on the eight roles and the 24 skills in the competing values framework. This preassessment is available in two forms: as a software package and as a written questionnaire. Either may be used. If your instructor desires that you do this preassessment, he or she will direct you in how to proceed.

REFERENCES

Ban, C., and S. R. Faerman. "Advanced Human Resources Development Program: Final Impact Report" (unpublished technical report). Rockefeller College of Public Affairs and Policy, University at Albany, SUNY, Albany, NY, 1988.

Bigelow, John D. (ed.) *Managerial Skills:Explorations in Practical Knowledge.* Newbury Park, CA: Sage Publications, 1991.

Boyatzis, R. E. *The Competent Manger.* New York: John Wiley & Sons, 1982.

Daft, R. L. *Management.* Chicago: Dryden Press, 1988.

Denison, D., R. Hooijberg, and R. Quinn. "Paradox and Performance: Toward a Theory of Behavioral Complexity in Managerial Leadership." *Organization Science* Volume 6, no.5, pp. 524–540, 1995.

DiPadova, L.N., and S. R. Faerman. "Using the Competing Values Framework to Facilitate Managerial Understanding Across Levels of Organizational Hierarchy." *Human Resource Management* 32(1) (1993):143–174.

Faerman, S. R., and T. D. Peters. "A Conceptual Framework for Examining Managerial Roles and Transitions Across Levels of Organizational Hierarchy." *Proceedings of the National Public Management Research Conference,* Syracuse, NY, September 20–21, 1991.

Faerman, S. R., and R. E. Quinn, "Effectiveness: The Perspective from Organizational Theory." *Review of Higher Education 9* (1985): 83–100.

Faerman, S. R., R. E. Quinn, and M. P. Thompson. "Bridging Management Practice and Theory." *Public Administration Review* 47(3) (1987): 311–319.

Flanders, L. R. Report 1 from the *Federal Manager's Job and Role Survey: Analysis of Responses.* Washington, D.C.: U.S. Office of Personnel Management, 1981.

Ghiselli, E. E. "Managerial Talent." *American Psychologist* 18 (1963): 631–642.

Giek, D.G., and P. L. Lees. "On Massive Change: Using the Competing Values Framework to Organize the Educational Efforts of the Human Resource Function in New York State Government." *Human Resource Management* 32(1) (1993): 9–28.

Hart, S., and Quinn, R. E. "Roles Executives Play: CEOs, Behavioral Complexity, and Firm Performance." *Human Relations* 46 (1993): 115–142.

Hooijberg, Robert, and Robert E. Quinn. "Behavioral Complexity and the Development of Effective Managers," in Robert L. Phillips and James G. Hunt (eds.), *Strategic Leadership: A Multiorganizational-Level Perspective.* Westport, CT: Quorum, 1992.

House, Robert J., and Philip M. Podsakoff. "Effectiveness: Leadership Past Perspectives and Future Directions for Research." Jerald Greenberg (ed.). Organizational Behavior: The State of the Science, 1994. Hillsdale, NJ: Lawrence Erlbaum,

Katz, R. L. "Skills of an Effective Administrator." *Harvard Business Review* 51 (1974): 90–102.

Kiechel, Walter, III. "A Manager's Career in the New Economy." *Fortune* (April 4, 1994): 68–72.

Livingston, J. S. "Myth of the Well-Educated Manager." *Harvard Business Review* 49 (1971): 79–89.

Luthans, F., and D. L. Lockwood. *"Toward an Observational System for Measuring Leader Behavior in Natural Settings,"* in J.G. Hunt, R. Stewart, C. Schriesheim, and D. Hosking (eds.), *Leaders and Managers: International Perspectives on Managerial Behaviour and Leadership.* Elmford, N.Y: Pergamon, 1984.

Miner, J. B. "The Real Crunch in Managerial Manpower." *Harvard Business Review* 51 (1973): 146–158.

Mintzberg, H. "The Manager's Job: Folklore and Fact." *Harvard Business Review* 53 (1975): 49–61.

Mirvis, P. H. *Work in the 20th Century: America's Trends and Tracts, Visions and Values, Economic and Human Developments.* Cambridge, MA: Revision, Rudi Press, 1985.

Pauchant, T. C., J. Nilles, O. E. Sawy, and A. M. Mohrman. "Toward a Paradoxical Theory of Organizational Effectiveness: An Empirical Study of the Competing Values Model." Working paper. Laval University, Administrative Sciences, Quebec City, Quebec, Canada, GIK 7P4, 1989.

Quinn, R E. "Applying the Competing Values Approach to Leadership: Toward an Integrative Framework," in J. G. Hunt, D. Hosking, C. Schriesheim, and R, Stewart (eds.), *Leaders and Managers: International Perspective on Managerial Behavior and Leadership.* Elmsford, NY: Pergamon Press, 1984.

———. *Beyond Rational Management: Mastering the Paradoxes and Competing Demands of High Performance.* San Francisco: Jossey-Bass, 1988.

Quinn, R. E., and K. S. Cameron. "Organizational Life Cycles and Shifting Criteria of Effectiveness: Some Preliminary Evidence." *Management Science* 29 (1983): 33–51.

Quinn, R.E., Joel A. Kahn, and Michael J. Mandl. "Perspectives on Organizational Change: Exploring Movement at the Interface," in Jerald Greenberg (ed.). *Organizational Behavior: The State of the Science.* 1994.

Quinn, Robert E., Neil B. Sendelbach, and Gretchen M. Spreitzer. "Education and Empowerment: A Transformational Model of Managerial Skills Development," in John D. Bigelow (ed.), *Managerial Skills: Explorations in Practical Knowledge.* Newbury Park: Sage Publications, 1991.

Quinn, Robert E., Gretchen M. Spreitzer, and Stuart Hart. "Integrating the Extremes: Crucial Skills for Managerial Effectiveness," in Suresh Srivastva, Ronald E. Fry and Associates, *Executive and Organizational Continuity: Managing the Paradoxes of Stability and Change.* San Francisco: Jossey-Bass, 1992.

Quinn, R. E., and J. Rohrbaugh. "A Spatial Model of Effectiveness Criteria: Towards a Competing Values Approach to Organizational Analysis." *Management Science* 29(3) (1983): 363–377.

Robins, S. P. *Management,* 2d ed. Englewood Cliffs, NJ: Prentice-Hall, 1987.

Sendelbach, N. B. "The Competing Values Framework for Management Training and Development: A Tool for Understanding Complex Issues and Tasks." *Human Resource Management* 32(1) (1993):75–99.

Senge, Peter. *The Fifth Discipline: The Art and Practice of the Learning Organization.* New York: Doubleday Currency, 1990.

Whetten, D. R, and K. S. Cameron. *Developing Management Skills,* 3d ed. New York: Harper-Collins, 1994.

Yukl, G. A. *Leadership in Organizations.* Englewood Cliffs, NJ: Prentice-Hall, 1981.

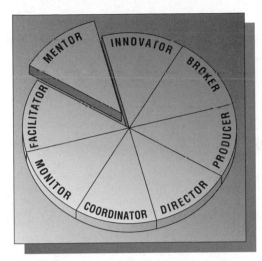

THE
MENTOR
ROLE

2

■ COMPETENCIES

Understanding Self and Others

Communicating Effectively

Developing Subordinates

We now turn to the human relations model. In this model the focus is on individuals and groups. We will also discuss commitment, cohesion, and morale as indicators of effectiveness. A central belief in this model is that involvement and participation in decision making result in outcomes such as high commitment. The climate emphasized in this model is characterized by teamwork, and the key managerial leadership roles are mentor and facilitator. The task is to establish and maintain effective relationships (Pfeiffer, 1994).

In Chapter 1 we pointed out that the **mentor** role might also be called the concerned human role. This role reflects a caring, empathetic orientation. In this role a manager is expected to be helpful, considerate, sensitive, approachable, open, and fair. In acting out the role, the leader listens, supports legitimate requests, conveys appreciation, and gives recognition. Employees are seen as important resources to be understood, valued, and developed. The manager helps them with individual development plans, and also sees that they have opportunities for training and skill building.

In Western society acts of caring and concern are sometimes seen as soft and weak. It is thought that to be a good leader one must be strong, powerful, and in control. Likewise, some individuals find that they have great difficulty with feelings and the expression of feelings. Given such societal and individual orientations, it is tempting to devalue the mentor role. This is a mistake. Great power can derive from attending to the "soft" issues (Nair, 1994). Social science has

BOX 2.1   THE DERAILED EXECUTIVES

A comparison was made between 21 "derailed" executives and 20 "arrivers" to try to determine why some people succeed and others fail to reach their potential. Several characteristics of the derailed executives stood out:

1. Insensitive to others; abrasive and intimidating.
2. Cold, aloof, and arrogant.
3. Betrayed the trust of others.
4. Overly ambitious; always trying to move up.
5. Could not delegate or build teams.
6. Could not get along with people who had different styles.
7. Overdependent on others.

Source: Morgan W. McCall and Michael M. Lombardo, "What Makes a Top Executive?" *Psychology Today* (February 1993), pp. 26-31. Reprinted with permission from Psychology Today Magazine, Copyright ©1983 (PT Partners, L.P.)

clearly demonstrated the importance of this role in overall managerial effectiveness (Bass, 1990). People who play the mentor role poorly do not fare well (see Box 2.1). The three competencies in this role are:

Competency 1   Understanding Self and Others
Competency 2   Communicating Effectively
Competency 3   Developing Subordinates

Competency 1   Understanding Self and Others

ASSESSMENT   Managerial Orientation Measure

Directions   Circle the level of agreement or disagreement that you personally feel toward each of the following 10 statements.

Scale

SA = Strongly Agree	A = Agree	U = Uncertain
D = Disagree	SD = Strongly Disagree	

1. People need to know that the boss is in charge.   SA   A   U   D   SD
2. Employees will rise to the occasion when an extra effort is needed.   SA   A   U   D   SD
3. Employees need direction and control or they will not work hard.   SA   A   U   D   SD
4. People naturally want to work.   SA   A   U   D   SD
5. A manager should be a decisive, no nonsense leader.   SA   A   U   D   SD

6. Employees should be involved in making decisions that concern them.　　SA　A　U　D　SD

7. A manager has to be tough minded and hard-nosed.　　SA　A　U　D　SD

8. A manager should build a climate of trust in the work unit.　　SA　A　U　D　SD

9. If a unit is to be productive, employees need to be pushed.　　SA　A　U　D　SD

10. Employees need the freedom to innovate.　　SA　A　U　D　SD

Scoring and Interpretation

Items	SA	A	U	D	SD
1, 3, 5, 7, 9:	1 point	2 points	3 points	4 points	5 points
2, 4, 6, 8, 10:	5 points	4 points	3 points	2 points	1 point

To determine your score, add up the total points for all 10 items. Scores can be between 10 and 50. As we'll see next, high scores suggest managerial attitudes in line with "Theory Y," whereas low scores would indicate attitudes that fit with "Theory X."

LEARNING   Understanding Self and Others

To be a successful mentor, managers must have some understanding of themselves and others. Although all members of a work group have something in common, each individual is also in some way unique. The challenge is to understand both the commonalities and differences and how these cause people to relate to one another in various ways. By being aware, you can better understand your own reaction to people and their reactions to each other. This understanding, should, in turn, make you more effective (Cotton, 1994).

The relationship between self-understanding and personal effectiveness is illustrated in an incident from the career of Jane Evans, president and CEO of InterPacific Retail Group. Earlier in her career, when she was announced as the new CEO of Butterrick/Vogue, seven division vice presidents, all male, immediately quit. What would your reaction be? The confident Evans met with the seven men and bet them that, within one year, they would agree that she was the best boss they ever had. Using her highly developed skills in the mentor role, she won the bet.

VALUES AND ASSUMPTIONS

The assessment activity you just completed is based on the work of Douglas McGregor (1960). He argues that people tend to make two very different sets of assumptions about the world. The first orientation, called **Theory X**, reflects a classical view of management that emphasizes control and close supervision. It assumes that people are predisposed not to work. The manager's job, therefore, is to control, push, and prod people into action. In contrast, the **Theory Y** approach assumes that people want to work, they want control over their own activities, and they want ever-increasing levels of responsibility. It views people as entirely capable of being innovative and of making important contributions to the organization. The manager's job is to listen, respond, inspire, and reward. A low score on the assessment activity you just completed suggests a Theory X orientation, whereas a high score suggests a Theory Y orientation.

In understanding ourselves and others, we start by looking at people's values and assumptions because of their great influence on behavior. Someone who has a Theory X view of the world, for example, will do very different things than someone who has a Theory Y view. Moreover, each will probably have difficulty understanding and working with the other.

Values are basic—the fundamental standards of desirability by which we choose between alternatives. They are our assumptions about the nature of reality. They differ from attitudes, traits, or needs. An *attitude* is a feeling about an object. A *trait* is a regularly occurring pattern of individual action. A *need* is a sensed lack of something desired. Values precede each of these.

Values are learned early and continue to develop throughout our lives. They are acquired and developed through relationships, initially with parents and family members, and later, outside the family.

Research (Rokeach, 1973) identifies two types of values: *instrumental values* (how you think things should be done) and *terminal values* (what your goals are). Instrumental values include such things as hard work, open-mindedness, competence, lightheartedness, and forgiveness. Terminal values include such things as a prosperous life, accomplishment, peace, and self-respect.

Although people tend to hold the same general values, research shows that people vary widely in how they prioritize the values they hold. A study by Clare and Sanford (1979), for example, found that managers tend to value sense of accomplishment, self-respect, a comfortable life, and independence more than others. Their highest instrumental value for managers was ambition, and their highest terminal value was sense of accomplishment. Clearly most managers tend to be very achievement oriented. Naturally, these values affect their view of the world. Managers who hold values such as these behave differently from managers who reject these values. A major challenge then is to know your own values and to know the values of other people. The more you do this, the more likely you are to choose the right strategy with the right person at the right moment.

VALUES AND UNDERSTANDING YOURSELF

The importance of understanding your own values and behaviors is obvious. If you don't understand yourself, it is nearly impossible to understand others. Yet there is evidence to suggest that many managers have considerable difficulty understanding themselves.

William Torbert (1987) uses a developmental model of behavior which suggests that people progress through a series of stages. In each stage they take on

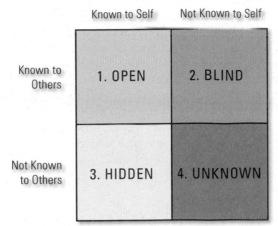

Known to Self   Not Known to Self

	Known to Self	Not Known to Self
Known to Others	1. OPEN	2. BLIND
Not Known to Others	3. HIDDEN	4. UNKNOWN

FIGURE 2.1
The Johari window.

different values and assumptions. One of these stages is what he calls the technician stage. It represents the most prevalent style of managing; 47% of senior managers and 68% of first-line managers fall into this category.

People in the technician stage are concerned with expertise. They focus on technical logic and on efficiency, often setting standards of perfection. They tend to work closely but impersonally with others. They are constantly checking up on details and do not hesitate to take over in an emergency. In terms of learning about themselves, they are very slow, perhaps resistant to taking feedback about their behavior. The feelings of others are simply not interesting or valid. People in this stage feel that technical facts rather than the norms and values of the group should guide behavior.

If so many managers are in fact in the technician stage, then learning about and understanding themselves is no small problem. For this reason it is useful to know about a concept called the Johari window.

The Johari window, developed by Luft and Ingham (1955), is a simple but helpful concept. As shown in Figure 2.1, it has four quadrants. In the upper left is the open area which represents the values, motives, and behaviors that are known to oneself and to others. In the upper right is the blind area. Here are the values, motives, and behaviors that are seen by others but are not recognized by you. In the lower left is the hidden quadrant. These are the things that you know but do not reveal to others. Finally, in the lower right is the unknown quadrant. Here are the motives and behaviors of which neither you nor others are yet aware; they exist, but no one has yet observed them or their impact on the relationship. Later, when they are discovered, it becomes obvious that they existed previously and did have impact.

The sizes of the four quadrants change over the course of time. In a new relationship, quadrant 1 is small. As communication increases, it grows large and quadrant 3 begins to shrink. With growing trust, we feel less need to hide the things we value, feel, and know. It takes longer for quadrant 2 to shrink in size because it requires openness to honest feedback. As we saw in Torbert's research, many people are not open to feedback about their blind spots. They feel defensive and use a variety of behaviors to close off feedback.

Quadrant 4 tends to change most slowly of all. It is often a very large quadrant that greatly influences what we do. Yet many people totally close off the possibility of learning about quadrant 4.

Some important lessons can be learned from the Johari window. People use a great deal of energy in order to hide, deny, or be blind to their own values, motives, and behaviors, particularly their inconsistencies and hypocrisies. As a result quadrant 1 begins to shrink and the others begin to enlarge.

When quadrant 1 increases in size, however, the others shrink: More energy, skills, and resources can be directed toward the tasks around which the relationship is formed. The more this occurs, the more openness, trust, and learning there is and the more the positive outcomes begin to multiply.

VALUES AND UNDERSTANDING OTHERS

The Johari window not only informs us of our own blind, hidden, and unknown areas, but it also makes us aware that these areas exist in others. If we appreciate that others have these three covert areas, then it is likely that they also will be defensive about them. And if we point out things in the three areas, it is likely that they will reject us and that the relationship will grow less trusting.

How then do we help others to learn? How do we build trust? How do we come to better understand others?

The paradoxical problem brings us back to ourselves. A key to positive change is not in focusing on others but on ourselves. In fact we need to be sensitive and respectful of the need of others to be defensive. The secret of overcoming defensiveness in others is to overcome defensiveness in ourselves. If we provide a role model of sensitivity, openness, and learning, we increase the probability of sensitivity, openness, and learning on the part of the other.

To provide such a role model, we need to feel secure enough to be open. Security, however, only comes by being open with ourselves. In other words, the key to understanding and helping others is to continuously increase our own awareness of those things we least want to know about ourselves, through openness to external feedback, and through sensitivity and respect for the defensiveness of others.

TABLE 2.1 Rules for Practicing Empathy

Empathy: The Ability to Experience the Feelings of Others

1. You must first examine yourself. If you do not truly want to understand others, if you are insincere, empathy will not work.
2. Communication is more than words. You must be sensitive to times when expressed thoughts and feelings are not congruent. You must read the nonverbal signals as well as the verbal ones.

3. Do not react too quickly to inaccurate statements of fact; listen carefully for the feelings beneath the statement before rushing in to correct facts.

4. You must allow the person to tell the emotional truth, which may include negative feelings about you. You must be ready to openly explore such negative feedback.

5. Use reflective listening (see Competency 2 in this chapter).

Integrity, security, and self-acceptance increase the ability to practice empathy, the key skill in helping others to grow. **Empathy** is truly putting yourself in the position of others and honestly trying to see the world as they see it. Table 2.1 lists five rules for helping you to practice being empathetic.

ANALYSIS   The Sherwood Holmes Case[1]

Directions   Your role for this activity is that of Sherwood Holmes, the American cousin of a certain famous detective. Although you are not as well known as your cousin, you are lucky to have inherited the same skills that have inspired numerous novels and films.

After reading the case, carefully study the room diagram. Then construct and complete the Sherwood Inference Sheet. In your small group compare your observations and inferences; a large discussion will follow.

Last month your department instituted the placement of suggestion boxes at all work sites. You came up with several suggestions, one of which was brought to the attention of your CEO. You have been called into the CEO's office to discuss how your suggestion could be implemented.

Always prepared, you reviewed your cousin's notes that stated:

Observation, knowledge, and induction and deduction are all any private investigator needs. Observation is what you see, hear, and so on. Knowledge consists of the meanings, facts, and information that is available to you. Induction is the process of reasoning from the specific to the general. For example, every tree I have seen has roots, therefore, all trees have roots. Deduction, on the other hand, is the process of reasoning from the general to the specific—all trees have roots; this is a tree; therefore, this tree has roots.

When you arrive at the office, the secretary tells you that the CEO will arrive in about 15 minutes. You are shown into the office to wait. Knowing you have several minutes alone in the office, your native curiosity becomes overwhelming. You begin to look around.

The office smells of Italian leather and the wooden parquet floor is stained a warm cherry. You sit in one of the two black leather club chairs to the left of the doorway. Between the chairs is a low wooden table on which is a large glass bowl and two smaller bowls. On the wall behind you is an imposing ebony and cherrywood clock. A rubber plant in a black globe-shaped container sits against the side wall next to the other chair.

Across from where you are sitting is a large cherrywood desk, with a black leather desk chair. An art print of one of Picasso's unidentifiable nudes hangs on the wall behind the desk, and below that sits a closed briefcase. The black wastebasket next to the wall by the desk chair is full of papers.

---

[1]*Adapted from* J.W. Pfeiffer and John E. Jones (eds.), *A Handbook of Structured Experiences for Human Relations Training*, Vol.VI, San Diego, CA.: University Associates, Inc. 1977. Used with permission.

You can see most of the objects on the desk. A matching pen-and-pencil stand and a letter opener are lying at the front of the desk. To one side of them is a calculator, and next to that is a brass desk lamp. In front of the lamp is a double metal photograph frame with photographs in it. One is of an attractive woman in her thirties with a young boy about eight years old. The other photograph is of a Dalmatian in a grassy field. In front of the frame is a stack of green file folders.

On the desk, in front of the desk chair, are a few sheets of paper and a felt-tipped pen.

On the other side of the desk is a clear glass teacup. In front of it are a leather-tabbed book and a legal-sized yellow pad. The book looks as if it is either an address book or an appointment calendar. Beside the yellow pad lies a pile of unopened mail—envelopes of many sizes. And partially on top of the pile and in back of it are half-folded newspapers: *The Wall Street Journal* and *The New York Times.*

Behind the desk and to one side is a credenza on which eight books are lined up. They are *Roget's Thesaurus,* the *Random House Dictionary, Basic Principles of Management, Marketing for Today, Diversity and the Organization, People at Work, You Are What You Eat,* and last year's *World Almanac.* On the far end of the credenza sits a bronze statue; it appears to be of a man sitting with his legs folded in a Yoga position, but it is slightly abstract. In the corner next to the credenza is a philodendron sitting in a deep red and black woven basket.

There is a window on the far wall, and you get up and go over to look out. Directly in front of the window is a sofa covered in smooth black leather. Two chintz throw pillows in contemporary prints lie against the arms of the sofa. The blinds on the window behind the sofa are an off–white. The view from the window is pleasant: a few tidy shops bordering a small park.

Your gaze turns to the square wooden table next to the sofa. Magazines are scattered in front of a heavy brass lamp. The magazines are varied: two recent editions of *Time,* and one copy each of *Sports Illustrated, The New Yorker, Psychology Today,* and *Ebony.* Next to the table is the philodendron.

As you turn to walk back to your chair, you notice that the papers on the desk in front of you are from your personnel file, and that a statement of your gender has been circled with the felt-tipped pen. Since the CEO may return at any moment, you sit in the chair to wait.

Directions for Inference Sheet   Read the description of the CEO's office and study the room diagram carefully. Construct the Sherwood Inference Sheet by drawing three columns on a piece of paper.

1. In the left-hand column (Observation) note data from your reading that you think are important clues about the kind of person who occupies the room.

2. In the middle column (Knowledge) note any experiences that you may have had that influence your observation.

3. In the right-hand column (Inference) note whatever conclusions you reach as a result of your observations.

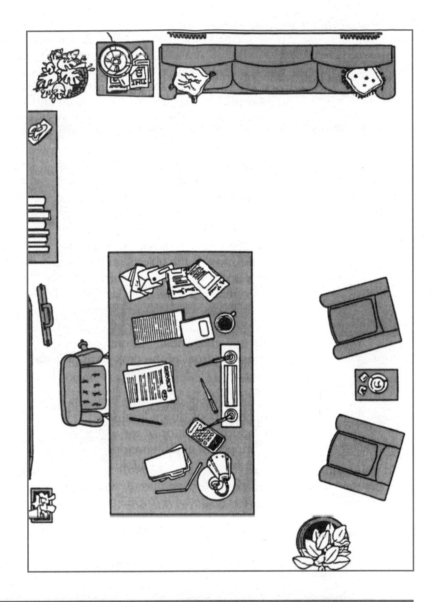

PRACTICE   The Marvins Are Missing Again

Directions   Read the case of each of the three Marvins. They are all absent from work, but for very different reasons. The performance of your unit is suffering as a result of these absences. Your manager is beginning to ask why you have so many reported absences in your unit.

Marvin Lowrey
Marvin Lowrey was one of your best workers until his wife was killed in a car accident several months ago. He asked for, and you approved, a two-week leave so that he could "think things out."

When he returned, it was obvious that this was not the same Marvin you knew several weeks before. He seemed absentminded, irritable, and was nearly injured in a shop accident because of his carelessness. He also has called in sick several times. You called him at home to see how he was doing, and he said it was just the flu. He has also used up all his vacation time. In the past, Marvin has been a good employee, and you are concerned with the situation.

Marvin Fletcher

Marvin is absent from work again today. He called in to say he would be a half-hour late because he had to run his daughter off to school. Marvin's wife also works, and running the kids around often falls under Marvin's responsibility. In Marvin's favor is the fact that his performance doesn't suffer from these short absences. When he is at work, he works harder than anyone else. His overall productivity is at least as good as anyone else in your unit. The problem is that you feel it doesn't look good to have people coming in whenever they want. Other employees also want increased flexibility "because Marvin gets to you." You feel you need to talk to Marvin, but feel a little guilty about it. Just last week your son was sick and you had to stay home with him. Marvin knows about it too.

Rita Marvin

Rita Marvin is also absent from work today. Rita has a degenerative bone disease that causes her a great deal of pain. The pain seems to occur in bouts that prevent her from coming to work.

Rita has volunteered to do some work at home, but union agreements and insurance regulations do not allow it. She is a fine worker and has a great sense of humor. She is a real morale booster in the unit. Unfortunately, in the past couple months Rita has been missing too much work. Her illness is getting worse. You have overheard some of the other workers say she should go on disability. You have mentioned the possibility of disability to Rita, but she pleads with you to keep her on. The job gives her life meaning, and all her friends are from work.

Discussion Questions   1. How would you deal with the Marvins' absences?

2. What strategy could you use in a discussion with each Marvin?

APPLICATION Understanding and Changing Relationships

1. Identify three people with whom you have to relate regularly.

2. Specify your first impression of each one.

3. List ways in which your perceptions have changed or been reinforced.

4. If there are problems in any of the relationships, identify ways in which you may have contributed.

5. Specify how you might use the concepts in this section to improve these three relationships.

Competency 2 Communicating Effectively

ASSESSMENT Communication Skills

Directions   Analyze the communication in two of your relationships: one that is very painful and one that is very pleasant. Next, analyze how your communication behavior varies in the two relationships and what areas of communication you might need to work on. Answer the questions by using the following scale.

Scale   Minimal Problem 1   2   3   4   5   6   7   Great Problem

Painful		Pleasant		
Other	Self	Other	Self	
_____	_____	_____	_____	1. Expresses ideas in unclear ways.
_____	_____	_____	_____	2. Tries to dominate conversations.
_____	_____	_____	_____	3. Often has a hidden agenda.
_____	_____	_____	_____	4. Is formal and impersonal.
_____	_____	_____	_____	5. Does not listen well.
_____	_____	_____	_____	6. Is often boring, uninteresting.
_____	_____	_____	_____	7. Is withdrawn and uncommunicative.
_____	_____	_____	_____	8. Is overly sensitive, too easily hurt.
_____	_____	_____	_____	9. Is too abstract and hard to follow.
_____	_____	_____	_____	10. Is closed to the ideas of the other.
_____	_____	_____	_____	Total score

Now go back and reexamine your answers. What patterns do you see?

Interpretation   1. How do you think your own communication behavior varies in these two relationships?

2. On what specific problems in the painful relationship do you most need to work?

Interpersonal communication is perhaps one of the most important and least understood competencies that a manager can have—and vital to playing the mentor role. Knowing when and how to share information requires a very complex understanding of people and situations (Zey, 1990).

Communication is the exchange of information, facts, ideas, and meanings. The communication process can be used to inform, coordinate, and motivate people. Unfortunately, being a good communicator is not easy. Nor is it easy to recognize your own problems in communication. In the exercise you just completed, for example, you may have easily ignored your own weaknesses in communicating and may have given yourself much lower scores than you gave to the other person in the painful relationship. Although most people in organizations tend to think of themselves as excellent communicators, they consider communication a major organizational problem, and they see the other people in the organization as the source of the problem. It is very difficult to see and admit the problems in our own communication behavior.

Despite this difficulty, analyzing communication behavior is vital. Poor communication skills result in both interpersonal and organizational problems. When interpersonal problems arise, people begin to experience conflict, resist change, and avoid contact with others. Organizationally, poor communication often results in low morale and low productivity. After all, organizing *requires* that people communicate—to develop goals, channel energy, and identify and solve problems.

A BASIC MODEL OF INTERPERSONAL COMMUNICATION

The exchange of information may take a variety of forms including ideas, facts, and feelings. Despite the many possible forms, the communication process may be seen in terms of a general model (Shannon and Weaver, 1948). See Figure 2.2.

The model begins with the communicator encoding a message. Here the person who is going to communicate translates a set of ideas into a system of symbols such as words or numbers. Many things influence the encoding process including the urgency of the message, the experience and skills of the sender, and the sender's perception of the receiver. The message is transmitted through a medium of some sort. A message, for example, might be written, oral, or even nonverbal. Once it is received, it must be decoded. This means that the message must be interpreted by the person who receives it. Like the encoding process, the decoding process is subject to influence by a wide number of factors.

The model includes a feedback loop between the receiver and the communicator. The **feedback** can take three forms: informational, corrective, or reinforcing. Informational feedback is a nonevaluative response that simply provides additional facts to the sender. Corrective feedback involves a challenge to, or

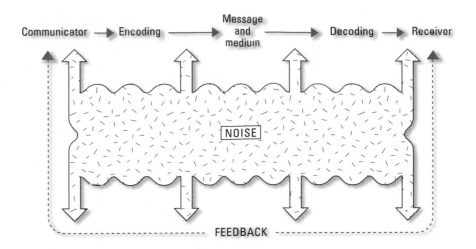

FIGURE 2.2
A basic model of communication.

*Source: Developed from C.
Shannon and M. Weaver,*
The Mathematical Theory
of Communication
*(Urbana: University of Illinois
Press, 1948).*
Used with permission.

correction of, the original message. Reinforcing feedback is a clear acknowledgment of the message that was sent. It may be positive or negative.

The final aspect of the model is noise. **Noise** is anything that can distort the message in the communication process. As indicated in Figure 2.2, it can occur at any point in the process. A sender may be unable to clearly articulate the ideas to be sent. In the medium, a document may leave out a key word. In the decoding process, the receiver may make wrong assumptions about the motive behind the message.

PROBLEMS IN INTERPERSONAL COMMUNICATION

Interpersonal communication problems occur in organizations for several reasons.

- *Defensiveness.* As indicated in the first competency of this chapter, people have defenses that prevent them from receiving messages they fear. All people have some insecurities, and there are certain things they simply do not want to know. This is especially true of issues that affect values, assumptions, and self-image. You, for example, may have been somewhat defensive in responding to the two questions at the end of this section's communication assessment.

- *Inarticulateness.* Communication problems may arise because the sender of the message has difficulty expressing the concept. If the receiver is not aware of the problem, completely inaccurate images may arise and result in subsequent misunderstandings.

- *Hidden agendas.* Sometimes people have motives that they prefer not to reveal. Because the sender believes that the receiver would not react in the desired way, the sender becomes deceptive. The sender seeks to maintain a competitive advantage by keeping the true purpose hidden. Over time, such behavior results in low trust and cooperation.

- *Status.* Communication is often distorted by perceptions of position. When communicating with a person in a position of authority, individuals often craft messages so as to impress and not offend. Conversely, when communicating with a person in a lower hierarchical position, individuals may be unnecessarily cold or insensitive to that person's needs, causing the receiver to reject or distort the message that is actually sent.

- *Environment.* The nature of physical space can greatly influence communication. Some environments may be too hot or too noisy. Others may provide an inappropriate setting for a particular type of message. Informal messages may be inappropriate in a setting that is highly formal, and formal messages may be inappropriate in settings that are highly informal.

- *Hostility.* In many cases the receiver is angry at the person who sends the message. When goodwill is lost in a relationship, all messages tend to be reframed in a negative way. Hostility makes it most difficult to send and receive accurate information. When trust is low and people are angry, no matter what the sender actually expresses, it is likely to be distorted.

Given the number and intensity of some of these barriers, how do people communicate effectively? Table 2.2 gives seven basic rules that will increase the quality of communication.

TABLE 2.2   Rules for Effective Communication

1. *Be clear on who the receiver is.* What is the receiver's state of mind? What assumptions are brought by the receiver? What is he or she feeling in this situation?

2. *Know what your objective is.* What do you want to accomplish by sending the message?

3. *Analyze the climate.* What will be necessary to help the receiver relax and be open to the communication?

4. *Review the message in your head before you say it.* Listen to the practice message from the point of view of the receiver. Then say it.

5. *Communicate in the language of the other person.* Use examples and illustrations that come from the world of the receiver.

6. *If the receiver seems not to understand, clarify the message.* Ask questions. If repetition is necessary, try different words and illustrations.

7. *If the response is seemingly critical, do not react defensively.* Try to understand what is happening in the receiver. Why is he or she reacting negatively? The receiver may be misunderstanding. Ask clarifying questions.

REFLECTIVE LISTENING

Managers often need to counsel a subordinate. Here effective communication is particularly important. Of all the skills associated with good communication, in such a situation, perhaps the most important is reflective listening. Most people fail to realize just how poorly they tend to listen.

Reflective listening is based on empathy (see Table 2.1). Reflective listening is a sincere attempt to experience the thoughts and feelings of the other person. In using empathy and reflective listening, instead of directing and controlling the thoughts of the other, you become a helper who tries to facilitate the other's expression. Instead of assuming responsibility for another's problem, you help him or her to explore it on his or her own. Your job is not to talk but to keep the other person talking. You do not evaluate, judge, or advise; you simply reflect on what you hear. In fewer words, you descriptively, not evaluatively, restate the essence of the person's last thought or feeling. If the person's statement is factually inaccurate, you do not immediately point out the inaccuracy. Instead of interrupting, you keep the person's flow of expression moving. You can go back later to correct factual errors.

The reflective listener uses open-ended questions like, "Can you tell me more?" or "How did you feel when that happened?" Evaluative questions and factual, yes-or-no, questions are avoided. The key is to keep the conceptual and emotional flow of expression. Instead of telling, the reflective listener helps the other person to discover. The practice exercise (below) will particularly help to illustrate this.

To the first time reader, reflective listening sounds very strange. Experience shows, however, that it can have major payoffs. Trust and concern grow with an ever-deepening understanding of interpersonal issues. More effective and lasting problem solving takes place, and people have a greater sense of impact. In short, communication greatly improves.

Reflective listening is not, however, a panacea. It is time consuming to really listen. It requires confidence in one's interpersonal skills and the courage to possibly hear things about oneself that are less than complimentary. There is also a danger that the sender will get into personal areas of life with which the listener is not comfortable and for which a professional counselor would be more appropriate. It is, nevertheless, a vital tool that is seldom understood or employed.

ANALYSIS   One-Way, Two-Way Communication

Directions   The following activities focus on several aspects of communication, including active listening, speaking, and one- and two-way communication. Choose a partner, with whom you will work. One of you will act as the speaker, giving instructions verbally, and the other will be the listener, drawing the figure on paper according to the information the speaker provides. Your instructor will provide the figure. You will remain in these roles for both activities. Sit so that you cannot hear the interaction between other participants. A large group discussion will follow.

Activity A

Objective: To have the listener draw the described figure. Time: 5 minutes.

1. *Speaker.* Sit back-to-back with the listener and describe one of the drawings you have chosen. You are to give drawing instructions without allowing the listener to see you or the figure. Do not answer any questions.

2. *Listener.* Sit back-to-back with the speaker and draw the figure as it is described to you. Correct your drawing as you think necessary. Do not look at the speaker; do not ask any questions.

Activity B

Objective: To have the listener draw the described figure. Time: 5 minutes.

1. Speaker and listener remain in the same roles.

2. *Speaker.* Sit facing the listener and describe the second drawing you have. You are to give drawing instructions while looking at the listener and at his or her drawing. Be careful not to show the drawing to the listener. You may shake your head and use your arms and hands. You may not touch the listener or the drawing he or she is doing. You may not draw the figures on a board or in the air.

3. *Listener.* Sit facing the speaker and draw the second figure as directed. Do not allow the speaker to touch the drawing; you may ask questions.

Discussion Questions

1. What problems did you experience?

2. What were your major impressions?

3. What do these activities show you about communication?

PRACTICE Reflecting Feelings and Ideas[2]

Directions Reflecting is demonstrating to the other person that his or her communication has been heard and understood. Read the following remarks and, as the listener, select the response that best reflects the feelings or ideas of the speaker. A large group discussion will follow.

Remark

1. The employee has been on a new crew for three months. During a counseling interview, he said, "I don't know why it is, but I just don't feel as

[2] *Adapted from Developing Managerial Skills,* by David A. Whetten and Kim S. Cameron. Copyright © 1984 by Scott, Foresman and Company. Used with permission.

though I'm one of the gang. They are all nice enough people, but somehow they seem to have a closed circle and make me feel like an outsider. Maybe it's me; I don't know."

Possible Responses to Reflect

a. Why don't you use the first chance you get to do the crew a favor?

b. It seems to you that the group doesn't accept you.

c. It seems that the others dislike you for some reason.

d. You don't think they will accept you, even if you give them some more time to learn that you are a nice fellow.

Remark

2. A manager with 10 years' experience missed a chance for a promotion because of a low score on a promotion exam. "I'm just going to do the minimum to get by until retirement," she told a co-manager.

Possible Responses to Reflect

a. You are discouraged about missing the opportunity for promotion.

b. You deserve to be upset. I would be too.

c. Those exams don't measure your ability correctly.

d. Your attitude had better change or you'll lose everything.

Remark

3. A clerical employee with 10 years' experience told his manager, "I've been doing this job for years now and nobody has ever complained. Now you send my work back and tell me to do it over. It isn't fair, and it doesn't make sense. Maybe I do make mistakes now and then, but nobody is perfect. And I don't know why I should get all the blame for what goes on around here."

Possible Responses to Reflect

a. You don't think it's fair to ask you to correct your own mistakes.

b. Suppose you check your work before you bring it to me.

c. You think you are being blamed for not being perfect.

d. You feel that I am too strict.

Remark

4. During an interview with his manager, an employee states, "I don't want to work with Jake anymore. He's lazy and is always taking a superior attitude, complaining about the rest of us not helping him as much as we should. He thinks he is too good for this kind of work and too good to work with the rest of us, and I'm sick of being around him."

Possible Responses to Reflect

a. You feel that Jake ought to be disciplined in some way.

b. Jake doesn't want to cooperate, is that it?

c. You feel Jake's attitude makes the work unpleasant.

d. You think Jake might fit in better somewhere else.

Remark

5. A young man whose work showed a sudden drop in quality was sent to the employment manager for an interview. One of the things he said on arriving was, "I don't know why I should be asked to talk to you about my work. I haven't complained and haven't time for this kind of chitchat. So give me what help you have in mind and I'll be on my way."

Possible Responses to Reflect

a. You came to see me because you were sent, not because you believe you have any need for help.

b. Don't you feel that with my experience in the company I might be of some help?

c. You feel irritated at coming here because you don't think I can help you.

d. You mustn't jump to conclusions. Often people need help when they are unaware of this need.

Remark

6. A manager met with her superior to report on a difficult performance appraisal meeting. "I hated to terminate that probationary employee but I had no other choice."

Possible Responses to Reflect

a. I hate doing those meetings myself.

b. How did the employee respond?

c. It was uncomfortable for you to fire someone.

d. It gets easier over time.

Remark

7. In the middle of a counseling interview with her boss, a 58-year-old woman said, "You don't want me here; you just want young women. I'm getting old; so I guess I should get out."

Possible Responses to Reflect

a. It's not true that I favor the young women employees.

b. You believe I'd like to have you leave because of your age.

c. You feel you have reason to believe that I prefer young girls.

d. I can see that I must have done something to hurt your feelings.

Remark

8. A manager was discussing the work of a young man who has been out of high school about a year. The manager was trying to determine why important details on procedures were often overlooked or clearly violated. Suddenly the young man shouted, "You're the worst manager I've ever had. If a person shows initiative, you work him over. I refuse to follow silly rules."

Possible Responses to Reflect

a. Why don't you check with me before you make a change in procedure?

b. You resent me for criticizing your work.

c. Perhaps it's my fault that I didn't train you on the correct procedure.

d. You feel I should have someone else go over your work.

Remark

9. In a conversation with a co-worker, a young woman talked at length about her husband's lack of consideration, going into considerable detail to justify why she should divorce him. After a pause she remarked that she never had long-term relationships with anyone. "Other people seem to have old friends, but I get tired of them after I get to know them. Maybe I expect too much of people."

Possible Responses to Reflect

a. You feel a divorce may be the solution to your problem.

b. You think perhaps you should reconsider your divorce.

    c. After you get to know people, they cease to be exciting and fun.

    d. You believe that expecting too much of friends may interfere with long-term relationships.

Remarks

10. Manager, age 35, says to a friend, "I'm determined to get ahead. I'm not afraid of hard work. I am not afraid to take a few hard knocks—if I can see my goal out there in front. And I'm not averse to climbing over a few people who get in my way, because this means a lot to me. I can't be satisfied with just a mediocre job. No, I want to be somebody."

Possible Responses to Reflect

    a. You feel that you just have to be out on top no matter what you may do to others.

    b. You see yourself as a deeply ambitious person, is that it?

    c. What do you suppose is behind this strong determination of yours to get ahead?

    d. Strong ambition can be a real asset to anyone. Are you really sure, though, that you mean it when you say you're not averse to climbing over those who get in your way? Couldn't that turn out to do you more harm than good?

APPLICATION   Active Listening[3]

You will be working with two other people for this activity. Assign yourselves the roles of *A, B,* and *C.* Then, follow these steps:

1. Participant *A* will be the first speaker and should choose the topic to be discussed from the list that follows. If none of the topics is appealing, additional topics may be substituted. Choose the topic about which you feel most strongly.

2. Participant *B* will be the first listener.

3. Participant *C* will be the first referee.

4. The speaker will then discuss the chosen topic for about 3 to 4 minutes. It is important to be sensitive to the needs of the listener. You can establish nonverbal cues for pacing the discussion.

[3]*Adapted from* J. William Pfeiffer and John E. Jones (eds.), *A Handbook of Structured Experiences for Human Relations Training,* Vol. I. San Diego, CA.: University Associates, Inc., 1974. Used with permission.

5. The listener will summarize the speaker's point of view in his or her own words and without notes (time: about 2 minutes).

6. If the summary is thought to be incorrect, both the speaker and the referee are free to correct any misunderstanding.

7. The referee is to make certain that the listener does not omit, distort, add to, respond to, or interpret what the speaker has said.

8. The total process of speaking and summarizing should take about 7 to 8 minutes in each round. The instructor will indicate when time is up.

9. In the second round, participant *B* becomes the speaker, participant *C* the listener, and participant *A* the referee. The new speaker should choose a topic and begin discussing that topic. Round 2 should also take 7 to 8 minutes.

10. In the final round, participant *C* becomes the speaker, participant *A* the listener, and participant *B* the referee. Again, this round should take 7 to 8 minutes.

Possible Topics

Capital punishment	Two-career couples
A memory from childhood	The AIDS epidemic
Drug use and abuse	All-volunteer army
Health care problems today	Vacation plans
Foreign policy	Soaring real estate prices
What I like about my job	Today's education system
What I dislike about my job	The open classroom
Rising food prices	The profit motive
Nuclear plant disasters	Expectations for this day
Slanted new stories in the press and on TV	The responsibility of the news media
Raising children	Tax reform
U.S. involvement in Central America	

1. What difficulties and barriers were encountered?

2. What did you learn about listening effectively?

3. How can you apply the principles in this section to your real-world problems?

Competency 3 Developing Subordinates

ASSESSMENT Assumptions About Performance Evaluations

Directions   Check off the statement in each of the following pairs of statements that best reflects your assumptions about performance evaluation.

Performance evaluation is:

_____ 1a. A formal process that is done annually.
_____ b. An informal process that is done continuously.
_____ 2a. A process that is planned for subordinates.
_____ b. A process that is planned with subordinates.
_____ 3a A required organizational procedure.
_____ b. A process done regardless of requirements.
_____ 4a. A time to evaluate subordinate performance.
_____ b. A time for subordinates to evaluate the manager.
_____ 5a. A time to clarify standards.
_____ b. A time to clarify the subordinate's career needs.
_____ 6a. A time to confront poor performance.
_____ b. A time to express appreciation.
_____ 7a. An opportunity to clarify issues and provide direction and control.
_____ b. An opportunity to increase enthusiasm and commitment.
_____ 8a. Only as good as the organization's forms.
_____ b. Only as good as the manager's coaching skills.

Interpretation   1. As you review your eight answers, do you see any patterns in your assumptions or in the assumptions you did not choose?

2. As you review the statements, can you explain why the performance evaluation process is disliked by most employees in the United States?

3. How would you design an effective process?

LEARNING Developing Subordinates

In a literal sense, *mentor* means a trusted counselor or guide—a coach. In this section we turn to this particular aspect of the role. It is interesting to note that the two previous competencies in this chapter did much to focus on the building of trust. Now we turn more specifically to coaching, or the notion of developing people by providing performance evaluation and feedback.

Feedback on performance is one of the most potentially helpful kinds of information that a person can get. It is critical to improvement, growth, and development. Yet, as implied in question 2 of the preceding exercise, performance evaluation is one of the most uniformly disliked processes in organizational America. Before we talk about how to do a performance evaluation, it might be useful to consider why performance evaluations so often fail.

THE MANY USES AND PROBLEMS
OF PERFORMANCE APPRAISAL

In the mentor role performance appraisal is seen as a tool to facilitate the development of subordinates, to clarify expectations, and to improve performance. This is not, however, the only view. A study of why organizations do performance appraisals revealed that high percentages of large organizations report other reasons for performance appraisal (Locher and Teel, 1977).

Compensation	62.2%
Performance improvement	60.6%
Feedback	37.8%
Promotion	21.1%
Documentation	10.0%
Training	9.4%
Staffing planning	6.1%
Discharge	2.2%

Although performance appraisal may serve some developmental functions for the individual, it is also an organizational tool (Swanson, 1994). It is often used to make systemwide decisions about rewards such as compensation and promotion. It may be used in cases of discharge. It may be used as a research base for developing selection and training strategies. Because of the importance of these formal functions, the organization is open to legal challenge. An employee, for example, may sue because of a given promotion decision. Hence issues of accuracy and fairness become increasingly critical, and much of the literature focuses on methods of forms design, statistical techniques, and sources of error. The objective, with good reason, is to build a generalized system that fits every situation in the organization and that is fair and defensible. This, of course, is a tall order, and in many organizations, performance appraisal becomes a source of high frustration or meaningless game playing. Often the result of the confrontation is a fairly meaningless procedure that is of little benefit to anyone.

In addition to the organizational problems, many personal pressures make performance appraisal difficult. The process often makes both managers and subordinates very uncomfortable. How well a person has performed over the past year is seldom as clear as the human resources staff would like to believe it is, and the form is seldom able to capture the complexity of real life. Subordinates sense that the quantitative evaluations are really a cover for subjective judgments and sometimes challenge what they are told. Managers feel uncomfortable admitting that the evaluation process often reduces to subjective judgment and they usually feel uncomfortable in the role of a "judge."

Both parties tend to fear being challenged with questions that they may not be able to answer. Managers often become frustrated when an angry subordinate becomes hostile or passive. In either case, they may lack the skills to know how to handle the problem. Because doing performance evaluation properly requires constant observation, recording, and feedback, it is seen by many managers as too time consuming to do right.

PERFORMANCE EVALUATION

In the assessment exercise at the beginning of this competency, you chose between options in eight pairs of assumptions about performance evaluation. In each pair of statements answer *a* reflected traditional control values—those normally associated with the evaluation process. Answer *b*, on the other hand, reflected values reflecting involvement, communication, and trust. In this section we will consider performance evaluation as a two-step process, one that mixes the *a* and *b* views of the world. Although the mixed view presented here differs from what is designed and practiced in most organizations, you may find it to be of some value.

PREPARATION

Performance evaluation starts long before the actual evaluation session. If you have the organizational freedom to do so, and if your situation is appropriate, you might even invite subordinates to join you in designing a program that will work. Their wisdom may surprise you. You might begin the planning session by discussing what program, if any, is currently in place and what is positive and negative about the system. You might review the value of feedback to individuals and the group and then consider the reasons that most programs fail. With these things in mind, you might as a group specify some guidelines that will work in your situation. Some samples are given in Table 2.3.

TABLE 2.3   Guidelines for Giving and Receiving Feedback

Giving Feedback

- Before giving feedback, examine your motivation and make sure the receiver is ready and open to hear you.
- While giving feedback, use "I" statements rather than "you" statements to indicate that these are your perceptions, thoughts, and feelings.
- Describe the other person's behavior and your perceptions of it.
- Ask the other person to clarify, explain, change, or correct.
- After giving feedback, give the receiver time to respond.

Asking for Feedback

- Before asking for feedback, make sure you are open to hearing information that may alter your perception.

- Be aware that the person giving you the feedback is describing his or her own perception of the situation, but realize that his or her feelings are real.

- Check your understanding of the feedback: Ask questions or give examples and share your reaction(s). Clarify issues, explain your actions, and correct perceptions people may have of you.

Giving and receiving feedback requires some self-confidence, trust in subordinates, and many of the skills and competencies discussed in the first two competencies of this chapter. If you feel uncomfortable, it may not be a good idea to try such a procedure. In any case, whether you generate your own guidelines or use existing ones, be sure, over time, to regularly observe the performance of subordinates and make notes of concrete incidents that would be useful to discuss at evaluation time. Feedback, however, should not be a onetime experience. There should be no surprises at the evaluation meeting. In fact, coaching sessions should be considered along the way, before a formal performance evaluation takes place.

Instead of walking into the evaluation cold, you may want to try another unique twist. At some specified time before the evaluation, exchange with the subordinate a written evaluation of the subordinate's performance. Spend some time reading the person's self-evaluation and use empathy to put yourself in the person's place. Use this process to prepare yourself for the evaluation session. In scheduling the session, be sure to set aside enough time and be sure that you have a private setting where you will not be interrupted.

In the actual evaluation, be sure that your own objective is clear. Know what you want to accomplish. Get into an appropriate frame of mind. Ask yourself how you really feel about the person, and most importantly, if you really want to help the person. Few managers enter the process in such a frame of mind.

Begin by focusing on positive behaviors. Ask the person to list the things that he or she has done well and contribute to the list as much as possible. When you turn to areas that might need improvement, again ask the person to begin, and in a supportive way, continue together until you agree on a list. At this point, if you have the skills discussed in the last two sections, you might ask how you as a manager are contributing to this person's problems. For example, you might suggest going through the list and asking what you could do differently. As the person responds, you might use reflective listening to explore the person's claim in an honest way. Make commitments to change your behavior where possible. Hence you are modeling the behavior in which you would like the subordinate to engage. After doing this you might again go through the list and ask the subordinate what changes he or she might make.

At the conclusion of the session, summarize what each of you might do differently during the next few months. Ask to see the person's career development plan. Review what progress has been made and what each of you can do to speed progress in the next period. If there is no such plan, one of the assignments should be to write a plan. You may need to help the person. After this, do an overall review and check the person's understanding of each action step. Do a final summary, and set a time for future reviews.

ANALYSIS ° United Chemical Company[4]

Directions   This exercise gives you a chance to analyze the principles of supportive communication and supportive listening you have read about in this chapter. Read the case and then answer the questions that follow.

The United Chemical Company is a large producer and distributor of commodity chemicals with five chemical production plants in the United States. The operations at the main plant in Baytown, Texas, include not only production equipment, but also the company's research and engineering center.

The process design group consists of eight male engineers and the manager, Max Kane. The group has worked together steadily for a number of years, and good relationships have developed among all members. When the work load began to increase, Max hired a new design engineer, Sue Davis, a recent master's degree graduate from one of the foremost engineering schools in the country. Sue was assigned to a project involving expansion of one of the existing plant facilities' capacity. Three other design engineers were assigned to the project along with Sue: Jack Keller (age 38, with 15 years with the company), Sam Sims (age 40, with 10 years with the company), and Lance Madison (age 32, with 8 years with the company).

As a new employee, Sue was enthusiastic about the opportunity to work at United. She liked her work very much because it was challenging and it offered her a chance to apply much of the knowledge she had gained in her university studies. On the job, Sue kept to herself and her design work. Her relations with her fellow project members were friendly, but she did not go out of her way to have informal conversations during or after working hours.

Sue was a diligent employee who took her work seriously. On occasions when a difficult problem arose, she would stay after hours in order to come up with a solution. Because of her persistence, coupled with her more current education, Sue usually completed her portion of the various project stages a number of days before her colleagues. This was somewhat irritating to her, and on these occasions she went to Max to ask for additional work to keep her busy until her fellow workers caught up to her. Initially, she had offered to help Jack, Sam, and Lance with their part of the project, but each time she was turned down tersely.

About five months after Sue had joined the design group, Jack asked to see Max about a problem the group was having. The conversation between Max and Jack was as follows.

[4]*Adapted from Organizational Behavior and Performance*, 3d ed., by Andrew D. Szilag; and Marc J. Wallace, Jr. Copyright © 1983, 1980 by Scott, Foresman and Company. Used with permission.

Max: Jack, I understand you wanted to discuss a problem with me.

Jack: Yes, Max. I didn't want to waste your time, but some of the other design engineers wanted me to discuss Sue with you. She is irritating everyone with her know-it-all, pompous attitude. She just is not the kind of person that we want to work with.

Max: I can't understand that, Jack. She's an excellent worker whose design work is always well done and usually flawless. She's doing everything the company wants her to do.

Jack: The company never asked her to disturb the morale of the group or to tell us how to do our work. The animosity of the group can eventually result in lower-quality work for the whole unit.

Max: I'll tell you what I'll do. Sue has a meeting with me next week to discuss her six-month performance. I'll keep your thoughts in mind, but I can't promise an improvement in what you and the others believe is a pompous attitude.

Jack: Immediate improvement in her behavior is not the problem, it's her coaching others when she has no right to engage in publicly showing others what to do. You'd think she was lecturing an advanced class in design with all her high-power, useless equations and formulas. She'd better back off soon, or some of us will quit or transfer.

During the next week, Max thought carefully about his meeting with Jack. He knew that Jack was the informal leader of the design engineers and generally spoke for the other group members. On Thursday of the following week, Max called Sue into his office for her midyear review. One portion of the conversation was as follows:

Max: There is one other aspect I'd like to discuss with you about your performance. As I just related to you, your technical performance has been excellent; however, there are some questions about your relationships with the other workers.

Sue: I don't understand—what questions are you talking about?

Max: Well, to be specific, certain members of the design group have complained about your apparent "know-it-all attitude" and the manner in which you try to tell them how to do their job. You're going to have to be patient with them and not publicly call them out about their performance. This is a good group of engineers, and their work over the years has been more than acceptable. I don't want any problems that will cause the group to produce less effectively.

Sue: Let me make a few comments. First of all, I have never publicly criticized their performance to them or to you. Initially, when I was finished ahead of them, I offered to help them with their work, but was bluntly told to mind my own business. I took the hint and concentrated only on my part of the work. What you don't understand is that after five months of working in this group I have come to the conclusion that what is going on is a "rip-off" of the company. The other engineers are "goldbricking" and setting a work pace much slower than they're capable of. They're more interested in the music from Sam's radio, the local football team, and the bar they're going to go to for TGIF. I'm sorry, but this is just not the way I was raised or trained. And finally, they've never looked on me as a qualified engineer, but as a woman who has broken their professional barrier.

Discussion Questions

1. What are the key problems?

2. How would you use the information in this chapter to redesign the meeting between Max and Sue?

PRACTICE   Giving and Receiving Feedback

Directions   Review the guidelines for giving and receiving feedback that were presented in Competency 3, then read the two roles that follow. At the indicated time, conduct a meeting, initiated by the person playing Schultz, that allows you to practice the guidelines.

Role for Klaus Schultz, Manager.   You are a parks maintenance manager at Winsome River State Park Campground. You are in your early forties and have been involved in campground maintenance since you were a child working summers at your parents' campground. You enjoyed those summers, so it seemed only natural to continue in this line of work.

Eight years ago you were made a manager. Your staff consists of eight full-time parks maintenance assistants. You have worked hard in this job and feel that you have had considerable success in building up your park's reputation over the past eight years. In fact, Winsome River has become the most popular campground in the state.

You are about to have a coaching session with one of your parks maintenance assistants, Martin LeFete. Martin also has had a lot of experience in the outdoors. He has done extensive backpacking and white-water rafting. He is a hard worker and very committed, but recently you have had several complaints from campers.

It seems that Martin has scolded several campers for littering and leaving fires unattended. Although these are fairly common occurrences in state parks, and they should be corrected, Martin's approach has been somewhat aggressive.

For example, a few days ago Martin followed a littering family, picking up their trash as they dropped it. When he arrived at their campsite, he threw the garbage in their tent. The campers were quite irate about the incident.

Although you do not think any severe action, such as firing Martin, is presently justified, you do feel the problems you have identified must be resolved.

Role for Martin LeFete, Parks Maintenance Assistant   After you were graduated from high school, you moved to Colorado to live with your older brother. You worked part-time but spent as much time as possible hiking through the Canadian Rockies. You also found time to raft down rivers in Colorado. When your money ran out, you decided to move back to New York. You applied for and got your present job at Winsome River State Campground. One of your goals in taking this job was to show ordinary citizens how wonderful the outdoors really is.

You like your boss, Klaus Schultz, and believe he respects your work. But workers at the park have been a little anxious lately. There has been little rain this season, and fire is a major danger. There have also been reports of bears lurking around the campground.

This is why it really angers you to see people being careless about fires and trash. They are endangering the safety of other campers, not to mention the spotless safety record built up by Klaus.

You realize you probably overreacted when you poured water all over a campfire blazing out of control last week. The camper complained that you ruined his steaks, but he could have ruined the entire campground. When you arrived, the flames were almost as high as the bottom branches of the pine trees.

You understand Klaus' position, but you do wish he would give you more backup support on this. Klaus has asked to talk with you this afternoon, and you are planning to bring the matter up.

Discussion Questions

1. At the conclusion of the role play, discuss each guideline. How well was each guideline implemented?

2. What did you learn from this role play?

APPLICATION   The Coach at Work

1. Select a parent, friend, teacher, or other associate with whom you spend time.

2. In what areas of life did the person coach you?

3. How well did he or she receive and give feedback? How did he or she think about objective setting? What were his or her strengths and weaknesses as a coach?

4. In a group of four to six students, make a list of the most common coaching mistakes made by people.

5. From the list you've made, choose the mistakes that also might be made by a manager.

6. Indicate what can be done to avoid such mistakes.

REFERENCES

Bass, *Bernard M. Bass and Stodgill's Handbook of Leadership: Theory, Research and Managerial Applications*. New York: Free Press, 1990.

Bennis, W. G., D. E. Berlew, E. H. Schein, and F. I. Steele. *Interpersonal Dynamics: Essays and Readings on Human Interaction*, 3rd ed. Homewood, IL: Dorsey Press, 1973.

Burack, E., and N. J. Mathys. *Career Management in Organizations*. Lake Forest, IL: Brace-Park, 1980.

Carnegie, D., and D. Carnegie. *How to Win Friends and Influence People*. New York: Simon & Schuster, 1981.

Carroll, S. J., and C. E. Schneier. *Performance Appraisal and Review Systems*. Glenview, IL: Scott, Foresman, 1982.

Clare, D. A., and D. G. Sanford. "Mapping Personal Value Space: A Study of Managers in Four Organizations." *Human Relations* 32 (1979): 659–666.

Cotton, J. *Employee Involvement: Methods for Improving Performance and Work Attitudes*. San Francisco: Jossey Bass, 1994.

Dalton, G. W., P. H. Thompson, and R. L. Price. "The Four Stages of Professional Careers—A New Look at Performance by Professionals." *Organizational Dynamics* 6 (Summer 1977): 19–42.

Fournies, F. F. *Coaching for Improved Work Performance*. New York: Van Nostrand Reinhold, 1978.

Hall, D. T. *Careers in Organization*. Pacific Palisades, CA: Goodyear, 1976.

Helmstetter, S. *What to Say When You Talk to Yourself*. New York: Pocket Books, 1986.

Hunt, R. G. *Interpersonal Strategies for System Management: Applications of Counseling and Participative Principles*. Monterey, CA: Brooks/Cole, 1974.

James, M., and D. Jongewood. *Born to Win*. Reading, MA: Addison-Wesley, 1977.

Kotter, J., V. A. Faux, and C. C. McArthur. *Self-Assessment and Career Development*. Englewood Cliffs, NJ: Prentice-Hall, 1978.

Kreitner, R. "People Are Systems Too: Filling the Feedback Vacuum." *Business Horizons* 6 (December 1977): 54–58.

Locher, Alan A., and Kenneth S. Teel. "Performance Appraisal—A Survey of Current Practices." *Personnel Journal* 56 (5) (May 1977): 245–247, 254.

Luft, Joseph. *Group Processes: An Introduction to Group Dynamics*, 2d ed. Palo Alto, CA: National Press Books, 1970.

Luft, Joseph, and H. Ingham. "The Johari Window: A Graphic Model of Interpersonal Awareness." University of California, Los Angeles Extension Office, *Proceedings of the Western Training Laboratory in Group Development* August, 1955.

Maslow, A. *Motivation and Personality*, 2d ed. New York: Harper & Row, 1970.

McCormick, E. J. *Job Analysis: Methods and Applications*. New York: AMACOM, 1979.

McGregor, D. *The Human Side of Enterprise*. New York: McGraw-Hill, 1960.

Nair, K. *A Higher Standard of Leadership: Lessons from the Life of Ghandi*. San Francisco: Berrett-Koehler Publishers, 1994.

Nierenberg, G. I., and H. H. Calero. *How to Read a Person Like a Book* New York: Pocket Books, 1973.

Pfeiffer, J. *Competitive Advantage Through People: Unleashing the Power of the Work Force.* Boston: Harvard Business School Press, 1994.

Progoff, I. *At a Journal Workshop: The Basic Text and Guide for Using the Intensive Journal.* New York: Dialogue House Library, 1975.

Reece, B. L., and R. Brandt. *Effective Human Relations in Business.* Boston: Houghton-Mifflin, 1981.

Rogers, C. R. *On Becoming a Person.* Boston: Houghton-Mifflin, 1961.

Rogers, Carl R., and Richard E. Farson. *Active Listening.* Chicago: Industrial Relations Center, University of Chicago, 1976.

Rogers, Carl R., and F. J. Roethlisberger. "Barriers and Gateways to Communication." *Harvard Business Review* 30 (4) (July–August 1952): 46–50.

Rogers, C. R., and B. Stevens. *Person to Person: The Problem of Being Human.* Lafayette, CA: Real People Press, 1967.

Rokeach, M. *The Nature of Human Values.* New York: Free Press, 1973.

Rusk, T., and R. Reed. *I Want to Change But I Don't Know How.* Los Angeles: Price/Stern/Sloan, 1986.

Sashkin, M. *Assessing Performance Appraisal.* San Diego, CA: University Associates, 1981.

Schein, E. H. *Career Dynamics: Matching Individual and Organizational Needs.* Reading, MA: Addison-Wesley, 1978.

Schoen, S. H., and D. E. Durand. *Supervision: The Management of Organizational Resources.* Englewood Cliffs, NJ: Prentice-Hall, 1979.

Shannon, C., and W. Weaver. *The Mathematical Theory of Communication.* Urbana, IL: University of Illinois Press, 1948.

Sheehy, G. *Passages: Predictable Crises of Adult Life.* New York: Dutton, 1976.

Sher, B. *Wishcraft: How to Get What You Really Want.* New York: Ballantine, 1983.

Swanson, R.A. *Analysis for Improving Performance: Tools for Diagnosing Organizations and Documenting Workplace Expertise.* San Francisco: Berrett-Koehler Publishers, 1994.

Torbert, W. R. *Managing the Corporate Dream: Restructuring for Long-Term Success.* Homewood, IL: Dow Jones-Irwin, 1987.

Watzlawick, P.J. Beavin, and D. D. Jackson. *Pragmatics of Human Communication.* New York: Norton, 1967.

Whetten, David A., and Kim S. Cameron. *Developing Management Skills.* NY: Harper Collins, 1994.

Zey, M. *The Mentor Connection: Strategic Alliances within Corporate Life.* New Brunswick, NJ: Transaction Publishers, 1990.

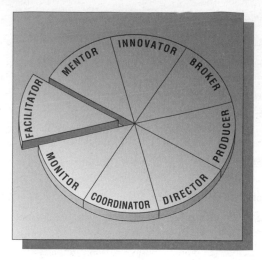

THE FACILITATOR ROLE

3

■ COMPETENCIES

Building Teams

Using Participative Decision Making

Managing Conflict

We have all spent a great deal of time working (and playing) in groups. Some of these groups seem to work very well together, and we sense that the group is able to accomplish something that none of the individuals could have accomplished on his or her own. In these cases, group members tend to identify with the group and may even surprise themselves in what they are able to accomplish individually when working with the group. Other groups, however, seem to function less effectively. In these cases, group members may dread spending time in the group and often feel that they could accomplish the task, or at least their part of the task, much more efficiently if they were left on their own.

Regardless of our past experiences working in groups, the expectation is that we can all expect to be spending a lot more time in groups. Organizational improvement processes, such as total quality management and process reengineering, rely heavily on work teams. In addition, organizations are relying more and more on task forces and other types of ad hoc, informal work groups to help solve organizational problems. Increasingly, people from different areas of the organization are being brought together to deal with issues with the expectation that by sharing their differing perspectives they will be able to develop a solution or an approach that none of the individuals could have imagined on their own. The message is clear: regardless of our job title, whether or not we are labeled as a managerial leader, we must all learn how to increase our skills as members of groups.

In this chapter we will focus on the role of the facilitator. The **facilitator role** falls in the human relations model of the competing values framework, and

60

focuses on the relationship between a managerial leader and his or her work group. In this role, the manager fosters collective effort, builds cohesion and morale, and manages interpersonal conflict. The facilitator uses some of the same competencies as the mentor, such as listening and being empathetic and sensitive to the needs of others. The role of facilitator, however, centers around the manager's work with groups.

In this chapter we will focus on three key competencies of the facilitator:

Competency 1   Building Teams
Competency 2   Using Participative Decision Making
Competency 3   Managing Conflict

Each of these competencies requires the manager to balance individual needs with group needs in order to create and maintain a positive climate in the work group. As you work through this chapter, however, you will see that these competencies are relevant to all group members, not just the individual who is given the title of leader.

Competency 1 Building Teams

ASSESSMENT   Are You a Team Player?[1]

Directions   The following assessment instrument asks you to examine your behavior as a team member in organizational settings. For each pair of items, place a check mark in the space in the column that best identifies how you behave in a working group at school, in student or community groups, or on your job.

	Very like me	Somewhat like me	Both describe me	Somewhat like me	Very like me	
Flexible in own ideas	____	____	____	____	____	Set in my own ideas
Open to new ideas	____	____	____	____	____	Avoid new ideas
Listen well to others	____	____	____	____	____	Tune out others
Trusting of others	____	____	____	____	____	Not trusting of others

[1]*Adapted from* training material for Income Maintenance Supervisors, Special Topics Workshop: "Motivation, Teambuilding, and Enhancing Morale," Professional Development Program, Rockefeller College of Public Affairs and Policy, State University of New York at Albany. Used with permission.

Prefer to raise differences and discuss them	___	___	___	___	___	Prefer to avoid discussing differences
Readily contribute in group meetings	___	___	___	___	___	Hold back from contributing in group meetings
Concerned for what happens to others	___	___	___	___	___	Not concerned for what happens to others
Fully committed to tasks	___	___	___	___	___	Have little commitment to tasks
Willing to help others to get the job done	___	___	___	___	___	Prefer to stick to my own task or job description
Share leadership with group	___	___	___	___	___	Maintain full control of group
Encourage others to participate	___	___	___	___	___	Expect others to participate without encouragement
Group needs come before my individual needs	___	___	___	___	___	My individual needs come before group needs

Interpretation   In each pair of items, the item on the left is associated more with team behaviors than is the item on the right.

1. In what ways do these team behaviors agree with your concept of team membership? How do they differ?

2. What strengths do you think you have working on a team? Weaknesses?

3. Are there times when you have performed more effectively as a team member? Alternatively, have there been times when you did not fully contribute as a team member? If so, what events or circumstances made you behave differently in the different situations?

LEARNING   Building Teams

In his recent book on team building, William G. Dyer (1995) tells a story about a management conference he had helped run. At the conference he asked approximately 300 managers whether they felt that teamwork and cooperation were essential in their organization and in their work unit. Without exception, managers reported that teamwork was essential. Dyer then asked how many were currently conducting programs to ensure that their team was functioning effectively—fewer than 25 percent responded positively. Finally, Dyer asked how many of their bosses were currently working on developing their team. At the third question, the response fell to below 10 percent. If teamwork is so essential to the proper functioning of the work unit, why do so few managers actively engage in team-building programs?

There are many reasons why managers do not do team building. In some cases, they simply do not understand the potential benefits that can occur from having the work unit function as a team. In other cases, they do not have the knowledge and skills required to turn a work group into a team, or may even believe that it is something that "just happens" without any effort. Toward the end of this section we will look again at barriers to team building and how they can be overcome. First, we will take a closer look at work groups and work teams and see how they function and identify some team building approaches.

WORK GROUPS AND WORK TEAMS

We have all experienced times when we felt that we were working on a "team." That team may have been a sports team, a work-related group, or a group within a community organization. What were the characteristics of that group that made it a team? Probably, the group was well coordinated, everyone had a role to play, and there was a commitment to a common goal. While there is no commonly accepted definition of team, and there are probably as many definitions of teams as there are researchers who study how teams function, there is some consistency in the characteristics generally used to differentiate teams from other types of groups.

First, **the group must be committed to a common goal or purpose.** In their book, *The Wisdom of Teams,* Katzenbach and Smith (1993) focus on having a meaningful purpose as part of the glue that holds the team together. It is the motivation that makes people want to contribute to their maximum ability. Just as important as having a common purpose, these authors assert, is that teams must have specific performance goals which are centered on the team work-product, the results. For example, they describe the team effort within the Peripheral Systems Group at Eli Lilly, a team that was developing an ultrasonic probe to help doctors locate deep veins and arteries in patients. In developing the probe, this team set specific goals for the performance quality of the product, the potential manufacturing rate of the product, and its production cost, as well as a goal "to develop the product in less than half the usual time frame for its division" (p. 54). Katzenbach and Smith argue that "[b]ecause each of [their] objectives was attainable and measurable, the team knew throughout where it stood" (p. 54).

Second, **members of the group must have clear roles and responsibilities that are interdependent**. One of the key reasons for having people work together in a team is to be able to draw on the different knowledge, skills, and abilities that people bring to the work place. In building a team, members must understand how they can draw on each other's experience, ability, and commitment in order to arrive at mutual goals. When Eric Doremus, who had spent seven years in marketing at Honeywell, was asked to lead a team developing data storage systems for a B2 bomber, he realized that "he would never have the technical skills of the engineers on the team" (Caminiti, 1995, p. 94). But he knew that he was good at motivating people and that he could "help the team communicate better with its customer...and see that the project was completed on time and within budget" (p. 94). Everyone does not have to know how to do all the jobs, but everyone should be clear about who is being asked to do what. Perhaps more important, people need to fully understand how their personal efforts contribute to the team work-product.

Third, **there is a communication structure that fosters the sharing of information**. The second characteristic indicated that one advantage of bringing people together to work in a team is that they can share the different, and sometimes unique, knowledge, skills, and abilities that they bring to the team. This can only happen, however, if people are willing to share their own ideas and listen carefully to the ideas of others. Larson and Fasto (1989, p. 56) identify four characteristics of an effective communication structure: (1) The information is easily accessible; (2) the information that is available must be seen as coming from credible sources, (3) in meetings, people must be able to raise issues of concern that may not have been on the formal agenda, and (4) there must be a system for documenting issues that have been discussed and decisions that have been made. A corollary to these four characteristics is that the communication structure must be supported by a climate of trust. People must feel that it is safe to raise controversial or difficult issues without being accused of attacking the other team members. Again, the team cannot benefit from the diversity of ideas if there is no opportunity to openly discuss the different perspectives.

Finally, **the group must have a sense of mutual accountability**. In many ways, this characteristic flows from the first three. If the team has common goals and members have clear roles and responsibilities, team members will have a sense of commitment to each other. They will see themselves as integral parts of the whole, where each person must perform in order for the whole to excel. Moreover, when one member of the team needs help, others are ready to provide that help so that the team can accomplish the goal. Katzenbach and Smith (1993, pp. 144–145) argue that "success or failure is a team event. No outside obstacle is an excuse for team failure, and no individuals fail. Only the team can fail." What is suggested here is that when team members are mutually accountable, the team functions as a whole, with each member feeling the full responsibility and gaining the full benefits when the team succeeds.

In this fourth characteristic, it is easy to see one of the paradoxes inherent in team functioning—that while each individual must have clear roles and responsibilities, each member must also be willing to take on the tasks of other team members in order to achieve the common performance goals. Thus, when team members are mutually accountable, they do not need to keep an "accounting system" of who has done what for whom. Individuals do not try to take personal credit for their efforts. Rather, they see their efforts as benefiting the team and, by definition, benefiting themselves. When all members understand what it means to be mutually accountable, no one takes advantage of other team members or becomes a free rider, and yet everyone reaps the benefits of the others' efforts.

Each of these four characteristics is essential to the effective functioning of the work team. The question that a managerial leader must ask, however, is: Does my work unit need to function as a team? That is, is it necessary for all members of the work unit to share a common goal or purpose? Does the nature of the work require people to be interdependent? In some sports teams, such as golf teams or gymnastics teams, individuals function quite independently. Although they may practice together and give each other pointers on how to improve their performance, there is no real need for coordination of effort. Other sports teams, such as basketball teams or volleyball teams, require a great deal of interaction and coordination among team members. Players must be in constant communication with each other; each player must be able to "predict" the next player's moves. The same is true of work teams. In some settings, individuals function independently and the work unit would not likely benefit from attempts to turn the work group into a work team. In many settings, however, the work depends on individuals working together and using each other's experiences, abilities, and commitments. In these cases, the managerial leader, in the role of facilitator, must make special efforts to help the work group develop into a work team. In this chapter we will focus primarily on team building efforts that help team members clarify their roles, responsibilities, and expectations.

ROLES OF TEAM MEMBERS

As was noted above in the discussion of the team characteristics, team members usually have specific, and sometimes very specialized, roles. A **role** is a set of expectations held by the individual and relevant others about how that individual should act in a given situation. For example, in basketball, the point guard is expected to bring the ball down the court and set up the play; the center is expected to get under the basket and to rebound. In the work place, an employee's role is defined by the specific tasks he or she is expected to perform. For example, in a factory there are production managers, machine operatives, and repair persons. In addition, there are health and personnel specialists, accountants and financial managers, maintenance staff, secretaries, and office clerks. Each of these individuals has a specialized role.

In pulling a new team together, people are usually expected to perform somewhat different roles on the team. Therefore, it is important to think about the specific competencies that people can bring to the task. These may be technical competencies, referring to substantive knowledge, skills, and abilities; or they may be personal competencies, referring to qualities, skills, and abilities to help the team work together. Some organizations, such as Apple Computer, have begun to develop computer systems that include a database of employee skills and abilities to help them find the best persons to bring together on a team (Dumaine, 1991).

In addition to the specific or unique competencies that can be used to select team members, team leaders might also consider general characteristics that all team members should possess. For example, when the Rogers Commission was pulled together to investigate the cause of the space shuttle *Challenger* disaster, Lieutenant Colonel Thomas Reinhardt, the Commission's executive secretary, identified the key criteria for deciding who might work on this investigative team.

> *Prospective staff members had to (1) have the technical knowledge, skills, and relevant background to unravel why the disaster occurred; (2) be honest and trustworthy and not allow any self-vested interests or outside constituencies to have a bearing on the facts gathered; (3) be willing to work hard and long hours in order to satisfy President Reagan's request that the project be brought to a conclusion within 120 days; (4) care about the tragic human side of the disaster; (5) understand that the future of the United States manned space flight program was at stake; (6) recognize that the National Aeronautics and Space Administration is a unique national asset and that therefore only the highest standards would be accepted in reaching the objectives of the project (Larson and Fasto, 1989, p. 61).*

While the first criterion clearly focuses on specific technical competencies, it is clear that Colonel Reinhardt thought about additional competencies that would determine how the team would operate. This example shows that whether we focus on technical or personal competencies, unique abilities or general characteristics that everyone on the team should possess, one of the important responsibilities of the manager, as facilitator, is to provide role clarity for his or her employees—to make it clear what is expected of each individual performing on the team.

ROLE CLARITY AND ROLE AMBIGUITY

Role clarity implies the absence of two stressful conditions: *role ambiguity* and *role conflict.* Role ambiguity occurs when an individual does not have enough information about what he or she should be doing, what are appropriate ways of interacting with others, or what are appropriate behaviors and attitudes. Consider the following story about four people: Everybody, Somebody, Anybody, and Nobody.

There was an important job to be done and Everybody was asked to do it. Anybody could have done it, but Nobody did it. Somebody got angry about that because it was Everybody's job. Everybody thought Anybody could do it, but Nobody realized that Everybody wouldn't do it. It ended up that Everybody blamed Somebody when actually Nobody asked Anybody.

New employees, who are not familiar with the work unit's norms and procedures, often experience role ambiguity if their manager does not clarify for them what is to be expected in their job. New managers, making the transition from worker to manager, also often experience role ambiguity because the role expectations for that individual have changed.

Role conflict occurs when an individual perceives information regarding his or her job to be inconsistent or contradictory. For example, if manager X tells employee Y to perform task A, and then manager X's boss tells employee Y to stop what he or she is doing and to perform task B, the employee is likely to experience role conflict.

There are several potential sources of role conflict. Role conflict may occur when one or more individuals with whom an employee interacts sends conflicting messages about what is expected. It can occur when an individual plays multiple roles that have conflicting expectations. For example, first-line managers represent their organization to their employees, informing them of rules and regulations or new policies and procedures. Managers, however, are also employees. In the employee role they may disagree with an organizational policy or directive. Role conflict can also occur when an individual's own morals and values conflict with the organization's mission or policies and procedures. For example, an environmental activist may find it difficult to work for a logging company or a company that produces toxic or nuclear wastes as a side effect of its primary production of goods. Role conflict also may occur when the expectations for a given role exceed the available time to complete those tasks. This is also sometimes referred to as *role overload* (Gordon, 1983).

Team leaders sometimes feel role conflict because they have not yet learned the new skills required of team leaders, and think they are supposed to behave as "the boss." In traditional organizations, managers were given both authority and responsibility for making decisions. But, as we discussed above, the value of using teams results from the team's ability to use the unique knowledge and skills that people bring to the team. Team leaders need to learn how to share power, how to decide when they should be "in charge" and when they should let others take charge (see the section on Using Participative Decision Making, later in this chapter), and that it is reasonable for them to not know everything. Put another way, team leaders need to learn the new set of expectations that employees and the organization have for managers (Dumaine, 1991).

Team building efforts that focus on clarifying roles help everyone in the work unit or work team understand what others expect. Later in this chapter we will present specific team-building techniques that focus on the clarification of roles. First, however, we discuss three general types of roles that employees play in teams, two that help the team to accomplish its objective and one the hinders the team.

TASK AND GROUP MAINTENANCE
ROLES VS. SELF-ORIENTED ROLES

Task and group maintenance roles focus on two necessary components of effective team functioning (Benne and Sheats, 1948, Dyer, 1995). In a task role, one's behaviors are focused on *what* the team is to accomplish. Performing in a task role is sometimes referred to as having a task orientation, or being task oriented. In a group maintenance role, one's behaviors are focused on *how* the team will accomplish its task. Performing in a group maintenance role is sometimes referred to as having a group maintenance, or process, orientation, or being process oriented.

A person may perform several different types of activities when taking on a task role. For example, a person may get the group moving by offering new ideas and suggesting ways to approach a task or a problem, or by simply reminding others that there is a task to be performed. In meetings, persons in the task role may raise or clarify important facts and opinions based on personal knowledge and experiences; encourage others to raise or clarify important facts and opinions based on their knowledge and experiences; pull together the range of ideas discussed in the group and restate them concisely, offering a decision or conclusion for the group to consider; or help the group to assess the quality of its suggestions or solutions, testing to see if the ideas will work in reality. A person in a task role also often brings together, schedules, and combines the activities of others.

Likewise we can identify different types of activities associated with a group maintenance orientation. People in this role tend to support team members, building cohesiveness and trust among them, alleviating tension and helping members find ways to see past their differences so that they can continue to work together. They also try to maintain an open discussion, and encourage others to pursue their ideas and suggestions. People who play this role in a team also often provide the group with feedback on how the group is functioning and suggest processes to ensure that all group members have sufficient opportunities to share their ideas and feelings.

Clearly these types of behaviors are consistent with the four characteristics of teams described above. There is, however, another type of role that some people may try to play in the team that is inconsistent with these team characteristics. This is a self or individual-oriented role. This role tends to be counterproductive to effective group functioning, and draws attention away from the team to personal needs that are not germane to the team's task or process. People in this role may oppose other members' ideas and suggestions, using hidden agendas to hinder group movement, or try to take over the group by manipulating the group or individual members and by interrupting others. They may also try to draw attention to themselves, either boasting of personal accomplishments, or acting in ways that indicate a feeling of superiority over other team members, or by separating themselves from the group and maintaining a distance from other group members.

Sometimes, people take on these roles naturally. You may find that one person consistently tries to bring the group back to its task. Another may be good at making sure that everyone has had an opportunity for input. Yet another may make sure that everyone knows what is to be accomplished by the next meeting and who has specific tasks to perform. The key is to make sure that task and group maintenance roles are appropriately balanced and that self-oriented roles are minimized. If the group tends to find itself completely focused on completing the task, but only a few team members are contributing, team members must ask themselves how they can get one or more people to play the group maintenance role. Alternatively, if the group is always focused on making sure that everyone is getting along, but work is not getting done in a timely manner, the group must think about how it can increase its task behaviors without sacrificing people's commitment to the team. Finally, if the group is not able to accomplish its tasks because it is constantly hindered by one or more individuals who are more concerned about their personal gains or accomplishments, rather than the team's work-product, the team must work with these individuals to get them to see how they are hindering the team (see the last section of this chapter on Managing Conflict), as well as to try to get them to accept the team's goals and purpose as their own. In the next section we look at how the appropriate balance between task and group maintenance behaviors may depend on how long the team has worked together, in general or on a particular task or problem.

TEAM DEVELOPMENT AND TEAM BUILDING

When a new work group forms, or an established work group undertakes a new task or problem, the group experiences different stages of team development before it can transform into a high performing team (Buchholz and Roth, 1987). For example, if team members do not know each other well or have never worked together before, it is important for team members to get acquainted with each other and to discuss what competencies each person brings to the team, and what types of preferences people have regarding how to approach the task. Alternatively, when an established team takes on a new project, team members are likely to have a good sense of the different competencies people have, but may still need to discuss various unique perspectives they have on the problem or different approaches team members may think are appropriate for the particular project. As you will see, we can identify four stages of team development, each of which requires team members to differently emphasize the various task and maintenance behaviors discussed above. The leader of a team (and also the team members) must be aware of how the team's needs evolve during these stages of development and encourage group members to perform different aspects of the task and group maintenance behaviors at the different stages.

STAGE 1: TESTING

At stage 1 the goals of the group are established and the task is defined. Group members ask themselves what is the purpose of this team and whether they want to be a member. (Of course, in most work-related situations, group members do not have a choice about their membership.) To create a climate where people can share ideas and feelings and begin to identify and align with a common goal, the group leader should encourage group members to offer new ideas and suggest ways to approach the task (task role), and should also make sure everyone's opinion is heard, creating a climate where people feel safe to offer opposing views (group maintenance role).

STAGE 2: ORGANIZING

At stage 2 the group establishes a structure. The group leader must emphasize the common purpose (task role) and establish norms and standards. In addition, the group must clarify issues regarding the sharing of information—how members will communicate with each other and what types of information need to be shared. If the group has no appointed leader, one of the group members will often emerge as an informal leader in this stage. Sometimes several people are identified as leaders, some focusing more on tasks and others on group maintenance. So that group members may ask more specific questions about what the group will do and how they will do it, the leader should encourage group members to continually question and assess the quality of suggestions and potential solutions (task role) and to resolve differences by helping others understand the differing perspectives that people bring (group maintenance role).

STAGE 3: ESTABLISHING INTERDEPENDENCE

Individual talents are drawn out and used and attention is focused on how to coordinate individual efforts in stage 3. The group leader should focus on member interdependence, discourage competition, and encourage individuals to take on informal leadership roles. The key question group members ask themselves concerns how they can coordinate their individual actions to accomplish the team's goals more effectively. At this stage, focusing on the task, the team needs members to raise and/or clarify important points and differences in perspective, and then to pull together and summarize or synthesize the range of ideas that have been expressed (task roles). Similarly, group maintenance behaviors that help the team to succeed focus on helping members see how the differing perspectives can potentially lead to a more creative or more productive proposal for action, and then encouraging others to pursue different ideas and suggestions.

STAGE 4: PRODUCING AND EVALUATING

If the group has successfully managed the first three stages, by stage 4 it should have transformed into a team and should be working together smoothly. Team members should be committed to a common goal or purpose, have a clear understanding of the different roles and responsibilities of individual team members, have a communication structure that allows for an open sharing of different perspectives, and have a sense of mutual accountability. At this stage, team members begin to evaluate the product of the team effort and also how well the individuals are working together as a team. To solicit input from all group members in evaluating goals, task output, productivity, and team process, the leader should encourage team members to ask questions regarding how it has approached its task and offer suggestions for improving team performance (task role), as well as feedback and observations on the team process (group maintenance role).

Again, one can see how the role that the team leader plays in helping the team develop is both critical and paradoxical. On the one hand, the team leader sets the climate and must be seen as someone with a strong personal vision. On the other hand, the leader must clearly demonstrate a belief in the team's purpose and in the notion that each person's contribution to the team is equally valuable. Thus, team leaders must simultaneously lead and give team members the opportunity to take a leadership role, suggest directions and listen to others' suggestions, and be appropriately involved in the day-to-day work while not micromanaging. In addition, they must find ways to value differences and reward successes, while never allowing some individuals to shine at the expense of the other team members. In the next two sections, we suggest some specific approaches to team building, approaches that build on the notion of maintaining a balance between task and group maintenance focus in the team.

FORMAL APPROACHES TO TEAM BUILDING

Although a team may reach the producing and evaluating stage of its development, it will likely cycle back through the various stages as it meets new challenges. Indeed, most work groups experience frequent, if not constant, change. Sometimes these changes are associated with new group members; sometimes the changes are associated with new tasks and responsibilities. Sometimes the changes are the result of changes in the group's external environment and the group must adjust in order to adapt to a new focus of the organization or new trends in the industry. At this point it is often important to "stop the action" and involve the group in formal team-building activities.

You may have heard the expression, "When you are up to your hips in alligators, you forget that you came to drain the swamp." Sometimes it is important to step out of the swamp and think about what you are doing. Formal team-building activities allow the group to put aside the work of the day, evaluate how well the group is performing as a team, and make any necessary changes. But team-building activities should not be seen as isolated experiences or events. Rather, they should be part of an integrated approach to team building that involves regularly scheduled sessions to allow the team to address whatever issues it is currently facing (Dyer, 1995). At Goodyear Tires' radial tire plant in Lawton, Oklahoma, work teams meet regularly to discuss goals, problems, and improvement ideas (Robbins, 1989).

When team members are interdependent, there is a need for effective communication among them. Periodic meetings that focus on information exchange may be the most effective way to enhance communication among team members. Many managers hold periodic off-site meetings to help keep employees enthusiastic and energized. The key is to encourage input from everyone regarding problems they are experiencing and questions or concerns they might have. Managers can also bring information about anticipated changes to these meetings. Sometimes it is important to clarify how much and what types of information individuals need in order to effectively perform their job. A group meeting to examine current information flows, and whether these flows meet each individual's needs, can enhance team functioning. (The section on Using Participative Decision Making later in this chapter will provide more information on how to conduct effective meetings.)

A fairly simple, but effective, team building technique involves setting aside a day or two, away from the work-site if possible, to examine three questions: (1) What do we do well?; (2) What areas need improvement?; and (3) What are the barriers to improvement? Starting with an examination of what the team does well reminds the group that while there may be some problems or issues to deal with, the team also has strengths upon which to build. This sets a positive climate for the team-building session and gets people involved in the discussion. Depending on time between team-building sessions, the list of areas for improvement may be short or long. This is a good reason to schedule regular team-building sessions. If the list is too long, the team may need to set priorities regarding which issues should be handled first. The last question reminds the team that team building is more than short-term problem solving. It involves taking a larger look at the system and examining if specific problems are indeed isolated events, or rather the result of an underlying structural issue. If there is an underlying structural issue, it will likely need to be dealt with before the improvement can be made. The final team-product of such a session should be an action plan to deal with whatever problems or issues are raised in the session. The action plan should include a statement of objectives or what the team wants to accomplish with this improvement effort, a time frame for addressing the issue, and a clear assignment of who is responsible for organizing the improvement effort (remember Anybody, Everybody, Nobody, and Somebody!).

As mentioned earlier, one key to effective team functioning is for each team member to know his or her role and how that role fits into the larger team effort. Several techniques are available. Role analysis technique (RAT) focuses one-by-one on the various roles in the group. This technique was first used by KP Engineering Corporation, a manufacturer of welding electronics, and is useful when team members are performing different functions (Dayal and Thomas, 1968). In this activity the person performing in the role to be analyzed states his or her job as he or she sees it. Other group members then comment on and make suggestions for changes in this job description. The individual in that role then lists expectations of other members who affect how the job is performed. There is open discussion until agreement is reached on a job description and the

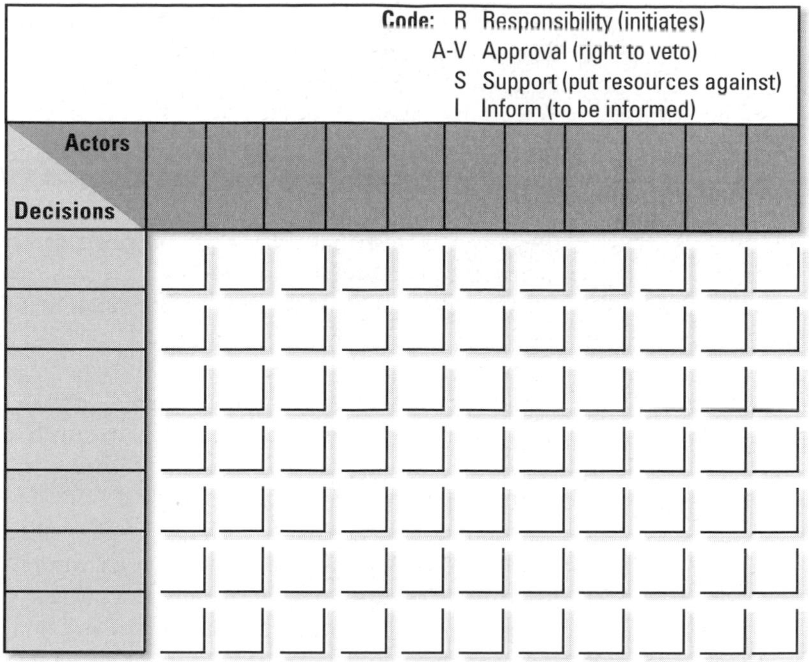

FIGURE 3.1
Responsibility chart.

Source: R. Beckhard and R.T. Harris, *Organizational Transitions: Managing Complex Change* (Reading Mass.: Addison-Wesley Publishing Company, 1977), p.78, Figure 6.1. Used with permission.

	Code:	R	Responsibility (initiates)
		A-V	Approval (right to veto)
		S	Support (put resources against)
		I	Inform (to be informed)

Actors / Decisions										

associated expectations of others. This process is then repeated until everyone has had his or her job analyzed.

A similar technique is role negotiation (Harrison, 1972). Here all members simultaneously list what expectations they have of others in the work group, focusing on what they feel others should do more or better, do less or stop doing, and maintain as is. Lists are exchanged, and individuals negotiate with each other until all team members agree on those behaviors that should be changed and those that should be maintained. A master list of agreements is later circulated to the group.

Responsibility charting (Beckhard and Harris, 1977) involves creating a large chart that lists the group's decisions and activities along the left side of the chart and each employee's name along the top of the chart (see Figure 3.1). Codes that indicate whether the individual has the responsibility for the activity or decision (R), has the right to approve or veto a decision (A-V), provides support or resources for the activity or decision (S), needs to be informed of the activity or decision (I), or has no role in the activity or decision (-) are then inserted into the boxes. The chart allows the group to see explicitly if some members of the group are overloaded and some could be given additional tasks and responsibilities.

INFORMAL APPROACHES TO TEAM BUILDING

As indicated, team building is not an event, but an ongoing process. In between formal team building sessions, the team can use informal techniques to encourage team development. Often when people think about team building they assume that it has to do with getting people to like each other, but as Dyer notes, "The fundamental emotional condition in a team is not liking but *trusting*. People do not need to like one another as friends to be able to work together, but they do need to trust one another" (1995, p. 53, emphasis added). They need to trust that other team members are equally invested in accomplishing the team's goals; they need to trust that other team members will share information appropriately; and they need to trust that other team members will be willing to work out disagreements in a professional manner.

How do you establish trust among team members? First and foremost, team members need to understand that each person's willingness to trust other team members will likely be influenced by that person's observations of the other team members' actions. If team members consistently produce and are willing to help others when they need assistance, trust is likely to develop among the team members. One key element here is ensuring that each person believes in the common goals and so is willing to "go the extra mile" when necessary.

Second, a managerial leader must work to create an atmosphere where it is safe to trust others. Trust is a behavior that recreates itself. That is, team members are more likely to trust other team members when they, themselves, feel trusted—when they feel that others are being open and honest in their communications. In the previous chapter you used the Johari window as a tool for thinking about self-awareness. The Johari window also tells you something about how you relate to others. When an individual has a large facade (information that is known to self, but unknown to others), others have a hard time trusting that individual because they do not feel trusted by the person. Alternatively, when an individual has been candid and sincere with others, that person will more likely be seen as approachable and trustworthy. Thus a managerial leader must begin by trusting the team members and set an example by sharing key information with the team.

Finally, although we indicated that the purpose of team building is not to create a situation where everyone likes everyone else, we do believe that social interaction can create opportunities for people to get to know each other, thereby creating greater potential for trust among team members. For example, a manager may encourage group interaction by suggesting that the group meet for a meal after work, or during a meal break, where possible. Don Martin, CEO of Cal-Surance Companies, one of the largest privately held insurance brokerage firms in California, suggests using rituals and traditions to create a sense of unity. Celebrations of people's accomplishments lets team members know that their work is appreciated. Annual picnics and holiday celebrations, as well as celebrations of personal events, such as birthdays or parenthood, communicate to employees that they as individuals are important to the organization. At Cal-Surance, the anniversaries of the dates people were hired are also celebrated. Every year employees are given gifts as evidence of the company's appreciation for their work. Martin notes, "Whether serious or silly, rituals and traditions become part of the company's culture and contribute profoundly to creating a sense of unity and belonging. They also enable everyone to step away from the pressures of business and have fun as a group. These experiences translate into good feelings toward your organization and help keep people with you" (Martin, 1993, p. 99).

BARRIERS TO TEAM BUILDING

When we began this section we noted that team building is not as regularly practiced in many organizations as one might expect, given what we know about the potential for team performance. What we need to ask here is "What are the barriers to team building?" and "How do we overcome them?" Of course, one important reason why team building programs are not more widely used in work organizations is time. Often the need to get the job done leads work groups to focus on specific tasks, rather than on planning and coordination. Further, when group members focus on their own parts they sometimes find it difficult to see the whole picture, or to recognize that they are not currently seeing that picture. There is no way to give people more time. Team members and organizational leaders must see the value of team building and recognize that this is a long-term investment. A day or two spent away from the work-site may save the team much more in both time and money in the long run.

A second reason may be a lack of knowledge about how to build a team. Some people assume that "team" is something that does or does not happen. They may not realize the many and varied techniques that can enhance team functioning. It is a manager's responsibility to examine the need for team building in his or her work unit, and if such a need exists to determine which formal or informal approaches would be most effective.

A final, but perhaps the most important, reason is organizational culture. Effective team building requires an environment that values differing opinions and open resolution of conflict (see the last competency in this chapter on Managing Conflict. In an organization where there is mistrust or negative feelings among co-workers, it is difficult to establish a team spirit. In cases such as these, one should consider bringing in an objective outside consultant to do formal team-building or organization development activities.

Similarly, the organization may not reward team behaviors or team-building activities. An organization may prescribe team building for its employees, but if managers are not evaluated on the implementation of such activities, there may be little incentive to take the time to do team–building. In a similar fashion, some organizations will hold team–building sessions, but then reward employees for their individual performance. If a sales representative is compensated based on individual sales, there is little incentive to share "best practices" with others in the work unit. Here, organizations need to examine their performance and reward systems to ensure that they do not run counter to team-building efforts. Further, upper-level managers need to demonstrate by their own actions their commitment to and support for team-building activities (Dyer, 1995).

ANALYSIS   Stay-Alive Inc.[2]

Directions   Read the case study and respond to the questions that follow.

Stay-Alive Inc., a small not-for-profit social service agency, hired Jean Smith to design, implement, and coordinate halfway house living programs for young adults.

When Jean arrived, the agency had an informal organization with little hierarchical structure and extensive participative decision making. The prevailing ideology that shaped virtually all decisions and interpersonal relationships was that a democratic system would be most effective and would lead to a higher level of job satisfaction for workers than would a more rigid hierarchical structure. The staff members attended at least five meetings weekly. Incredibly, the group devoted the majority of time at each one to exploring interpersonal problems.

Most staff people were young and had recently finished college. They often remarked that they sought a place to belong and feel accepted. Stay-Alive met that need in many ways; the group acted as a surrogate family for many employees. Even their life outside of work revolved heavily around activities with other Stay-Alive members. Salaries were low, and so the agency hired inexperienced people. Although the employees were bright, enthusiastic, and motivated, they lacked the skills needed for effective performance in their jobs. Organizational leaders, therefore, defined success on the job in terms of the employees' ability to relate well to others at work instead of their ability to work with clients.

Within three months of her arrival Jean submitted her plan for implementing the program. Her manager praised it, calling it a remarkable piece of work. Soon after the program was implemented, however, it became clear that it was not working. Still the agency members responded by patting her on the back and told her what a great job she was doing. Jean soon became frustrated and angry and left the agency.

Discussion Questions

1. Was Stay-Alive Inc. an effective team? Why or why not?

2. How were task and maintenance behaviors being performed in this agency?

3. Rather than leaving, how might Jean have helped Stay-Alive to become a more effective organization?

4. What other suggestions would you give to the management team at Stay-Alive to help them to improve?

5. If you were the director of Stay-Alive, what issues would you want to see addressed in a team-building session?

[2]*Adapted from* Judith R. Gordon, *A Diagnostic Approach to Organizational Behavior* (Boston: Allyn and Bacon, 1983), pp. 304–305.

PRACTICE   "Students as Customers" Task Force

Directions   Divide into groups of approximately six people. Each group will compose a new university task force that is part of the university's total quality management effort. Read the memo from the university president and begin your first meeting according to the suggested agenda provided below. Respond to the agenda questions as if you, yourself, were attending the meeting. When your task force has completed the two tasks on the agenda, each person should individually respond to the discussion questions. Your instructor will then lead a large group discussion.

MEMORANDUM

FROM: President Adams
TO: "Students as Customers" Task Force
SUBJECT: Task Force Charge
DATE: January 22, 1996

First, I want to welcome you back to a new semester and thank you for agreeing to sit on this exciting new task force. I think you will find this task force rewarding, and the University will certainly benefit from your input.

As you know, our University has been working since the Fall semester with a team of management consultants to develop a total quality management (TQM) program on this campus. As part of this effort, we are beginning to look at "customer satisfaction," recognizing students as our customers. We believe that the best people to help us decide how to gather customer satisfaction data are the students themselves. The members of this task force have been carefully chosen from among our best students. Your charge is to make a recommendation, by the end of this semester, regarding how we might gather such data. You are, of course, free to choose from among many available data-gathering approaches, for example, surveys, interviews, focus groups, and use of existing course evaluation data. You should make your recommendations based on your assessment of how we can get the best information.

I look forward to seeing your recommendations.

Task Force Meeting Agenda

  1. Briefly discuss the president's charge.

  2. Discuss the following questions:

    a. What unique skills or abilities does each person bring to the task force?

    b. What skills do members share in common?

c. What specific team or organizational strengths does each person possess?

d. What team or organizational weaknesses or areas of discomfort does each person possess?

e. How can the team make best use of each individual's skills and abilities?

f. How can team members benefit from their time on the task force?

Discussion Questions   1. How satisfied were you with the group's discussion? Did you feel comfortable discussing your team and organizational strengths and weaknesses in this first meeting of the group?

2. How well did the task force do at discussing how it could make best use of each person's abilities? Did everyone participate in the discussion?

3. Think about the stages of team development. What elements of stage 1 (Testing) did you accomplish in your task force? What elements of stage 2 (Organizing) or stage 3 (Establishing Interdependence) were accomplished? What member behaviors provided support for the team's development?

4. What issues still need to be dealt with to allow this task force to develop as a team?

5. Did a leader emerge? If so, what specific events identified that person as a leader? Who in the group might have emerged as a team leader at a later time?

APPLICATION   Team-Building Action Plan

Think about a student group, a work unit, a task force, or a committee of which you are currently a member, where you could do some informal or formal team building.

1. Consider carefully which team-building activities are most appropriate. For example, you may feel that the roles and responsibilities of group members are not clear and that you would like to try one of the role clarification techniques. Or you may decide you need to personally practice using task and maintenance roles in group meetings. If you are a group leader, think about whether it is appropriate to meet privately with individuals who have been exhibiting self-oriented behaviors. Wherever possible, try your team-building effort.

2. Write a three- to five-page report describing the design for your team-building effort. Include a description of the group, as well as what you would do. In your report you should carefully explain why you have chosen this team-building approach. If you are describing an ongoing group, discuss also the stage of the group's development and how this would affect your team-building effort.

Competency 2 Using Participative Decision Making

Directions   Think of a meeting of a student organization, a study group, or a meeting at work that you recently attended. If you have not recently attended any such meetings, think about the "meetings" of your groups when working on small group exercises in this or other classes.

Rate the overall effectiveness of the meeting as: (5) very effective, (4) moderately effective, (3) neither effective nor ineffective, (2) moderately ineffective, or (1) very ineffective. Then respond to the items below using the following scale:

Scale

Strongly Disagree	Disagree	Undecided	Agree	Strongly Agree
1	2	3	4	5

_____ 1. I was notified of this meeting in sufficient time to prepare for it.

_____ 2. I understood why this meeting was held (e.g., information sharing, planning, problem solving, decision making, open discussion) and what specific outcomes were expected.

_____ 3. I understood what was expected of me as a participant and what was expected of the other participants.

_____ 4. I understood how the meeting was intended to flow (e.g., agenda, schedule, design) and when it would terminate.

_____ 5. Most participants listened carefully to each other.

_____ 6. Most participants expressed themselves openly, honestly, and directly.

_____ 7. Agreements were explicit and clear, and conflicts were openly explored and constructively managed.

_____ 8. The meeting generally proceeded as intended (e.g., the agenda was followed, it ended on time) and achieved its intended purpose.

_____ 9. My participation contributed to the outcomes achieved by the meeting.

_____ 10. Overall, I am satisfied with this meeting and feel that my time was well spent.

Scoring and Interpretation   Add your responses to each of the questions and divide the sum by 10. The closer your score was to "5," the more your meeting could be considered very effective; the closer your score was to "1," the more your meeting could be considered very ineffective.

1. How close was your initial evaluation of the meeting to your rating based on the questions in the meeting-evaluation scale?

2. Review the meeting-evaluation scale. What were the meeting characteristics that made the meeting more effective? Less effective?

[3] *Adapted from* Frank Burns and Robert L. Gragg, "Brief Diagnostic Instruments," in *The 1981 Annual Handbook for Group Facilitators,* John E. Jones and J. William Pfeiffer (eds.) (San Diego: University Associates, Inc. 1981), p.89. Used with permission.

3. What were the specific events at the meeting that made the meeting more effective? Less effective?

4. How can you make your next meeting more effective?

LEARNING   Using Participative Decision Making

In the past decade, there has been increasing attention to a wide variety of techniques and practices that involve employees in organizational decision making. Extending the concept of democracy to the workplace (Weisbord, 1987), participative management techniques are built on the assumption that employees should have the opportunity to have input into decisions that affect their lives. More recently, some researchers have argued that although the participative management approach is consistent with national values of democratic decision making, the more compelling reasons for adopting this type of approach are economic—that organizations that employ participative management approaches will have a competitive advantage (Lawler, 1992).

Indeed, largely as a result of global competition and other external pressures, organizations in both the public and private sectors have begun to experiment with a variety of approaches, ranging from simply encouraging managers to listen to employees' ideas about work improvements; to the creation of large-scale participation programs such as quality circles, labor-management quality of work life committees, and self-managed work teams; to organizationwide changes to accommodate new work systems, policies, and procedures. In many cases, organizations that have adopted such changes have found that they have been able to lower costs and raise productivity, produce higher quality products and services, and respond more quickly, as well as in more innovative ways, to the needs of customers. Moreover, they have found that their employees are more motivated and have a greater sense of organizational commitment (Lawler, 1992, Osborne and Gaebler, 1992).

In the 1990s, few would dispute the notion that involving employees in organizational decisions that affect their lives makes both social and economic sense. The issue at hand is identifying which decisions affect employees' lives. At some level, all organizational decisions that have an impact on organizational performance will affect the lives of the employees. From an organizational perspective, two things are clear: First, in many situations front-line employees are closer to the information necessary to make a decision and should therefore be allowed to make those decisions. This is where organizations can gain competitive advantage by being able to respond more quickly to customer needs. Second, the more organizational information is shared with employees, the greater will be their ability to make decisions that are in the interest of the entire organization. For example, at Chaparral Steel, workers are trained "to understand how the whole business operates. [The] course. . . not only describes what happens to a piece of steel as it moves through the company, but also covers the role of finance, accounting and sales" (Dumaine, 1990, p. 58). Thus, workers can be involved in decisions about new product machinery, and make those decisions based not only on an understanding of how their particular job works, but also on an understanding of how their job relates to the welfare of the whole organization.

Nevertheless, there are times when it is not feasible or it is inappropriate to involve employees in an organizational decision. Thus managerial leaders need to be able to decide in specific circumstances whether it is appropriate to involve employees, as well what issues need to be considered when involving employees. Although we have talked about the advantages to be gained by using participative approaches, we should be clear that participative decision making is not a single technique that can be universally applied to all situations. As indicated above, there are a wide variety of participation approaches and managers can involve employees in making decisions in a variety of ways. Which way is most appropriate to use depends on the manager, the employees, the organization, and the nature of the decision itself.

A RANGE OF DECISION-MAKING STRATEGIES

Managers constantly encounter situations where they must make decisions about their work units and their employees. Most often, the manager has the option of involving or not involving employees in these decisions. Indeed, even team leaders will encounter situations where a decision must be made about the team, and it is not certain that the entire team needs to be involved in the decision. In reality, the choice is not simply between involvement and no involvement. Rather, there is a wide range of options available to the manager.

Tannenbaum and Schmidt (1973) were among the first to consider the process of participative decision making. They proposed that decision-making processes vary with respect to the amount of authority held by the boss and the amount of freedom held by employees; an increase in the authority held by the manager, by definition, results in a decrease in the amount of freedom held by employees (see Figure 3.2).

At one extreme of the continuum are processes that are considered to be boss-centered. In these situations, the manager makes the decision and announces it, or maybe tries to sell the decision. At the other extreme are processes that are considered to be subordinate-centered. In these situations, employees make decisions, generally within limits set by upper management. Between these two extremes is a series of options by which managers may elicit input from employees, involving them by asking them for ideas and suggestions. Similarly, Lawler (1986, 1992), referring to these two approaches as control-oriented versus involvement-oriented, discusses both advantages and disadvantages of each approach, and indicates that the choice of management approach must be made within a context of sociocultural values, the nature of the work force, the type of product being produced, and the organization's external environment.

FIGURE 3.2
Leadership-behavior continuum.

Source: Reprinted by permission of Harvard Business Review. *An exhibit from "How to Choose a Leadership Pattern" by Robert Tannenbaum and W.H. Schmidt, March/April 1958. Copyright © by the President and Fellows of Harvard College, all rights reserved. (May–June 1973), p.164.*

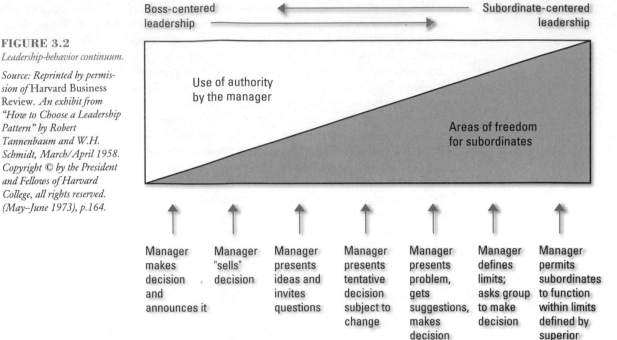

Choosing from the range of options available to managers regarding the extent to which employees should be involved in decisions requires a careful examination of the advantages and disadvantages associated with involving employees in the decision-making process, as well as an analysis of the particular situation. We begin with a brief examination of the general advantages and disadvantages. Note that some of these parallel the advantages and disadvantages of using team processes discussed in the previous section.

Advantages

1. When more individuals are involved in the decision-making process, there is generally greater knowledge or expertise being brought to bear on the problem. Involving employees in the decision-making process increases the probability that important issues affecting the decision will surface.

2. When employees are involved in decisions, they tend to generate a wider range of values and perspectives, representing the range of issues and concerns at stake in the decision. Increasingly, we are aware that neither the labor force nor the market place is homogeneous in background, values, or needs. Reflecting the customer profile in the decision-making group can be a competitive advantage (Cox, 1993, Loden and Rosener, 1991).

3. Employees have a greater commitment to implementing a decision in which they were involved, because they understand the reasons behind the decision.

4. Employees involved in the decision-making process will often be able to identify potential obstacles to implementing the decision, as well as ways to avoid them. James Houghton, chairman of Corning Glass Works, says, "If there is one thing our company and others like us have learned from our efforts to enhance quality, it is that the person on the job knows more about the job and how to improve it than anyone in the organization" (The *New York Times*, 1987).

5. Involving employees in the decision-making process enhances their skills and abilities and helps them to grow and develop as organizational members.

Disadvantages

1. Participative decision making takes time. As the number of people who are involved in a decision increases, so does the time it takes to reach a decision.

2. If the group is involved in a decision for which it does not have the proper expertise, participative decision making will likely result in a low-quality decision.

3. If group meetings are not well structured, individuals with the appropriate expertise may fail to contribute to the discussion, whereas those with little or no knowledge may overcontribute and dominate the discussion.

4. When group members are overly concerned with gaining consensus in participative decision making, groupthink occurs (Janis, 1972). Recall that groupthink is a situation where group members avoid being critical of others' ideas and thereby cease to think objectively about the decision at hand.

WHO SHOULD PARTICIPATE—AND WHEN

As noted above, the decision to involve employees in the decision-making process should be a function of the relative importance of the relevant advantages and disadvantages in each situation. A model that allows managers to examine the questions of *when* to involve employees in the decision-making process, and when they decide to do so, *how* to do it most effectively was developed by Vroom and his colleagues (Vroom and Jago, 1974, Vroom and Yetton, 1973). This model is the basis of Kepner-Tregoe's TELOS, a two-day management development program. The model identifies five decision-making strategies that are relevant here. These five strategies can be classified as autocratic (A), consultative (C), or group (G) decision-making strategies. It should be noted, however, that Vroom and Jago's work also included a sixth strategy, delegation, where complete authority and responsibility for the decision is given to a group of employees. The five relevant strategies are:

AI   You solve the problem or make the decision yourself, using information available to you at the time.

AII   You obtain any necessary information from subordinates, then decide on the solution to the problem yourself. In getting the information from them, you may or may not tell subordinates what the problem is. The role played by your subordinates in making the decision is clearly one of providing specific information which you request, rather than generating or evaluating solutions.

CI   You share the problem with the relevant subordinates individually, getting their ideas and suggestions without bringing them together as a group. Then you make the decision. This decision may or may not reflect your subordinates' influence.

CII   You share the problem with your subordinates in a group meeting. In this meeting you obtain their ideas and suggestions. Then, you make the decision which may or may not reflect your subordinates' influence.

GII   You share the problem with your subordinates as a group. Together you generate and evaluate alternatives and attempt to reach agreement (consensus) on a solution. Your role is much like that of chairperson, coordinating the discussion, keeping it focused on the problem, and making sure that the critical issues are discussed. You do not try to influence the group to adopt "your" solution and are willing to accept and implement any solution which has the support of the entire group (Vroom and Jago, 1974, p. 745).

Selecting the appropriate decision-making strategy requires the manager to ask seven questions that focus on (1) the required quality or rationality of the decision, (2) the necessity of group acceptance or commitment to the final decision, and (3) the time available to make the decision.

Figure 3.3 shows a decision tree with the seven questions displayed across the top. In deciding which decision-making strategy to employ, a manager asks the seven questions sequentially, following the appropriate path to a set of feasible decision-making strategies. The set of feasible strategies are shown at the bottom of Figure 3.3. Each set of feasible strategies is arrayed so that, reading from left to right, the strategies require an increasing commitment of time and allow for an increasing involvement of subordinates in the process. Thus, if you have great time constraints, you would likely choose the first strategy presented in the feasible set. If you have fewer time constraints, but are concerned about group commitment to the solution and therefore want to maximize input from the group, you should choose from the latter strategies within the feasible set.

Problem Attributes

A. Is there a quality requirement such that one solution is likely to be more rational than another?

B. Do I have sufficient information to make a high-quality decision?

C. Is the problem structured?

D. Is acceptance of the decision by subordinates critical to effective implementation?

E. If I were to make the decision myself, is it reasonably certain that it would be accepted by my subordinates?

F. Do subordinates share the organizational goals to be attained in solving this problem?

G. Is conflict among subordinates likely in preferred solutions?

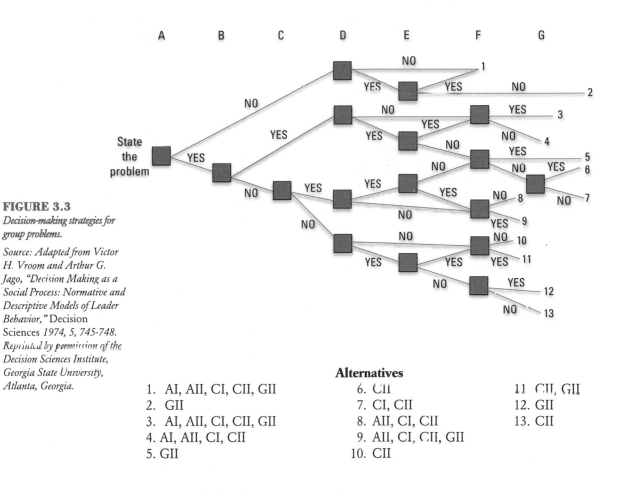

FIGURE 3.3
Decision-making strategies for group problems.

Source: Adapted from Victor H. Vroom and Arthur G. Jago, "Decision Making as a Social Process: Normative and Descriptive Models of Leader Behavior," Decision Sciences *1974, 5, 745-748. Reprinted by permission of the Decision Sciences Institute, Georgia State University, Atlanta, Georgia.*

Alternatives

1. AI, AII, CI, CII, GII
2. GII
3. AI, AII, CI, CII, GII
4. AI, AII, CI, CII
5. GII
6. CII
7. CI, CII
8. AII, CI, CII
9. AII, CI, CII, GII
10. CII
11. CII, GII
12. GII
13. CII

In deciding whether to involve employees in the decision-making process, time plays a critical role. You should be careful, however, not to avoid group decision-making strategies because you believe that meetings tend to be inefficient and wasteful of both your own and your employees' time. Although a meeting may take a greater amount of employees' time overall, it may be possible to reach a decision within a shorter time period by bringing everyone together. Moreover, while a decision may take a bit longer in the short run, it may save a lot of time in the long run if the decision-making process has been designed so that employees feel committed to the decision outcome. Jack Stack, CEO of Springfield Remanufacturing Corporation, was faced with a decision that could have resulted in layoffs of 100 employees. After almost three months of trying to make the decision on his own, he held "town meetings" at all company sites and found that his employees were willing to work to bring on new products and jobs, rather than see fellow workers laid off. He later commented, "The neat thing about it was to realize that I couldn't make the decision myself. It was not a manager's decision. It was their future and their company" (*INC*, 1988). The most important element in gaining employees' commitment to a decision is to ensure that each person feels that his or her opinions and ideas have been heard. The next section provides some guidelines for running effective face-to-face meetings which allow everyone to participate. The last section discusses some telecommunications technology that can help elicit input from employees when it is not possible for everyone to meet in the same room at the same time.

INCREASING MEETING EFFECTIVENESS

No doubt you have attended some pretty horrible meetings in your life. You have also attended some good meetings. What characteristics differentiate good meetings from bad meetings? First, good meetings accomplish the desired task. Second, in good meetings there is appropriate input from group members, and everyone feels that he or she contributes in an important way.

Note the similarity of these characteristics to the task and group maintenance roles played in transforming a work group into a work team. This is no accident! One key to effective meeting management is the ability to balance the focus between task and group maintenance roles—making sure the group stays on track while ensuring that everyone has an opportunity for appropriate participation. Here are some guidelines for effective meeting management; the guidelines focus on preparing for the meeting, running the meeting, and following up on the meeting.

Preparing for the Meeting
1. *Set objectives for the meeting.* If you are not clear about the purpose of the meeting, it is unlikely that you will feel that you have accomplished something at the end of the meeting.

2. *Select appropriate participants for the meeting.* Invite individuals who are affected by, or have an important stake in, the outcome of the decision. Where appropriate, choose participants with the intent of maximizing knowledge and perspective diversity.

3. *Select an appropriate time and place to meet.* Choosing the appropriate time depends on individuals' work schedules, the amount of time required for the meeting, and what time of day is most appropriate: the fresh early morning or the work-focused end of day. Choosing an appropriate location

depends on how large the group is, whether you will need special equipment (such as a chalkboard, flip chart, overhead projector, videotape machine, etc.), and how much privacy or formality is necessary. Holding a meeting in your office will carry a very different message to your employees than holding the meeting in a conference room.

4. *Prepare and distribute an agenda in advance.* Like setting the objectives for the meeting, preparing and distributing an agenda in advance increases the likelihood of accomplishing the objectives of the meeting. Include the time and place of the meeting and an estimated time for dealing with each major item on the agenda. Sequence the items so that there is some logic to the flow of topics. This gives participants a better sense of direction for the meeting. It also allows individuals to gather whatever information or resources they may feel will be important for the meeting.

Running the Meeting

1. *Start on time.* Starting on time allows for the best use of everyone's time.

2. *Make sure that someone is taking minutes where necessary.*

3. *Review the agenda and check if there are any necessary adjustments.* Again, this provides a sense of direction for the meeting and will increase the likelihood of task accomplishment.

4. *Make sure that participants know each other.* The atmosphere in the meeting will be much more pleasant when people know others with whom they are meeting.

5. *Follow the agenda.* Pace the meeting. Make sure that each topic is carefully discussed; individuals should not go off on tangents or take the focus away from the item at hand.

6. *Minimize (or eliminate) the number of interruptions.* Show respect to others in the meeting by keeping telephone calls, papers to be signed, and people walking in with questions to a minimum. After all, if you were away from the office, these interruptions would likely have to wait until you could get to them. Treating your employees and peers as you would a customer demonstrates that you value their input.

7. *Be aware of everyone's contributions.* Encourage participation by all. Remember, you selected the participants because you felt they had something to contribute to the decision. If some individuals dominate the discussion, politely ask them to give others an opportunity to contribute. If some are reticent to contribute, try to ask for their opinions or suggestions without embarrassing them.

8. *Conclude the meeting by reviewing or restating any decisions reached and assignments made.* In order to ensure agreement and to reinforce decisions, it is helpful to review or restate all decisions at the conclusion of the meeting. Clarification of decisions and assignments will increase the likelihood that the next meeting will be productive. You may also want to schedule the next meeting at this time.

Following Up on the Meeting

1. *If minutes have been taken, distribute them in a timely manner.* This reminds people (or informs them, if they were unable to attend the meeting) of what happened in the meeting and what the group accomplished, as well as what their responsibilities are for the next meeting.

2. *If assignments have been made, periodically check with individuals as to their progress.* It is best not to wait until the next meeting to find out that someone has been delayed in completing an assignment.

GROUPWARE—COMPUTER AIDS TO GROUP DECISION MAKING

Earlier we discussed several of the advantages and disadvantages to participative decision making. Implicit in some of the disadvantages was an assumption that participation involved bringing employees together to meet and discuss the issues at hand. Sometimes, however, not everyone who should have input into the decision is available at the same time and/or the same place. As organizations become increasingly reliant on the input of employees in decision-making processes, they also need to find better ways to support employee participation.

Over the past two decades, new approaches to participative decision making have emerged from advances in computing technology in general, and the emergence of groupware in particular (Pardo and Nelson, 1994). The term *groupware* generally refers to "any information system designed to enable groups to work together electronically. [It includes] a variety of different products . . . that help groups communicate better, reach faster and better decisions, plan and track a series of actions to reach a goal, and produce reports and other documents as a collaborative effort" (Opper and Fersko-Weiss, 1992, p. 4). Some researchers have extended this definition to include nonelectronic tools as well, suggesting that it is the process, rather than the tool, that is fundamental in enhancing the group's decision making (Johansen, Sibbet, Benson, Martin, Mittman and Saffo, 1991). Given our general focus on the potential gains associated with group decision making, here we will assume this broader definition.

One type of groupware that emerged during the 1980s, called *decision conferencing* (Quinn, Rohrbaugh and McGrath, 1985, Reagan-Cirincione and Rohrbaugh, 1992) or *group (decision) support systems* (Jessup and Valacich, 1993), decreases some of the disadvantages of group decision making by using computer technology and a group facilitator to structure the discussion. These types of meetings range from those that only use the computer technology to track the discussion but otherwise resemble more traditional meetings, to those that allow everyone to "talk" at once through networked personal computers. Users of this latter type of groupware argue that this improves productivity because people have increased opportunity for input. For example, at Boeing users of this type of groupware claim to have "cut the time needed to complete a wide range of team projects by an average of 91%, or to *one-tenth* of what similar work took in the past" (Kirkpatrick, 1992, p. 93, emphasis in original). In one case, a group of engineers, designers, machinists, and manufacturing managers completed a job that normally would have taken more than a year in just 35 days with 15 electronic meetings. Managers who use this software also indicate that in addition to each person having more physical (clock) time for input, people often feel freer to contribute since the source of the comment is generally kept anonymous; participants can feel free to disagree with others, even their boss, without the others knowing who is disagreeing.

A useful framework for understanding the potential benefits of groupware builds on the notion that traditional meetings require people to be at the same place at the same time. Stanley M. Davis, in his book *Future Perfect* (1987), essentially argues that in order to remain viable, organizations will need to shift their thinking from "same time/same place" approaches to organizing to "any time/any place" approaches. That is, in order to meet customer needs more effectively, organizations will need to be unconstrained by time and place; they will need to shorten their production cycles and broaden their geographical boundaries to compete in a global marketplace. The proliferation of mail order companies that promise next-day or two-day delivery provides but one example of how organizations have begun to move to an any time/any place manner of thinking. This same logic applies to organizational decision making. Thus, if organizational decision-making processes are to remain viable in this type of environment, they must be able to gather input from employees any time/any place. Tools that support same time/same place meetings include copyboards, PC projection systems, and group decision-support systems. Group decision-support systems can also support same time/different place meetings, as can audio conference calls and videoconferences. Tools that support different time/different place (any time/any place) meetings include electronic mail and voice mail systems, where the use of a distribution list can deliver a message to all meeting participants simultaneously and virtually instantaneously for use when the participants are available.

While groupware technology is currently developing at a rapid pace, researchers agree that it is just at the beginning. As indicated above, as organizations recognize a greater need to have employees participating in organizational decision making, their need for new technology to support this input will evolve. Indeed, Opper and Fersko-Weiss (1992, p. 5) state:

> Today's groupware products will one day be seen as equivalent to one and two-celled creatures in the animal kingdom. Future groupware, like higher forms of life, will be adaptable and intelligent, with a rich mix of well-delineated features. Users

will be able to combine video images with scanned-in photographs, computer-generated graphics, textual data, voice and other technologies. The programs will be more intuitive and intelligent—resembling complex, many-celled animals. These programs will be able to suggest solutions, explore the ramifications of decisions, minimize miscommunications and even promote effective work group dynamics.

While this vision of future groupware is certainly provocative, it is the last sentence that is particularly striking in the context of participative decision making. It reminds us that no matter how we enhance our decision making through the use of technology, ultimately the group makes the decision and it is those individuals who must be certain that those participating in the decision fully understand others' input and that each person feels that his or her perspective has been heard.

ANALYSIS   Decision by the Group[4]

Directions   Read the following story and answer the questions that follow.

John Stevens, plant manager of the Fairlee Plant of Lockstead Corporation, attended the advanced management seminar conducted at a large midwestern university. The seminar, of four weeks' duration, was largely devoted to the topic of executive decision making.

Professor Mennon, one of the university staff, particularly impressed John Stevens with his lectures on group discussion and group decision making. On the basis of research and experience, Professor Mennon was convinced that employees, if given the opportunity, could meet together, intelligently consider, and then formulate quality decisions that would be enthusiastically accepted.

Returning to his plant at the conclusion of the seminar, John decided to practice some of the principles which he had learned. He called together the 25 employees of department B and told them that production standards established several years previously were now too low in view of the recent installation of automated equipment. He gave the employees the opportunity to discuss the mitigating circumstances and to decide among themselves, as a group, what their standards should be. John, on leaving the room, believed that the employees would doubtlessly establish higher standards than he himself would have dared proposed.

After an hour of discussion, the group summoned John and notified him that, contrary to his opinion, their group decision was that the standards were already too high, and since they were given the authority to establish their own standards, they were making a reduction of 10 percent. These standards, John knew, were far too low to provide a fair profit on the owner's investment. Yet, it was clear that his refusal to accept the group's decision would be disastrous. Before taking a course of action, John called Professor Mennon at the university to ask for his opinion.

[4]*Source:* Reprinted with permission from John M. Champion and John H. Jones, *Critical Incidents in Management* (Homewood, Ill.: Richard D. Irwin, Inc., 1975 ©).

Discussion Questions

1. What went wrong?

2. Was John's style of participative decision making appropriate for the situation? Why or why not?

3. What style of participative decision making would you have advised John to use initially? How did you come to this conclusion?

4. What would you suggest that John do now? Be specific in your suggestions!

5. Given the current situation, what advice would you give John about using participative decision making with his employees in the future?

PRACTICE   Ethics Task Force

Directions

The class will be divided into several small groups to consider an organizational dilemma. In your meeting to discuss the dilemma, think about which participative decision-making skills you can practice.

Directions for the Small Groups

You are members of a task force that has been called in to discuss and make suggestions for policies and procedures to deal with the use of work time (and telephone) for personal business. Recently, some employees have reported to their managers that they feel that some individuals spend a substantial amount of time doing personal business from work and that this affects their work load. A few managers who have confronted employees have indicated that their employees argue that they can only do business with some companies during office hours, and it is not fair to expect them to take personal leave for a few minutes here and there. Other managers have indicated that the amount of time lost is not sufficient to make a big deal about it. Furthermore, they argue, raising the issue will result in negative feelings toward the organization. The division director has asked you to come up with a list of recommendations in which you recognize the need for optimum employee productivity, as well as the potential costs, both financial and personal, of monitoring and attempting to change such behaviors.

Discussion Questions

1. What happened during the meeting of the ethics task force?

2. Did you feel prepared for the meeting? If not, what additional information or material would have been helpful?

3. Did all task force members participate in the meeting?

4. Did the discussion stay on track, or was there a tendency to go off on tangents?

5. Did your group discuss any necessary follow-up measures?

6. What suggestions would you make to the meeting chair about running future meetings?

7. What suggestions do you have for yourself for the next time you chair a meeting?

APPLICATION Meeting Management

During the next few weeks, try to attend and observe meetings of several groups with which you are involved. Ideas for meetings that you might attend are student organization meetings, sports team meetings, dorm meetings, and meetings where you work. After you have attended several meetings, choose one and write a three- to five-page paper describing the following aspects of the meeting:

1. What decisions were made at the meeting?

2. Were these decisions appropriate for group or participative decision making? Why or why not?

3. Who led the meeting?

4. Was an agenda distributed prior to, or at the beginning of, the meeting? Were specific time parameters set for the meeting?

5. Were people properly prepared for the meeting?

6. Was participation of all members encouraged?

7. Did the discussion remain focused on the main issues?

8. Was there proper closure to the meeting (i.e., summarizing accomplishments and allocating follow-up assignments)?

9. If this was a meeting you called, how well did you do at implementing new skills for participative decision making? If it was a meeting called by someone else, what advice can you give the group leader for future meetings?

Competency 3 Managing Conflict

ASSESSMENT How Do You Handle Conflict?[5]

Directions Think of a friend, relative, manager, or co-worker with whom you have had a number of disagreements. Then indicate how frequently you engage in each of the following described behaviors during disagreements with that person. For each item select the number that represents the behavior you are *most likely* to exhibit. There are no right or wrong answers. Please respond to all items on the scale. The responses from 1 to 7 are:

[5]*Adaptation of* the Organizational Communication Conflict Instrument (OCCI), Form B, developed by I. L. Putnam and C. Wilson. Reprinted in Wilson, Steven R. and Michael S. Waltman, "Assessing the Putman-Wilson Organizational Communication Conflict Instrument (OCCI)," Management Communication Quarterly. 1(3), pp. 382-384, copyright © by Sage Publications. Reprinted by permission of Sage Publications, Inc.

Scale

	Always 1	Very Often 2	Often 3	Sometimes 4	Seldom 5	Very Seldom 6	Never 7

_____ 1. I blend my ideas to create new alternatives for resolving a disagreement.

_____ 2. I shy away from topics which are sources of disputes.

_____ 3. I make my opinion known in a disagreement.

_____ 4. I suggest solutions that combine a variety of viewpoints.

_____ 5. I steer clear of disagreeable situations.

_____ 6. I give in a little on my ideas when the other person also gives in.

_____ 7. I avoid the other person when I suspect that he or she wants to discuss a disagreement.

_____ 8. I integrate arguments into a new solution from the issues raised in a dispute.

_____ 9. I will go 50-50 to reach a settlement.

_____ 10. I raise my voice when I'm trying to get the other person to accept my position.

_____ 11. I offer creative solutions in discussions of disagreements.

_____ 12. I keep quiet about my views in order to avoid disagreements.

_____ 13. I give in if the other person will meet me halfway.

_____ 14. I downplay the importance of a disagreement.

_____ 15. I reduce disagreements by making them seem insignificant.

_____ 16. I meet the other person at a midpoint in our differences.

_____ 17. I assert my opinion forcefully.

_____ 18. I dominate arguments until the other person understands my position.

_____ 19. I suggest we work together to create solutions to disagreements.

_____ 20. I try to use the other person's ideas to generate solutions to problems.

_____ 21. I offer trade-offs to reach solutions in disagreements.

_____ 22. I argue insistently for my stance.

_____ 23. I withdraw when the other person confronts me about a controversial issue.

_____ 24. I sidestep disagreements when they arise.

_____ 25. I try to smooth over disagreements by making them appear unimportant.

_____ 26. I insist my position be accepted during a disagreement with the other person.

_____ 27. I make our differences seem less serious.

_____ 28. I hold my tongue rather than argue with the other person.

_____ 29. I ease conflict by claiming our differences are trivial.

_____ 30. I stand firm in expressing my viewpoints during a disagreement.

Scoring and Interpretation

Three categories of conflict-handling strategies are measured in this instrument: solution oriented, nonconfrontational, and control. By comparing your scores on the following three scales, you can see which of the three is your preferred conflict-handling strategy.

To calculate your three scores, add the individual scores for the items and divide by the number of items measuring the strategy. Then subtract each of the three mean scores from 7. The closer your score is to 0, the less likely you are to use that type of strategy; the closer your score is to 7, the more likely you are to use that type of strategy.

Solution oriented: Items 1, 4, 6, 8, 9, 11, 13, 16, 19, 20, 21

Nonconfrontational: Items 2, 5, 7, 12, 14, 15, 23, 24, 25, 27, 28, 29

Control: Items 3, 10, 17, 18, 22, 26, 30

Solution-oriented strategies tend to focus on the problem rather than the individuals involved. Solutions reached are often mutually beneficial, where neither part defines himself or herself as the winner and the other party as the loser.

Nonconfrontational strategies tend to focus on avoiding the conflict by either avoiding the other party or by simply allowing the other party to have his or her way. These strategies are used when there is more concern with avoiding a confrontation than with the actual outcome of the problem situation.

Control strategies tend to focus on winning or achieving one's goals without regard for the other party's needs or desires. Individuals using these strategies often rely on rules and regulations in order to "win the battle."

Discussion Questions

1. Which strategy do you find easiest to use? Most difficult? Which do you use most often?

2. How would your answers to these items have differed if you had considered a different person than the one you chose?

3. Would your answers differ between work-related and non-work-related situations? Between different types of work-related situations?

4. What is it about the conflict situation or strategy that tells you which to use in dealing with a particular conflict situation?

LEARNING   Managing Conflict

Over the past three decades, the topics of conflict and conflict management have become increasingly important to managers within organizations of all sizes. In the 1980s, research on organizational conflict indicated that managers were spending between 20 and 50 percent of their time dealing with conflict, with managers at the lower levels of the organizational hierarchy reporting more time than managers at the higher levels (Lippitt, 1982). In the 1990s, one might expect these numbers have increased. Considering the nature of changes that are occurring within organizations as they attempt to adapt to and/or anticipate changes in their external environment, it would seem inevitable that conflict will increase, as individuals disagree over how work should be organized, who should participate in various decisions, and what strategies should be used to accomplish organizational goals. Although these statements may at first seem to suggest that organizational anarchy is imminent, you will see in this chapter that conflict over these types of decisions can potentially lead to stronger organizational performance. When managed appropriately, conflict can be a positive and productive force in decision making.

DIFFERENT PERSPECTIVES ON CONFLICT

Most people in our society see conflict between individuals or groups as harmful. In both work-related and non-work-related situations, people often try to avoid conflict because they believe it will create bad feelings among people that will then lead to a negative atmosphere in which to work or play. This view of conflict, sometimes called the traditional view of conflict (Robbins, 1974), assumes that the most effective approach to conflict management is the elimination of the sources of conflict. Thus, if two employees in a work unit tend to consistently engage in conflict, the solution is to separate them and structure their work so that they do not have to interact.

A second view of conflict, sometimes called the behavioral or human relations view of conflict (Robbins, 1974), views conflict as inevitable. Given the differences in individuals' personalities, needs, goals, and values, there is bound to be conflict; it simply cannot be avoided. Strategies for conflict management under this scenario focus on recognizing conflict when it surfaces and attempting to resolve whatever issues caused the initial conflict in a way that recognizes the different personalities, needs, goals, and values of the parties in conflict. Interestingly, people who hold this view believe that positive outcomes can arise when conflict is managed appropriately, but still tend to see the actual conflict as a negative force in the organization.

In this section we will assume a third view of conflict. Sometimes referred to as the interactionist view (Robbins, 1974), this third view differs from the first two because it does not view conflict as either good or bad, but as appropriate or inappropriate, functional or dysfunctional, for the particular situation. This view of conflict recognizes that not only is conflict inevitable, but it should sometimes be encouraged in order to allow new ideas to surface and to create positive forces for innovation and change. As William Wrigley, Jr. noted, "When two [people]. . . always agree, one of them is unnecessary" (cited in Tjosvold, 1993, p.133). Viewing conflict from this perspective requires us to seek challenges to our thoughts and ideas, and to value those challenges over unquestioning acceptance. Jerry Harvey's famous story of the Abilene Paradox (see shaded Box) provides a clear example of when a challenge can be more valuable than acceptance.

THE ABILENE PARADOX

The July afternoon in Coleman, Texas (population 5,607) was particularly hot—104 degrees as measured by the Walgreen's Rexall Ex-Lax temperature gauge. In addition, the wind was blowing fine-grained West Texas topsoil through the house. But the afternoon was still tolerable—even potentially enjoyable. There was a fan going on the back porch; there was cold lemonade; and finally, there was entertainment. Dominoes. Perfect for the conditions. The game required little more physical exertion than an occasional mumbled comment, "Shuffle 'em," and an unhurried movement of the arm to place the spots in the appropriate perspective on the table. All in all, it had the makings of an agreeable Sunday afternoon in Coleman—that is, it was until my father-in-law suddenly said, "Let's get in the car and go to Abilene and have dinner at the cafeteria."

I thought, "What, go to Abilene? Fifty-three miles? In this dust storm and heat? And in an unair-conditioned 1958 Buick?"

But my wife chimed in with, "Sounds like a great idea. I'd like to go. How about you, Jerry?" Since my own preferences were obviously out of step with the rest I replied, "Sounds good to me," and added, "I just hope your mother wants to go."

"Of course I want to go," said my mother-in-law. "I haven't been to Abilene in a long time."

So into the car and off to Abilene we went. My predictions were fulfilled. The heat was brutal. We were coated with a fine layer of dust that was cemented with perspiration by the time we arrived. The food at the cafeteria provided first-rate testimonial material for antacid commercials.

Some four hours and 106 miles later we returned to Coleman, hot and exhausted. We sat in front of the fan for a long time in silence. Then, both to be sociable and to break the silence, I said, "It was a great trip, wasn't it?"

No one spoke.

Finally my mother-in-law said, with some irritation, "Well, to tell the truth, I really didn't enjoy it much and would rather have stayed here. I just went along because the three of you were so enthusiastic about going. I wouldn't have gone if you all hadn't pressured me into it."

I couldn't believe it. "What do you mean 'you all'?" Don't put me in the 'you all' group. I was delighted to be doing what we were doing. I didn't want to go. I only went to satisfy the rest of you. You're the culprits."

My wife looked shocked. "Don't call me a culprit. You and Daddy and Mama were the ones who wanted to go. I just went along to be sociable and to keep you happy. I would have to be crazy to want to go out in a heat like that."

Her father entered the conversation abruptly. "Hell!" he said.

He proceeded to expand on what was already absolutely clear. "Listen, I never wanted to go to Abilene. I just thought you might be bored. You visit so seldom I wanted to be sure you enjoyed it. I would have preferred to play another game of dominoes and eat the leftovers in the icebox."

After the outburst of recrimination we all sat back in silence. Here we were, four reasonably sensible people who, of our own volition, had just taken a 106-mile trip across a godforsaken desert in a furnace-like temperature through a cloud-like dust storm to eat unpalatable food at a hole-in-the-wall cafeteria in Abilene, when none of us really wanted to go. In fact, to be more accurate, we'd done just the opposite of what we wanted to do. The whole situation simply didn't make sense.

Source: Reprinted by permission of publisher, from *Organizational Dynamics,* Summer 1974, 1974. All rights reserved.

While we will spend part of the chapter talking about how to encourage or stimulate conflict, we will begin by focusing on conflict that emerges naturally. First, we will present some basic definitions and frameworks for understanding the sources and progression of naturally emerging conflict. We will then look at strategies for managing these conflicts that increase the likelihood that positive outcomes will result. Finally, we will look at a technique for stimulating conflict for the purpose of encouraging innovation.

LEVELS, SOURCES, AND STAGES OF CONFLICT

In order to use conflict constructively, it is important to understand how conflicts arise and how they develop. Although the primary focus in this chapter is on conflicts that arise between individuals or between groups (and that is, in fact, where most conflicts of consequence to organizations arise), it is important to recognize that conflict occurs at all levels of the organization. For example, conflicts may occur between two different organizations, or between units of an organization, when the first organization or unit senses that the second organization or unit is working against the goals or interests of the first.

In addition, individuals often experience internal, or intrapersonal, conflicts. Lewin (1935) identified three types of intrapersonal conflict: (1) those that occur when an individual must choose between two desirable outcomes or courses of action, such as when a manager must choose between two good job candidates; (2) those that occur when an individual sees a goal or outcome as having both positive and negative consequences, such as when one chooses a new job because it potentially has more promotional opportunities, knowing that it also requires leaving the security of one's present job; and (3) those that occur when an individual must choose between two negative outcomes or courses of action, such as during a fiscal crisis when management must decide whether to totally eliminate a single project or program or to cut the budget across the board.

Although this chapter does not discuss at length conflicts at the intrapersonal or interorganizational levels, it is important to be aware of their existence because of their potential impact on interpersonal or intergroup conflicts.

Conflicts in organizations develop for a wide variety of reasons. Often conflicts develop because of individual differences, such as differences in values, attitudes, beliefs, needs, or perceptions. Conflicts also develop between individuals when there are misunderstandings or communication errors, which lead individuals to believe that there are differences in values, attitudes, beliefs, needs, or perceptions. As organizations expand their use of participative decision making, there will be more and more situations where conflict can arise. In addition, as the workforce becomes increasingly culturally diverse, conflict may arise out of misperceptions that are related to differing world views held by different cultural groups (Cox, 1993). The tremendous benefits that derive from diverse people bringing differing perspectives to the decision-making process are not likely to occur without conflict over how the decision should be made, who should have input into the decision, how information about the decision should be disseminated, and what the actual decision should be.

Organizational structures may also increase the likelihood of conflict within or between groups. For example, when two or more units perceive that they are in competition with each other for scarce resources, there is likely to be conflict among the units. Similarly, conflicts can arise when two or more units see themselves as having different goals. For example, in large organizations, units associated with cost or quality control, or with setting organizational policies and procedures, often find themselves in conflict with other organizational units. While this appears to be a natural consequence of the differing focuses of the units, of the checks and balances that organizations build into the system, Tjosvold (1993) reminds us that our assumption that conflicts arise out of opposing interests and goals is only partly true, and that, most often, conflicts arise out of interdependence. That is, conflicts do not arise because two departments or work units have incompatible long-term interests or goals, but because they disagree on the path or means to accomplish the goal and, more importantly, one cannot accomplish the goal without the other.

STAGES OF THE CONFLICT PROCESS

Regardless of the level or the source of the conflict, conflicts usually follow a set sequence of events or stages. In the first stage, the conflict is latent. Neither part senses the conflict, but the situation is one in which individual or group differences or organizational structures have created the potential for conflict.

When the potential conflict situation is perceived by one or more of the individuals or groups, the conflict moves into the second stage. In this stage, individuals become cognitively and emotionally aware of the differences. Here, each of the two parties may attribute intentional and unjustifiable acts to the other. Emotional reactions may take the form of anger, hostility, frustration, anxiety, or pain.

In the third stage the conflict moves from a cognitive and/or emotional awareness to action. It is in this stage that the conflict becomes overt, and the individuals or groups implicitly or explicitly choose to act to resolve the conflict or to escalate it. Actions to escalate the conflict include various forms of aggressive behaviors, such as verbally (or physically) attacking the other persons or group, acting in ways that purposefully frustrate others, attainment of goals, or attempting to engage others in the conflict by getting them to take sides against the other party. Actions to resolve the conflict generally require both parties to take a positive problem-solving approach that allows both of their needs and concerns to be heard and handled. If the two parties believe that they are bound by a common long-term goal, it is more likely that they will take a positive problem-solving approach.

The fourth stage of conflict is the outcome or aftermath. Actions taken in the third stage directly affect whether the outcomes are functional or dysfunctional. Functional outcomes include a better understanding of the issues underlying the conflict, improved quality of decisions, increased attention to the use of creativity and innovation in solving and resolving future problems, and a positive approach to self-evaluation. Dysfunctional outcomes include continued anger and hostility, reduced communication, and a destruction of team spirit. More important, conflicts that result in dysfunctional outcomes often snowball, setting the stage for new conflicts that will potentially be more difficult to resolve because their source will be more complex.

CONFLICT MANAGEMENT STRATEGIES

In the assessment activity, you identified your preference among three conflict-handling strategies within a particular situation. These three strategies can be represented along two dimensions that show how individuals think and act in approaching situations where there is conflict (Thomas, 1976). The first dimension represents cooperativeness, or the extent to which you are willing to work in order to meet the other party's needs and concerns. The second dimension represents assertiveness, or the extent to which you are willing to work in order to meet your own needs and concerns. Figure 3.4 shows how these two dimensions define five conflict management approaches. Nonconfrontational strategies are associated with avoiding and accommodating approaches; control strategies are associated with a competing approach; solution-oriented strategies are associated with collaborating and compromising approaches.

FIGURE 3.4
Dimensions of conflict-handling orientations.

Source: K. Thomas "Conflict and Conflict Management," Handbook of Industrial and Organizational Psychology, *Marvin D. Dunnette, ed. New York: John Wiley and Sons, 1976, p.900. Used with permission.*

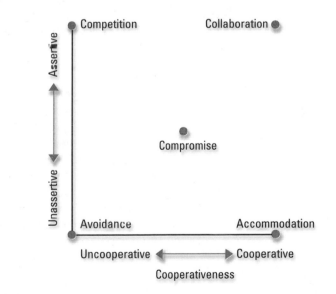

1. *Avoiding approaches.* Avoiding approaches are those for which individuals recognize the existence of a conflict but do not wish to confront the issues of the conflict. In avoiding the issues, they work neither to satisfy their own goals nor to satisfy the other party's goals. Individuals may avoid by withdrawing and creating physical separation between the parties, or by suppressing feelings and attempting not to discuss the issues of the conflict. This approach is often useful when some time is needed to allow two parties engaged in a conflict to "cool off." In the long term, however, if the conflict is not dealt with, it is likely to surface again. Moreover, avoiding conflict increases the likelihood that important management issues will be similarly avoided. For example, the information leakage that occurs when lower-level managers report only favorable information to their superiors, and screen out information that is less favorable, may avoid a conflict but may also lead to larger problems in the long run. Similarly, the bankruptcy of the Penn Central Railroad has been attributed to mismanagement and a tendency by the company's board of directors to avoid conflict and to not question management's actions (Binzen and Daughen, 1971).

2. *Accommodating approaches.* Accommodating approaches are those for which individuals do not act to achieve their own goals, but rather work only to satisfy the other party's concerns. This approach has the advantage that it preserves harmony and avoids disruption. In the short term, this approach is useful when the issue is not seen as very important, or when the other party is much stronger and will not give in. In the long term, however, individuals may not always be willing to sacrifice their personal needs so that the relationship can be maintained. In addition, accommodating approaches generally limit creativity and stop the exploration for new ideas and solutions to the problem. Many unnecessary "trips" have taken been to Abilene by individuals believing that they were helping the situation by accommodating.

3. *Competing approaches.* In direct contrast to accommodating approaches, competing approaches are those for which individuals work only to achieve their own goals. In these cases, individuals often fall back on authority structures and formal rules to win the battle. Although competing approaches are appropriate when quick, decisive action is necessary or when one knows that certain decisions or actions must be taken for the good of the group, these approaches often result in dysfunctional outcomes. Competing behaviors set up a win–lose confrontation, in which one party is clearly defined as the winner and the other as the loser. In addition, like accommodating approaches, the use of competing behaviors generally limits creativity and stops the exploration for new ideas and solutions to the problem.

4. *Compromising approaches.* Compromising approaches are the first of the solution-oriented strategies. Individuals using these approaches are concerned both with their own interests and goals and with those of the other party. These approaches usually involve some sort of negotiation during which each party gives up something in order to gain something else. The underlying assumption of compromising strategies is that there is a fixed resource or sum that is to be split, and that through compromise, neither party will end up the loser. The disadvantage to this approach, however, is that neither party ends up the winner, and people often remember what they had to give up in order to get what they wanted.

5. *Collaborating approaches.* The second solution-oriented strategy is collaboration. Individuals using collaborating approaches are concerned with their own interests and goals as well as those of the other party. The difference is that there is no underlying assumption of a fixed resource that will force everyone to give up something in order to gain something else. Rather the assumption is that by creatively engaging the problem, a solution can be generated for which everyone is the winner and everyone is better off. Clearly these approaches have great advantages with respect to cohesion and morale; the great disadvantage is that they are time consuming and may not work when the conflict involves differences in values.

ADVANTAGES AND DISADVANTAGES OF CONFLICT MANAGEMENT APPROACHES

Each of the conflict management approaches has advantages and disadvantages that make it more or less appropriate for a given situation. Table 3.1 presents the five approaches and the appropriate situations for using each. Clearly your approach will also depend on your own comfort in using the various approaches. Research has shown, however, that collaborating approaches are associated with such positive outcomes as decision-making productivity and organizational performance (Thomas, 1976). In addition, as we discussed in the beginning of this section, the interactionist perspective suggests that a certain amount of conflict is to be encouraged to allow new ideas to surface and to create positive forces for innovation and change. Collaborating approaches are, in fact, the most effective of the conflict management approaches for allowing new and creative ideas to surface.

TABLE 3.1 When to Use the Five Conflict Management Approaches

Conflict Management Approach	Appropriate Situations
Competing	1. When quick, decisive action is vital.
	2. On important issues where unpopular actions need implementing.
	3. On issues vital to the organization's welfare, and when you know you are right.
	4. Against people who take advantage of noncompetitive behavior.
Collaborating	1. To find an integrative solution when both sets of concerns are too important to be compromised.
	2. When your objective is to learn.
	3. To merge insights from people with different perspectives.
	4. To gain commitment by incorporating concerns into a consensus.
	5. To work through feelings which have interfered with a relationship.
Compromising	1. When goals are important, but not worth the effort or potential disruption of more assertive modes.
	2. When opponents with equal power are committed to mutually exclusive goals.
	3. To achieve temporary settlements to complex issues.
	4. To arrive at expedient solutions under time pressures.
	5. As a backup when collaboration or competition is unsuccessful.
Avoiding	1. When an issue is trivial, or more important issues are pressing.
	2. When you perceive no chance of satisfying your concerns.
	3. When potential disruption outweighs the benefits of resolution.
	4. To let people cool down and regain perspective.
	5. When gathering information supersedes immediate decision.
	6. When others can resolve the conflict more effectively.
	7. When issues seem tangential or symptomatic of other issues.
Accommodating	1. When you find you are wrong—to allow a better position to be heard, to learn, and to show your reasonableness.
	2. When issues are more important to others than to you—to satisfy others and maintain cooperation.
	3. To build social credits for later issues.
	4. To minimize loss when you are outmatched and losing.
	5. When harmony and stability are especially important.
	6. To allow subordinates to develop by learning from mistakes.

Source: Kenneth W. Thomas, "Toward Multi-Dimensional Values in Teaching: The Example of Conflict Behaviors," *Academy of Management Review* 2, no. 3 (1977): p. 487. Used with permission.

HOW TO USE COLLABORATIVE APPROACHES TO CONFLICT MANAGEMENT

As indicated above, collaborative approaches have been found to be most effective, especially in the long run. These solutions fall under the solution-oriented strategies. This should indicate to you that these approaches require the parties to work together to find a solution, or multiple solutions, that meet both sets of needs.

The first step in collaboration is to face the conflict. One party must recognize that a conflict exists, face his or her feelings about the conflict, and be willing to approach the second party to talk about his or her feelings about the conflict. People often find this to be difficult because it requires that they put aside any anger or hostility they are feeling and also that they be willing to face the anger or hostility that may be presented by the other party. Moreover, if there has been a long history of conflict, the second party may not yet be willing to try to collaborate. If you want to try the collaborative approach, you will need to think in advance about how to handle this situation. Decide how to approach the other person. Be persistent, but give the other person whatever time and space he or she needs to agree to collaborate.

It is often a good idea to meet with the other party in a neutral environment. This will promote the atmosphere that you are willing to work together on generating positive solutions. When you meet, it is important that you examine your feelings, as well as the actual source of the conflict. Each person should state his or her views in a clear, nonthreatening way. Make use of the reflective listening techniques presented in Chapter 2.

After both parties have had a chance to surface their personal feelings and views of the conflict, the parties should move to a mutual definition of the conflict in terms of needs. It is important that both parties share a definition of the conflict before attempting to resolve it; otherwise, you may be focusing on two separate and distinct issues. Again, it is important that you use reflective listening to come to a mutual definition of the conflict.

The next step is to generate potential solutions. Search for solutions that address the needs of both parties. Use creative thinking techniques (see Chapter 9 for a discussion of creative thinking) to increase the likelihood of finding a solution that meets everyone's needs; avoid making judgments about any of the solutions. Instead of asking yourself "what about this solution will not work?" ask "what about this solution will work?"

After both parties have listed all possible solutions, it is time to select an alternative. Both parties should identify their preferred solutions and think about why these solutions best meet their needs. The two parties should then see if any of the preferred solutions coincide, or what sorts of compromises are required to allow the two parties to come to a mutually acceptable agreement.

Once the solution has been identified, decide who will do what and when it will be done. That is, make sure you have an action plan that outlines the steps to carry out the solution. As discussed in the previous section on Using Participative Decision Making, at the end of a meeting everyone should be clear about what decisions have been reached and what assignments have been made. You may also want to identify steps to evaluate your success in implementing your solution. As a final step, it may be appropriate for both parties to identify what they learned from this conflict and what they will do in the future to avoid having the same situation surface again.

When using a collaborative approach, it is important to keep in mind this maxim: Confront the conflict; confront the problem; do not confront the person. That is, if the two parties in conflict can see the problem as their enemy, rather than each other, it will be easier to come to a mutually acceptable solution.

HOW TO STIMULATE CONFLICT AND MANAGE AGREEMENT

In the beginning of this section, we discussed the notion that sometimes unquestioning or unhealthy agreement can be more harmful to the organization than overt conflict. Indeed, as was evident in the case of the Abilene Paradox, unhealthy agreement can lead organizations to "take actions in contradiction of what they really want to do and therefore defeat the very purposes they are trying to achieve" (Dyer, 1995, p. 37). Similar to the notion of unhealthy agreement is Irving Janis's (1972) notion of *groupthink,* a phenomenon that occurs when decision-making groups become too cohesive and develop norms that actively suppress conflict. Janis's work, focusing on foreign-policy-making groups, led to a number of suggestions to help all types of decision-making groups avoid the pitfalls of groupthink, including several techniques for stimulating conflict.

While there are a number of techniques for stimulating conflict in groups (Faerman, forthcoming), here we present one that builds directly on Janis's proposal that "the policy-making groups should from time to time divide into two or more subgroups to meet separately. . . and then come together to hammer out their differences" (p. 213). This technique divides the larger group into two smaller groups and assigns both groups the task of developing a set of recommendations. The assumption here is that higher quality decisions will emerge from the juxtaposition of two (or more) opposing sets of recommendations, allowing a synthesis of the best of each set of recommendations. The following set of guidelines, adapted from Johnson, Johnson, and Smith (1989), who refer to these groups as advocacy groups, provides a way for decision-making groups to structure the discussion to guarantee that differing perspectives will be presented.

Guidelines for Advocacy Groups
1. Groups (two or more) are assigned different positions to adopt.

2. Groups gather data and structure a case for their position and present the case to all other groups.

3. Each presentation is followed by a discussion where the group is challenged by

others who present opposing positions. (It should be noted that these discussions are referred to as controversy, rather than debate, because the goal is not to win, but to hear the different ideas, information, theories, conclusions, etc.)

4. More information is sought to support and refute positions presented, as well as to understand others' positions.

5. A synthesis of the different alternatives is sought. This involves creative (divergent) thinking to see new patterns and integrate the various perspectives.

The similarity between this technique and the collaborative method of conflict resolution presented above should be noted. Both require that two groups present differing ideas, defend their ideas, remain open to opposing ideas, and ultimately search for a solution that is mutually beneficial to the different parties. The implication of this similarity, of course, is that most organizational conflicts do not involve a "right" and a "wrong" side, or a "correct" and an "incorrect" way of doing something. Rather there are numerous alternatives that can be chosen, with the best often being a synthesis of the various possibilities.

ANALYSIS   Zack's Electrical Parts [6]

Directions   Read the following case study and answer the questions that follow.

Bob Byrne's ear was still ringing. Bob was director of the audit staff at Zack's Electrical Parts. He had just received a phone call from Jim Whitmore, the plant manager. Jim was furious. He had just read a report prepared by the audit staff concerning cost problems in his assembly plant.

Jim, in a loud voice, said that he disagreed with several key sections of the report. He claimed that had he known more about the audit staff's work, he could have shown them facts that denied some of their conclusions. He also asked why the report was prepared before he had a chance to comment on it. But what made him particularly angry was that the report had been distributed to all the top managers at Zack's. He felt top management would get a distorted view of his assembly department, if not his whole plant.

Bob ended the call by saying that he'd check into the matter. So he called in Kim Brock, one of his subordinates who headed the audit team for the study in question. Kim admitted that she had not had a chance to talk to Jim before completing and distributing the report. Nor had she really had a chance to spend much time with Dave Wells, who headed the assembly department. But Kim claimed it wasn't her fault. She had tried to meet with Jim and Dave more than once. She had left phone messages for them. But they always seemed too busy to meet and were out of town on several occasions when she was available. So she

[6]*Reprinted from* Henry L. Tosi, John R. Rizzo, and Stephen J. Carroll, *Managing Organizational Behavior* (New York: Harper & Row), p. 504. Copyright © 1986 Henry Carroll. Used with permission.

decided she had better complete the report and get it distributed in order to meet the deadline.

That same day, Jim and Dave discussed the problem over lunch. Dave was angry too. He said that Kim bugged him to do the study, but her timing was bad. Dave was working on an important assembly area project of his own that was top priority to Jim. He couldn't take the time that Kim needed right now. He tried to tell her this before the study began, but Kim claimed she had no choice but to do the audit. Dave remembered, with some resentment, how he couldn't get Kim's help last year when he needed it. But the staff audit group seemed to have plenty of time for the study when he couldn't give it any attention. Jim said that he'd look into the matter and agreed that they had been unnecessarily raked over the coals.

Discussion Questions

1. What were the sources of conflict between the staff audit group and the managers in the plant?

2. What were the differences between the interpersonal conflict and the intergroup conflict in this case?

3. How would you describe the conflict in terms of the stages it went through?

4. What should Bob and Jim do now to resolve this conflict?

5. What might Bob do to avoid future conflict situations between the staff audit group and other line managers?

PRACTICE   Win as Much as You Can[7]

Directions

Your instructor will place you in groups of eight (or more). Each of these groups should divide into four smaller groups, trying to keep the small groups evenly balanced. If you have exactly eight, you will be in four dyads; if you have more than eight, you will have some small groups with three or four people. Once you have decided on the small groups, seat yourself so that people in each small group can talk among themselves without being heard by the other small groups.

You will play ten rounds. In each round, your small group will tell the instructor whether you would like to say 'X' or 'Y.' You will win points based on the configuration of X's and Y's according to the following payoff schedule. Rounds 5, 8, and 10 are bonus rounds. In Round 5, your points are multiplied by 3; in Round 8 they are multiplied by 5; and in Round 10 they are multiplied by 10. The objective of the exercise is to win as much as you can.

[7]*Adapted from* "Win As Much As You Can," by William Gellermann, Ph.D., in *A Handbook of Structured Experiences for Human Relations Training*, Vol. II, Revised, J. William Pfeiffer and John E. Jones (eds.) (San Diego: University Associates, Inc. 1974), pp. 62-67. Used with permission.

PAYOFF SCHEDULE

4 X's	Each small group loses 1 point
3 X's	Each small group that said X wins 1 point
1 Y	Small group that said Y loses 3 points
2 X's	Each small group that said X wins 2 points
2 Y's	Each small group that said Y loses 2 points
1 X	Small group that said X wins 3 points
3 Y's	Each small group that said Y loses 1 point
4 Y's	Each small group wins 1 point

In each round, confer within your small group and make a group decision. In rounds 5, 8, and 10 you may confer with the other small groups before making your decision. Use the following scorecard to keep track of your points.

SCORECARD

Round	Time Allotted	Your Choice	Pattern of Choices	Payoff	Balance
1	1 ½ mins.	X Y	___ X ___ Y		
2	1 min.	X Y	___ X ___ Y		
3	1 min.	X Y	___ X ___ Y		
4	1 min.	X Y	___ X ___ Y		
5	1 ½ mins.	X Y	___ X ___ Y	x 3	
6	1 min.	X Y	___ X ___ Y		
7	1 min.	X Y	___ X ___ Y		
8	1 ½ mins.	X Y	___ X ___ Y	x 5	
9	1 min.	X Y	___ X ___ Y		
10	1 ½ mins.	X Y	___ X ___ Y	x 10	

Discussion Questions

1. Who was "you" in the phrase "win as much as you can"?

2. What does "win" mean in that phrase?

3. What did you assume that your instructor did not say to you?

4. What, if any, conflicts arose within your small group? How did you resolve these conflicts?

5. Does this resemble any real-life experiences you have had? If so, how might you approach this type of conflict differently in the future?

6. Does this exercise tell you that conflict is inherently bad?

APPLICATION Managing Your Own Conflicts

Select a situation that exists for you (or that you have dealt with in the recent past) where the level of conflict is inappropriate. That is, select a situation where (1) there is (was) a high level of unquestioning agreement so that encouraging conflict might lead (have led) to a better solution or (2) there has been much negative conflict with little willingness on the part of either party to resolve the conflict in a positive way.

Analyze the situation and how it was or is managed, using the concepts and skills learned in this chapter. Describe the situation in a three- to five-page report. Regardless of whether it is a situation where there is not enough conflict or one where there is too much negative conflict, think about a strategy that could be used in order to enhance parties' willingness to work together to find innovative solutions. If it is a conflict that has passed, think about how you might have handled the situation differently now. Make sure you address the following topics:

- The nature of the situation and underlying issues.
- Your feelings about the situation.
- Your behavior in the situation.
- The other party's (parties') behavior in the situation.
- The outcome of the situation.
- Your plan for dealing with this type of situation in the future.

If there has been too much negative conflict, discuss:

- The current stage of the conflict.
- The conflict management strategies used by you and the other party (parties) and the appropriateness, advantages, and disadvantages of those strategies.

If there has not been enough conflict, discuss:

- Why you think people have avoided open discussion of the issues.
- What needs to change in order to get the parties to examine this situation from several different perspectives.

REFERENCES

Beckhard, R., and R. T. Harris. *Organizational Transition: Managing Complex Change.* Reading, Mass: Addison-Wesley, 1977.

Benne, Kenneth D., and Paul Sheats. "Functional Roles of Group Members," *Journal of Social Issues* 4, no. 2 (1948): 41–49.

Binzen, P., and J. R. Daughen. *Wreck of the Penn Central.* Boston: Little, Brown, 1971.

Buchholz, Steve, and Thomas Roth. *Creating the High-Performance Team.* New York: John Wiley and Sons, 1987.

Caminiti, Susan. "What Team Leaders Need to Know," *Fortune* (February 20, 1995): 93–100.

Cox, Taylor, Jr. *Cultural Diversity in Organizations: Theory, Research and Practice.* San Francisco: Berrett-Koehler Publishers, 1993.

Davis, Stanley M. *Future Perfect.* Reading, Mass.: Addison-Wesley, 1987.

Dayal, I., and J. M. Thomas. "Operation KPE: Developing a New Organization," *Journal of Applied Behavioral Science* 4 (1968): 473–506.

Dumaine, Brian. "Who Needs a Boss," *Fortune* (May 7, 1990): 52–60.

———. "The Bureaucracy Busters," *Fortune* (June 17, 1991): 36–50.

Dyer, William G. *Team Building* (3rd edition). Reading, Mass.: Addison-Wesley, 1995.

Faerman, Sue. "Managing Conflicts Creatively," in *The Handbook of Public Administration* (2nd edition), James L. Perry (ed.). San Francisco: Jossey-Bass, forthcoming.

"For Better Quality, Listen to the Workers," *The New York Times* (October 18, 1987).

Gordon, Judith R. *A Diagnostic Approach to Organizational Behavior.* Newton, Mass.: Allyn and Bacon, 1983.

"Getting to Know You," *INC* (1988): 167–169.

Harrison, Roger. "Role Negotiation: A Tough Minded Approach to Team Development," in *The Social Technology of Organization Development,* W. Warner Burke and H. A. Hornstein (eds.). La Jolla, Calif.: University Associates, 1972: 84–96.

Janis, Irving. *Victims of Groupthink.* Boston: Houghton Mifflin, 1972.

Jessup, Leonard M., and Joseph S. Valacich. *Group Support Systems: New Perspectives.* New York: Macmillan, 1993.

Johansen, Robert, David Sibbet, Suzyn Benson, Alexia Martin, Robert Mittman, and Paul Saffo. *Leading Business Teams: How Teams Can Use Technology and Group Process Tools to Enhance Performance.* Reading, Mass.: Addison-Wesley, 1991.

Johnson, David W., Roger T., Johnson, and Karl Smith. "Controversy within Decision Making Situations," in *Managing Conflict: An Interdisciplinary Approach,* M. Afzalur Rahim (ed.). Westport, Conn.: Praeger, 1989.

Katzenbach, Jon R., and Douglas K. Smith. *The Wisdom of Teams.* New York: HarperCollins, 1993.

Kirkpatrick, David. "Here Comes the Payoff from PCs," *Fortune* (March 23, 1992): 93–102.

Larson, Carl E., and Frank M. J. La Fasto. *TeamWork: What Must Go Right/What Can Go Wrong.* Newbury Park, CA: Sage Publications, 1989.

Lawler, Edward E., III. *High-Involvement Management*. San Francisco: Jossey-Bass, 1986.

———. *The Ultimate Advantage: Creating the High-Involvement Organization*. San Francisco: Jossey-Bass, 1992.

Lewin, Kurt. *A Dynamic Theory of Personality*. New York: McGraw-Hill, 1935.

Lippitt, Gordon L. "Managing Conflict in Today's Organizations," *Training and Development Journal* (July 1982): 67–74.

Loden, Marilyn, and Judy B. Rosener. *Workforce America! Managing Employee Diversity as a Vital Resource*. Homewood, Ill.: Business One Irwin, 1991.

Martin, Don. *TeamThink: Using the Sports Connection to Develop, Motivate, and Manage a Winning Business Team*. New York: Penguin Books, 1993.

Opper, Susanna, and Henry Fersko-Weiss. *Technology for Teams: Enhancing Productivity in Networked Organizations*. New York: Van Nostrand Reinhold, 1992.

Osborne, David, and Ted Gaebler. *Reinventing Government: How the Entrepreneurial Spirit is Transforming the Public Sector*. Reading, Mass.: Addison-Wesley, 1992.

Pardo, Theresa, and Mark Nelson. "Groupware Technology Testbed," *Center for Technology in Government Project Report* 94-2, Albany, NY: University at Albany, SUNY, 1994.

Quinn, Robert E., John Rohrbaugh, and Michael R. McGrath. "Automated Decision Conferencing: How It Works," *Personnel* (November 1985): 49–55.

Reagan-Cirincione, Patricia, and John Rohrbaugh. "Decision Conferencing: A Unique Approach to the Behavioral Aggregation of Expert Judgment," in *Expertise and Decision Support*, George Wright and Fergus Bolger (eds.). New York: Plenum Press, 1992.

Reilly, A. J., and John E. Jones. "Team Building," in *The 1974 Annual Handbook for Group Facilitators*, J. William Pfeiffer and John E. Jones (eds.). San Diego, Calif.: University Associates, 1974.

Robbins, Stephen P. *Managing Organizational Conflict: A Nontraditional Approach*. Englewood Cliffs. N.J.: Prentice-Hall, 1974.

———. *Organizational Behavior: Concepts, Controversies, and Applications*. Englewood Cliffs, N.J.: Prentice-Hall, 1989.

Tannenbaum, Robert, and W. H. Schmidt. "How to Choose a Leadership Pattern," *Harvard Business Review* (May–June 1973): 164–197.

Thomas, Kenneth W. "Conflict and Conflict Management," in *Handbook of Industrial and Organizational Psychology*, Marvin D. Dunnette (ed.). Chicago: Rand McNally, 1976: 889–935.

Thomas, Kenneth W. "Toward Multidimensional Values in Teaching: The Example of Conflict Management," *Academy of Management Review* (1977): 484–490.

Tjosvold, Dean. *Learning to Manage Conflict: Getting People to Work Together*. New York: Lexington Books, 1993.

Vroom, Victor H., and Arthur G. Jago. "Decision-making as a Social Process: Normative and Descriptive Models of Leader Behavior," *Decision Sciences* 5 (1974): 743–769.

Vroom, Victor H., and Philip W. Yetton. *Leadership and Decision-Making*. Pittsburgh: University of Pittsburgh Press, 1973.

Weisbord, Marvin R. *Productive Workplaces: Organizing and Managing for Dignity, Meaning, and Community*. San Francisco: Jossey-Bass, 1987.

The Mentor and Facilitator Roles

We have just completed the first two roles of the Competing Values Managerial Leadership Framework. As you read the description of each role, you may have been tempted to think that you should apply this role to all situations. Depending on your beliefs about the relative importance of the various organizational effectiveness criteria, you may have thought about the role as right or wrong, good or bad. Instead, you should be thinking about what types of situations call for using this role and its associated competencies. The best way to do this is to place these roles in the context of the full framework.

Looking at the roles in the context of the full framework will allow you to think about how the roles complement other roles in the model and so you can begin to think about when it is most appropriate to call on each role, as well as how you might blend the roles to use them in synergistic ways. As we complete each pair of roles in the model, we will pause to reflect briefly on how these roles fit into the context of the full framework.

A BRIEF REVIEW

The mentor and facilitator roles are in the human relations model. Recall from Chapter 1 that the desired ends in the human relations quadrant are commitment and morale. The assumed means to these ends have to do with discussion, participation, and openness. This model assumes that all individuals are unique; they all have their own needs, values, and assumptions. But the team cannot function if each individual is focused solely on personal goals and aspirations. Thus, the manager's job is to help each individual develop his or her own abilities, while simultaneously bringing these unique individuals together to build the team. The competencies of the mentor and facilitator roles focus on developing individuals and developing the group or team.

WHEN THE MENTOR AND
FACILITATOR ROLES ARE APPROPRIATE

To understand when these two roles are appropriate, let's begin by reviewing the two axes that define the human relations model. On the horizontal axis, the model is defined by an internal focus, which suggests less external pressure for action; time is available before action needs to be taken. The vertical axis is defined by high flexibility, which suggests that these roles are most suitable in situations where the basic problems are ambiguous and not easily understood. In such situations, it is appropriate to bring people together to share their observations and opinions, to air all the different perspectives, and then to try to develop an action strategy to which people are committed. This process is often time consuming and may bring to the surface underlying conflicts, and thus may be uncomfortable for some people. However, to rush in, take charge, and make command decisions (as might be suggested by the roles in the rational goal quadrant), when it is clear that no one person has sufficient information about the situation, may result in a situation where the decision has little credibility and will likely face resistance.

You should also note that some of the competencies associated with the mentor and facilitator roles will be useful in other situations as well. Knowing yourself is perhaps the most important competency for a manager. This is the starting point for being able to develop as a managerial leader, for if you are not aware of your own strengths and weaknesses, you will not likely be open to learning new skills. Similarly, communicating effectively is a competency that will help you in your personal as well as professional life. Thus you can see that the competencies here may be useful in any situation that involves working with other people.

COMPLEMENTARY ROLES

The fact that the competencies may be useful in any situation that involves working with people should not imply that it is inherently "right" or that you, as a managerial leader, should always be focused on the human relations aspects of your work. Indeed, as you will see with all the roles, overuse of the roles can also lead to problems. As you saw in Chapter 1, one can enter a "negative zone" where overusing any one role or perspective is just as harmful as not having the ability to use it at all. Some managers become so concerned about the needs and feelings of subordinates that they become overly permissive, allowing almost total freedom. In these cases, there is insufficient concern for productivity and goal accomplishment. A productive team orientation then becomes an unproductive "country club" orientation.

The mentor and facilitator roles must be balanced and blended with the other roles that you will learn about in subsequent chapters. In particular, it is useful to look at the mentor and facilitator roles together with the director and producer roles, because they are seen as conceptual opposites. This can be seen by looking at a situation that occurred at Honeywell during the 1980s. There they introduced the need to practice participative decision making and managers interpreted this to mean that they should simply abdicate all decision-making authority to subordinates. The result was organizational chaos and a major intervention was necessary in order to help managers understand how to use participative decision making and still provide direction.

Clearly the roles in the human relations quadrant must be seen in context and must be used appropriately. People in the organization should feel individually valued and should certainly have personal goals, but they should also value the organization's goals and want to contribute to the overall product or service output. It is the managerial leader's job, in the roles of mentor, facilitator, direction, and producer, to see to it that these orientations are appropriately balanced.

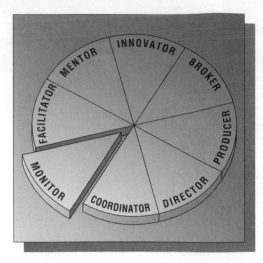

THE MONITOR ROLE

4

■ COMPETENCIES

Monitoring Personal Performance

Managing Collective Performance

Managing Organizational Performance

The next role we turn to is the monitor role. On the face of it, this role appears less interesting than others in the Competing Values Framework. The word "monitoring" connotes the watchful and intrusive gaze of the bureaucrat, the snooping supervisor, or the principal who stalked the halls when we were in grammar school. Monitors sound like people who get paid for catching others enjoying their work and putting a stop to it. Monitoring may sound like a controlling and nosey activity, but monitoring, in the way we describe it, is essential to maintaining high performance in both individuals and groups.

MONITORING IS NOT SURVEILLANCE

A colleague of ours, who is now an executive in the insurance industry, began his career in a large regional office of an insurance firm in the northeastern United States. The first person he heard about was the chief claims examiner. This man's office was located on the top floor of the office building, affording a full view of the firm's parking lot. Always one of the first to arrive at work, he would do a visual check of the lot every 15 or 20 minutes. He liked to notice which employees arrived early to work, and those who came late. He mentally noted the identity of those arriving between 8:30 and 8:45. After 8:45, if he happened to see a car pull past the security gate into the parking lot, he would record (no joke) its license number, have his secretary check with her friend at the Department of

Motor Vehicles on the name and address of the owner, and call the supervisor of that employee to make certain the tardiness was officially noted and, if "unexcused," disciplined.

Thus, the chief claims examiner made his contribution to building a culture of trust, integrity, and continuous improvement. Many employees escaped his surveillance by driving several blocks out of the way and entering through the south exit of the parking lot. This leader, who prided himself on his professionalism and vigilance, was the most frequent topic of stories told at the water cooler and the most frequent target of obscenities written on company toilet stalls. This bizarre tale has two points: First, no monitoring system is tamper proof. People will always find the south exit of the parking lot. People will eventually find a way to get around a system inspired by distrust and a need to control their behavior. Second, the stereotypic view we have of the monitor role, especially in American culture, is almost totally negative. When most of us think of "monitoring" we think of "control freaks" like our claims examiner. Our purpose in this chapter is to cast the skills of monitoring in a more favorable light and encourage you to learn how to monitor your own work more effectively.

Good monitoring is nothing more nor less than effective information gathering. The problem is that it is often done poorly and for the wrong reasons. Monitoring should be done to answer such questions as:

- What are the core processes—the activities, transactions and outputs—that are most essential to my effectiveness and that of my work unit, or organization?

- How effectively are we conducting those activities? How do we know?

- Are we getting better at them? How do we know?

In this chapter we will cover the core competencies of the skilled monitor. These competencies include:

Competency 1 Monitoring Personal Performance
Competency 2 Managing Collective Performance
Competency 3 Managing Organizational Performance

The logical place to begin is with yourself. No matter what career you pursue, what jobs you hold or subjects you study, much of your success will depend upon your own ability to monitor your performance and convert the swirl of data around you into information you can use and learn from. As a student, you cannot rely solely on the feedback your instructor gives at the end of a term, or, as an employee, the feedback your boss gives you once a year on the performance assessment form. You need more personal, candid, and frequent feedback on how you are really doing.

Competency 1 Monitoring Personal Performance

ASSESSMENT Data Overload and Information Gaps

Directions Listed below are some questions about the amount of data and information you have to handle and make sense of. A couple of the questions focus on the kind of information you receive on your own performance—as a student and employee. Respond to these questions individually and then be prepared to discuss them as a class.

1. Has the amount of paper and documents with which you've been confronted at school, work, and in your personal life increased or decreased over the past three years?

2. Do you feel you have become more skillfull in sorting, storing, transmitting, and using information via paper?

3. What are your major sources of overload in managing information via paper? What can you do about the overload?

4. How confident do you feel about the information you have on your current performance as an employee? As a student? Do you know where you stand with your supervisor or boss? With your instructors?

5. What further information would you like to have on these roles?

LEARNING Monitoring Personal Performance

If managers today agree on anything, it is that the competitive forces in the global economy have made their lives more complex. Information is coming at them at an ever accelerating rate. Managerial success depends upon speed and agility, not just thoroughness and accuracy. Managers simply do not have the time to study every message, piece of paper, and report that comes their way. They have to cut through the pile of data and access the information they need to improve their own performance and the performance of their work units. This section is devoted to sharpening the skills required to monitor your own performance. Specifically, we will deal with converting data to information and actively seeking helpful feedback.

THE PAPERCHASE: TWO STEPS FORWARD, ONE STEP BACK

Literally a ton of paper crosses a manager's desk each year. We are generating over 750 million pages of computer output, 234 million photocopies, and 76 million letters per day in the United States alone (Alesandrini, 1992, p. 59). And this kind of paper barrage is hitting not only business and government offices, but our homes, apartments, and dormitories. "Over 60 billion pieces of third-class or junk mail weighing 4 million tons are sent each year, amounting to 41 pounds for each adult American" (Alesandrini, 1992, p. 59). By anyone's standard, paperwork is simply out of control in most organizations. According to a report published by Facts on File, nearly half of most workers' days, in nearly all industries, is spent handling paper. In the spring of 1992, an article in the *Washington Post* reported that 24 cents out of every dollar spent on health care in North America is spent on processing paper. Our colleagues in the airline industry tell us that the paperwork generated by the design and manufacture of the first jumbo jet weighed more than the prototype of the plane itself. How do we handle the paperchase?

High technology is finally helping. We have made incredible progress in our capacity to store and retrieve data through such methods as optical scanning and "data compression." For example, the entire contents of the *Encyclopedia Britannica* can be transmitted over a fiber optic line in less than one second, and the same amount of information can be stored on a single CD-ROM disk. Some companies are now investing in "electronic paper," the process of scanning the data off of forms and storing it electronically. This information can then be called up in seconds and displayed on a computer screen. The paper it was originally printed on does not have to be filed and eventually warehoused. We recently toured the offices of a major insurance company that has not yet moved to any electronic document storage process. The storage room in which it inventories its policies is the largest single room in the company's national headquarters. This high-ceilinged room has over 6,000 square feet of floor space. Within two years, the adoption of electronic scanning will allow the company to store and transmit the same amount of information through an electronic "file server" no larger than a telephone booth. Insurance companies, publishing firms, hospitals, and government offices will exploit the power of optical scanning, and replace at least some of the paper mountain. One insurance firm, USAA, now destroys 99 percent of all the documents it receives.

And yet, the paper continues to stack up. And the promise, so frequently heard in the 1970s, that we would all be working in a "paperless office" by 1990, has not been realized. That term, "paperless office," has been changed to the more realistic "less-paper office." Shipments of office paper have actually increased 51% since 1983 (Tetzeli, 1994, p. 60). We now know that such a goal was unrealistic to begin with. Paper is still an ideal medium through which to transfer and store some types of information. The problem is that paper tends to be overused. A better goal is for an office to have no more paper documents than it really needs. Most of the written information handled by organizations is still on paper, as is most of the information used by students. Students read books and articles; they write term papers and exams; they take "objective tests" on scantron forms; they take lecture notes and trade study notes with other students in study groups. Recently, the power of desk top publishing has turned all of us into amateur designers, typesetters, and printers. We spew out documents that then have to be revised and reprinted. No wonder the demand for paper continues to run far ahead of the gross national product.

One unforeseen development is the popularity and convenience of the fax machine. Most manufacturers of fax machines believe the number of units in operation will increase by nearly three times over the next six years. Every fax message sent results in at least one additional piece of paper crossing someone's desk. Clearly, today's manager must either learn to handle paper or be buried under it.

THE TRAF SYSTEM: TOSS, REFER, ACT, FILE

Without a system, you may not be able to wade through the insignificant stuff to find the information you need, when you need it. So the first task a monitor must undertake is information management—setting up a system that forces you to do something with every piece of paper that hits your desk. "Traffing," a method recommended by personal efficiency expert Stephanie Winston (Winston, 1983, pp. 40–47), is the remedy for doing nothing with the same piece of paper many times. The metaphor of traffic control is wisely chosen because in order to control traffic we have to give it places to go. Likewise, paper has to be given a few basic routes or streams in which to flow.

Imagine that you receive in the morning mail a copy of a report from a quality control committee. This report is being circulated to all departments. The document looks interesting, but you're too busy to read it now. You're not even sure why it came to you, but you're intrigued enough to keep it. The quarterly report from the design unit comes with it along with some advertising copy on new office equipment. There's a memo from the vice president for operations on the increase in shop floor accidents. The invitation to the design unit's holiday party is an R.S.V.P., and this list of training films that must be previewed before the end of the month is still stuck on your desk. There are four signed contracts being returned for your final approval, a memo requesting agenda items for the next staff meeting, and a signup sheet for the next blood drive.

What do you do with all this stuff? Traffing gives you four options:

1. **Toss** papers into the wastebasket or recycling bin if they are not immediately valuable. Most of us are too conservative when deciding which things to save.

2. **Refer** papers to other people (secretary, staff, colleagues). You should probably set up files for the people you most often refer things to. If you're not using routing slips, start immediately. If you're writing a little note on each piece of paper you refer, you're wasting time.

3. **Act** by putting papers requiring your personal action (for example, writing a response letter or a brief report) in an action box or folder.

4. **File** documents by indicating on the document itself the name of the file

into which it should go. Put the paper in a box or file labeled "to file." Keep in mind that reading, in terms of this system, is a form of acting. If a document takes more than five minutes to read, put it in the "act" box. Don't let reading short-circuit your traffing, or you'll never get the papers sorted. Finally, make a clear distinction between traffing and acting, and schedule time for doing both.

Our entry onto the information superhighway may well prove a mixed blessing to our efforts to separate information from data. The volume of data pouring into our homes and offices will increase exponentially over the next decade. This "revolution" is now being made possible by what information technologists call "convergence." Until now, film, books, television programs, newspapers, and radio all existed in different media, as different modes of information. Now, all the information in these various media can be converged into digital data, the native, binary code of the computer. Another part of this convergence is the creation of alliances among cable television, computer, and telephone companies, which, through their combined resources and expertise, will be able to "wire" homes and institutions to the information superhighway through fiber-optic systems. These systems will carry phenomenal loads of data to computers and television screens around the developed world. Fiber wire can now carry 150,000 times as much information as copper wire, and the carrying capacity of these systems will only increase with time.

Where the revolution is really headed is uncertain. Much of the hype now surrounding the information superhighway is reminiscent of the predictions made in the early 1970s about cable television. The backers of cable told us that it would revolutionize education and the way Americans shop, learn, and work (Gomery, 1994). Even with the success of such ventures as CNN, C-SPAN, and QVC (a home shopping network), cable television has not brought about a revolution in working and learning. But the new technology does seem to offer most of us, who can afford to be "wired," some tantalizing opportunities. communi cate with our workplaces; do more shopping online; order any film we wish to see when we wish to see it; access any kind of information that would traditionally be available in libraries anywhere in the world; play ever more spectacular video games; send one another electronic mail and chat online with anyone willing to communicate with us; and talk to and look at each other via video telephone. Virtually all of these services are now available, though in some cases they are too expensive for most of us. They will soon be affordable to most middle-class people everywhere in the world.

The net effect of this wave of digital data will probably mean our being even more overwhelmed by it, and our having an even more difficult time being "unavailable" or inaccessible when we want to be.

As an article in *Fortune* magazine describes it, the tidal wave of data hitting managers' desks may be, to managers who do not know how to monitor it effectively, a load of garbage traveling at the speed of light.

If people keep clambering on the Internet at the current pace, every human on the planet will be connected by 2001. And get this, we're sending even more mail via the U.S. Postal Service and spending more time talking on the telephone (the desktop variety). The quality of what we're getting has not necessarily improved. . . . Much of what fills up new information outlets is dreck. . . . Babson College dean of faculty Allan Cohen has worked as a management consultant for many Fortune 500 companies. He says, "Managers everywhere are finding it harder to keep up. They have to learn about other parts of the organization, even as the pace of knowledge accumulation within their own field is accelerating. In addition, they need to think strategically and know what's going on in the rest of their industry" (Tetzeli, 1994, pp. 60-61).

And today's managers are more harried than ever before, not only because of all this information coming at them, but because many of them are now working without secretaries. Secretaries have traditionally filtered a lot of information and transactions for managers, but many of these positions have been eliminated from contemporary organizations.

E-mail is itself a current example of how technology can become overwhelming. One of the authors recently spent several weeks in the Far East, away from the university where he teaches. Upon his return, he realized that his office assistant had not been checking his e-mail messages, saving those that seemed important, and deleting the rest. When he accessed his electronic "mailbox," he found that he had accumulated over 600 separate messages. Most of them were left unread because of the time it would have taken to read and respond. The strength of this technology—speed and easy access to the person you want to communicate with—are the very things that lead to data overload. We can dump too many messages on each other. But the strengths of e-mail are apparent in many instances. Teams whose members need to be linked and communicate frequently find groupware a great asset.

Many companies are now linking their teams and department members through some kind of groupware application such as Lotus Notes. This kind of software allows people not only to communicate online, but to work on documents together, adding editorial comments and building sections of a document from different parts of the world.

We are also making good progress with audio and video conferencing software, which allows people to hold meetings without sitting in the same room. They can see and hear one another from remote sites and save thousands of dollars and hours of time by not having to travel to meetings.

This kind of "connectivity" is made possible by the corporate "net," the network of linked computers that has become the central nervous system of many organizations. The computer network is an example of how technology can change the structures of organizations. A typical computer network in a global company such as AT&T or Boeing can connect people who need to work on a project and give them instantaneous access to one another. Consider what this kind of connectivity does to the nature of work and to traditional notions of hierarchy and "chain of command." If you are a design engineer working for Boeing Aircraft in Seattle, you might be involved in the development of a new air-conditioning compressor for the next generation of Boeing airliners. This project is a joint effort with Airbus, an alliance of European aircraft manufacturers, and two or three smaller high-tech companies in Western Europe. You don't send letters to these people, and you seldom send Fed-Ex packages to them. You chat with them on groupware software that enables you to save travel time by holding meetings online with them. True, you still have the time differences to take into account, but you hold meetings through your computer. You can see one another and hear one another. Once a month, the team gathers in one place to have a meeting. But the ability to communicate instantaneously saves time. Some companies are reducing by 30% the time it takes to get new products and services to market.

In addition to speed, another benefit of networks is the access they provide to knowledge and expertise. Networks move information laterally, not vertically. As the design engineer on the Boeing project, you don't ask people's bosses if you can ask them to do something. You go directly to those people. You may be working with ten people, some of whom are in "lower" positions than you, and some of whom are in higher positions. But you are all linked, talking to one another several times a week, sometimes several times a day. If you need to ask Lisa Meuller, an aeronautics engineer with Airbus, to do an airflow analysis in her lab in Dusseldorf Germany, you don't have to check with her boss before making the request. You just do it. Lisa has the authority to respond, just as you have the authority to request. As for feedback on your job performance, everyone on this team will have something to tell you if you ask them. Supervisors and managers are not the only people in a position to provide feedback. This means that managers lose some of the power they once had: being the sole person in their unit with access to certain information, and with "signoff" authority on who can work on what. At Sun Microsystems, a company that makes workstation computers for scientists and engineers, people often just "troll" for information and help by putting messages up on e-mail: "Does anyone know anything about...?" Invariably, someone in the company does and that person has an automatic entree onto a project.

The network lifts the lid on a lot of information. People can plug into it and decide for themselves what it means. Mangers also lose the role of being the person that has to be checked with all the time in order to run the business. People who are linked make decisions faster and more effectively than can a manager who is sitting outside the flow of transactions. The result is that supervisors end up doing less managing and monitoring of the content of people's jobs, and more influencing of people's overall performance and careers (Stewart, 1994, p. 54).

This kind of lateral linking eliminates what Lotus Corporation's Jim Manzi calls "The slowest cycle in any company, the vertical processing of information—up the chain to somebody's boss and then down again" (Stewart, 1994, p. 47). Networked, cross-functional teams move information laterally.

What are some of the things managers need to do to take advantage of this technology and not be swallowed up by it? Here is some advice from people who have used this technology effectively.[1]

---

[1] *Adapted from* Thomas A. Stewart, "Managing in a Wired Company,." *Fortune*, July 11, 1994, pp. 44–56.

Don't fight the net. You can't deal with a network by ignoring it. Managers who sit on the sideline and have their secretaries handle their e-mail are usually left completely out of the conversation. The conversation is relentless and often very candid. Communication experts who have studied how the use of networks affects human behavior seem to agree that people are less diplomatic and more direct in the messages they send. E-mail messages are often curt and blunt, and we have seen many misunderstandings arise because the readers often assume the writers are being more critical or cynical than really intended. Managers who pull rank and use the command and control style will lose with a network. The only way you can control information with a network is by limiting the access people have to it, and that defeats the network's purpose.

Create an atmosphere of trust. People in "wired" organizations need to trust one another. The information is more dispersed—more people know the numbers and the data about organizational performance—and people must be trusted, and be trustworthy in how they use the information. Cooperation is more important than obedience, because of the number of people constantly working on projects. Trust seems to have two components. One deals with integrity, the other with competence. We really trust someone if we believe that person has our interest and welfare at heart. But we also need to feel that the person can be trusted to do a competent job with the task at hand. Cross-functional teams and networks represent substitutes for hierarchy. They bring a lot of social pressure to bear on their own members—pressure that used to be exerted by supervisors and bosses. Managers need to trust people to work out their own trust issues and hold one another accountable.

Manage the people, not the work. The legal department of a major company recently learned when it installed a network that the junior attorneys needed less information from senior partners because they could find what they needed in databases, and had access to other people through the net. The role of senior partners quickly changed from one of answering specific questions to coaching and mentoring the junior attorneys, and monitoring the development of their careers.

Don't neglect human contact. E-mail is very transactional, not social. That's why we see a lot of interpersonal problems caused by e-mail messages. Managers need to meet with their people, listen to them, talk to them.

Don't drown in the infoglut. Most of us have become pretty cynical about the volume of junk mail we receive everyday. E-mail is starting to look a lot like junk mail. It is too easy to dump information on a network. People send electronic documents, sometimes 20 or 30-page documents, just "FYI." Managers cannot read it all. At Sun Microsystems, employees each receive an average of 120 messages per day, which represents an increase of 50% in 18 months (Stewart, 1994, p. 56). These messages come in addition to the wave of faxes, Fed-Ex packages, beeper vibrations, and phone calls that wash over people every day. Occasionally, leaders must challenge their people to streamline information and focus on implications—more on meaning, and less on raw data.

Miniaturization will allow us to carry ever better personal data assistants, such as Apple's Newton, and Sharp's Wizard line of machines. By the end of the 1990s, more than a third of us will have our own cellular phones. Perhaps the most serious difficulty posed by this amazing technology is that it will increase the social distance between those who can afford it and those who cannot. In the next decade, a much greater number of jobs will require access to a computer (or some kind of converged communication device) at home that can be linked to machines at work. In fact, there is ample evidence that the nature of "the job" itself is being transformed from a fixed position within a particular organization to a much more mobile and shortlived series of projects. The end of the job as we have perceived it for the past 100 years may require even greater challenges to our ability to monitor our own performance and convert waves of data into useful information.

ARE YOU IN DATA OVERLOAD?

Russel Ackoff, an international consultant on managerial problem solving and a designer of complex information systems, says that a major problem confronting managers is too much irrelevant information. Managers are surrounded by data that do not tell them what they need to know but which demand attention anyway. The smart managers learn to watch the helpful data and ignore the irrelevant stuff. Less sophisticated managers drown in information anxiety. Richard Wurman, an expert on making information accessible, says, "Information Anxiety is produced by the ever widening gap between what we understand and what we think we should understand. [It is] the black hole between data and knowledge. It happens when information doesn't tell us what we want or need to know" (Wurman, 1989, p. 34).

See if you identify with some of these symptoms of information overload as a student or employee:

1. Chronically talking about not keeping up with what's going on around you.

2. Nodding your head knowingly when someone mentions a book, an artist, or a news story that you have actually never heard of.

3. Blaming yourself for not being able to follow the assembly instructions for a bicycle, a barbecue grill, a bookcase, and so on.

4. Thinking that the person next to you understands everything and you don't.

5. Calling something that you don't understand "information." It isn't information if you don't understand it (Wurman, 1989, pp. 35–36).

The fashion of referring to virtually any kind of data as "information" emerged when we started using the word to describe anything that was transmitted over an electrical or mechanical channel (Campbell, 1982, p. 17). The term *information* meant anything sent by any channel to any receiver, whether the receiver found it informative or interesting or not. Information has since become virtually the most important term in our society; however, much of the information we receive is really just unformed data. We are inundated with bits and pieces of stuff disconnected from any coherent picture, but we still feel guilty when we can't assimilate it. Information is probably best thought of as "that which reduces uncertainty." If the information we use is only feeding our uncertainty, it is probably data that has not yet been converted to information.

MONITORING THE MESS: BUILDING YOUR OWN INFORMATION NETWORK

Wurman suggests that most of us need to get beyond the anxiety of not knowing so we can begin to understand. He wants us to relax, feel less guilty about our ignorance, and begin to play with information instead of being controlled and intimidated by it. We agree that managers need to feel less intimidated by things like the mountains of paper on their desks, and all the documents they "have to read." A manager shouldn't feel too guilty about being interrupted, because managerial life is usually cut up into five-to-ten-minute chunks, each interrupted by another chunk. In fact, managerial life is a "mess" because it deals with human and technical interconnections that will never stay in a stable condition. We have met many frustrated "clean desk" managers whose goal is to finally get the mess cleaned up so they can live a normal life. One of the first things we coach managers to do is to give up on the idea that there is such a thing as normality.

But however we describe the work of managers, we know that most of them do a great deal of monitoring. They observe, they listen, and they track performance in their work units. Managers trust what they see, touch, and hear. They also trust the people who have come through with reliable information in the past. Thus, every manager builds his or her own information network, most of it informal. This is why we disagree with the statement that managers need to spend more time monitoring their in-basket and reading their mail more carefully. Most of the information managers really use is verbal, word-of-mouth, and informal. A phone call, a question at the water cooler or in the plant cafeteria, a walkthrough on the shop floor—these are the richest sources of "management information." A major misconception about what managers do is that they spend most of their time monitoring data and making plans. They spend far more time interacting with people—sending and receiving information through conversation. Effective managers can tolerate moving from one activity to the next dozens of times each day. We have found that many managers, in their preoccupation with time, paper, and data, insulate themselves from the relationships and information they need to be effective. The term *management by walking around* (MBWA), made popular by Tom Peters and Bob Waterman in their book *In Search of Excellence* (1982), refers to a style of leadership and learning that has been going on for centuries. Good leaders have contact,—

personal, face-to-face contact,—with the people they lead. A study conducted in the mid-sixties on effective management practices revealed that the most effective managers had very high levels of contact with their people. Effective managers monitor tasks and relationships simultaneously. The results of this study, still applicable today, include the following: [2]

1. Superior managers spent between four and six hours each day interacting with other people. Less effective managers spent less time interacting with people or spent too much time in reading, planning, and doing paperwork.

2. Superior managers tended to distribute their contacts with people widely; ineffective managers ignored certain people and paid attention to others.

3. While effective managers spent more time with superiors than subordinates, often two or three times as much (these results might now be different with the emergence of cross-functional teams), the ineffective managers spent *even more time* with superiors, becoming cut off from the issues of workflow and the "feel" or climate of the work units.

4. The best managers seemed to customize the length and depth of their contact with people to fit the situation. The ineffective managers seemed to have a one-size-fits-all approach with subordinates. Their interviews and contacts were all about the same length.

5. The best managers also varied the way they brought people together, in meetings, in one on one interviews, and small group sessions. The least effective managers seemed to use the same forum, such as a meeting, for every purpose.

GOOD MONITORING VERSUS MICROMANAGING

This discussion of how managers need to engage their people leads us to a crucial point about "micromanagement." This is a term one hears frequently. The manager who gets into details and asks specific questions about operations and involves herself in them might quickly be labeled a micromanager. But this label is often misused, and managers who understand the intricacies of workflow issues are often falsely accused of micromanaging. Leaders who insist on having all information flow through them, who monitor the calls from the work unit to the central office, and want to now why someone went "to the top" for information instead of coming to them—these leaders deserve the title of micromanager. They are afraid to have other people make decisions, and they are too insecure to learn from people "below" them. Good leaders, however, know enough about

[2]*Adapted from* Leonard R. Sayles, *Leadership: Managing in Real Organizations* (2nd ed.), New York: McGraw-Hill,1989, p. 72.

workflow issues to ask good questions. These leaders are appreciated for their understanding of operational issues, and they don't preside from on high and ask for things that are impossible to do, or are detrimental to the overall work of a unit.

Effective managers know that a profound knowledge of how a system is supposed to fit together is essential to supporting that system. They also know that systems are not stable; they are constantly moving out of equilibrium. As the chaos theorists are teaching us, one tiny change in the system can have massive effects on other places in that system. Good monitors do not put *people* under surveillance; they put the *system* under surveillance. Less effective leaders work in the system; more effective leaders work on it, and help teach their people how to work on it. When problems arise, they look first for problems in the system, not in people.

THE FACTS ARE FRIENDLY: PURSUING THE TRUTH ABOUT YOUR OWN PERFORMANCE

No matter what our monitoring efforts tell us we need to improve, we must begin with the attitude that the "facts are friendly." This phrase, used by the psychologist and educator Carl Rogers, is one of the major themes of this chapter. Facts about our own performance provide the starting point for improvement and personal mastery. When we are uneasy or anxious about how we are "really" doing, we naturally tend to avoid feedback on our performance, fearing bad news or criticism. Ironically, this is the point at which we most need feedback. When students are not performing well in classes, their tendency is to avoid contact with instructors and even classmates. When workers are not performing up to standards, they avoid the very information that can help them improve their performance. They become trapped in a downward spiral of poor performance, which is further eroded by a lack of relevant information (feedback), which further erodes performance. A good self-monitor is a person who stays out of that spiral and believes that the facts, even if negative in the short-run, are friendly in the long run.

WHY WE DON'T NECESSARILY LEARN FROM EXPERIENCE

We are told that experience is the best teacher. Experience comes from doing things, making decisions, trying things out, becoming familiar with a process. But, as Peter Senge points out, it is impossible to learn from experience *if we are not getting feedback on how effective our choices and actions are.* "We learn best from experience," says Senge, "but we never directly experience the consequences of many of our most important decisions" (Senge, 1990, p. 23). This absence of feedback on what the real effects of our decisions or actions are is what Senge calls the central dilemma of organizational life. But most of us face this kind of vacuum, not only in making big decisions, but in simple conversations as well. Without feedback, we are left to draw our own conclusions about how our decisions, words, tone of voice, and facial expressions have affected the person we just talked to. The way out of this problem is to seek feedback—to monitor our performance and not wait for others to provide that information.

Susan Ashford of the University of Michigan's Business School has spent years studying how people at all levels in organizations obtain and use feedback on their performance. Her research has demonstrated that those who actively seek feedback are perceived as far more competent and motivated than those who wait for someone to offer feedback on their performance (Ashford and Tsui, 1991). This is a lesson worth remembering. Pursue the facts about how you're doing. You cannot solve a problem until you know it exists.

Not only do we encourage you to seek feedback on how you're doing in a job, in a class, or in a relationship, we encourage you not to feel discouraged if the assessment you receive disagrees with your own. Our colleague, Margaret Carlson of the University of North Carolina, has studied situations in which an individual's self-assessment is more positive than the assessment of a manager, peer, or subordinate (direct report). Most of us would think that if we rated ourselves higher than the other person or persons, that "rating error" proves we must have a blind side that will cause us serious problems. Not necessarily; Carlson has learned that those who see their performance in a positive light, even if it disagrees with the assessments of others, often have the confidence to move ahead with decisions, recover from difficulties and failures, and make adjustments in their performance. Not all "illusions" are negative. If you encounter discrepancies between how you view your performance and how others view it, we think it's better if the discrepancy is on the positive side rather than the negative side. In any case, the challenge is to seek specific, concrete feedback, discuss it, and make adjustments you think are most appropriate.

WHAT ARE THE "FACTS" ABOUT YOUR PERFORMANCE?

The "facts" about your performance on the job usually come in the form of perceptions formed by people who evaluate, judge, and reward your work, or assign you tasks. Such facts are human constructs. It is almost pointless to argue about them. Perceptions are the only reality we have, and we seldom change perceptions through argument. When you seek feedback, accept it with a mature and open sense of appreciation. "Thanks for pointing that out. I think your insights will help me improve my work." You can then ask questions and provide clarifying information to the person doing the evaluating. Allan Cox, a prominent consultant in team development, shares this experience about giving and receiving feedback in a very candid and personal way.

I'm sitting across the table from my client. He's hosting me for lunch at his downtown club. This is a client in whom I truly take delight. Time spent with him is a joy because he has a bountiful sense of humor while the workings of his mind are something to behold. When it comes to the art of managing people in a large organization, this is the most imaginative person I've ever met.

Though I'm the guest, this luncheon was my idea. I requested it because I wanted to share some views of mine with this man who might take what I say as bad news. Though I like him a great deal, we haven't been working together very long, I don't know him all that well, and he just might be offended enough to terminate our relationship.

Since he is vice-president of human resources of his large specialty chemicals company, this could spell a loss to me of many thousands of dollars in fees. Counted up over a number of years, that number could be staggering.

...I said that my host is extraordinarily imaginative... Where he gets hung up, unfortunately, is his all-too-frequent seeking of "strokes" from his associates. He seeks more attention and praise from his boss for his initiative than is good. He seems to be saying by his actions, "See, what ya think of that? Aren't I a good boy? How about a pat on the back?"

I'm here to tell him I believe that if he keeps this up, he'll get into trouble. His career with the company will be cut short. People will lose patience with him no matter how talented he is.

I tell him. But I begin the conversation this way: "Sam, if you don't mind, I'd like to spend some time talking about your management style. I think you know I'm a fan. I've learned a lot from you that I've been able to use here, and elsewhere as well. I want to hear from you about how you think things are going for you, but again, if you don't mind, I'd like to talk first."

Sam usually smiles a lot and his enthusiasm is boundless. On this occasion, however, he is appropriately subdued. He looks at me straight in the eye and says, "It's all yours."

After I tell him, he remains quiet. He nods slowly several times and bites his lower lip, all the while staring at the tablecloth. He picks up his cup of coffee and just before putting it to his lips, says, "You're right." We then make good on my introduction to the conversation, that is, he talks about his management style. Only now, he's focusing on what purpose his attention getting serves; how that purpose is negative and gets in the way of his otherwise standard-setting performance.

Near the end of our time together he asks me a question: "Does Will (his boss and CEO) know we're having this conversation?" I reply truthfully..."No, but in hanging around him and some others, I've been picking up signals."

On the street in front of his club, we part company. Just before we do, we shake hands and he says, "Thanks for being a friend" (Cox, 1990, pp. 41-42).

This example of free and open exchange captures the spirit of giving and receiving feedback appropriately. Allan Cox, the person who gave the feedback, demonstrated candor, courtesy, and loyalty to a client whom he admired. The client also demonstrated courage, and an openness to hear important feedback—some of the most important feedback of his career. This person was wise enough to know that the facts were friendly. He didn't try to explain them away or fight them. He listened, clarified, and then made some vital changes. He sought to understand before he sought to be understood. That's what good self-monitors do. They don't pass up a chance to learn how they are doing.

CONTINUOUS IMPROVEMENT
AT THE INDIVIDUAL LEVEL

We hear a lot about building a culture of "continuous improvement" in organizations, but that ambitious goal requires continuous improvement in individuals.

Quality and effectiveness are often very personal concepts. What kinds of things can individual managers do to improve their own performance? If they are open to giving and receiving feedback, they will be able to answer those questions, but they may need a process for tracking their improvement in the areas they have decided to work on. For example, we have found that managers benefit from tracking things like punctuality to meetings, time taken in responding to phone messages, and not allowing too much time to pass without being in contact with their people. These are simple goals, but can make a big difference in personal effectiveness.

Some of these goals may be even more personal, such as regularly getting exercise, reducing fat intake, and staying with a reasonable diet. They might include working on personal traits, such as a need to control a hot temper or impatience under pressure, failing to listen and ask questions before making a snap judgment, or letting your voice be heard in a tactful, rational way instead of being silent during conflict or criticism and then later resenting the situation or person involved. A program of personal growth and improvement can do more than all of the corporate campaigns in the world because it is designed by the individual and is an outgrowth of personal commitment. It's easy to set goals, but difficult to keep them. A simple method for monitoring personal performance can be a big help. The little form shown in the table on page 130 was used by a manager who committed himself to working on three target behaviors. In several one-on-one coaching sessions, we had not been very successful in helping him focus on specific behaviors. Our discussions were indirect and vague. We decided to challenge him to track and monitor his behavior for two weeks. Notice from the form that he kept track of successes as well as failures. We wanted him to include the date of a critical event and a brief discussion of it. The "evaluation" column was for him to use however he wished, but we asked him to consider such things as:

- How did he feel about the success or failure?

- What suggestions would he make to himself?

- Is he improving? How does he know that?

This manager was shocked to realize how many times he was losing his temper or becoming impatient, and the act of recording these events made him more aware of the impact his behavior was having on others. For example, after the May 4 incident in which he got very angry at a service representative, he realized that the secretary from his office had found the person before he left the building and personally apologized for the manager's behavior. On May 8, when he swore at an umpire during a Little League game he was coaching, he noticed that the boys on his team were unusually quiet in the dugout for the rest of the game. "That was painful," he said, "and I knew I was making a big mistake as soon as I opened my mouth. I decided I would stay in the dugout the next time I felt myself getting steamed." This event had come on the same day as one in which he kept his cool during a very difficult review session with his division manager. "I start feeling like I have things

Target Traits and Behaviors	Date	Event	Evaluation
Punctuality	May 2	10 minutes late for team meeting,	Being teased, but team is frustrated.
	May 7 May 8	10 minutes late for interview with S. Diez,	He was ticked. Bad.
	May 10	Made all contract briefings on time!	Teased about being on time. Good sign.
	May 14	20 minutes late for dinner,	Broke promise to Jennifer to be on time.
	May 15	Missed dentist appointment.	Makes me mad! Wasted time.
Patience	May 4	Got mad at network services rep.	Gwen apoligized for me later. (Embarrassing.)
	May 8	Did OK when Diez pushed me about upgrade deadline.	Mark was suprised I didn't get mad.
	May 11	Swore at umpire (Little League game).	Saw it coming and didn't stop. Lousy.
	May 15	Kept cool in program review meeting.	They said I must have been sick. Good move.
Organization/ Responsiveness	May 4	Didn't get back to Lloyd on schedule change.	Forgot. Do I need a cellular phone?
	May 12	Had all calls done before Chicago trip.	Good.
	May 14	Called Gwen twice for fax numbers.	Keep using electronic organizer. Don't quit.

under control and the same old problem pops up." The discipline of tracking those events on paper, thinking about them, and then having to "report" to someone else on them can be a powerful tool for personal improvement.

WORKING FROM THE LEFT-HAND COLUMN: MAKING UNDISCUSSABLE ISSUES DISCUSSABLE

Chris Argyris of the Harvard Business School uses a term for the thoughts and feelings that are relevant to a conversation but which we do not express. Argyris calls these "left-hand column issues" (Senge et al., 1994, pp. 246–250). Suppose we were to imagine a conversation we might have with a person at work. The person might be our boss, a co-worker, or someone who reports to us. Before we begin writing this conversation, we draw a vertical line down the middle of the paper. In the left-hand column we would write the thoughts, feelings, questions, and concerns we might have, but which we would not express. In the right-hand column we would write the actual words spoken by us and the other person. Here's an example of such a conversation:

Left-hand Column	Right-hand Column
Terry: I don't want to wait any longer on getting this position filled. We've already waited too long as it is.	**Terry:** Have you had a chance to look at the memo with the list of candidates? If you have any questions or hesitations about who ought to be on the list, just let me know. I want you to be comfortable with the people we bring in to interview.
Me: I knew Terry wasn't going to add Michelle LaFleur to that list. We talked about it and he knows I wanted her to be interviewed.	**Me:** I think it looks pretty good. Have you gotten any feedback from the rest of the team?
Terry: I know what he's thinking. "Does anyone else agree with me that LaFleur should be interviewed." Why doesn't he just say it? That bugs me.	**Terry:** I haven't heard from anyone yet, but we've got three people out of town till Friday. They may get back to me before then on e-mail. I'd like to interview these people next week. Do you think that's possible?
Me: Right, another question from the guy who doesn't listen to my suggestions anyway.	**Me:** I don't see why not. Let's move ahead with it. The last thing we want is to get stuck in a hiring freeze before we get someone in the door.
Terry: I know Troy is miffed about this process. He gets frustrated because we don't follow his proposals, but he keeps putting unqualified people in front of us because he wants to work with them. He's always looking for friends instead of someone to get the work done.	**Terry:** I agree. Thanks Troy. I think we're making progress.

Clearly, these two people are not saying what they are thinking or feeling, but those feelings are influencing the "deep structure" of their behavior. The conversation on the surface is not as powerful as the silent conversation taking place beneath the surface. Argyris contends that organizations' left-hand column issues are "expensive" to maintain. We work around them, we avoid them, we make things up and say things we don't mean or believe. We go through these pretences often to avoid offending people or having to deal with a difficult situation. But when the list of undiscussables becomes larger than the list of discussables, the organization begins to suffer. Trust erodes and lots of covering up and avoidance make it difficult for people to improve their performance because they have no idea where they stand with one another. Important information is lost or kept concealed.

People need to be trained to surface left-hand column issues in ways that are non–punishing and positive. In the example from Allan Cox, the consultant could have easily kept his concerns to himself, but he cared enough to be candid with his colleague. He also had the skill to express his concerns in a way that helped the other person want to hear what he had to say. In the monitor role, a manager will often encounter issues that may be sensitive or even threatening to another person. For this reason, a good monitor must also be an effective facilitator and mentor, or the information gained from good monitoring will best remain "undiscussed."

We have found that co-workers and teammates appreciate this kind of effort in a manager. A person who is working on personal quality improvement doesn't have to make a big, public issue out of the effort. But sharing some of these goals with others will usually increase one's commitment and provide a little extra motivation.

ANALYSIS A   Why Was Allan So Effective?

Take a few minutes and read the Allan Cox example on pages 127–128 again. Why was Allan so effective in surfacing a left-hand column issue with this client? What are some of the mistakes Allan might have made in his approach? What about the client? What was effective about his response? Is such a response typical? Why?

ANALYSIS B   Monitoring Your Own Behavior

Select one or two target behaviors you would like to work on and use a simple form such as the one we have presented. Track your behavior for at least two weeks. Respond either in writing or in discussion to the following questions:

What patterns or trends do you observe in your behavior?

What kinds of situations or circumstances seem to trigger the problem behaviors?

What efforts at improvement seem to be most effective? Why? Where do you hope to go from here with these behaviors?

PRACTICE   Monitoring Your Performance by Inviting Feedback

Directions   This exercise is designed to give you more experience in seeking feedback. Think of a "performance domain" in your life about which you would like to receive some feedback and coaching from a person you respect and trust. You are free to choose the domain. You might wish to consider such areas as the following:

- Your effectiveness as a presenter.

- Your effectiveness in interpersonal communication.

- Your overall effectiveness in terms of work habits, consistency, motivation, and so on. (This choice would involve seeking a global performance assessment from someone who has observed your work quite closely.)

- Your effectiveness in one of the eight managerial roles discussed in this book.

Select a person whose judgment you trust and who has had some opportunity to observe your performance in the domain you have chosen. Develop a few simple questions you would like to ask the person, or some specific areas you would like feedback on. For example, if you choose the domain of interpersonal communication, ask for specific feedback in areas such as your ability to listen effectively; to sense other people's concerns and read the cues that come to you nonverbally; to advocate a need or belief you have in a persuasive and thoughtful way without being dogmatic or intimidating. The more specific the feedback, the more valuable it will be. What advice would this person give you for improvement? What are your greatest strengths and weaknesses in this domain?

Take good notes from your interview and write a one-page memo to your instructor discussing what you learned from this interview and how it will (or will not) influence your performance in the future.

APPLICATION   Working in the Left-hand Column: Stacy Brock and Terry Lord

This application exercise is designed to help you enhance your ability to surface left-hand column issues and clarify roles and expectations with another person—a boss, peer, or direct report. The two people in this case, Stacy Brock and Terry Lord, have gotten themselves into a box in their working relationship. They've already had one blowup, and may have another if they don't handle themselves effectively. Both need some feedback, and both have things they need to say.

Directions   Read the case carefully, and be prepared to act in either role.

Role for Stacy Brock (Manager)

You are the manager of a unit of 15 people in a human services agency in a large county government in the southeastern United States. The unit has been down-sized during the past year from 18 people, but you are not complaining; many of the units in your agency, the Department of Human Services, took a much worse hit during the budget crisis. You also feel you have a pretty good group of employees to work with. Many of the people in your unit are top-notch; most others are good, solid workers who perform well but tend not to take as much initiative as you would like; a few are just "not motivated" in your opinion. Terry Lord is a person you have classified as a good, solid worker, but over the past year you feel Terry has not been working up to her potential.

For example, several months ago you handed Terry a project that you think should have taken a couple of weeks to complete, but Terry took over a month. Moreover, every time you asked Terry about the project, her response was, "It's coming along." When the project was finally completed, you were disappointed with the results, though you said nothing to Terry about it. Instead you tried to give Terry a little closer supervision on the next project, and encouraged her to come to you with any problems or frustrations she might have. This strategy back-fired, however, and the situation just seemed to get worse. Terry seemed to take even less initiative than before, and you sensed she was avoiding even talking about the project.

Last week you did a performance review with Terry, and most of the ratings you gave her fell at average. At the one-on-one meeting in which you planned to discuss the performance review, you tried to discuss these issues with Terry but the conversation got out of hand. Terry insisted that the ratings should have been higher and that you were biased in your evaluation. About half-way through the things you wanted to discuss, Terry ended the meeting by saying that there was no point in discussing the matter further because you really did not understand her or how to mentor employees. "You either ignore people and let them drift without any support, or you watch over them like a hawk and drive them nuts," Terry said. At that point, you suggested that both of you take some time to cool off.

It is now time to have your follow-up meeting with Terry.

Role for Terry Lord (Employee)

You are in a unit of 15 people, some of whom work pretty hard and some of whom slack off. Up until last year, you put in a great deal of effort and always tried your hardest. At times your efforts seemed to pay off, and at times you felt your efforts were not fully appreciated, but overall you were pleased with the work environment.

Last year some of that changed. As a result of cutbacks, you were asked on several occasions to carry what you thought was far more than your fair share of the workload. To make things worse, there was no recognition given for all this extra effort. The last straw was last week when you received your performance review. Almost all of the ratings fell at average and there was no recognition or expressions of appreciation for your extra work. Your manger did not mention one project that you had carried completely on your own.

To some extent the evaluation did not surprise you. You have been feeling for several months that your supervisor, Stacy Brock, has been under a lot of stress this year and has not been providing the type of mentoring you have been used to. You have felt that Stacy has gone from one extreme to the other, first providing no guidance, and then at times micromanaging everything you do. You really lost it at the review discussion, and everything just stopped. You now feel that it was a mistake to show so much anger, but you still believe that Stacy needs to know that you have been unhappy with her leadership this past year. Stacy was shocked with your outburst and suggested you take time to cool off. Now you have to meet with Stacy again.

Competency 2 Managing Collective Performance

ASSESSMENT What Went Wrong and Why?

Directions   Break into learning teams of no more than six people each. Think of situations in which a process, a project, or some event did not go well. The situation might actually be a disaster, such as an industrial accident. It might also be a project that went so far over budget it was abandoned. It might be a case in which a product or service turned out to be unsafe or significantly defective. The example need not be a dramatic one, such as the Chernobyl disaster or the Challenger space shuttle explosion, though these events offer interesting specimens. A group member may have an example from a summer job, a service organization, or an athletic team.

After the group has identified two or three examples that sound interesting, choose one you want to examine in more detail. With that example in mind, try to do some "root cause analysis" on how the project went awry. Consider these questions:

- What processes or practices were not watched carefully enough?

- Did anyone in the organization try to draw attention to problems or defects?

- How were the efforts of this individual (if there were such efforts) accepted by leaders in the organization?

- How could the problems have been avoided?

- Based upon what you know, were the problems primarily technical or social?

- What do you believe the organization learned from this experience? Has behavior changed as a result?

Appoint a member of your group to give a three-minute report on the case your group discussed.

LEARNING	Managing Collective Performance

Traditionally, many managers and supervisors have used their role as monitors to keep score of how individuals are doing. The manager sets the bar at a certain height, and if the employee doesn't reach it, some kind of "managerial action" then has to be taken. But good managers do their monitoring at the "seams," the places where people and workflows have to connect. They aren't trying to catch people making mistakes; they are trying to find flaws in the system. When a manager sees frequent arguments erupting in a work unit, or too much time occuring between a request and a response, or far too many people having to be involved in solving a problem, a signal goes on inside his head that says, "Look for a workflow breakdown." Fix the system before you "fix the people" (Sayles, 1983, p. 38). Unfortunately, it is far too easy to observe individual people than it is to really understand how their jobs are supposed to fit together. After all, a manager's job involves looking at the overall output of the unit, not just his own output, and that requires an understanding of workflow. Workflow is more than the sum of individual tasks.

WE MONITOR "OUTPUT"—BUT WHAT IS THAT?

Andy Grove, President of Intel, likes to ask newly promoted managers this question: "What is a manager's output?" He always gets interesting answers. Here are a few (Grove, 1985, p. 39):

judgments and opinions	products planned
allocation of resources	commitments negotiated
decisions	courses taught
mistakes detected	

Grove points out that this is really a list of activities—descriptions of what managers do as they attempt to create a final result or output. A surgeon's output is a healed patient living an active life; a fifth-grade teacher's output may be a student prepared with the skills, information, and confidence necessary to move to the next grade. Some activities are vital to achieving outputs, but if we focus too much on activities, they become ends in themselves and we lose sight of outputs. Sometimes, managers lose control of outputs altogether because they are so busy managing tasks.

Contemporary organizations are moving from a product and selling focus to a customer and marketing focus. That focus means that we are looking *outside* our boundaries first. Businesses are working to discover what customers need and want, and then redesigning their business practices to meet those needs. That may sound like an obvious thing to do, but for many decades, particularly in North America, business leaders were looking in the opposite direction. They organized practices around internal needs (convenience, cost, tradition) and then tried to meet customer needs without changing existing processes. Businesses are now becoming *customer-centered* or *customer driven* in ways we have never before imagined. This new focus requires monitoring skills that go far beyond anything we have seen before. How do businesses create greater customer value? For one thing, they try to eliminate work that doesn't promote value. For another, they try to put the job of serving customers into the hands of local, well-trained teams. The local group, not the CEO sitting in corporate headquarters, is in the best position to know what customers want, how markets are working, and what the competition is doing. That's why it's so important to monitor and support group (team) performance.

MONITORING THE VALUE CHAIN: HOW DO WE KNOW HOW WE'RE DOING?

To help businesses distinguish between things that add value and things that do not, Michael Porter, an expert on business strategy, proposes a model called a *value chain* (Figure 4.1). The value chain is a picture of all the activities a business uses to produce and deliver something its customers will value. Porter lists nine value-creating activities, five of which he calls primary and four of which are support. The five primary activities involve the following:

1. Bringing materials or information into the organization (inbound logistics).

2. Operating on them (operations) .

3. Sending them out (outbound logistics) .

4 Marketing them (marketing and sales) .

5. Servicing them (service).

The four support activities that surround these primary activities and help them operate more effectively are:

1. *Firm infrastructure* (the planning, legal, financial and accounting transactions used to add value to materials and information).

2. *Human resource management* (the hiring, training, compensating, and socializing of people who do the work).

3. *Technology development* (the equipment, tools, and information that make value adding possible).

4. *Procurement* (acquiring the equipment, tools, ideas, and information necessary to maintain and improve the primary activities).

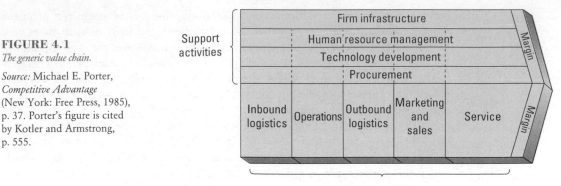

FIGURE 4.1
The generic value chain.

Source: Michael E. Porter, *Competitive Advantage* (New York: Free Press, 1985), p. 37. Porter's figure is cited by Kotler and Armstrong, p. 555.

All of these activities must be monitored and continuously improved, but they must also be orchestrated to deliver maximum value to the customer or clients (and other publics) of the organization. For example, if manufacturing has to wait for weeks for a procurement department to purchase a new graphics computer, the customer will ultimately lose some value by having to wait or settle for lower quality or higher price. If a credit department prides itself on writing only low-risk contracts with customers, it may take too long to approve credit applications and lose good customers in the process. All of these activities must be integrated and made to "face the customer." Some of these activities, which are subsets of primary activities, are listed in the following (Kotler and Armstrong, 1994, pp. 557–558):

- **Product development process:** all the activities involved in identifying, researching, and developing new products with speed, high quality, and reasonable cost.

- **Inventory management process:** all the activities involved in developing and managing the right inventory levels of raw materials, semifinished materials, and finished goods, so that adequate supplies are available while avoiding the costs of overstocks.

- **Order-to-payment process:** all the activities involved in receiving orders, approving them, shipping the goods on time, and collecting payment.

- **Customer service process:** all the activities involved in making it easy for customers to reach the right parties within the company to obtain service and resolve problems.

Managing these activities brings competitive advantage to a firm. Wal-Mart gains competitive advantage through superior inventory management. They restock shelves twice weekly, instead of the industry average of less than once a week. When customers go to the shelves they can usually find what they want instead of being told the item is "back ordered." Wal-Mart managers know what to restock because all stores are linked by satellite to one another, and to many suppliers, so orders are instantaneously placed. Managers also know right away what products are selling quickly or slowly in a given region. Wal-Mart also has its own fleet of trucks, enabling it to avoid delays with trucking companies and slow suppliers.

REENGINEERING THE PROCESS

Within these core processes, businesses carry out "events" or routines. Some events are vital, some are not; some are internal to the organization, some are external. Such routines might include: visiting customers, determining the cost of an insurance claim, cutting a reimbursement check for an employee, ordering a product, receiving payment from a customer, packing merchandise for shipment, and training employees in using presentation software. Recently, with the advent of faster and more powerful technology, many businesses have simply automated the conduct of these events. If an organization continues to reimburse its employees the way it always has, and just hooks the old process up to a computer, the new process will not necessarily get better. It may, in fact, become worse. Automation allows us to make more mistakes per minute than manual processes do because the machine does not know how to handle exceptional cases. Often what we need to do is start over and begin, as process engineers say, "with a blank piece of paper." But a nagging question is, what processes do we choose to work on? Not every event is critical to our survival. Some events, such as filing our taxes with the federal government, are required, but being world class at them will hardly make us competitive (Denna and Perry, p. 8). So how can organizations decide where to direct their efforts at redesigning and monitoring core events or processes?

Lee Perry, an expert on business strategy, suggests that business leaders place each of their major events or processes into one of these four categories:

1. **Unit of competitive advantage (UCA),** or the work and capacities that create distinctiveness for the business in the marketplace.

2. **Value-added support work,** which facilitates the accomplishment of UCA work.

3. **Essential support work,** which neither creates advantage nor facilitates the work that creates advantage, but must be done if businesses are to continue to operate.

4. **Nonessential work,** or activity that has lost its usefulness but continues to be done because of tradition (Denna and Perry, p. 8).

Obviously, UCA activities provide the greatest benefit, so we should reengineer them first. Value-added support activities should also be reengineered and tightly integrated along with UCA activities. Essential support work should be reengineered, but it does not require tight integration with UCA and value-added activities. Nonessential work represents wasted time and resources. If we find any nonessential activities we should stop doing them.

KEEPING THE BALL IN PLAY: SOME PRINCIPLES OF PROCESS REENGINEERING

Several years ago, two managers at IBM had the task of making the firm's finance department more effective and efficient. Sales representatives would close a deal on a big mainframe computer and then call the credit department to arrange for financing. The process would sometimes take up to 50 days. In a business that deals with high-ticket items, these delays can be disastrous. Customers can change their minds, the competition can move in, and the customer's initial impressions of the company's commitment and responsiveness can be soured for good.

The managers had a simple but brilliant idea. They pretended they were a credit application form and proceeded to walk themselves through the system. The process usually involved five steps. At each step, the managers asked the person in charge to stop whatever he or she was doing and process the application as usual, only without the delay of having it sit in the pile on the desk. They were astonished to learn that the whole procedure took about 90 minutes! The rest of the time was spent in handing off the form from one department to the next, and having the form sit in various in-baskets. The process was like a baseball game. The game might last nearly three hours, but the ball is actually in play less than five minutes. The job the managers took on was to "reengineer" the system to keep the ball in play.

They replaced their credit specialists, the credit checkers and pricers, with generalists. Now, instead of passing the ball from one department to the next, one person, who is now called a deal structurer, processes the entire application with no handoffs. The major problem with the old system, say Michael Hammer and James Champy, experts on process reengineering, is that it was based on a false assumption:

> ...that every bid request was unique and difficult to process, thereby requiring the intervention of four highly trained specialists. In fact this assumption was false; most requests were simple and straightforward. [The mangers found that] most of the work the specialists did was little more than clerical. . . .In really tough situations, the new deal structurer could get help from a small pool of real specialists, experts in credit checking, pricing, and so forth (Hammer and Champy, 1993, p. 38).

Hammer and Champy give us some principles for attacking a reengineering problem. Here are the major ones.

- **Combine multiple jobs into one where possible.** We are still enthralled by the image of the assembly line where one worker does one small thing to a line of products moving by, and the next worker does the next little thing. In process reengineering, the assembly line is often replaced. Recall the IBM credit example where the jobs of specialists, such as credit checkers and pricers, were combined into a single job, that of "deal structurer." The greater the number of jobs, the greater the number of hand-offs, transfers, and misunderstandings. Products and services sit in baskets and on warehouse floors, waiting for someone to get them to customers.

It is not always possible to reduce several complex jobs into one. The solution may be to create "case teams" whose members all have the skills required to perform all the tasks required to complete a job. Bell Atlantic created case teams to establish digital circuits for customers. These teams reduced the number of days required to establish high-speed service links from 30 days to three. The process is not only much faster, but simpler, less costly, and less error prone than the assembly line process used earlier.

■ **Workers make decisions.** Traditionally, workers have had to stop the process when a problem occured and wait for leaders to make a decision so the work could continue. Now, we have teams making the decisions as part of the work. Instead of having the "worker bees" do all the routine stuff, and sending in managers to figure out what to do with exceptional problems, teams learn how to deal with exceptions and communicate their needs and insights in all directions—up, down, and laterally. This process of flattening the organization and having fewer layers of checkers and monitors is a powerful way of improving quality and reducing costs at the same time.

■ **The steps in the process are performed in a natural order.** We often see processes that follow a linear order that makes little sense. With simple adjustments, step two in a process might be simultaneously done with step one. Some steps can be eliminated altogether. A major goal of reengineering is to put things in a logical, natural order that best serves the needs of customers. The elimination or reordering of steps reduces waste, error, and time consumed.

■ **Processes have multiple versions.** Have you ever had the frustrating experience of waiting for days or even months for a request or an application to be approved because the organization had only one megaprocess for granting the approval? Hammer and Champy use the example of a friend of theirs who waited six months for the city board of a small community to approve a request for making some improvements on his home. This request was handled in the same way as requests for major commercial construction projects, through a public hearing. Hammer and Champy suggested, "Why not 'triage' the application process by handling simple home improvements, medium size projects, and major commercial projects that require careful study?" For example, the simple home projects, could be approved by a single qualified administrator who could have recourse to a committee for special cases. The medium size projects could be handled by two or three people who could also refer special cases or issues to the city council. The full-scale commercial projects could be handled by the existing public hearing process. This method would be much more efficient, and could have built-in procedures for making appeals and handling special cases. In wartime, emergency medical unit personnel often categorize incoming wounded into three classes: those who will live regardless of how soon they are treated; those who will die no matter how soon they are treated; and *those who will live or die depending upon how soon they are treated.* Obviously, the third category is the most urgent. Systems need to be designed to allow for flexibility. One standard process is usually not enough.

- **Checks and controls are reduced.** We hope this chapter has made it clear that the best monitoring is done on the local level. Centralized, specialized checking and monitoring is often very expensive, demotivating to the people whose work is being checked, and sometimes just plain silly. For example, companies have traditionally had the purchases and expenses of all their business units checked by an accounting department. Every signature on a purchase order is verified, then the amount of the purchase is checked against the amount of money available in the unit's budget. But many companies have learned that this process often costs more than the item being purchased. They have also learned that there are easier, more rational ways of making sure that abuses and unintentional errors are identified. The managers of these units can check expenses from a computer-generated list once a month, and deal with any special issues. Insurance companies have learned that it is much less expensive and much faster to not send claims adjusters out to examine a damaged car every time a claim is filed by a customer. It is cheaper to trust their approved body shops to offer estimates, do the repairs, and then bill the insurance companies. The insurance company can periodically review the bills submitted by the body shops to note any irregularities. This process is better for everyone involved. (All of these examples are taken from Hammer and Champy, 1993, pp. 53–61.)

So, let's suppose we succeed in doing all this. We find the nonessential activities and eliminate them; we figure out what our units of competitive advantage are and support them with great energy and commitment. Is our system now self-sustaining? No. All systems seem to obey the second law of thermodynamics: They move from an organized state to a disorganized state. Processes run down, sharp instruments dull with use, and people forget why a process was designed the way it was. Systems need monitoring and fine tuning; however, that monitoring must be done in the right way. That's part of the art of management.

WHAT DO WE WATCH AND WHY?

Organizations will always have core processes or routines for getting their products and services to the people who need them. Those processes have to be monitored. When an organization is sick, the people most concerned about its health will often call in an outsider to improve its performance. These people often bring a fresh perspective to the organization's problems, but they face a stiff challenge:

they have to figure out what's going on and move quickly to make changes. George Fisher was hired in 1992 to turn Eastman Kodak around. Kodak was losing market share to global competitors and falling behind in product innovation. Fisher said he used the "80/20 rule" of Italian economist Vilfredo Pareto. Pareto said that 80% of an organization's problems are rooted in 20% of its practices and methods. If you identify that 20% accurately and then improve them, you've made great progress. How did Fisher find out where the crucial practices were? He asked people in the organization. He held town meetings with people at all levels; he took secretaries and other support staff to lunch and personally interviewed Kodak customers and suppliers (Dumaine, 1993, pp. 63–67). This information helped Fisher decide what activities needed the most attention. Fisher, and many other leaders who specialize in turning failing organizations around, know that good monitoring is mostly just good listening and careful watching. As we discuss in Chapter 8 (the Broker Role), good managers also work hard to share what they've learned from all these conversations. James Champy is emphatic in saying, "Today's successful manager is not a person who is entrusted with secrets, but one who wins trust by sharing what he or she knows" (Champy, 1995, p. 47).

Jan Carlzon, CEO of SAS, one of the world's most successful airlines, learned from his efforts at monitoring the experience his customers were having that the performance of flight attendants, gate receptionists, and baggage handlers had the greatest impact on how customers evaluated their flying experience (Carlzon, 1989, p. 55). These were the roles and processes the company put great energy into supporting and improving—without allowing the quality of other crucial factors, such as safety and timeliness, to erode. Customer satisfaction, and hence business profits, have grown dramatically under Carlzon's leadership. Similarly, Dr. Mitchel Rabkin, president of Boston's Beth Israel hospital, concluded that nursing care was the most underemphasized but powerful determinant of patient comfort and satisfaction. His exit interviews with patients revealed that people would indirectly choose a hospital because of the reputation of a physician, *but once in the hospital*, the most powerful factor was the quality of nursing care they received. Rabkin revolutionized nursing care by hiring Joyce Clifford as a nurse-in-chief. Clifford developed a system of assigning each patient to a primary nurse who is accountable for everything that happens to that patient while in the hospital. With this new system virtually every measurement of quality the Beth Israel staff uses has gone up. In addition, at a time when hospitals in North America have reeled from the effects of nursing shortages, Beth Israel has continued to attract excellent nurses (Shapiro, 1991, pp. 225–226). Careful monitoring and observation helped both Carlzon and Rabkin decide what processes needed the most improvement and support.

Businesses today are far more sophisticated at monitoring their operations than they were even a decade ago. The reason is simple: competitive pressure. The pressure came first in the manufacturing sector, but it is now invading the service sector. In manufacturing, many Japanese companies, following the advice of Americans W. Edwards Deming and Joseph Juran in the 1960s and 1970s, simply rewrote the books on quality. Japanese achievements in the auto and electronics industries are now well known. In the past decade, Western companies have responded intensely to improve their competitive position by improving the quality of their products.

With the quality standard now sitting very high, overall customer satisfaction has become even more important. The so-called intrinsic qualities of the product, such as durability, ease of use, and so on, are important, but they do not guarantee high customer satisfaction. Quality and customer satisfaction are now seen as "complex values." The values have many dimensions, such as speed, cost, durability, attractiveness, and (in the case of the huge service industries) courtesy, helpfulness, and creativity. In the 1990s, offering a high-quality product or service now only admits an organization into the game. Superior customer/client satisfaction will allow the organization to play the game. We believe that as the 1990s progress, the ability to offer high-quality products that satisfy customers, but at the *lowest relative cost,* will be the criteria that win the game. Eileen Shapiro, an internationally recognized consultant on strategy, says that business strategy amounts to this:

> The ongoing process of figuring out how to give a group of customers a better deal than the competition can, and still make money, and continuing to do so even as the environment changes (Shapiro, 1991, p. 111).

Shapiro displays this process as a simple triangle (Figure 4.2).

FIGURE 4.2
The Strategic Triangle.

Source: Shapiro, p.112.

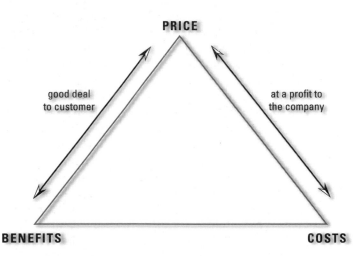

Thus, an organization must be expert at monitoring its processes, inside and outside. Every organization must decide, over and over, what its core tasks are, how to do them better, and how to do them cheaper.

THE NEXT REVOLUTION: SERVICE-SECTOR PRODUCTIVITY

The area in which the battle will be fought most intensely is in the service and knowledge industries. For the past 120 years, productivity in manufacturing, mining, farming, construction, and transportation—the crafts of making and moving things—have continued to improve at about 3% to 4% per year. That growth has fueled the improvements in our standard of living in the western world. Because of this productivity, the working class of the nineteenth century, which worked nearly 3,000 hours per year, became the middle class of the twentieth century. But the *percentage* of the population in the industrialized world that is now engaged in making and moving things has dropped dramatically. According to Peter Drucker, they account for only one-fifth of the workforce (Drucker, 1991, pp. 69–79). The majority of us now work in the "service and knowledge industries." Engineers, surgeons, data-entry operators, custodians, dishwashers, and hamburger flippers are in this huge sector. This is the largest job sector in the modern world, and if we are to increase productivity in the future, that increase will have to come primarily from this service sector. Insurance companies, hospitals, schools, financial companies, information services, and software designers will have to become more productive. The intelligent and innovative monitoring of core processes is a key to the productivity gains required.

We once thought that technology alone would bring the gains we sought. For example, the authors of this textbook were taught in the late 1960s to believe that computers would bring enormous productivity gains to the service sector. We believed that computers would replace millions of clerks and office staff, reducing overhead and creating a need to train the displaced workers to do other things. On that promise, organizations invested billions in automated systems. But as a result, says Peter Drucker, "office and clerical forces have grown at a much faster rate since the introduction of information technology than ever before. There has been virtually no increase in the productivity of service work" (Drucker, 1991, p. 71). The computer has helped immensely, especially in the knowledge industries, but many of the productivity gains in service industries have not yet been realized, or are only now beginning to be realized. We have also learned that machines alone will not transform productivity. High-tech machinery, especially in industries that require human judgment and team work, are tools. They help do the job, but they cannot perform the job without human beings. General Motors, at the end of the 1980s, invested billions in high technology but did not realize dramatic gains in productivity as a result. Most experts believe the problem was the failure to integrate *people* into the process intelligently and sensitively. But Drucker and many others believe there is a productivity revolution underway in both the knowledge and service industries, a revolution that builds on what we have learned about process innovation in manufacturing.

BOILING EGGS: LOOK FOR THE LIMITING STEP AND DESIGN AROUND IT

A good place to start in improving a process is to understand it in its present form. The things we do every day are loaded with inefficiencies that we may not notice. We can use an example most of us are familiar with: the task of cooking a simple breakfast in a restaurant. Let's assume that the breakfast consists of a three-minute soft-boiled egg, buttered toast, and coffee. The task is to deliver such a breakfast at a scheduled delivery time (within five minutes of the customer's giving us the order), at an acceptable quality level (egg is not hard boiled, or too runny; toast is buttered but not lathered with butter; toast is not burned etc.), and at the lowest possible cost. The customer wants a good deal; we have to deliver the deal and still do it at a profit over time. Here is how Andy Grove describes the process from a "manufacturing" standpoint.

> *The first thing we must do is to pin down the step in the flow that will determine the overall shape of our operation, which we'll call the* limiting step. *The issue here is simple: which of the breakfast components takes the longest to prepare? Because the coffee is already steaming in the kitchen and the toast takes only about a minute, the answer is obviously the egg, so we should plan the entire job around the time needed to boil it. Not only does that component take the longest to prepare, the egg is also for most customers the most important feature of the breakfast.*
>
> *What must happen is illustrated in this simple flow diagram. To work back from the time of delivery, you'll need to calculate the time required to prepare the three components to ensure that they are all ready simultaneously.*
>
> - *First you must allow time to assemble the items on a tray.*
>
> - *Next, you must get the toast from the toaster and the coffee from the pot, as well as the egg out of the boiling water.*
>
> *Adding the required time to do this to the time needed to get and cook the egg defines the length of the entire process—called, in production jargon, the total throughput time.*

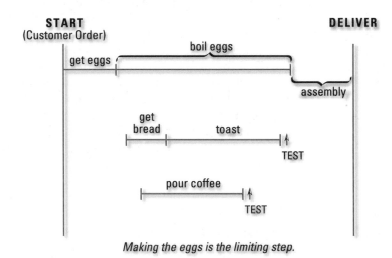

Making the eggs is the limiting step.

> *Now you come to the toast. Using the egg time as your base, you must allow yourself time to get and toast the slices of bread. Finally, using the toast time as your base, you can determine when you need to pour the coffee. The key idea is that we con-*

struct our production flow by starting with the longest (or most difficult, or most sensitive, or most expensive) step and work our way back. Notice when each of the three steps began and ended. We planned our flow around the most critical step— the time required to boil the egg—and we staggered each of the other steps according to individual throughput times; again in production jargon, we offset them from each other (Grove, 1985, pp.4-5).

Don't let the simplicity of this example deceive you. The idea of a limiting step has very broad application. We have seen more than one manufacturing or service process poorly designed because people were not focusing on the limiting step. Grove uses the process of recruiting college graduates to his company, Intel, to illustrate how important it is to design processes around the limiting step. Intel managers visit campuses, interview many candidates (as many as 50), and then invite the more promising ones to visit the company. Intel pays for the candidates' travel and each one is interviewed in greater detail by managers and other technical people. After careful consideration, and usually a meeting of the people who met the candidates, the company offers employment to one or more candidates. Clearly, the limiting step in this process is the students' visit to the plant, because of the cost of travel and the time taken by Intel employees to interview them and show them around. The goal is to have the tightest possible ratio between the number of people invited to visit and the number of people who are offered employment with Intel and accept it. To limit the number of people brought in for visits, Intel managers use phone interviews and correspondence, as well as some follow-up on references to screen the final pool of candidates. This process is difficult and expensive, but far less expensive than bringing too many candidates in for plant visits. The process saves money, increases the ratio of hires per plant visit, and reduces the need to use the expensive limiting step (Grove, 1985, pp. 5–6).

Notice that Intel managers also have to use the principle of time offsets here. They have to think backwards and be sure they alert campuses to their visits for interviews; they have to interview as many candidates as possible while on campuses, and build in time to do phone screening and then plant visits with the best candidates—all before graduation.

As you observe various processes, try to notice areas where the system is "soft." Look for bottlenecks and logjams. Look for indications that the process is not centered around the limiting step, or where other processes are not offset, but are run in linear fashion, one after the other. Are people boiling eggs and *then* making toast, or making toast while the eggs are boiling? Look for examples of how problems in a process are not found in the low-value stage, but only later when time and money have been spent on the process. For example, is it better to detect a rotten egg before it is boiled and delivered to the customer or after? You also need to think about what the primary or core indicators are that tell you how effectively a process is operating. What about inventory—the availability and quality of supplies needed? Does inventory stack up, wasting money and space, or do supplies run out, making it impossible to fill orders and resulting in lost customers? What about downtime on equipment? And finally, is the system stable? Does the process produce a product or service within a range of variability that is tolerable—given the needs of your customers? Questions such as these can help you decide what to monitor in order to improve the process.

MONITORING VARIATION, THE ENEMY OF QUALITY

W. Edwards Deming, an industrial statistician who died in 1993, taught the Japanese for decades that every process is subject to variation in its functioning. Variation is the enemy of quality because variation reduces our ability to predict an outcome. Deming made a great contribution to improving the quality of goods and services by teaching managers how to detect variation, reduce it, and continue to reduce it, thus continuously improving quality.

One of the bedeviling problems with variation is that it can have two different kinds of causes. Deming called these "common" and "special." Common causes of variation are those that are built into the system. For example, in a manufacturing plant that makes automatic transmissions for automobiles and light pickups, the teeth in the gear sets will vary slightly in the smoothness of their edges. This variation may be caused by slightly worn tool bits that cut the smooth metal shafts into gear teeth. It may be caused by unevenness of the fit of the steel shaft on the lathe when the teeth are cut out of the shaft to make the gear. The problem is to find the source of the variation. This is a serious problem because the unevenness causes friction that wears out the gears faster, causing the transmission to fail. In this case, the variation is within a certain range, so it is statistically predictable. The system is thus "stable," and the cause of the variation is "common" to the system. The quality level, however, must be improved. Lathe operators must check the settings frequently; the diamond bits that cut the teeth might be improved, and so forth.

Another source of variation is from "special" causes. An example of a special cause is a run of warped steel shafts used to make the gear sets. This is not a problem with the stability of the system. The problem is a batch of defective material, or a machine that has suddenly gone way out of its setting. Special causes of variation are usually easier to discover than are common causes because their effects are more dramatic.

Another example of a common cause and a special cause is that of a driver heading down a country road in a sports car. If we were able to measure the amount of variation in how close the driver stays to his side of the white line, we would see a good deal of variation, but within a boundary or parameter of not more than about three feet. Some of the causes of the variation include: driver reaction time to curves in the road, slight slippage in the steering system, wear in tires that results in temporary loss of traction, and so forth.

However, if the driver suddenly veered all the way over into the oncoming lane, we would say the system is suddenly "unstable." This instability would be from a special cause, such as a blown tire, the driver falling asleep at the wheel, or a deer jumping onto the road causing the driver to swerve (Gabor,

1990, p. 48). Special causes are exceptional; *common causes are the ones caused by the design of the system* and they have to be worked on continuously if the system is to be improved. The driver must be trained better; the tires replaced; the steering system inspected for defects; the windshield cleaned to improve visibility. Managers are responsible for making systems better. It will not suffice to exhort the driver to be more careful if her tires are worn out or the suspension system on the car is sloppy. Deming insisted that managers are not paid to exhort people, *but to help perfect the systems in which their people work.* The system is the problem; the employees are the solution. Unfortunately in American industry, we have too often viewed employees as the problem and the system as the solution. We are seeing more system improvements being made by the teams who operate them. People are being trained to monitor systems while they use them.

Managers need to help the people in their units gain what Deming called a "profound knowledge" of their systems (Neave, 1990, p. 259). People must monitor the system by using specific statistical tests that will reveal wether the system is stable, and whether the causes of variability are common or special. If special, that one dramatic cause must be found and eliminated. If common, the cause or causes must be found and their impact lessened by improving the system itself. This latter process is often slow and tedious, but it is the key to continuous improvement in small increments. Many people who have studied Japanese manufacturing methods say much of their success is rooted in their patience in staying with a process and gaining a profound knowledge of it while making a thousand small improvements. The disposition of westerners is to go for the big gain, the breakthrough in improving the system, and then let it run as is for a long time. Westerners seem naturally to be a little less effective as monitors, perhaps preferring the innovator and broker roles. Companies now realize that they are engaged in an endless battle to reduce variation thereby improving quality and reducing costs (Neave, 1990).

ANALYSIS   Can This Process Be Improved?

State Automobile License Renewals

Henry Coupe, the manager of a metropolitan branch office of his state's Department of Motor Vehicles, attempted to perform an analysis of the driver's license renewal operations. Several steps are performed in the process. After examining the license renewal process, he identified the steps and associated times required to perform each step, as shown in the following table:

State Automobile License Renewals Process Times

Step	Average Time to Perform (seconds)
1. Review renewal application for correctness	15
2. Process and record payment	30
3. Check file for violations and restrictions	60
4. Conduct eye test	40
5. Photograph applicant	20
6. Issue temporary license	30

Coupe found that each step was assigned to a different person. Each application was a separate process in the sequence shown above. Coupe determined that his office should be prepared to accommodate the maximum demand of processing 120 renewal applicants per hour.

He observed that the work was unevenly divided among the clerks, and the clerk who was responsible for checking violations tended to shortcut her task to keep up with the other clerks. Long lines built up during the maximum demand periods.

Coupe also found that jobs 1, 2, 3, and 4 were handled by general clerks who were each paid $6.00 per hour. Job 5 was performed by a photographer paid $8 per hour. Job 6, the issuing of a temporary license, was required by state policy to be handled by a uniformed motor vehicle officer. Officers were paid $9.00 per hour, but they could be assigned to any job except photography.

A review of the jobs indicated that job 1, reviewing the application for correctness, had to be performed before any other step could be taken. Similarly, job 6, issuing the temporary license, could not be performed until all the other steps were completed. The branch offices were charged $5 per hour for each camera to perform photography.

Henry Coupe was under severe pressure to increase productivity and reduce costs, but he was also told by the regional director of the Department of Motor Vehicles that he had better accommodate the demand for renewals; otherwise, "heads would roll."

Discussion Questions

1. What is the maximum number of applications per hour that can be handled by the present configuration of the process?

2. How many applications can be processed per hour if a second clerk is added to check for violations?

3. How would you suggest modifying the process in order to accommodate 120 applications per hour?

Source: Sasser, W. Earl, Paul R. Olson, and D. Daryl Wyckoff, *Management of Services Operations: Text, Cases, and Readings,* Boston: Allyn & Bacon, 1978.

PRACTICE   A Better Way to Handle Loan Applications

1. A Customer Service Team (in this case, the top management of a bank) looked at its core processes. They identified many processes and then selected the one that was most doable, the one they had control over and that benefited their customer. To do this they asked, "What's going well and what could be improved?" They asked their customers. They asked themselves. They asked management.

   They did a Things Gone Right/Things Gone Wrong chart. They listed their processes. . . what they did a lot of, they needed to do well.

Source: This exercise is taken from "Quickstart: Foundations of Team Development," pp.6–11 to 6–15, developed by the Praxis Group, Provo, Utah. Used by permission.

PROCESSES
- Approve budgets
- Review performance reports
- Meet with staff
- Make presentations at conferences
- Approve loans
- Etc.

SELECTED PROCESSES
- Loan Approval

2. They then worked to flowchart the process. This made the steps and tasks visible. In flowcharting, they asked:
   - What is the product or service?
   - What are the standards the customer wants?

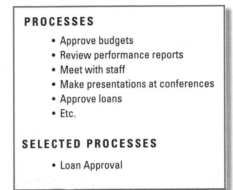

	DOCUMENT REVIEW	VALIDATION	SUBMIT TO LOAN COMMITTEE	LOAN DECISION	LOAN PROCESSING	
INPUT (Trigger) →	1. Check to see if complete	1. Credit check	1. Loan packets to secretary	1. Loan committee approves	1. Process review	**OUTPUT FOR CUSTOMER** →
	2. Request for additional information	2. Income verification		2. Loan committee requests more information	2. Check request/audit approval	
Loan forms submitted	3. Verify complete package	3. Reference check		3. Loan committee reports	3. information management	*Money to Customer*
	4. Verify standard format					

- What is the trigger for this process?
- What are the major steps?
- What are the tasks for each of these steps?

3. Next they used basic quality tools to see where they could improve. Essentially, they asked:

- How are we doing?
- How do we know how we are doing?
- What could we do better, faster, cheaper?
- Do we have this process in control?

To answer these questions, they asked:

- Where are the value-added parts and non-value-added parts?
- Where are the bottlenecks, delays, barriers, or errors?
- Where do we hear complaints?
- When is the process out of control?

They added their analysis to the flowchart to make value-added issues visible.

	DOCUMENT REVIEW	VALIDATION	SUBMIT TO LOAN COMMITTEE	LOAN DECISION	LOAN PROCESSING	
INPUT (Trigger) →	1. Check to see if complete	1. Credit check	1. Loan packets to secretary	1. Loan committee approves	1. Process review	OUTPUT FOR CUSTOMER →
	2. Request for additional information	2. Income verification		2. Loan committee requests more information	2. Check request/audit approval	
Loan forms submitted	3. Verify complete package	3. Reference check		3. Loan committee reports	3. information management	Money to Customer
Total time	½ day	½ day	0	8 days	2 days	11 days
Value-added time	20 minutes	30 minutes	5 minutes	$\frac{12 \text{ minutes}}{120 \text{ minutes}}$	60 minutes	3 hours 55 min.
Cost	4.25	7.00	1.68	80.00	28.00	121.93

4. To help them identify and work on significant causes instead of minor causes or symptoms, they used the fishbone diagram.

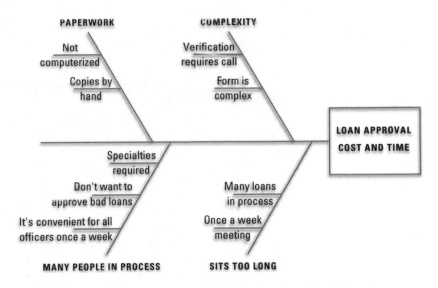

They also used the Praxis Empowerment Model to do a 6-cell analysis of causes.

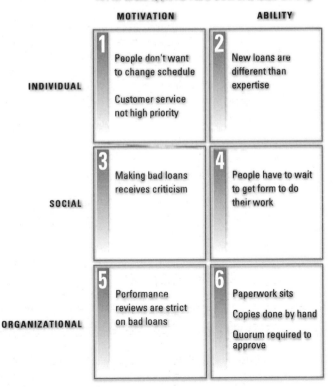

5. Once they had a clear picture of the process and the opportunities for improvement, they brainstormed solutions and studied solutions used by other banks.

This is now your task: make any recommendations you believe would improve the loan approval process and meet customer needs for speed, convenience and accuracy. Although you do not have "profound knowledge" of this process, not having worked with it, you will probably have some insights into how it can be improved.

Work in teams of three people. Try to get "out of the box" and think creatively about some approaches that would save time, avoid bottlenecks, and reduce the handling of paper as well as the decision time necessary for approval. Please write your recommendations in a simple memo to the Board of Trustees of Civic Trust Savings and Loan. You are members of the Customer Service Team. Try to make your message as visually accessible as possible by using diagrams or visuals and a simple narrative. Try to help your readers see the process and what steps have been eliminated or combined.

APPLICATION   Mapping and Improving a Process Yourself

Directions   In learning teams of four to five people, select an organization that conducts a process you can map. The organization need not be a formal one. The easiest processes to map are those that recur. Try to observe the process and not just hear about it. Don't be intimidated by the fact that you are not an expert on the process. Your ignorance will be a major resource because it allows you to look at the process with a fresh perspective. Draw a map of the process and discuss how it could be improved. Consider the following suggestions.

- Think about steps that can be collapsed or simply eliminated.

- Look for places in which a product or service sits idle in the "value chain" with no value being added.

- Look for those expensive and time-consuming "hand-offs" and consider ways of eliminating them.

Competency 3   Managing Organizational Performance

ASSESSMENT   Take the Role of the Customer

Directions   Your instructor will create groups of six people each. This group will be a "focus group" of buyers who make purchases in a certain market niche. You as a group will choose the niche. You can select consumer electronics (portable disk players or tape players), computers, cars, clothes, athletic shoes, and so on. Choose one product you want to focus on.

Now appoint a person to act as a facilitator. With the facilitator's help, begin listing the four or five factors (there can be more or less) you take into account in deciding to buy one brand or model over another. Now, assign a specific weight to each factor you choose, and make sure that the sum of all factor weights equals 100.

For example: Your focus group might choose athletic shoes as its product, and might come up with four factors:

appearance	30
functional performance (foot support, maneuverability)	20
cost	30
durability	20

Finally, pick three major brands of the product you have chosen, and rate each brand on each of the four or five factors you have chosen on a scale of one to ten, with 1 being very poor and 10 being superior. Multiply each brand's score on each factor by the weight of that factor, and add the results to get an overall customer satisfaction score.

You may prefer to use a service instead of a manufactured product example. Fast food restaurants or banking services might be a good choice. Think about factors such as cost, speed, courtesy of personnel, variety of services (breadth of menu) offered. How would you rate these respective dimensions of quality? How do several restaurants or banks compare to one another?

When you report to the class as a whole in a five-minute presentation, consider some of these questions:

- How much agreement was there among group members in choosing the factors for making purchase decisions? Did the group have trouble coming up with terms or phrases for the factors they wanted to list?

- Were you surprised by any of the factors? Did you learn anything about the product you were discussing? (You might have discovered that some of you were very cost driven while others were feature or quality driven.)

- If you went to work tomorrow in a retail store selling this product, would you be better prepared to discuss its features and benefits to a potential customer? Do you have any suggestions to offer the manufacturer of this product or provider of this service?

LEARNING   Managing Organizational Performance

If you are in your early twenties or older, you have witnessed first hand some of the benefits of the quality revolution in both goods and services we have witnessed in the past decade. Auto manufacturers are now unveiling engines that need to be tuned up about every 100,000 miles instead of every 30,000. We now expect to get 200,000 miles or more out of the new cars we buy, whereas ten years ago, most American cars made it only half that far. Ten years ago it took anywhere from one to three months to have a mortgage approved in the United States or Canada—if you had excellent credit. Today, some banks, such as

Citicorp, can approve a mortgage application in half an hour and process the application in less than 15 days. We have all benefited from the quality revolution.

QUALITY: BEYOND CONFORMANCE TO INTERNAL STANDARDS

But the companies that are ahead in this race with no finish line are the ones that not only do great work inside their walls, but have a profound knowledge of what their customers need and want. We have learned during the quality revolution that it is possible to have a "zero defect" product, and still lose out to competitors who understand customers better than we do. Great quality in our products and services gets us into the game, but profound knowledge of customers and the ability to respond to their needs are required to win the game. Products free of defects will not necessarily please customers. A company may be designing the wrong features into their product, or ignoring certain support services that go with it. The first stage of quality requires a company to monitor the degree of variation it has from established standards. In the first stage, if your products comply with standards you have set internally, you are a quality company. Until you have your processes sufficiently under control to enable you to produce a good product, on time, for a price people are willing to pay, there is no point in gaining profound knowledge of what customers want, or how your product compares with the best competition. Internal quality, defined by tight conformance to internal standards, is a good beginning, but only the beginning. The next step is to focus outside on the customers you are serving. What do they tell you about how you're doing?

In this brief section, we will present some core principles for monitoring the needs of customers. Some of the most important monitoring you will do in your career will be focused on the people who use what your organization has to offer. A lot of mistakes have been made in this role. We'll try to help you avoid the big ones.

Traditionally, companies have set up customer satisfaction programs that ask questions such as:

- What are the things you consider most important in making a decision to buy a _____ (product type)?

- What relative importance would you attach to each one of these factors?

- How would you rank the performance of our product on each of these factors—poor, fair, good, or excellent?

But as Bradley Gale, an international authority on managing customer value, points out:

Two key issues are missing from these surveys. First, they fail to obtain data from noncustomers who are buying the competition's product. Thus they don't track the opinion of the market as a whole. Second, customer satisfaction surveys usually do not measure the product's performance relative to competitors' products. If your performance is improving, your customers will probably say they are satisfied. But if your competitors are improving faster, customers will soon realize they could be even more satisfied if they bought from your rival (Gale, p. 13).

When we see a company losing ground to competition, or a public agency facing increased criticism from its clients, we sometimes assume they are not paying attention to their customers and clients. But on closer examination, we often find that these companies are running intense customer satisfaction programs. The problem is that they are doing a good job of asking the wrong questions. Companies must monitor an entire market segment, not just the people who have bought their products. If you sell consumer electronics, you ask a broad spectrum of people who tend to buy those products what they are looking for and what makes them choose one brand or model over another. You don't limit yourself to your own customers. Second, companies must ask people how their products compare with the competition in the attributes that are most important, such as cost, durability, user friendliness, attractiveness of design, and so forth. So, what do we want to monitor? We don't want to monitor how satisfied our current customers are. We want to monitor what our current customer value is as compared to all major competitors, and *become the preeminent provider of customer value in our market.*

What we are really monitoring is value. Quality, as defined by conformance to certain standards, is a good place to start, but in the final analysis the customer decides what quality is. Customers buy when they find the value they want. Value is determined by how the customer balances perceptions of quality with perceptions of cost. Value is "quality however the customer defines it, offered at the right price" (Gale, p. 26). Even "price" is sometimes more complex than we realize. For example, in the luxury car market, the selling price of an automobile is only part of the cost. Customers often take into account such factors as resale value, trade-in value, and cost of financing. Of course, companies don't know these things unless they ask.

In the mid-1980s, American Telephone and Telegraph Co. (AT&T) prided itself on its commitment to monitoring customer satisfaction.[3] The General Business Systems (GBS) unit of the company made and installed small business telephone switching systems. GBS spent a lot of energy and money asking customers to rate their performance as either excellent, good, fair or poor on the following quality attributes:

Equipment	Repair
Marketing and Sales	Training
Installation	Billing

The results were always satisfying to management. The entire company defined "customer satisfaction" as the percentage of "good" and "excellent" responses earned on these surveys. The two categories were combined into one. Unit managers usually came close to 90% and sometimes exceeded it. The company used

[3]This account of AT&T's work in customer value management is adapted from Bradley Gale's *Managing Customer Value*, New York: Free Press, 1994, pp. 73–94

this data to help them make decisions on recognition programs, promotions, and performance assessments for managers in general. Often, the focus of each manager was to beat another manager in another region of the company rather than to beat a competitor in the same market niche.

In 1987, a special team of managers and market researchers within the company were brought together to solve a puzzle for the company. Despite continued high scores on customer satisfaction, the company was losing market share to competitors in several areas such as customer equipment business and even long distance service. Two team members, Ray Kordupleski and West Vogel, started digging into the huge AT&T database on customer satisfaction. There was a lot of data, but not enough information. They developed a few additional questions and pulled together groups of customers who were willing to talk about AT&T products and services and complete a brief questionnaire. One new question they asked was, "How willing would you be to *repurchase* from AT&T?" The managers found that among those who rated AT&T's products and services as "good," 40% indicated they would like to "shop around" before making another purchase decision. But only 10% of those who gave an "excellent" rating said they would shop around before buying again.

This simple but powerful finding let executives at AT&T know that the "good was the enemy of the best." A more careful analysis showed that customers who gave a "good" rating were, indeed, likely to abandon AT&T at the next point of purchase. A "good" rating was actually bad news! The challenge was thus to turn customers who rated the company as "good" into customers who would rate it as "excellent." This change needed to happen in a matter of months, or customers would probably vote with their feet.

But the insights on how to monitor customer satisfaction were just beginning. By working with "customer value" experts such as Bradley Gale, AT&T executives learned that they needed to compare how their customers rated AT&T *relative to how they rated AT&T's competitors*. The company had learned that it was of little value to ask customers to rate them alone. They needed to know the relative values customers attached to their goods and services. Quality is a relative thing. "What ultimately matters is not the percentage of customers *satisfied* but the extent to which customers are *more satisfied by your product than by the competition's product*" (Gale, p. 80). They also learned that they had to survey the customers of competitors to see if those customers were looking for the same kinds of values. For example, AT&T learned that their own customers placed more weight on equipment quality and billing services, but competitors' customers placed more weight on maintenance and repair and marketing and sales. This data indicated that AT&T customers were attracted to what they perceived to be better-quality equipment and efficient billing. Perhaps this was because competitors had won over people who wanted to pay less for equipment and were probably then having more contact with their vendors on service and repair issues. It was unclear why the competition's customers placed more weight on marketing and sales. Perhaps people who had chosen another company had done more shopping around first and had stronger opinions about how effectively the sales processes functioned. We include these points because even good customer value methods do not provide data whose meaning is intuitively obvious. This kind of monitoring requires digging and rethinking.

In the midst of all this work, AT&T also discovered a powerful question to ask all their customers: *Considering the products and services that your vendor offers, are they worth what you paid for them?*

They then began comparing this "worth what they paid" data with the same data from competitors' customers. With all this relative data available, Kordupleski and West began using these better measures of customer satisfaction to predict market share in the short run—often three months. For example, in 1987 their customer value data showed the Long Distance Service Division was headed for trouble, and for two reasons. First, customers across the long distance market were indicating that they saw little difference in quality across MCI, Sprint, and AT&T. Because AT&T had always pushed for a slight price advantage because they had a reputation for having the edge in quality, this was frightening news. Second, customers perceived the cost differences between AT&T and its competitors as greater than it actually was—15% as opposed to 5%. AT&T responded in two ways. They poured immense capital into expanding their fiber optic network. (Sprint and MCI had actually outpaced them in fiber optics and had clearer voice transmission than AT&T.) This step required writing off $6 billion in obsolete plant and equipment years ahead of schedule, and increasing the budget for capital improvements by an additional $2 billion per year for several years. Second, AT&T launched a very successful "I came back" ad campaign in which customers explained that the savings they had anticipated in switching from AT&T to Sprint or MCI were not realized. Further research showed that long distance callers began to see a narrowing difference in cost between AT&T and its competition. Further work enabled the company to establish with great precision the quality attributes their customers were most interested in. The breakdown for these quality attributes, in descending order of importance, looked like this:

Equipment Quality	30%
Marketing and Sales	30%
Bills and Billing	15%
Repair	15%
Installation	10%

What remained to be done was to identify the exact processes within their business that drove relative performance on each of these attributes. For example, what exactly does "equipment quality" mean? Interviews with customers, and some translation help from technical specialists in the company, showed that equipment quality really meant three things: reliability, ease of use, and the cluster of features and functions provided. How does the company monitor its performance on reliability of equipment? It tracks the percentage of all installed pieces that have repair calls made on them. You can see that discovering what customers find important is only the first step. A company then has to translate that information into a map of which processes are responsible for delivering that value to customers. It must then monitor those core processes and continuously improve them. The table on page 160 summarizes this data.

Performance Monitoring Matrix

Source: Raymond E. Kordupleski, Roland T. Rust, and Anthony J. Zahorik, "Marketing: The Missing Dimension in Quality Measurement," *California Management Review,* Spring 1993.

Main Attributes and Weight		Key Subattributes and Weight		Internal Metrics
Equipment	30	Reliability Ease of Use Features-Functions	40 20 40	% Repair Call % of Help Calls Function Performance Test
Sales	30	Knowledge Response Follow-up	30 25 10	Supervisor Observations % Proposals Made on Time Installed on Due Date
Installation	10	Delivery Interval Does Not Break Installed When Promised	30 25 10	Average Order Interval % Repair Reports % Installed on Due Date
Repair	15	No Repeat Trouble Fixed Fast Kept Informed	20 35 10	% Repeat Reports Average Speed of Repair % Customers Informed
Billing	15	Accuracy, No Surprises Resolved on First Call Easy to Understand	45 35 10	% Billing Inquiries % Resolved on First Call % Billing Inquiries

*The numbers assigned to the subattributes are at first confusing. They are not percentages or parts of some base such as 100, so they do not add to 100. They were apparently generated by team members who were asked to assign a relative value to each subattribute. So, in the first category, "Equipment," the factor of "reliability" is twice as important as "easy to use."

When companies begin to engage in this kind of organizational learning, they often discover that they can't improve their processes without tearing down the walls and "silos" that separate their functions—manufacturing, marketing, sales, installation—and they begin using cross-functional teams. These teams bring people from across functions to focus on everything the customer needs from a specific service or product. The point we are making here is that good monitoring influences and guides everything a company does. Good monitoring is really strategic navigation, not just checking on little details. When a few leaders at AT&T began looking carefully at what customers really wanted from their company, they realized they had been asking the wrong questions and monitoring the wrong activities.

CUSTOMER MANAGEMENT DATA IS A MORE POWERFUL PREDICTOR THAN FINANCIAL DATA

The kind of data we have been describing is really more fundamental, and has more predictive power, than the traditional financial data like that found in profit and loss statements. Before changes occur in a company's profitability, there are usually signals from customers that all is not well, that something is happening in the marketplace that will affect market share, costs, and eventually profitability. Most financial data gives us a look in the rear-view mirror. Good customer management data let us look into the present and even the future. Master managers are beginning to push for perceived quality profiles for all their products, and a more systematic way to track how their companies win and lose specific customers and accounts. This is the kind of information that tells a company where it's headed, long before the profit-and-loss statement says "We must have made a wrong turn somewhere; look at all the money we've lost."

But most companies still do not have the kind of monitoring discipline that enables them to read these signals. As a current or future member of an organization, you can make a great contribution by helping your colleagues discover what the customers or clients of your organization really need and want, and then developing some simple metrics for tracking performance on meeting those needs. Gaining a profound knowledge of customers not only requires some analytical skills, it requires a dogged determination and consistency. It also requires relationships of trust and mutual respect with customers and clients. Good monitoring requires good mentoring, facilitating, and brokering. As we have often said in this book, the competencies of the master manager cannot be isolated. They function in concert.

SEEING THE FUTURE FIRST: ANTICIPATING WHAT CUSTOMERS WANT BEFORE THEY ASK FOR IT

A final point we make in discussing this third competency, Monitoring the Needs of Customers and Stakeholders, is that customers cannot always tell us what they want, because what they want may not yet exist. Customers, like all of us, are good at making comparisons among existing choices, but they have a much harder time articulating a need that no existing product yet fills. There is a difference between studying how customers feel about what is currently on the market, and studying what the market needs but does not yet have. Gary Hamel and C.K. Prahalad, who consult with global companies on emerging trends, put it this way:

> *Customers are notoriously lacking in foresight. Ten or 15 years ago, how many of us were asking for cellular telephones, fax machines, and copiers at home, 24-hour discount brokerage accounts, multivalve automobile engines, compact disk players, cars with onboard navigation systems, hand-held global satellite position receivers, automated teller machines, MTV, or the Home Shopping Network? As Akio Morita, Sony's visionary leader puts it: Our plan is to lead the public with new products rather than ask them what kind of products they want. The public does not know what is possible, but we do. So instead of doing a lot of market research, we refine our thinking on a product and its use and try to create a market for it by educating and communicating with the public (Hamel and Prahalad, 1994, p. 67).*

Hamel and Prahalad like to ask the leaders they consult with to identify what they believe are the major forces at work in their industry that have the potential to "profoundly transform industry structure." One such macrotrend that is frequently mentioned is virtual reality. Others include the increase in the number of people working out of their homes, the dramatic increase in the number of Americans and Western Europeans over the age of 75, and the aroused concern of young adults and adolescents for environmental issues. Some trends are more specific to a particular industry. Once they have a list in front of them, they then ask the group if they could sustain a day-long debate about the implications of this trend to the company. They ask specific questions such as the following:

- Do you understand how fast this trend is emerging in different markets around the world, the technologies that are propelling it, and the technological choices your competitors are making in response to the trend?

- Do you know which companies in your industry have the most to gain or lose by this trend, and who is now riding the edge of it?

- Do you know what would be required for your company to respond to this trend in order to benefit from it or even lead it?

Often, executives respond by saying that these questions are simply unfair, that no one in the industry knows enough to debate these issues for eight hours. Then, Hamel and Prahalad ask the group if they could talk all day about how the company manages its overhead, sets prices, or tracks its sales. "Now this," they say, "is something we can talk about for days" (Hamel and Prahalad, 1994, p. 67). The point is that a company is not in control of its destiny unless and until its leaders are willing to study the future with the same kind of intensity and care with which they study its present. Another implication of Prahalad and Hamel's advice is that monitoring an organization's market and environment requires the skills of the innovator and broker. Monitoring of this kind, which attempts to anticipate change before it occurs, is a very creative and free-form kind of activity. Thus, we reinforce a point we have been making throughout this book: All the roles in the Competing Values Framework are vital to an organization's success.

Capturing leadership in creating the future requires more than careful and intelligent monitoring; however, monitoring customer reactions and monitoring in a general way the trends, themes, and developments that are emerging around us is a good foundation on which to build. This means reading good periodicals, talking to informed people, and keeping the antennae up.

ANALYSIS   Constructing a Real Customer Value Profile

Directions   The next task is to build a customer value profile with people in a real organization. We recommend that you perform this task in pairs or threes. Find a company that manufactures a product, or a service company that offers a specific service or line of services. The type of company is not important. It does not have to be a large firm. In fact, there are advantages to working with a small company because they lack the staff to conduct this kind of analysis.

Ask permission to meet with three or more people in the company, preferably people in different jobs and at different levels in the company. Explain that you are doing a project on how people make sense of how their customers decide about buying their products or services. This process takes about half an hour, and could be very beneficial to the firm.

With the group in place, ask them to choose one of the products or services their company offers as the focus of this analysis. Next, ask them to list two or three of the major competitors who offer similar products or services. Then ask them to indicate what they believe are the three or four major factors customers use in buying that product or service. Remember, the focus is not only on the company's product, but on comparable products offered by their major competitors.

Your goal is to come out of the discussion with the form completed. It won't be perfect and people would make lots of changes in it if they had the time, but you should give them only half an hour to complete the task.

Try to force the group to limit their factors to no more than four. In the assessment exercise we listed these factors as an example:

- Appearance
- Functional performance
- Cost
- Durability

But we suggest that you not list these unless the group fails to come up with their own criteria. *You next need to have the group assign weights to each factor, with the sum of the weights adding to 100.* If the group tries to list four factors and then simply divide by four to create the weights, challenge their logic. The factors are probably not weighted equally in the minds of customers.

Finally, ask the group to rate their product or service against the product or service of two major competitors. Each member of the group may assign a raw score of 1 to 10, with 1 being terrible and 10 being best in market. But remember each raw score is then multiplied by the weight number. If the group assigns a weight of 40 (out of 100 possible) to cost, and one individual rates her company's product at 7 points for its cost attractiveness, then that score ends up being 280.

Each person can then add his or her scores to get an overall customer satisfaction score for the group's product and the products of the competitors. You can also average the scores of the group, but the differences are probably more significant than the average scores.

How does the group's product rate (using the same factors) in comparison to the competition? How does the group account for differences in scores?

You want to come out of this session with the following things:

- A list of factors.
- Weights assigned to them.
- Strong agreement by the group that the factors are the right ones and the weights are appropriate for each factor.
- An average score of the performance of the group's product, by factor, compared to the competition.

It might help to use a table that looks like this for presenting the individual results and the average scores assigned by the group.

Here are a few things to look for and to look out for in conducting this analysis. Don't be embarrassed or apologetic if, at first, the group thinks you're doing a cute little "real-world" exercise for one of your management classes. Most managers in most companies are surprised

Factors	Weights per Factor	Our Product's Score (multiplied by weight)	Competitor One's Score (multiplied by weight)	Competitor Two's Score (multiplied by weight)
Factor 1				
Factor 2				
Factor 3				
Factor 4				
Total				

to discover that they do not agree among themselves what factors customers use to make purchase decisions—and these people serve the same kinds of customers every day! This question, "How do our customers choose between us and our competitors?" is a vital one.

Another point: The process is a kind of solution. This little exercise, if you do it effectively, will stimulate the thinking of the people you talk to. Ideally, the next step would be for them to ask you or have someone in the company begin to survey customers on these very questions. Ideally, these questions are asked of potential customers, but beginning with members of the company itself is a good way to start. Lots of consultants and business analysts take executives through a very similar exercise. Just bringing people together to struggle with the question of how customers make decisions will strengthen the focus on customer service.

PRACTICE   A Role Play for Challenging Customer Service Situations

Directions   In groups of three people each, choose an example of a very challenging customer service situation. This may be taken from your own experience. It might be a case where a customer was in a very difficult situation and needed help above and beyond what is normally expected. It might be a situation you have observed or heard about in which a customer was simply more demanding and confrontational than most people are. The task is to enact the situation. One of you needs to be in the role of the customer and another in the role, or roles, of the people who provided the service.

Be prepared to lead the class in a discussion of the situation. Why was it so challenging? Did the person providing the service react appropriately? Are these situations unusual? What can we learn from them about improving service in organizations?

APPLICATION A   Creating Customer Value Profile with Real Customers

Now it's time to do what many companies all over the world are now doing: creating a customer value analysis. The task is to conduct a customer value analysis with real customers. This is essentially the same task you performed in the Analysis exercise on pages 162-164, and we strongly recommend that you choose the same product or service offered by the company you worked with in doing that exercise. The benefit to using the same product you studied with a focus group inside the company is that you can then compare the kinds of ratings employees of the company give to those given by external customers. Sometimes, the gaps are dramatic.

The process is virtually the same you used inside the company. But with external customers, be sure to ask one or two open-ended questions, such as:

> What recommendations would you make on how the company can improve its services or products?

> If you were to choose not to do business with this company again, what would be the reason for leaving?

> How can this company win your loyalty?

If you choose a service organization, such as a hospital or a government entity, you may not be able to gather comparative data (the state Department of Motor Vehicles does not have a competitor), but customers can still rate the service of the organization on the factors they think are most important.

You will need to decide the best way of surveying these customers. You may choose to go on-site and interview some people on the premises of the company or organization. This would be an effective method to use if you are studying a public institution such as a hospital or a government agency. If you choose a company whose products are bought by a large segment of the population you could probably gather a group of people on the campus and conduct the session anywhere that is convenient. Don't worry too much about sample size, but try to gather data from at least twice as many external customers as you did internal employees when you did the Analysis exercise. If you had four employees in your focus group, try to gather data from ten external customers for this Application exercise.

When you have your data, the best possible use for it would be to share it with the company that provides the product or service. This could be done in a short written report, but the most effective way would be to give the company a brief presentation. Consider some of these questions:

- What are the major gaps between what employees think customers value about the product, and what customers say they value?

- Assuming there are some factors that were identified by both employees and customers, what are the biggest gaps between the ratings employees gave on those factors and the ratings customers gave?

Again, you will need to do this task in teams of two to four people. If you have the opportunity of presenting the data to the company, be sure to prepare some simple but cogent graphics on your data.

APPLICATION B   Analyzing Customer Service

It's time to observe some companies at work. This week, your task will be to watch three customer service transactions. You can be the customer yourself, or you can choose to observe how other people are handled as customers. Try to observe a "significant" transaction—something more complex than ordering a quick meal or buying a retail item in the store. Ideally, this is a transaction which requires a thorough and satisfying response because the customer has a complaint, has returned a product, or is asking for a little extra attention from the company. Notice at least the following things:

- Was the customer treated with courtesy and professionalism? Was the company's representative empathetic and patient? How could you tell?

- Did the customer have a long wait, or was the response quick?

- Did the representative have the authority to solve the problem, or was it necessary to go up the line to a manager or supervisor?

- How would the customer feel about doing repeat business with this company? If not, why not? Do you feel the company representative knew how the customer felt about the transaction? How?

REFERENCES

Argyris, Chris. "Good Communication That Blocks Learning," *Harvard Business Review,* (July–August 1994), 77–85.

Ashford, Susan J., and Ann S. Tsui. "Self-regulation for Managerial Effectiveness: The Role of Active Feedback Seeking," *Academy of Management Journal,* 34, no. 2 (1991).

Alesandrini, Kathryn. *Survive Information Overload: 7 Best Ways to Manage Your Workload By Seeing the Big Picture.* Homewood, Ill. Business One Irwin, 1992.

Band, William A. *Creating Value for Customers: Designing and Implementing a Total Corporate Strategy.* New York: John Wiley & Sons, 1991.

Bernstein, Aaron. "How to Motivate Workers: Don't Watch' Em," *Business Week* (April 29, 1991) 52.

Byrne, John A. "The Horizontal Corporation," *Business Week,* no. 3351 (December 20, 1993): 76–81.

Campbell, Jeremy. *Grammatical Man: Information, Entropy, Language and Life.* New York: Simon and Schuster, 1982.

Carlzon, Jan. *Moments of Truth.* New York; Perennial Library, 1989.

Champy, James. *Reengineering Management: The Mandate For New Leadership.* New York: Harper Business, 1995.

Cox, Allan. *Straight Talk for a Monday Morning: Creating Values, Vision and Vitality at Work.* New York: John Wiley & Sons, 1990.

Dumaine, Brian. What's So Hot About Outsiders? *Fortune,* November 29, 1993, (vol. 138 no. 14) pp. 63–67.

Drucker, Peter 4. The New Productivity Challenge. *Harvard Business Review,* November/December 1991 pp. 69–79.

Gale, Bradley T. *Managing Customer Value: Creating Quality and Service that Customers Can See.* New York: Free Press, 1994.

Gabor, Andrea. *Deming: The Man Who Discovered Quality: How W. Edwards Deming Brought the Quality Revolution to America.* New York: Random House, 1990.

Gomery, Douglas. "In Search of the Cybermarket," *Wilson Quarterly,* 18, 3 (Summer 1994): 9-17.

Grove, Andrew S. *High Output Management.* New York: Vintage Books, 1985.

Halbertasm, David. *The Reckoning.* New York: Avon, 1987.

Hamel, Gary, and C.K. Prahalad. "Seeing the Future First," *Fortune,* (September 5, 1994): 64–70.

Hammer, Michael, and James Champy. *Reengineering the Corporation: A Manifesto for Business Revolution.* New York: Harper/Collins 1993.

Kanter, Rosabeth M., Barry Stein, and Todd D. Jick. *The Challenge of Organizational Change: How Companies Experience It and Leaders Guide It.* New York: Free Press, 1992.

Kotler, Philip, and Gary Armstrong. *Principles of Marketing* (6th ed.). Englewood Cliffs, N.J.: Prentice Hall.

Kordupleski, Raymond E., Roland T. Rust, and Anthony J. Zahorik. "Marketing: The Missing Dimension in Quality Measurement," *California Management Review* (Spring 1993).

McKinnon, Sharon M., and William J. Bruns. *The Information Mosaic.* Boston: Harvard Business School, 1992.

Neave, Henry R. *The Deming Dimension.* Knoxville, Tenn.: SPC Press, 1990.

Ohmae, Kennichi. *The Borderless World: Power and Strategy in the Interlinked Economy.* Harper Business, 1990.

Perry, Lee and Eric Denna. *Retrofitting Process Reengineering.* (Unpublished manuscript, Brigham Young University, November 1993).

Peters, T.J., and R.H. Waterman, Jr. *In Search of Excellence.* New York: Harper and Row, 1982.

Rice, Faye. "The New Rules of Superlative Service," *Fortune,* Special Issue (Autumn/Winter 1993): 50–53.

Rosenbluth, Hal F., and Diane McFerrin Peters. *The Customer Comes Second: And Other Secrets of Exceptional Service.* New York: William Morrow and Company, 1992.

Sasser, W. Earl, Paul R. Olson, and D. Daryl Wyckoff. *Management of Services Operations: Text, Cases, and Readings.* Boston: Allyn & Bacon, 1978.

Sayles, Leonard R. *The Complete Book of Practical Productivity.* New York: Boardroom Books, 1983.

Sayles, Leonard R. *Leadership: Managing in Real Organizations.* New York: McGraw-Hill, 1989.

Sayles, Leonard R. *The Working Leader: The Triumph of High Performance Over Conventional Management Principles.* New York: The Free Press, 1993.

Senge, Peter. *The Fifth Discipline: The Art and Practice of the Learning Organization.* New York: Doubleday, 1990.

Senge, Peter, Richard Ross, Bryan Smith, Charlotte Robers, and Art Keller. *The Fifth Discipline Fieldbook: Strategies and Tools for Building a Learning Organization.* New York: Doubleday, 1994.

Shapiro, Eileen C. *How Corporate Truths Become Competitive Traps.* New York: John Wiley & Sons, 1991.

Stewart, Thomas A. "Managing in a Wired Company," *Fortune* (July 11, 1994): 44–56.

Tetzeli, Rick. "Surviving Information Overload," *Fortune* (July 11, 1994): 60–64.

This account of AT&T's work in customer value management is adapted from Bradley Gale's *Managing Customer Value,* New York: Free Press, 1994, pp. 73–94.

Winston, Stephanie. *The Organized Executive: New Ways to Manage Time, Paper, and People.* New York: W.W. Norton, 1983.

Wurman, Richard S. *Information Anxiety.* New York: Doubleday, 1989.

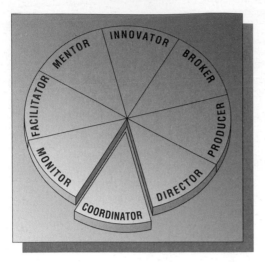

THE COORDINATOR ROLE

5

■ COMPETENCIES

Managing Projects

Designing Work

Managing Across Functions

In Chapter 1 we discussed the emergence of the Internal Process model of organizational effectiveness during the first quarter of the twentieth century and indicated that the primary focus of this model is the efficient flow of work and information (with the coordinator primarily responsible for the flow of work and the monitor primarily responsible for the flow of information). When the model first emerged, Henri Fayol's work on the general principles of management articulated a way of organizing work that was believed to result in continuity and stability in the workflow. The scientific management approach, developed by Frederick W. Taylor (1911), argued that work could be accomplished more efficiently if workers performed a minimal number of tasks and managers identified the one best way to perform these tasks. At the time, the internal process model clearly called for routinization of work.

Today, although the Internal Process Model still focuses on the efficient flow of work and information, and on stability and continuity in the organization, the underlying principles have changed dramatically. Computing technology and the globalization of the economy, as well as other economic forces, have changed the nature of work and hence our very understanding of the concept of "efficient flow of work." In 1994, *Fortune* ran a story entitled "The End of the Job." In that article, William Bridges asserted that "The job is an idea that emerged early in the 19th century to package work that needed doing in the growing factories and bureaucracies of the industrializing nations. Before people

168

had jobs, they worked just as hard but on shifting clusters of tasks, in a variety of locations, on a schedule set by the sun and the weather and the needs of the day . . . Now the world of work is changing again: The conditions that created jobs 200 years ago—mass production and the large organization—are disappearing. . . . With the disappearance of the conditions that created jobs, we are losing the need to package work in that way" (1994, p. 64). As this world of work changes, we must look at the role of the coordinator in a new way.

The role of the coordinator involves coordinating the work of two or more employees, work groups, or work units that act interdependently. In the coordinator role, the manager's task is to make sure that work flows smoothly and that activities are carried out according to their relative importance with a minimum amount of friction among individuals, work groups, or work units. But this no longer means that work must be routinized. Nor does it mean that the manager, in the coordinator role, makes all the decisions regarding work design and workflow. Instead, it means that it is the responsibility of the coordinator to see to it that the right people are at the right place at the right time to perform the right task, potentially involving employees in any or all aspects of this task as appropriate. Managers performing in this role must be concerned with the resources needed to do the work, including the necessary tools of the job and the physical space where the work is to be done; but they may also give the individual or work team responsibility and authority for carrying out this task. Finally, when several people or groups are working together, the coordinator is responsible for making sure that the output of one work group is available as input for the second work group when that group is ready. Again, in today's world of work, the coordinator is likely to involve the two work groups in planning how this is to be accomplished.

In this chapter we focus on three interrelated competencies that are key to this new role of the coordinator:

Competency 1 Managing Projects
Competency 2 Designing Work
Competency 3 Managing Across Functions

As you will see in this chapter, these three competencies are vital to accomplishing the organization's work. They are basic to the day-to-day functioning of the organization and the maintenance of its stability and continuity. They do not, however, necessarily assume that maintaining stability and continuity need be achieved at the cost of flexibility and adaptability. Rather, in the new world of work, the competencies are concerned with maintaining smooth work processes so that the organization can respond to change in a way that is simultaneously flexible and controlled when necessary.

Competency 1 Managing Projects

ASSESSMENT Project Planning

Directions Think about a project or event you have worked on, preferably one where you had some leadership responsibility. (Note that having leadership responsibility does not mean that you were the sole project leader.) Think about the planning and coordination, and respond to the questions below.

1. To what extent were goals and objectives made explicit? What role did you play in clarifying goals and objectives?

2. To what extent was the project explicitly divided up into smaller, more manageable activities? Describe the process by which the project was divided up. What role did you play in dividing up the project into the smaller activities?

3. To what extent was there a clear understanding regarding a schedule or time line? What role did you play in devising the schedule?

4. To what extent was there a need to coordinate resources (money, equipment, supplies), as well as people? What role did you play in the coordination of resources?

5. Overall, how well was this project or event coordinated? What were the key successes? Where were some needed details overlooked?

LEARNING Managing Projects

In Chapter 3 we discussed the increasing use of teams in organizations. Project teams are one type of team that has become a necessity in organizations that need to bring specialists from several different organizational areas to work more efficiently on a single, time-limited activity. Although they were originally used primarily in the areas of research and development and construction, changes in the economy, heightened competition, increased complexity in the organizational environments, and rapid technological changes have created ideal conditions for project teams to spread to other organizational areas. Indeed, project teams are seen as an ideal approach to deal with the need to respond more quickly to changes in the environment.

In many ways, managing projects is similar to managing long-term programs, and you will find that virtually all of the competencies presented in this book are useful to the project manager. There are, however, some specific skills that are associated with the work of the project manager. Many of these specific skills focus on managing the flow of work, and so we include managing projects within the coordinator chapter. We should note that students also find these skills to be useful when coordinating complex group or team projects.

PROJECTS AND PROJECT MANAGEMENT: A DEFINITION

As noted above, there are many similarities between project management and line management. What then differentiates the two? Let us start with a definition of the terms *project* and *project management*. Harold Kerzner, considered to be one of the leading authorities on project management, defines a project as

> *"any series of activities and tasks that:*
>
> * *Have a specific objective to be completed within certain specifications*
>
> * *Have defined start and end dates*
>
> * *Have funding limits (if applicable)*
>
> * *Consume resources (i.e., money, people, equipment)"*
>
> *(Kerzner, 1989, p. 2)*

Thus projects primarily differ from ongoing programs in that they have a specific end point, in terms of both product and time. Some authors also add that a project should be a unique, nonrepetitive endeavor; that is, it should not be an activity that recurs. Kerzner goes on to define project management as:

> *"involv[ing] project planning and project monitoring and includ[ing] such items as:*
>
> * *Project planning*
>
>   * *Definition of work requirements*
>
>   * *Definition of quantity of work*
>
>   * *Definition of resources needs*
>
> * *Project monitoring*
>
>   * *Tracking progress*
>
>   * *Comparing actual to predicted*
>
>   * *Analyzing impact*
>
>   * *Making adjustments"*
>
> *(Kerzner, 1989, pp. 2-3)*

In point of fact, the various tools of project planning and project monitoring are closely tied. Planning clarifies the work to be accomplished and sets priorities for task completion. Planning involves scheduling—establishing timetables and milestones for completion—and resource allocation—developing a budget that forecasts the amount of labor and equipment that will be needed. Alternatively, monitoring tracks progress to see whether the project is proceeding as planned. Is the schedule being adhered to? Are milestones being met? How likely is the project to be completed within, or even under, the projected budget? In the next two sections we will present several key planning and monitoring tools. Again, it should be noted that the monitoring tools will be useful only if the planning has been conducted carefully, with sufficient attention to detail.

PLANNING TOOLS

"Planning is determining what needs to be done, by whom, and when" (Kerzner, 1989, p. 578). It should make clear the path the project is expected to take, as well as the destination. Consequently, the planning process should focus attention not only on the goals and objectives of the project, but also on such issues as the technical and managerial approach, resource availability, the project schedule, contingency planning and replanning assumptions, project policies and procedures, performance standards, and methods of tracking, reporting, and auditing (Badiru, 1993). It is thus evident that planning is far more complex than scheduling. Indeed, while scheduling is considered a key element of coordination, it is actually the last step of the planning process and depends on the existence of a precise statement of goals and objectives, accompanied by a detailed description of the scope of work. Below we present some of the key planning tools available to the project manager, with the order of presentation based on the order in which they are likely to be used.

STATEMENT OF WORK

The statement of work (SOW) is a written description of the scope of work required to complete the project. It should include a statement regarding the objectives of the project, brief descriptions of the services to be performed and the products and documents to be delivered, an explanation of funding constraints, specifications, and an overall schedule. Specifications should be included for all aspects of the project and are used to provide standards for determining the cost of the project. The overall schedule should be more general, including only start and end dates and key milestones.

The statement of work may also include brief descriptions of the tasks necessary for project completion, as well as a description, where appropriate, of how individual tasks will be integrated into the whole. Alternatively, this information may be included in the work breakdown structure.

WORK BREAKDOWN STRUCTURE

The work breakdown structure (WBS) shows the total project divided into components that can be measured in terms of time and cost. It may be presented in tabular or graphical form, or both (see Figure 5.1). Whether in tabular or graphical form, the WBS divides the project into a series of hierarchical levels; in graphical form it resembles an organizational chart of tasks (rather than positions). The complexity of

PROJECT: ORGANIZING THE OFFICE PICNIC		
TASK	**ESTIMATED TIME (DAYS)**	**RESPONSIBLE PERSON**
TASK 1: Do invitations and determine number of guests	5	Sam
Activity 1.1: Get material from last year's picnic		
Activity 1.2: Edit last year's invitation	.5	Sam
Activity 1.3: Set up invitation log	.5	Sam
•		
•		
•		
Activity 1.X: Do final estimate on number of guests	.5	Sam
TASK 2: Plan and purchase food		
Activity 2.1: Plan snack food	.5	Marty
Activity 2.2: Plan main meal	2	Pat
Activity 2.3: Plan beverages	.5	Chris
•		
•		
•		
Activity 2.X: Purchase beverages	.5	Chris
TASK 3: Plan picnic activities		
Activity 3.1: Do informal poll of activities enjoyed at last year's picnic	5	Linda
Activity 3.2: Find out where sports equipment is held	.5	Marty
•		
•		
•		
Activity 3.X: Buy new equipment, as necessary	1	Linda
TASK 4: Plan and purchase supplies		
Activity 4.1: Plan food supplies (plates, cups, plasticware, etc.)	.5	Marty
Activity 4.2: Plan decorations	.5	Chris
•		
•		
Activity 4.X: Pick up decorations from Picnic Store	.5	Marty

FIGURE 5.1A
Work breakdown structure: Tabular form.

the project and the degree of control desired during project monitoring will determine the number of levels. Badiru (1993) suggests starting with three levels, with Level 1 being the final or total project, Level 2 being the major tasks or subsections of the project, and Level 3 containing definable tasks or subcomponents of Level 2. Again, if the project is very complex, the WBS should include additional levels, until the final level specifies discrete activities that can be examined in terms of the time and cost required to complete the activity.

At the final level, the work breakdown structure should include at least two pieces of information that are needed for coordination of effort: the estimated time to complete the activity and the name of an individual who is responsible

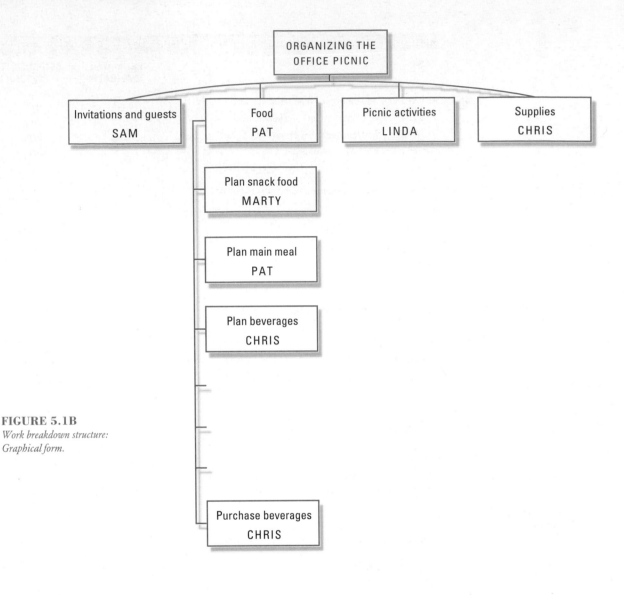

FIGURE 5.1B
Work breakdown structure: Graphical form.

for seeing that the activity is completed. Often a third piece of information, the estimated cost of completing the activity, is also included. This allows for better integration of cost and schedule information needed to monitor the project. When cost information is included, people refer to the work breakdown structure as a *costed WBS*. It should be noted that time and cost estimates should be developed by the persons most knowledgeable about those specific activities. Thus, if project team members come from different functional areas, the project manager should likely consult with managers from those different functional areas before making time and cost estimates.

PROGRAM EVALUATION AND REVIEW TECHNIQUE AND CRITICAL PATH METHOD

The WBS provides information on the estimated time of completion for each individual activity, but it does not indicate the order in which the activities can or will take place. It does not indicate if Activity A must be completed before Activity B can proceed, or if the two can proceed concurrently. When a project is fairly simple, these interrelationships are not difficult to discern and a schedule can be constructed directly from the WBS by laying out the activities in the order in which they are to be carried out (see the section on Gantt charts, later in this chapter). Alternatively, when a project is complex, it is almost impossible to construct a schedule before the interrelationships among the various activities are made explicit. Network diagrams are graphical tools for making explicit these interrelationships. Until recently, the most popular network diagramming techniques have been *Program Evaluation and Review Technique* (PERT) and *Critical Path Method* (CPM).

PERT was introduced by the Special Projects Office of the United States Navy in 1958 as an aid in planning (and controlling) its Polaris Weapon System, a project that involved approximately 3,000 contractors. At virtually the same time, a similar technique, Critical Path Method (CPM), was introduced by DuPont Company. The methods are very similar and essentially show the flow of activities from start to finish. Over the years, the two methods have essentially merged and people often refer to PERT/CPM diagrams and/or analysis. More recently, with the increased use of project management computer software, other similar approaches have been developed and have gained some popularity and acceptance (Spinner, 1989). Because the basic logic of network diagramming is essentially the same across the various techniques, we will present the more traditional approaches.

As was implied above, PERT/CPM diagrams allow the project manager to see the flow of tasks associated with a project by showing the interrelationships between activities. They allow the project manager to estimate the time necessary to complete the overall project given the interdependencies among tasks, and to identify those critical points where a delay in task completion can have a major effect on overall project completion. In performing the PERT/CPM analysis, one assumes that all tasks or activities can be clearly identified and sequenced, and that the time necessary for completing each task or activity can be estimated.

Figure 5.2 shows a simple PERT/CPM diagram. In the diagram, activities are designated by arrows. The circles at the beginning and end of the arrows are referred to as nodes; they designate starting and ending points for activities. These points in time are called events and consume no time in and of themselves. An activity is referred to as Activity *i,j* or Activity *i-j*, where *i* is the start node and *j* is the end node. Because of the way the diagram is constructed, the PERT/CPM diagram is sometimes referred to as an arrow or activity-on-arrow network diagram. Alternatively, activity-in-node network diagrams, as the name implies, place the activities within the node (usually drawn in boxes) and use the arrows simply to show the necessary ordering of activities. In activity-on-arrow diagrams the numbers along the arrows indicate the expected time for the activity to be completed.

FIGURE 5.2
PERT network with critical path.

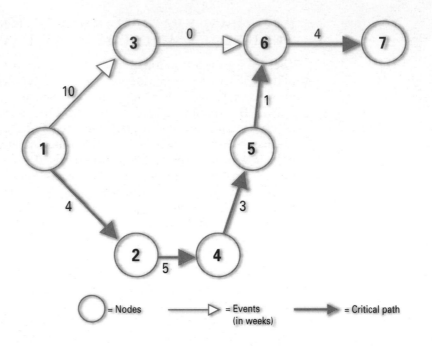

Although these numbers may come directly from the WBS, it is customary to calculate an expected time for activity completion (t_e), using a weighted average of an optimistic time (t_o), a pessimistic time (t_p), and the most likely time (t_m) using the following equation:

$$t_e = (t_o + 4t_m + t_p)/6$$

Note that Activity 3,6 has an expected time of zero weeks. This type of activity is called a dummy activity, as used to indicate that Activity 6,7 cannot begin until Activity 1,3 is complete.

The critical path is that chain of activities that takes the longest time through the network. In Figure 5.2 the path is 1-2-4-5-6-7, which takes 17 weeks from start to finish. It indicates the least possible time in which the overall project can be completed, and it is the path that needs to be watched most carefully to ensure that the project stays "on track."

To identify the critical path, it is necessary to understand the concept of *slack* or *float*. In Figure 5.2, the critical path, 1-2-4-5-6-7 takes 17 weeks from start to finish. Note, however, that there is another path, 1-3-6-7, which only takes 14 weeks from start to finish. This means that Activity 1,3 could begin three weeks later than Activity 1,2 and the project would still be completed on time, assuming, of course, that the time estimates are fairly accurate. We then say that Activity 1,3 has a total float or slack of 3 weeks. While this is easy to see in Figure 5.2, it requires more effort when the diagram is more complex.

The first step in identifying the critical path is to identify the earliest start and finish times. Start at the first node of the diagram; this has an earliest start time of zero. For the other nodes, the earliest start times equals the earliest finish time of the previous activity. For all activities, the earliest finish time is the sum of the earliest start time plus the estimated time of the activity.

Next, take the largest finish time for the last node and calculate the latest start and finish times by starting at the last node and subtracting the estimated time for completion of that activity from the latest finish time of the previous activity. To identify the critical path, make a list of latest finish times and earliest start times. Time available is then calculated as the difference between the earliest start time and the latest finish time. If time available is equal to the estimated time for completing the activity, there is no float and that activity is on the critical path. Table 5.1 shows the calculations.

TABLE 5.1   Identifying the Critical Path

Activity	Latest Finish Time	(–)	Earliest Start Time	(–)	Time Estimate	(=) Float
1, 2	4		0		4	0*
1, 3	13		0		10	3
2, 4	9		4		5	0*
3, 6#	13		10		0	3
4, 5	12		9		3	0*
5, 6	13		12		1	0*
6, 7	17		13		4	0*

* Critical path
\# Dummy activity—has no time duration

As indicated above, the critical path is important because it is that path that must be most closely monitored. It is the path for which there is no slack, and activities must begin and end on time in order for the project schedule to be met. Alternatively, activities that are not on the critical path can begin any time between the earliest and latest start dates. The determination is usually made in accordance with the availability of resources, primarily human resources.

RESOURCE LEVELING

The ultimate purpose of project management is to obtain the most efficient use of resources. Efficient use of resources can be a problem, however, if there are wide swings in resource needs. House asserts that "There will be times when team members feel they can't get enough done. Times when they can't get enough to do. Even when it is carefully planned, a project will not need the same amount of time from the same amount of people throughout" (1988, p. 10). One approach to maximizing the use of people is to use the information from the WBS together with the information regarding the amount of float to schedule activities that are not on the critical path.

Kimmons defines resource leveling as "the process of scheduling work on noncritical activities so that resource requirement on peak days will be reduced" (1990, p. 79). Although in this sense *resources* refers to all project resources that are limited within a specified time period, including personnel, equipment, and materials, resource leveling is most often used to allocate personnel to different project activities.

To determine the optimal use of resources, the project manager needs to begin by assuming that all activities will begin at their earliest start dates. Based on this assumption, the project manager can then draw a graph showing the required personnel, by job type (title) over time. This graph will show peaks, times where there is a great amount of work to be done, and valleys, times when there is less work to be done. Using the PERT/CPM diagram and the table that gives the float associated with each activity, the project manager can then level the resources by moving the start dates for some of the activities that have float to a later time (but prior to the latest start date). The process continues until the changes in personnel requirements from one time period to the next are minimized, that is, until the peaks and valleys are evened. Of course, with large, complex projects, the project manager would want to rely on computer software to perform this type of analysis.

GANTT CHARTS

The project manager is now ready to schedule the activities, that is, to set dates on which the various project activities are expected to begin and end. The most popular tool for showing this type of schedule is the Gantt chart, developed by Henry L. Gantt in the early part of the twentieth century. These charts are essentially bar charts that allow you to see at a glance how the different activities fit into the overall schedule.

To develop a Gantt chart, make a list of each of the major activities, grouped as they are in the work breakdown structure and sequenced as they are expected as a result of the PERT/CPM and resource leveling analyses. Construct the Gantt chart by drawing the time line for the project along the horizontal axis of a graph and placing the list of activities along the vertical axis of the chart. For each activity, draw a bar showing the time commitment (see Figure 5.3). The Gantt chart is most useful when each activity time is commensurate with the units of time drawn on the horizontal axis. That is, if the horizontal axis is drawn in terms of months, most activities should take at least two months. You can also identify specific milestones, or points of accomplishment, within each task by using a circled number within the bar. In Figure 5.3 the milestones could represent first drafts of status reports due at the end of the activity.

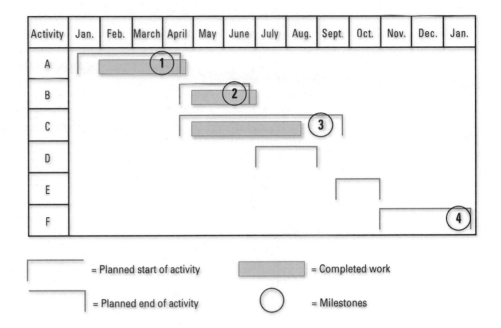

FIGURE 5.3
Gantt chart.

Specialized Gantt Charts. Once the Gantt chart is constructed, it can be used to integrate information about projected use of time with information about projected use of other resources. Two types of Gantt charts are commonly used. The first shows personnel task assignments. By listing each individual along the vertical axis, followed by all of the tasks/activities to which that individual is assigned, the project manager can see at a glance which tasks/activities each person is assigned to at each time period of the project (see Figure 5.4). If the task distribution across individuals is uneven or if some individuals were mistakenly assigned to too many work assignments during a single time period, this chart gives the project manager another chance to redistribute task assignments.

The second type of integrated Gantt chart is the Bar Chart Cost Schedule. This Gantt chart simply shows the projected cost of each activity below the bar showing that activity in the overall Gantt chart. This allows the project manager to have some sense of how much money is projected to be spent in each time period. It also allows the project manager to calculate the cost slope by dividing the cost of the activity by the duration of that activity (in whatever unit of time is being used). Thus, for example, if Activity A cost $4,500 and is expected to take three weeks to complete, the cost slope in dollars per week is $1,500. While this piece of information is not interesting in isolation, it becomes interesting when the project manager compares it to the cost slopes of other activities because it gives a sense of the relative cost of activities per time period.

Gantt Charts as Monitoring Tools. The Gantt chart is also a useful project monitoring tool. By using different colors or different symbols, the Gantt chart can

FIGURE 5.4
Personnel Task Assignments

help the project manager track how closely the project is keeping to the planned schedule. When a given task runs over the allotted time, the Gantt chart can be used to determine whether or not the schedule needs to be rethought. Figure 5.3 shows that Activities A and B ran over schedule approximately one week each, whereas Activity C was completed almost one month ahead of schedule.

HUMAN RESOURCE MATRIX

One final planning tool is the human resource matrix. As with the Gantt chart used to show the personnel task assignments, this matrix can be used to see whether workload is evenly distributed across individuals. The human resource matrix lists the tasks/activities along the vertical axis and the names across the top of the matrix (see Figure 5.5). For each task/activity one person is designated

FIGURE 5.5
Human Resource Matrix.

TASK	CHRIS	LINDA	MARTY	PAT	SAM
1				P	
2	S		S	C	P
3		P	S	C	
4	P		S	C	

as having primary responsibility (P), and others may be designated as having secondary responsibility (S). Other designations can be also be added as needed. For example, one can label an individual as (C) if that individual needs to be consulted, or (B) if a person can provide backup, and so on. Project teams need to be able to adapt the project management tools to best meet their needs.

One advantage of this chart over the personnel task assignment chart is that it is clear whether or not time spent on the project is time in a leadership capacity. Further, it makes it clear at a glance if someone has too many leadership (primary) assignments. Alternatively, while it tells who is assigned to which task/activity, it is not as informative as the personnel task assignment chart with respect to how much time is being spent during each time period by each person. Thus it is probably wise to use the two charts together for keeping track of how human resources are being utilized.

PROJECT MONITORING

As indicated in the beginning of this section, monitoring is essentially keeping track of progress over the life of the project. There are four primary resources that need to be monitored: time, money, people, and materials. Monitoring involves looking at actual expenditure of resources, comparing actual with estimated, and, where necessary, deciding what adjustments need to be made in the work plan to accommodate discrepancies between actual and planned.

In the section on project planning we gave examples of planning tools that can be used in monitoring the use of human resources and time. Here we will focus on the project budget and time. Note that the tools provided here can be used to look at the total budget or at specific components of the budget, and so they are applicable to monitoring the use of human resources and materials as well.

COST/SCHEDULE INTEGRATION

While project success is generally defined in terms of project completion within constraints of time and cost, and at an appropriate level of performance, Roman argues that "Often [the project manager] will be rated a success or failure as a project manager according to whether the project comes in under budget, on budget, or over budget" (1986, p. 156). The project manager therefore has good incentives to closely monitor the project budget.

In monitoring the budget, the project manager is concerned with two types of information. The first focuses on the amount of money budgeted for the work to be performed (budgeted cost of work performed—BCWP) versus the actual cost of performing the work (actual cost of work performed—ACWP). The difference between the two quantities (BCWP – ACWP) is referred to as the cost variance and is an indication of how close the estimated costs were to actual costs, with a positive number indicating monetary savings and a negative number indicating budget overrun. (Again, note that these variances can be calculated for the total budget or by category of expenditure. Below we will use the acronyms for both situations.)

The second piece of information looks at the amount of money projected to be spent on the actual work performed during the time period (budgeted cost of work performed—BCWP) versus the amount projected to be spent during the time period (BCWS). The difference between the two quantities (BCWP – BCWS) is referred to as the schedule variance and is an indication of whether the money is being spent according to the projected schedule. Here a positive number is an indication of the project running ahead of schedule—that is, more work is being performed than was originally scheduled—whereas a negative number is an indication of the project running behind schedule—less work is being performed than was actually scheduled. Alternatively a negative number could be an indication that some work is being performed out of its scheduled sequence. Harrison (1992) suggests that schedule variance should not be looked at separately from the formal scheduling system; that is, this information should be examined in conjunction with the Gantt chart or PERT/CPM network diagram to determine the actual status of specific activities or milestones.

Cost and schedule variances can be examined graphically or in a table. To examine these variances graphically, the project manager needs to calculate at each time period a cumulative BCWS, BCWP, and ACWP. That is, for each reporting period (usually monthly) the project manager needs to calculate the total projected budget up to that time period (cumulative BCWS), the total projected budget for the work that has actually been performed up to that time period (cumulative BCWP), and the total budget actually spent up to that time period (cumulative ACWP). The three amounts are plotted at each time period along the vertical axis, with time across the horizontal axis. The points are then connected to make a smooth curve (see Figure 5.6). Note that the cumulative BCWS curve extends from the lower-left corner, where no money has been budgeted to be spent before the beginning of the project, to the upper-right corner, where all the money is budgeted to be spent by the end of the project. When the cumulative BCWP curve lies above the cumulative ACWP curve, then the project is running under budget. Alternatively, if the cumulative ACWP lies above the cumulative BCWP curve, the project is running over budget and the project manager needs to understand why. Similarly, if the cumulative BCWS lies below the BCWP, then the project may well be running ahead of schedule. Alternatively, if the BCWS lies above the BCWP, then the amount that you expected to spend up to that time period is less than the amount you are actually spending and you may be behind schedule. In Figure 5.6, the project was initially running under budget, but is now running considerably above budget. It was also initially behind schedule, but is catching up.

Performance analysis reports present cost and schedule variance in a tabular form. These reports are usually generated on a monthly basis, although, depending on the complexity of the project, they could be done more or less often. The report includes two tables, one with information about performance in the current time period and the second with information about cumulative performance. The first

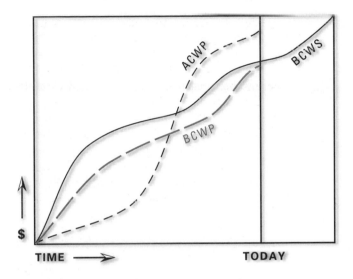

FIGURE 5.6
*Cost/Schedule
Integration Chart.*

table presents five pieces of information for each category of expenditure: the amount budgeted for this time period (BCWS), the amount budgeted for the work performed (BCWP), the amount actually spent in the current time period (ACWP), and the schedule and cost variance. The second table repeats this format providing cumulative information. Again, the project manager should be concerned when the performance analysis reports negative cost or schedule variances.

THE HUMAN SIDE OF PROJECT MANAGEMENT

As was indicated earlier in this chapter, many of the competencies that are presented throughout this book are relevant to the project manager. In particular, you should be aware that the tools associated with the managerial leadership roles in the human relations quadrant are important to managing a project team. One reason why interpersonal skills are so important in project management is that the project often lies outside of the usual organizational structure. Thus, while projects can be undertaken within a functional area, they are more often undertaken across functional areas in an organization. (Note that the last section of this chapter is on managing across functions.) Depending on the permanent department structure of the organization, the job of the project manager will have different requirements. Since Chapter 6 (the Director Role) discusses the different types of department structures, we will not go extensively into this topic here. It is, however, important to note that the definition of project management includes both projects that are undertaken within a work unit and those that require people to be brought together from across several different work units. Further, while bringing people from different functional areas together makes good sense from a creativity perspective, it may also create priority conflicts if members of the project team are also involved in other work over which the project manager has no authority (Kimmons, 1990).

Here it is particularly important for the project managers to have good negotiation (see Chapter 8) and conflict management (see Chapter 3) skills in working with line managers (Thornberry, 1987).

In House's (1988) book, *The Human Side of Project Management,* she discusses interpersonal skills that are needed with clients as well. She argues that internal and external integration (coordination) are two project management tools that are generally given far less attention than the formal planning and control tools. In particular, she argues that when the outcomes of the project are not well defined and/or the project team's experience with project technology is high, there is a greater need to depend on tools of integration than on tools of planning and control. House gives the following rules of thumb regarding the choice of management tools that will most contribute to the project's success:

> *When a project is* large *and has* well-defined outcomes *but there is only* low experience *behind it, a project manager should expect to depend heavily on formal planning and control techniques.*
>
> *When a project has* well-defined outcomes *and* high company experience *behind it, [the project manager] should expect to draw heavily on internal integration.*
>
> *When a project is* large *and has* only loosely-defined outcomes *with* low company experience *behind it, [the project manager] should expect to emphasize external integration, formal planning, and formal control.*
>
> *When a project has* only loosely-defined outcomes *but* high company experience *behind it, the project manager will find . . . people skills at peak demand . . . [and] will rely heavily on external integration and internal integration (House, 1988, p. 44, emphasis in original).*

While it is of course preferable to have well-defined outcomes, this is not always possible. In this case, it is very important to be in close contact with the client, perhaps even including the client on the project team, and communicating on a regular basis, both formally and informally, regarding project progress. In addition, it is important to communicate regularly with key people in your own organization regarding project progress. Similarly, tools of internal integration involve regular formal and informal communication within the project team, using many of the skills of the mentor and facilitator presented earlier in this text.

ANALYSIS   Project Planning

Directions   Read the following scenario and respond to the questions that follow. Your instructor may have you work individually or in small groups.

Congratulations! You have your first project manager assignment. You were asked to be the project team leader for the team that is going to design a new management training course in your organization. Here is the background information:

Last week your boss found your copy of *Becoming a Master Manager* sitting on your shelf and decided to borrow it. After reading through the book, your boss shared it with the head of the Training and Development Unit (T&D), and they both agreed that it would provide an ideal foundation for the new management training course that was being discussed. Even though you do not know much about training, they decided that you would be an ideal project manager for the team designing the training since you are familiar with the framework. After giving you the assignment, you met with the head of T&D and you agreed on a few basic concepts regarding the training program: (1) the program should run either one week or two; (2) the curriculum should be accompanied by two types of evaluation, one based on participant reaction and one based on the actual changes in work behavior when the participants return to the job; (3) the project team should conduct a needs assessment (i.e., you should interview managers) in the three divisions that will be the heaviest users of the training program to determine what they would like to see included in the curriculum; (4) you should develop some new cases or exercises based on the outcomes of the needs assessment; and (5) you should set up an advisory committee of upper-level managers from across the organization to approve the curriculum and the evaluation instruments.

Fortunately you have some good people on your team from the training unit and after meeting with them a few times, they volunteered to put together an initial schedule. This morning you found a memo on your desk explaining that they had developed a schedule based on a proposed list of activities with estimated times and a PERT/CPM analysis. The memo indicated that the list of activities, the PERT/CPM network diagram, and a proposed schedule were all attached to the memo, but all you could find was the following list of activities with time estimates:

Activity	Description	Estimated time (in weeks)
1,2	Track literature on evaluation	4
1,4	Set up steering committee	1
1,5	Develop needs assessment questionnaire	2
2,3	Develop reaction evaluation instrument	1
2,10	Dummy activity	0
4,9	Meet with advisory committee to discuss curriculum	1
5,6	Conduct needs assessment in first division	4
5,7	Conduct needs assessment in second division	2
5,8	Conduct needs assessment in third division	2
6,9	Analyze data and develop cases and exercise	3
7,9	Analyze data and develop cases and exercise	2
8,9	Analyze data and develop cases and exercise	2
9,10	Develop first draft of curriculum	10
10,11	Develop behavior evaluation instrument	3
10,12	Advisory Committee reviews curriculum	2

Activity	Description	Estimated time (in weeks)
11,13	Advisory Committee reviews evaluation instruments	2
12,14	Curriculum revisions based on Advisory Committee input	2
13,14	Evaluation revisions based on Advisory Committee input	1
14,15	Conduct two pilot training courses	4

When you tried calling the team members who drafted the memo you were told that they were away for the next two days at a training conference and no one else knew anything about what they were working on. You have a breakfast meeting scheduled with your boss and the head of the training unit tomorrow morning to discuss the schedule.

1. Based on the list of activities, prepare a PERT/CPM network diagram. What is the critical path?

2. Create a chart of earliest and latest start and finish times. Determine the critical path. What is the shortest time from start to finish?

3. What are your current scheduling concerns? Assuming that you do not have unlimited resources, make a few suggestions for resource leveling and set up a Gantt chart.

4. What concerns do you have about internal and/or external integration? How do you think you should handle these concerns?

PRACTICE   The Job Fair

Directions   Your instructor will divide you into teams to work on a project.

The president of the student association has asked for volunteers to organize a Job Fair, to be held in conjunction with the annual meeting of the Regional Management Association, and you think this is a great opportunity to try out your project management skills. The job fair was discussed during the last meeting of the student association and there was a fair amount of consensus that:

• The job fair should take place during the first morning of the annual meeting.

• It should provide an opportunity for graduating students to meet potential employers and vice versa. Therefore, potential employers in the private, public, and nonprofit sectors will be invited.

- Organizations (potential employers) will be expected to "rent" a table so they can advertise their organization.

- Students (potential employees) will be expected to submit an updated resume to be placed in a resume book that will be distributed at the job fair to all organizations that rent a table.

The job fair is three months away.

1. Start by thinking about all the activities that need to occur in order to make the job fair a success. (Here are some major tasks to keep in mind: advertising the job fair, contacting potential employers, organizing the resume book and getting it printed in advance, arranging for the setup of tables. You may think of others.)

2. Create a Work Breakdown Structure

3. Propose a Gantt chart.

APPLICATION Managing Your Own Project

Choose a complex project or a program in which you are involved at school or work, or in a community organization to which you belong. If you cannot think of any such projects, think about a complex project you would like to undertake, such as organizing a family reunion or conducting a fundraising event for a non-profit organization that you think does good work.

Write a three- to five-page paper describing the project planning for the project or event. Start with a brief description of the project and what you consider to be the most challenging aspects of planning this project. Then, using the planning tools presented in this chapter (SOW, WBS, PERT/CPM, Gantt charts), show how you would plan to complete the project on time and within cost. If there are important issues of internal and external integration that will affect the success of the project, discuss how these issues will be handled.

Competency 2 Designing Work

ASSESSMENT Your Ideal Work Situation

Directions Write a one- to two-paragraph description of your ideal work situation when you complete your current degree program (if you plan to go on for an additional degree immediately after completing your current degree, write about your ideal work situation when you complete the higher degree). Try to be as realistic as possible; you will not learn much from this exercise if you write that your ideal work situation is one where you do not have to do any work, but get paid large amounts of money.

1. List 5 to 10 characteristics of this ideal work situation.

2. To what extent do the characteristics you have listed focus on the type of work itself, the feelings of accomplishment you will have doing this work, and/or the extent to which you feel the work will give you opportunities to develop personally and professionally?

3. To what extent do the characteristics focus on physical working conditions, such as the physical space, the geographic location, and so on?

4. To what extent do the characteristics focus on work relationships with others, for example, supervisors, co-workers, employees, customers/clients?

5. To what extent do the characteristics focus on work-related privileges, such as autonomy with respect to what you do, how you do it and/or when you do it?

6. To what extent do the characteristics focus on financial rewards and/or non-work-related privileges of the work, such as pay and/or bonuses, fringe benefits (health insurance, other types of insurance, education, etc.), special parking privileges?

7. What other types of characteristics did you use to describe your ideal work situation?

8. Knowing what you know now (assuming you have not yet read the rest of this chapter), what would you tell an upper-level manager about the design of work in today's organizations?

LEARNING   Designing Work

In the Assessment exercise, we asked you to describe your ideal work situation. Perhaps your ideal work situation described a specific job within an organization, but there is a good chance that it did not. While a decade ago most people would have considered the terms "work" and "job" to be virtually synonymous, the world of work is changing. Today more and more people are self-employed and/or have only a temporary or part-time employment relationship with an organization. Even those who have a "full-time job" with an organization are not necessarily spending much time at a centralized work site (an office) or working what would be considered "regular" hours; they can telecommute through the use of computers and fax machines, working hours that are personally convenient rather than working traditional "9 to 5" hours.

In the introduction to this chapter we quoted from a *Fortune* article, entitled "The End of the Job," which argued that the world of work is changing and so must our ideas about the way work is packaged. At about the same time, *Business Week* ran a special report, entitled "Rethinking Work," in which they proclaim "The job, certainly, is not dead. There's still a robust need for relationships between employer and employed that rely on stability, security, and shared economic interests. . . .[But t]he relationship isn't what it was" (*Business Week* October 17, 1994, p. 76). Whether or not the notion of "job" is dead, it certainly is experiencing some profound changes. In particular, changes in the economy and in technology have resulted in the need to think very differently about the nature of work and the relationship between the organization and the employee. In this section we will explore these issues, focusing on the implications of the changing nature of work for managers who are concerned with the design of work for employees. We begin with a brief history of job design, and then explore both individual job and work team approaches to designing work, focusing on two popular techniques: job enrichment and self-managed work teams. While neither of these approaches is new, they both provide means for organizations to rethink how work is organized.

A BRIEF HISTORY OF JOB DESIGN IN THE TWENTIETH CENTURY

As noted in the introduction to this chapter, for most of the twentieth century we have accepted the notion that work is performed most efficiently when large, complex tasks are broken down into smaller, more specialized tasks. In general, this is not an unreasonable assumption (note that this is exactly the process followed in the planning phase of project management), but as the nature of work and the nature of the work force has changed, this notion needs to be reexamined. To some degree this assumption is the legacy of Adam Smith, whose treatise, *The Wealth of Nations*, written in 1776, set forth the notions that work could be accomplished more efficiently if it were divided into its component tasks and workers were specialized so that each individual had responsibility for completing only one of the component tasks. In the early 1900s, these principles were reinforced by Frederick Winslow Taylor and Frank and Lillian Gilbreth, whose research in the area of scientific management argued that work should be broken down so that workers performed a minimal number of tasks, and that through scientific study, one could determine the one best way to perform each task so that motions that caused fatigue and/or reduced productivity were reduced to a minimum.

While the notion that dividing up work into specialized tasks has persisted, the assumption that this approach is the most efficient way to do work has been questioned since the 1930s (Lawler, 1992). As the negative effects of task specialization on the individual employee became apparent, efforts to develop techniques to redesign jobs began to appear. In the 1950s and 1960s, various approaches to job design were tried in an effort to improve worker motivation, performance, and satisfaction. Perhaps the best known among these approaches was based on Fredrick Herzberg's (1968) work on employee motivation, which suggested that what motivated people at work was different from what demotivated them. Herzberg and his associates argued that while the absence of such factors as pay, supervisory competence, and good working conditions could demotivate employees, the presence of those factors would not necessarily motivate them. Instead, to motivate employees, jobs should be "enriched"; that is, they should be designed so that they are seen as giving individuals opportunities for achievement, recognition, responsibility, and advancement. In organizations like AT&T, which had been notorious for standardizing and routinizing work processes across the United States (Lawler, 1992), efforts were made to give workers greater responsibility for deciding how the work was to be done and to hold them accountable for how well they did it. Although Herzberg's theory of motivation has often been criticized on methodological grounds, this work laid the foundation for much of the job redesign that was carried out in the 1970s, and we will come back to this approach in the next section. Interestingly, an underlying theme in many approaches to job redesign has been to make whole the work that was previously broken down into specialized tasks.

A fundamental issue raised here is "Who controls how work is organized and managed at the lowest levels of the organizational hierarchy—the organization or the employee?" The organizational purpose of breaking down work into specialized tasks is to increase organizational efficiency. Lawler asserts, however, that research on job design has shown that these approaches can instead lead to inefficiencies. He argues that when organizations control the design of work processes there is a tendency to assume "that work should be simplified, standardized, and specialized, and that supervision and pay incentives should be used to motivate individuals to perform their tasks well. In essence, the thinking and controlling part of the work is separated from the doing of the work" (1992, p. 28). In separating the thinking from the doing, workers become inflexible and unable to do any work that does not fit into their narrowly written job descriptions. This can result in loss of productivity when the worker is suddenly unavailable. Not only are the workers inflexible, the entire work process is inflexible, leading to a loss of productivity when the process must be adapted or changed to accommodate changes in economic and/or technological conditions. In addition, the less the workers know about the work process, the more coordination is required to produce the product. When workers are not responsible for an entire product, there tends to be a greater need for quality control.

Alternatively, when employees have greater control over how work is organized and managed, the work tends to be more challenging, interesting, and motivating. When employees are given the opportunity to both think and do, they take ownership over the whole process and therefore are more likely to invest in finding ways to make the process more efficient. In his book, *Crazy Times Call for Crazy Organizations,* Tom Peters gives a variety of examples of employees finding better ways to perform their work, noting "[t]he average employee can deliver far more than his or her current job demands" (1994, p. 71). Later he adds, "if bosses could appreciate the responsibility and pride people take in doing things most of us would be tempted to dismiss as mundane, we'd know how to tap a very profound power" (1994, pp. 83–84).

Over the past few decades there have been two major streams of effort to redesign work to give employees more control over the process. The first focuses on the individual job, and includes efforts to add tasks, responsibility, and/or autonomy. The second stream focuses on redesigning the whole work process to create self-managed work teams. Here we look at these two streams and suggest some guidelines for deciding whether either can be used to redesign the work within a work unit.

JOB DESIGN (REDESIGN): MOTIVATIONAL CRITERIA

As noted above, much of the work on job design has emerged as a result of research on motivation. While the efficiency approach of Adam Smith and Fredrick Taylor focused on the specific tasks, the motivational approach has focused on the subjective characteristics of the job, or how the individual perceives the job. Again, this assumes that rather than using pay and close supervision as incentives to motivate people to do their work, the work itself could become the incentive. If employees feel positively about the work they are doing, they will not need to be closely supervised; rather they will manage themselves.

The most frequently used approach to measuring the subjective characteristics of a job derives from a model developed by Hackman and Oldham (1975). The model posits five core job characteristics, or dimensions, that are said to lead to three critical psychological states that influence personal and work outcomes (see Figure 5.7). The five job characteristics are:

FIGURE 5.7

Core job characteristics and individual work outcomes in a diagnostic model of job enrichment.

Adapted from: *J. Richard Hackman and Greg R. Oldham, "Development of the Job Diagnostic Survey,"* Journal of Applied Psychology *60 (1975): 161. Copyright © 1975 by the American Psychological Association and the authors.*

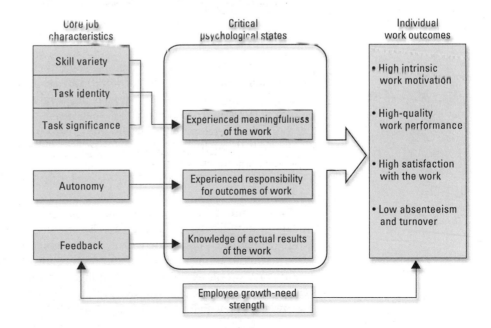

1. *Skill variety.* The degree to which the job requires the individual to perform a wide range of tasks.

2. *Task identity.* The degree to which the job requires completion of a whole piece of work that employees can identify as resulting from their individual effort.

3. *Task significance.* The degree to which the job is seen as having an impact on the lives or work of other people.

4. *Autonomy.* The degree to which employees have discretion in determining work schedules and procedures.

5. *Feedback.* The degree to which the job provides employees with clear and direct information about job performance.

The three critical psychological states are:

1. *Experienced meaningfulness of the work.* The degree to which the person experiences work as important, valuable, and worthwhile. This is influenced by the degree of skill variety, task identity, and task significance.

2. *Experienced responsibility for outcomes of the work.* The degree to which the employee feels personally responsible for making decisions regarding work processes and work outcomes. This is influenced by the degree of autonomy.

3. *Knowledge of actual results of the work.* The degree to which the employee is able to see, on a regular basis, the effect of his or her performance on the work outcome. This is influenced by the degree of feedback.

As shown in Figure 5.7, the extent to which these five core job dimensions of work influence employees' internal work motivation, work performance, job satisfaction, absenteeism, and turnover is moderated by employees' degree of "employee growth-need strength," or their need for personal accomplishment and individual development. That is, the greater the individual's need for self-actualization through work, the stronger the influence of the job characteristics on personal and work outcomes.

Hackman and Oldham (1975) proposed this as a multiplicative model, so that the degree to which a job has motivating potential is calculated as the multiplicative product of the degree to which the three psychological states are present. In a multiplicative model, low levels of one variable cannot be compensated for by high levels of another. Thus, for example, if the individual experiences low meaningfulness in a particular job (as a result of low skill variety, low task identity, or low task significance), the motivating potential of this job will not be high, regardless of how high the levels of experienced responsibility for outcomes or knowledge of actual results. The five core characteristics are usually measured by the Job Diagnostic Survey (JDS) which was developed by Hackman and Oldham as well.

JOB DESIGN STRATEGIES

Over the past few decades, as workers have begun to expect more from their jobs than a paycheck, organizations have increasingly begun to recognize the importance of motivational criteria in job design and have experimented with various techniques that focus not just on increasing job performance, but also on increasing employee satisfaction. Interestingly, while job enrichment techniques were originally seen as primarily applicable to production work, organizations are more frequently applying this approach to white-collar sales and service jobs as well (Lawler, 1992). Indeed, as service workers make up one of the fastest-growing segments of the U.S. labor force, many organizations are finding that one key to their survival is to redesign the work so that the delivery of superior service is a motivator for employees, as well as a way of satisfying customers. Carla Paonessa, an Andersen Consulting partner in Chicago, goes so far as to say that "You cannot expect your employees to delight your customers unless you as an employer delight your employees" (quoted in Henkoff, 1994, p. 116).

Below we list a variety of job design approaches. Some are considered more effective than others; some may work with certain types of workers betters than with others. Recall that in the Hackman and Oldham (1975) model, the relationship between the five core job characteristics and the outcome variables is moderated by the degree to which the employee is motivated by the need for accomplishment and challenging work.

Job Enlargement. **Job enlargement** increases the skill variety and task identity by redesigning the job to increase the number of tasks the person performs. It is also sometimes referred to as horizontal loading, because it increases the number of tasks performed within the production or service process, tasks otherwise performed by co-workers at the same level of organizational hierarchy. Opposite to task specialization, job enlargement requires employees to perform a greater number of tasks, and so increases their ability to complete a whole piece of work. This approach is, however, often criticized because the work may be no more challenging than when the employee performed only one task. That is, performing many boring tasks may be no better than performing only one boring task, if the person has no ability to make decisions regarding how the task will be performed.

Job Rotation. Similarly, **job rotation** increases the skill variety by allowing individuals to shift among a variety of tasks, based on some time schedule. Like job enlargement, this approach has both advantages and disadvantages. Job rotation can be used to reduce boredom. When there is a monotonous job that must be done, job rotation is one way to share the boredom so that no one employee is assigned solely to that job. Here, job rotation, like job enlargement leads to increased skill variety, but not necessarily to increased autonomy or feedback. It thus may have limited ability to influence individual and work outcomes. It can, however, also be used to expose people to different parts of the organization, thus giving them more knowledge about how the organization is run. This use of job rotation allows the individual to have a better understanding of the interdependencies among work units and the need for cooperation across units; it also allows managers to see how well a person adapts to the various situations and is therefore sometimes used to test interpersonal skills that may be required for promotion.

Job Enrichment. **Job enrichment** is considered the most effective of the various job design techniques in that it can potentially increase all five subjective job characteristics. Whereas job enlargement and job rotation focus primarily on skill variety and, to a lesser extent, task identity, job enrichment focuses on task significance, autonomy, and feedback as well. That is, instead of merely increasing the number and variety of job activities, job enrichment generally increases the responsibility and decision making regarding one's work practices, as well as enhances the nature of job relationships with managers, co-workers, and clients.

One of the earliest and best known job enrichment projects was conducted with keypunch operators at the Travelers Insurance Companies (Hackman et al., 1975). It was not until the 1980s, however, that American industry, facing a shortage of skilled labor, began to take job enrichment more seriously than it had previously. For example, Lechmere, a retail chain store owned by Dayton Hudson, began to offer raises based upon the number of jobs an employee could perform. In 1985, when National Steel lost nearly $150 million, the company struck an agreement with the United Steelworkers Union to consolidate 78 job classifications into 16, and to broaden worker responsibilities and participation (Alster, 1989). Today, as noted above, most organizations in the service industry are recognizing that to keep the best service workers they need to create jobs that employees enjoy and find challenging. Here we identify several specific approaches to job enrichment.

1. *Forming natural work units.* This means distributing work according to a logic that is based on workflow and completion of a whole job. By forming natural work groups, jobs have greater task identity and task significance because employees experience their work as a whole, rather than seeing only a small piece. (This is similar to the creation of work teams, which will be discussed in the next section.)

2. *Establishing client relationships.* Wherever possible, employees should be given direct contact with the ultimate user of the product or service provided. When employees have direct contact, they also need to have the ability to make decisions to help customers (see next item, on vertical loading). At the Ritz-Carlton Hotel chain, every employee, beginning with junior bellhops, is given the authority to spend up to $2,000 to fix a guest's problems (Peters, 1994). At Marriott Hotels, guest service associates (GSA) perform work that was once done separately by bellhops, doorpersons, front-desk

clerks, and concierges. In addition, they can make decisions that they once had to refer up to a supervisor. Says one GSA at the Marriott Hotel in Schaumberg, Illinois, "I have more responsibilities. I feel better about my job, and the guests get better service" (quoted in Henkoff, 1994, p. 110). Thus, direct contact increases the likelihood of feedback, as well as increasing skill variety and autonomy.

3. *Vertical loading of jobs.* Vertical loading is simply the redesign of jobs so that employees have greater responsibility and control over work schedules, work methods, and quality checks, and therefore have greater autonomy. In the previous paragraph, examples were given regarding employees' ability to make decisions to help customers. Employees also need to be able to make decisions regarding work processes. They thus need to be trusted with the organizational information they need to make intelligent decisions. Steve Sheppard, CEO of Foldcraft, a restaurant-seating manufacturer, shares financial information with all employees through weekly department meetings. He believes that if employees are to manage for increased profitability, they need to know how money is spent and what is the result of various sales and cost-saving techniques (Peters, 1994).

4. *Opening feedback channels.* Increasing feedback to employees increases their opportunity to adjust and improve their performance. The more frequent the feedback, the greater the likelihood that job performance will improve. Efforts to open feedback channels should focus on job-provided feedback rather than manager-supplied feedback. Many quality programs stress the importance of employees working with their customer(s), whether it be an internal or external customer. Working with customers increases the likelihood that the employee will value the importance of satisfying them. Thus, while manager-supplied information can be valuable to the employee, job-supplied information is often information provided by the person (work unit) who is actually receiving the product or service. Note also that job-supplied feedback is more accessible when the employee is completing a full piece of work; try to imagine a trip to a restaurant where you are served each course by a different waiter or waitress. How would you decide how much tip to leave if the service is inconsistent? Thus, opening feedback channels also often involves vertical loading and establishing client (customer) relationships as well.

SELF-MANAGED WORK TEAMS

Self-managed work teams grew out of the sociotechnical approach to work design, which was originally developed in the 1950s at London's Tavistock Institute. The sociotechnical approach was basically built on two assumptions: The first is that the accomplishment of a task requires both a technology, which includes methods and tools, and a social system, which includes the people who work together to get the task done. The second assumption is that these two components need to fit each other if the task is to be done effectively. Thus, in contrast to the job designs that focus on individual jobs, the sociotechnical approach sees the group as the basic unit of work design. Despite this difference, there is great similarity in the underlying beliefs of these two approaches in that both focus on producing a whole piece of work and both suggest that workers should be given greater autonomy in decision making regarding the work process.

As was the case with participative decision-making approaches discussed in Chapter 3 (the Facilitator Role), there is a wide range of decision-making discretion that can be given to self-managing work teams. They are thus called by a variety of names besides self-managing work teams, including autonomous work teams, semiautonomous work teams, process teams, and shared-management teams, often based on how much autonomy in decision making they have (Lawler, 1992). Thus, in some cases, work teams are fully responsible for managing the process, and have the authority to make decisions on work methods, quality standards, purchasing (dealing directly with suppliers) and inventory, hiring and firing, salaries and bonuses, and so on. In other cases, the team may set production goals and make decisions regarding work methods, but does not make human resources decisions. Lawler argues, however, "A team must be given responsibility for enough of the creation of a product or service so that it controls and is responsible for a clear input and a clear output. All the factors that influence how successfully a particular transformation is done should be included within its scope of responsibility" (1992, p. 90).

One issue that must be resolved in order for a work team design to be successful is that of how much cross-training there should be. That is, should team members be trained to perform all the jobs for which the team is responsible or is it expected that each person brings unique skills and responsibilities that are appreciated, but not performed, by others? In some cases, work team designs do indeed call for everybody to be fully able to perform all the tasks required of the work team. For example, work teams in automobile manufacturing plants typically train all members in all aspects of their team's work. But this does not need to be the case.

In Chapter 3 we discussed roles and responsibilities of team members and the notion that people bring unique skills and abilities to work teams and yet are expected to share the work. This issue is particularly important in thinking about work design. In their book, *Reengineering the Corporation,* Hammer and Champy talk about process teams—"groups of people working together to perform an entire process" (1993, p. 66)—and discuss the difference between being individually responsible for completing a task and being collectively responsible for a process. They state:

Process team workers . . . have a different kind of job. They share joint responsibility with their team members for performing the whole process, not just a small piece of it. They not only use a broader range of skills from day to day, they have to be thinking of a far bigger picture. While not every member of the team will be doing the exact same work—after all, they have different skills and abilities—the lines between them blur. Each team member will have at least a basic familiarity with all the steps in the process and is likely to perform several of them. Moreover, every-thing an individual does is imbued with an appreciation of the process as a whole (Hammer and Champy, 1993, p. 68).

At Kodak, for example, products are designed by teams that include specialists—shutter designers, lens specialists, manufacturing experts, and others. But, as Hammer and Champy note, "A lens designer who used to concentrate strictly and narrowly on lens design now designs lenses in the context of the camera as a whole, which means that he or she inevitably contributes to other aspects of the design and that his or her design will be influenced by what others have to say" (1993, pp. 68–69). Thus we again see the paradox of needing to have clearly defined roles and responsibilities while simultaneously asking people to step out of their narrow roles and participate in the full process, of asking employees to contribute their special skills and abilities while expecting them to develop a broader range of skills and abilities.

CHOOSING BETWEEN JOB AND TEAM APPROACHES

If an organization decides to use semiautonomous work teams, it must make this decision for an entire work unit. While the decision does not have to be inclusive of the entire organization, it cannot have some people working on teams and others working individually in a given work situation. Thus, an organization must decide if more traditional, specialized work designs are preferred or if the organization will choose a work design that gives employees greater responsibility and greater autonomy. To a large degree, this should be determined by the organization's external environment and its technology. If labor costs are low and the environment is fairly stable, a traditional work design may be preferred. If work processes are simple and cannot be made complex, it may not be possible to create enriched jobs, although it may be possible to redesign jobs using job enlargement or job rotation.

Alternatively, if the organization's environment is changing and decisions need to be made quickly, there is a greater necessity to give employees the ability to make those decisions in a timely fashion. In these cases, the choice between job enrichment and work teams will depend more on the technology. Can an individual take a process from beginning to end or does the process require that a variety of tasks be accomplished simultaneously? In the former case, job enrichment approaches may be preferred as these are often less costly. In the latter case, employees are interdependent and need to be able to interact effectively with others working on the same process. In these cases, work team designs are preferable since the only way for an individual to have a good sense of the full process is to be a member of a team that is given the full responsibility for a whole piece of work.

SOME FINAL CONSIDERATIONS

Underlying the discussion of work design has been the notion that people will perform their work roles more effectively if they have ownership of the work. Creating an environment where people have ownership requires that managers value the potential that each person brings to the work environment. In the introduction to this section we noted that employees are often capable of contributing more than we generally ask of them. At DuPont, there is a famous story about "an hourly worker who responded to an employee survey by writing, 'For some twenty years, you have paid for my hands and you could have had my head for free, but you didn't ask'" (Gundry, Kickul and Prather, 1994, p. 35). In designing jobs, organizations need to be more cognizant of workers' capabilities and less focused on the immediate requirements of the task.

Similarly, in designing jobs, organizations (managers) need to consider that job design can (should) be a learning experience. The core job dimensions do not directly address the issue of challenge, the extent to which a job gives a person the opportunity to try something he or she has never done before. Recent attention to total quality management, however, has also brought attention to the notion of continuous learning and the need for ongoing training and development. While in many cases, training and development is an essential part of work team design, this is not always so with individual job design. We would argue that development should be an integral part of all work designs, and that employees should not only be evaluated on how they currently perform, but also on what they do to prepare for future roles. Training and development need not take place within a formal course or workshop; however, the changing nature of work suggests that the new relationship between employers and employees may be based more on a contract of employability than on a promise of job security. As stated in the *Business Week* article on "Rethinking Work," "job skills, like businesses, are ephemeral, and . . . employees themselves must be continually reinvented . . . . [The organization] has a responsibility to help workers sharpen existing skills or take on new ones" (1994, p. 86). Over the next few years, the design of work will focus more and more on learning, which is one of the key tasks of work.

ANALYSIS   What's My Job Design?

Directions   Think about a job that you currently have or one you had in the recent past. Describe the job design in terms of the five core job characteristics. (If you cannot describe a job of your own, use a job with which you are familiar, such as the job of a family member or close friend.)

Now think about the job outcomes of internal work motivation, quality performance, general job satisfaction, absenteeism, and turnover presented in Figure 5.7 and describe how the five job characteristics affect these outcomes. Is this job a good candidate for job redesign? Why or why not? Is this a job that could be altered to create a work team design? Why or why not?

Think about how (if at all) this job was performed 10 years ago. How (if at all) will it be performed 10 years from now? What caused the changes in the nature of this work over the past 10 years? What are the expected changes that you foresee that influence your perception of the changes to occur over the next 10 years?

PRACTICE   Redesigning Work

Directions   For this exercise, work in groups of two. If you described someone else's job in the previous exercise you may want to find a partner who described his or her own job. Share the results of the previous exercise with your partner. Review the five core characteristics and your responses to the questions regarding redesigning the job or integrating it into a work team design. (For the purpose of this exercise you should probably choose the one that you agree has the greatest need for change.) Decide on which approach is best and create a new design. Then respond to the following questions:

1. In what ways does the new design give the individual greater opportunity for ownership of the work?

2. What are the personal and/or organizational drawbacks to this design?

3. What about the design would make it difficult to implement in the current organization?

APPLICATION   Designing the Work Team

Find an organization that uses work teams to accomplish some of its key tasks. Interview several members of the work team about how decisions regarding work methods, quality standards, purchasing and inventory, hiring and firing, salaries and bonuses, and/or any other key work decisions are made. If you can, observe the team in action. Write a three- to five-page paper describing your findings. Also include any suggestions you might have regarding how to improve the work design of this team.

Competency 3 Managing Across Functions

ASSESSMENT   Student Orientation

Directions   You are president of the University Students Services Association (USSA). USSA is a student-run organization that coordinates the activities of all other student-run organizations on campus. USSA monitors scheduling of all extracurricular activities, tracks consistency of student organization activities with University Policy and attempts to provide resource support whenever possible.

In the past, each major University organization, such as Academic Support Services, the USSA, the Student Health Services, the Honor Society, and so on, conducted its own new student orientation during the general orientation prior to the beginning of the Fall semester. These orientations typically lasted anywhere from one to three hours and included speeches, presentations, videotapes, and workshop-type activities. For most organizational units, these orientations were seen as an opportunity to publicize the way in which they contributed to the students' experience of university life. Organizational units gave a great deal of time, effort, and attention to preparing their individual orientations, as they felt it was important for students to learn about how they might take advantage of the services provided. Great pride was taken in conducting a professional presentation and organizational units paid close attention to the evaluations that students completed for each orientation session. In fact, there was somewhat of an informal competition among the units, with each unit trying to be the most innovative in its presentation.

This year, the Provost has decided to try a new approach and has declared that all student orientation sessions will be centrally coordinated and run over a three-day period during the first week of classes. You have been asked to head the team that coordinates this orientation.

Your first task is to prepare a one-page outline on how you will approach this new responsibility. After you have completed the outline, respond to the process questions below.

Process Questions

1. What work- or task-related issues need to be addressed in order to carry out the Provost's request?

2. What people-related issues do you foresee?

3. What issues of internal and external integration will need to be addressed in carrying out this task?

4. What was better about the previous format for student orientations? What is better about the new format?

LEARNING   Managing Across Functions

In the previous section, we discussed the design of work from the perspective of the changing world of work. Consistently, the theme of global competition surfaced as a primary cause of the need to rethink how we organize work. *Made in America* (Dertouzes et al., 1989), a summary of the report of the MIT

Commission on Industrial Productivity, identifies six factors that distinguish U.S. companies that are successful in competing globally from those that are not. They found that the companies that were more successful engaged in simultaneous improvement efforts in quality, cost, and speed; built close ties to customers; built close ties to suppliers; integrated technology into manufacturing and marketing strategies and linked them to organizational changes that promote teamwork, training, and continuous learning; did continual training; and had greater functional integration and less organizational stratification. Three of these factors focus on breaking down barriers that have been created by organizational bureaucracies. They suggest that we not only need to rethink the world of work from the perspective of the individuals who are performing the jobs, but that we also need to rethink work from the perspective of how we divide up work in organizations. They suggest that the separations that are caused by grouping work by functional specialties can result in inefficiencies in communication and coordination, the very functions that hierarchical structures are supposed to support.

In recent years, more attention has been paid to organizational processes that cross functional boundaries (see, for example, Hammer and Champy (1993) and Rummler and Brache (1990)). One approach that has gained a fair amount of popularity, partly because it can be used without creating excessive disruptions to the current organizational structure, is the *cross-functional team*. Cross-functional teams are made up of specialists from different functional areas, often brought together on an ad hoc basis, to perform some organizational task in a more effective, more timely manner. In the preface to his book on cross-functional teams, Parker notes that "In many organizations, eight or more disciplines are working together on cross-functional teams to bring a new product to the market, develop a next generation computer system, design a new layout for a factory floor, produce an important new drug, engineer a complex telecommunications network, prepare a long-term corporate strategy, or implement a procedure to upgrade service in a government agency" (1994, p. xii). While cross-functional teams may begin to sound like a panacea, they also pose new challenges for managers who must figure out how to manage a cross-functional team whose members still often report to a functional manager on the organizational chart.

In the next section, we discuss some of the specific challenges that are raised when cross-functional teams are used within traditional work structures. This is followed by an illustrative example of the use of a cross-functional product development team. The chapter concludes with some guidelines for managing cross-functional teams.

CROSS-FUNCTIONAL TEAMS WITHIN TRADITIONAL WORK STRUCTURES

In the Chapter 6 (the Director Role), one of the competencies focuses on organizational design. Because some of these issues are germane to our present focus on cross-functional management, we briefly present some key concepts and assume that you will explore them in greater depth in the next chapter. We also explore specific challenges for managing cross-functionally in an organization that is more traditionally structured.

Following the principles of Adam Smith and Henri Fayol, organizations have tended to create departments that handle the different functions of the organizations. When departments within a single organization are structured differently so that they can each approach their own task in a way that is most efficient for that particular department, we refer to this as *differentiation*. In traditionally designed organizations, differentiation is accomplished through the creation of specialized jobs and work units that are then hierarchically organized. Thus, the organization's work is performed by individual contributors. Performance management and reward systems focus on the individual performer. Job evaluations and job descriptions clearly specify who does what and who reports to whom. Status differentiations are made clear by labels such as "labor" and "management," "bonus eligible" and "bonus ineligible," and so on. Organizational subunits typically consist of individuals with similar expertise performing similar tasks—engineers engineering, marketers marketing, and manufacturing experts manufacturing. Careers are focused on moving up the hierarchy, rather than on adding value to the output of the organization. The size of budget and number of people one manages are symbols of position and power, and may suggest that the organization is more interested in hierarchical control than in the delivery of products or services to a customer (Mohrman, 1993).

When an organization is so differentiated as a consequence of its traditional structure, there is a need for *integration*, or the coordination of work across units. Integration is primarily accomplished by processes inherent in the organizational hierarchy. Processes and procedures are standardized and formalized, and specify how the work is to be done and the sequence by which it is to proceed through the organization. Individual contributors are managed, directed, controlled, and coordinated by middle-level managers who receive strategic guidance from senior-level executives. Galbraith (1973), however, points out that while these types of integrative processes work for relatively simple and static situations, their effectiveness is limited in complex, dynamic, and turbulent environments. The rules of competition and the characteristics of organizations that are successfully competing in today's global market suggest that the current organizational environment is anything but static and simple. Mohrman states that the situation faced by today's organization is characterized by "complexity and extreme performance pressures" (1993, p. 113). Consequently, the challenge confronting organizations in the next decade is to "simultaneously" accomplish the following (1993, p. 113):

> Achieve multiple focuses (on product, market, customer, and geography) without dysfunctionally segmenting the organization.

> Align individuals and groups that are task-interdependent in a manner that fosters teamwork in pursuit of shared overall objectives.

Enable quick, low-cost, high-quality performance while responding to a highly dynamic environment that calls for ongoing change.

Respond to ongoing increases in competitive performance standards by learning how to be more effective.

Attract, motivate, develop, and retain employees who are able to operate effectively in such a demanding organizational environment.

While some organizations are "throwing away their organizational charts in favor of ever-changing constellations of teams, projects, and alliances" (Dumaine 1991, p. 36), many organizations are attempting to manage these challenges within a more traditional structure. The challenge is then to identify processes and devices that are consistent with the complex and dynamic environment that the organization faces, and that allow organizations to integrate and coordinate their efforts within the constraints of what may still be a traditionally designed and structured organizational chart. It is the challenge of trying to create ad hoc structures that both transcend and operate within a traditional organizational design. This is the challenge of managing across functions.

Here we list several specific challenges that are faced by cross-functional project teams. Because many cross-functional teams are formed as a result of a need to respond quickly to competitive pressures, the list focuses on challenges associated with forming a team of strangers (Parker, 1994) to work together in an integrated fashion to produce a product faster than was previously possible when management coordinated the work across the different functional areas.

The need for a clear charter and consistent support from senior management.

The need for a project or product champion, as well as functional champions.

The need for early involvement of all relevant functional areas.

The need to co-locate cross-functional teams.

The need for efficient allocation of work across functional areas.

The need for speed in the focusing of energy and resources.

The need for new and better ways to hear the "voice of the customer."

The need for a clearly defined process for cross-functional decision making.

The need for process disciplines and schedule integrity, that is, a need for well-defined, time-based approaches for performing the work.

In the next section, these challenges will be illustrated by a specific example of a cross-functional product development team in the late 1980s.

AN ILLUSTRATION OF THE NEED FOR MANAGING CROSS-FUNCTIONALLY: THE STORY OF HEWLETT-PACKARD'S DESKJET PRINTER

In this section we present the story of Hewlett-Packard's development of the Deskjet printer to illustrate the potential of a well-managed cross-functional team. The illustration draws largely from the chapter on Hewletts-Packard in the book *The Perpetual Enterprise Machine* (Bowen et al., 1994), and is a good example of how team members from different functional areas can put aside those differences when they have a clear goal and an understanding that a quick response to competitive pressures requires an integrated focusing of energy and resources.

Prior to 1982, Hewlett-Packard, Digital Equipment Corporation, and IBM each sold their printers (along with other peripherals) with their computer products. In that year, Japanese competitors began to market a standalone printer and within a few years, one company, Epson, dominated the general-purpose low-end market with 80 percent of market share. In 1985, prototype inkjet printers hit the market. HP had the edge on this market since the inkjet technology was invented at HP labs, but these printers made little progress since they were more expensive, were not as reliable as impact printers, and, initially, required special paper. While they offered better resolution and increased flexibility in type style, inkjet printers could not compete against the increasingly sophisticated dot-matrix printers. Shortly after that, laser printers became available and became the best quality (and highest cost) option, offering the highest resolution.

In 1979, HP's Vancouver Division had been formed to build and market impact printers (printers where a lettering device hits the page). By 1985, however, given the changing market, the division was facing increasing competitive pressures and profits were steadily declining. That year, the division's charter was expanded to include development of printers using HP's proprietary inkjet technology, and by the end of the year, the division, with the support of group management, embraced a new "charter"—to focus on the development of a printer for the low-end personal and office market.

The division reacted quickly and placed all its energy and resources on one machine—the Deskjet. The strategic objective was to wedge a niche between lower-priced and lower-quality impact printers and higher-priced, higher-quality laser products by building an inkjet printer with resolution approximating that of a laser printer, but with a price that was significantly lower. In fact, the intention was to market the printer at a price that was so low it would essentially eliminate sales of impact and dot-matrix printers for general computer usage. The division was confident that it could accomplish this goal knowing that: (1) the technology was invented at HP labs; (2) two key managerial leaders in the "puzzle," the Vancouver division R&D manager and the Deskjet project manager, were champions of the technology; and (3) the Deskjet project team had been experimenting with the technology for a few years. Nevertheless, there was still a huge challenge ahead—developing a product that could come close to laser-quality printer standards at a low cost.

The life cycles for printers in the low-end niche of the business were short, averaging about two years. The next generation of printer following the Deskjet would be ready in 15 months; the Deskjet was seen as an interim step in the development of a longer-term strategy for the low-end printer business. Although senior management at HP did not micromanage, they left no doubts that the future of the division was riding on the Deskjet printer. Their charter to the division was to find a path to solid footing in the market. They allowed the project team to identify specific goals. The team formulated one very specific goal that everyone on the division could understand and relate to—create a printer with laserlike quality with a retail price below $1,000. The manager of the division reinforced the group's goal by stating, "If you are not working on Deskjet, then you are just rearranging the deck chairs on the Titanic" (quoted in Bowen et al., 1994, p. 420).

Execution of the project required the most effective management of a cross-functional team. A key component of the product, the print head, required major development work. It was to be developed and manufactured by the components operation in Corvallis, Oregon—a two-hour drive from Vancouver by car. Because of this, the team decided to lower its risks and take as much pressure as possible off of the print head effort by assuming additional design tasks in Vancouver. Another major challenge was to cut costs by maximizing the extent to which the product was designed for manufacture. The principle strategy the team adopted for doing this was to minimize the total number of parts in the printer, thereby simplifying assembly, the handling of parts, and purchasing. This meant that manufacturing and suppliers had to be involved early.

Perhaps the greatest challenge that the team faced was confronting a marketplace in which it had virtually no experience. The Deskjet would compete in the fiercely competitive high-volume, dealer-oriented marketplace. If the Deskjet was to accomplish its role in winning the market, the inexperienced marketing team would have to rely heavily on its fellow functions operating in new ways, taking on roles that they had never taken on before. Team members from marketing, R&D, and manufacturing and suppliers would have to operate in a highly integrated cross-functional mode if they were to have any chance of succeeding in this new situation.

Marketing made what was considered extraordinary efforts to hear and understand the voice of its potential customers. HP realized that Deskjet would appeal to ordinary and typical computer users, and so it sought out those customers in an ordinary and typical place—the shopping mall. HP team members actually asked potential customers how they felt about proposed features. While the design engineers were initially reluctant and disbelieving, they became convinced when they went out to the malls themselves and personally talked with potential customers. R&D understood the importance of early involvement of manufacturing and arranged for a dedicated manufacturing engineering group to be assigned only to the Deskjet. From the very beginning, materials engineers had compiled a "materials checklist," which by its presence alone served as a cost focal point for the team, in particular with suppliers.

The team also followed a strict process discipline during the prototyping process. Each month, regardless of whether R&D had completed its share of work on a prototype, manufacturing performed its role—building 50 prototype units. This represented a major cultural shift at HP. In the past, design engineers dominated the prototyping schedule, allowing themselves to tweak many last-minute changes into a prototype before it was tested. A positive outcome of this new process discipline was that marketing and manufacturing could confidently use the prototyping process to focus on customer needs rather than on the whims of the designers.

Perhaps the most critical aspect of the team's success was its success at integration. From the project's beginning, marketing and manufacturing people were moved into the lab to sit with the R&D engineers. This "co-location" resulted in very strong integration among the three functional teams, something that had previously been atypical at HP where R&D engineers had typically led the charge alone. In this case, R&D saw itself as the champion for resources for manufacturing. The R&D functional manager occupied a dual role of managing the R&D engineers and as a member of the "core group," the key decision-making body that was made up of one person from each of the three functions—R&D, marketing, and manufacturing. While taking a lead role in this group, the R&D functional manager always emphasized the equality of all team members.

Overall, the team had striking drive and energy. The reality that the division's future rested heavily on the project's success or failure generated much commitment and ownership. There was also a unique synergy between top management and the team via the guiding vision of the project. Senior management had provided a clear goal: steal back market share. But they had also given another clear message: It was the responsibility of the division to make decisions that would make the goal a reality.

KEY GUIDELINES FOR MANAGING CROSS-FUNCTIONALLY

The story of the HP's success in developing the Deskjet printer provides several practical lessons regarding key aspects of effectively managing across functions. Here we present a list of guidelines that, although derived largely from other sources (Dumaine, 1991, Meyer, 1993, Parker, 1994), are well-illustrated by the story of the Deskjet.

1. **Clarify goals and charter and get team buy-in.** The cross-functional team will generally take the formal charge from senior management, but the team must also feel ownership over the goals. In Chapter 3 (the Facilitator Role), we discussed the importance of being committed to a common goal or purpose and indicated that this is the glue that holds the team together. Sometimes the cross-functional team will need to meet with senior management to negotiate the goal or to make sure that there is a shared understanding. In the case of the Deskjet printer, senior management made it clear that it wanted to retrieve market share in the low-end printer market; the product development team then set a more specific goal of creating a printer with laserlike quality with a retail price below $1,000.

2. **Seek to create a critical mass of leadership.** While a single functional unit can generally get by with a single leader, most cross-functional groups cannot. If the ultimate purpose of cross-functional teams is to make optimal

use of people from across different functions, each of these functions must have a strong leadership voice. In addition, this is a good time to take advantage of team members' unique talents. Kenan Sahin, president of a software consulting firm in Cambridge, Massachusetts, asserts that in order for organizations to truly take advantage of each person's talents, managers will have to learn how to follow, allowing the person who knows the most about the subject to lead (Dumaine, 1991).

3. **Hold the team and its members accountable for its performance.** Once team members have bought into the goals, they must also buy into the process. Everyone must feel responsible for the team's performance. Team goals should be translated into clear short term objectives and milestones that are constantly visible and in the forefront of everyone's thinking. While senior management should avoid micromanaging, they should hold the team to standards. When standards are not met, questions should be raised in a way that team members feel supported, rather than attacked.

   At Becton Dickinson, a maker of high-tech medical equipment, a team was given responsibility to develop a new instrument to process blood samples. While the team developed the instrument 25 percent faster than its previous best effort, the CEO felt this was not fast enough. After some research, senior management found the problem in the decision-making structure. Rather than blame the group, they created a new decision-making structure (Dumaine, 1991).

4. **Keep cross-functional teams as small as possible with critical functional representation.** While the purpose of creating a team is to bring together a diverse set of perspectives, years of research on group processes shows that as group size increases there is a loss of productivity that results from increased time devoted to coordination and communication. One estimate of productivity loss indicates that in groups with as few as five people between 10 and 30 percent of team members' time is spent in communicating with other team members about the task (Parker, 1994). Alternatively, if there is not sufficient representation of all functional areas from the very beginning, the team will be not be able to perform effectively. One solution is to break up the large group into smaller groups, with each small group having representation on a central decision-making group. In the example of the HP Deskjet, the product development team had a small "core group" that made key decisions.

   In addition to determining the optimal team size, finding the right mix of people is critical. If all functional areas are represented, but one team member cannot see the value of working on a cross-functional team, size will quickly become a secondary issue.

5. **Provide the cross-functional team with constantly updated and relevant information.** If an organization is to make heavy use of cross-functional teams,

it must essentially "rewire" the information system so that cross-functional teams have ready access to the information they need to do their jobs. In the previous section on designing work, we emphasized the notion that in order for employees to make intelligent decisions, they need to have key information that will allow them to make those decisions. The term "informate" has been coined to describe the use of technology to provide people with information that will allow them to make decisions that were once only made by management (Peters, 1994). Again, optimal effectiveness of cross-functional teams will be achieved only if these teams are given what was formerly assumed to be the prerogatives of management: authority to make decisions and the information with which to make these decisions in the most reasonable way.

6. **Train members in teamwork and process management.** Operating in cross-functional teams with complex and fuzzy authority and reporting relationships necessitates that members know the core skills of teamwork. In Chapter 3, we presented some of these core skills, including defining roles and responsibilities, managing conflict, using participative decision making, and managing meetings. As was noted in that chapter, teamwork does not develop naturally. There needs to be a conscious effort to develop as a team, and organizations must often be willing to make the investment to give people training in interpersonal skills.

Similarly, people are not inherently knowledgeable about managing processes. As was made clear in the HP Deskjet example, a clear understanding of the various processes that must be mastered in the completion of a project or task is critical. The section on managing projects in this chapter provides an introduction to the key elements of managing processes.

7. **Clarify expectations within and between teams.** Each individual that is part of a cross-functional team has three responsibility perspectives: the team, the function, and the larger organization. Each of these should be clearly articulated before the start of the project. Moreover, leaders of cross-functional teams must have the ability to develop effective relationships with key stakeholders, including leaders of functional departments, senior management sponsors, and other resource people in the organization. In the section on managing projects, earlier in this chapter, we presented the notion of internal and external integration and suggested that regular communication with key project stakeholders was an important element of managing projects. It is even more so if the project is being carried out by a cross-functional team where the definition of who is internal and who is external can become somewhat blurred. While it is clear that all organizations have multiple and often competing goals, these competing goals cannot become a barrier to effective cross-functional team management. An organization will be able to use cross-functional teams effectively only if team members and others in the organization identify first with the larger organization, and secondarily with their functional units.

One step that is often useful here is the co-location of team members. That is, whenever possible, cross-functional team members should be located as close as possible, "in the same building, on the same floor, and in the same area" (Parker, 1994, p. 78). Physical proximity allows for more regular and more informal interactions. Co-locating team project members also sends a very clear message regarding the importance of the project.

8. **Encourage team members to be willing to step out of their roles.** As a corollary to the previous guideline, we suggest that people must not only be willing to step out of their functional identity to "put on an organizational hat," they must also be willing to step out of their status or rank identity in order to allow for more optimal use of everyone's unique skills and abilities. As noted in the second guideline, the increasing use of cross-functional teams suggests that more and more, "leaders" on one project will be "followers" on the next. As we discussed in the previous section on designing work teams, the most successful teams are ones that are able to manage the paradoxes that are associated with having clearly defined roles and responsibilities, while simultaneously expecting that everyone does everything that needs to be done.

ANALYSIS   Errors in the Design?[1]

Directions   Read the paragraph below. It comes from a real situation encountered in one of the Big Three automobile manufacturers. Diagnose the errors that might have been made in managing across the various functional areas that were involved in designing the automobile.

The total amount of electrical power in a vehicle is determined by the capacity of the alternator. The power must serve over twenty subsystems, such as the stereo, the engine, the instrument panel, and so on. These subsystems are developed and controlled by separate "chimney" organizations, and power allocations must be made for each subsystem. The problem was, in this vehicle program, when the requirements of all the chimneys and teams were added up, they equaled 125% of the capacity of the alternator. Keith, who had recently taken over as head of this vehicle program [which had made changes in direction and was behind schedule to begin with], called a meeting of the Program Steering Committee designed to resolve this conflict and reach a compromise. However, many of the chimney representatives who were members of the team came to this meeting with instructions from their bosses [who, incidentally, did their performance appraisals] *not* to make any compromises, but to make certain that their chimney "got what it needed" and "didn't lose out." After Keith presented the group with the problem and the need to reach a compromise solution, their response surprised him: "It's not our problem," they replied, "it's *your* problem."

Questions   1. What advice would you give Keith for dealing with the Program Steering Committee?

[1] *Source:* Denison, Dan, Stuart Hart, and Joel Kahn. "From Chimneys to Cross-functional Teams: Developing and Validating a Diagnostic Model," Working Paper, University of Michigan, 1993. Used with permission.

2. Which other key stakeholders should Keith deal with? What advice would you give him for dealing with these other key stakeholders?

3. If Keith could "turn back the hands of time," what advice would you have given him at the beginning of this project? Be as specific as possible in your advice.

PRACTICE   Student Orientation Revisited

Directions   In the Assessment exercise, you were asked to put together an outline on how you would approach coordinating a universitywide student orientation. In groups of five to ten people, role play a first meeting of the team organizing the orientation. One person should take the role of University Student Services Association president. Others should take the roles of representatives of other university organizations that had, in the past, run their own orientations.

By the end of your meeting you should have clarified your goal, determined a list of tasks to be carried out and assigned everyone specific responsibilities, and identified key external stakeholders with whom you will have to work.

APPLICATION   Examining a Cross-Functional Team

Identify a situation that you are currently in at school, at work, or in some other formal organization that has "cross-functional" elements to it. Analyze the situation in terms of the guidelines presented in this section. In analyzing the situation, find specific ways in which the situation is being managed well, as well as problems. When you identify a problem, try to determine its specific source(s). That is, instead of saying "Meetings do not accomplish anything," try to determine if the cause of the problem is that goals are not clear, the wrong people are attending the meeting, the person running the meeting has not appropriately organized the meeting, and so on. Suggest ways to improve the "operations."

REFERENCES

Alster, Norm. "What Flexible Workers Can Do," *Fortune* (February 13, 1989): 62–66.

Badiru, Adedji Bodunde. *Quantitative Models for Project Planning, Scheduling and Control.* Westport, Conn.: Quorum Books, 1993.

Bowen, H. Kent, Kim B. Clark, Charles A. Holloway, and Steven C. Wheelwright (eds.). *The Perpetual Enterprise Machine.* New York: Oxford University Press, 1994.

Bridges, William. "The End of the Job," *Fortune* (September 19, 1994): 62–74.

Business Week. "Rethinking Work," *Business Week* (October 17, 1994): 74–117.

Denison, Dan, Stuart Hart, and Joel Kahn. "From Chimneys to Cross-Functional Teams: Developing and Validating a Diagnostic Model," Working Paper, University of Michigan, 1993.

Dertouzes, Michael L., Richard K. Lester, Robert M. Solow, and the MIT Commission on

Industrial Productivity. *Made in America: Regaining the Productive Edge.* Cambridge, Mass.: MIT Press, 1989.

Dumaine, Brian. "Who Needs a Boss?" *Fortune* (May 7, 1990): 52–60.

———. "The Bureaucracy Busters," *Fortune* (June 17, 1991): 36–50.

Galbraith, Jay R. *Designing Complex Organizations.* Reading, Mass.: Addison-Wesley, 1973.

Gundry, Lisa K., Jill R. Kickul, and Charles Prather. "Building the Creative Organization," *Organizational Dynamics* 22 (Spring 1994): 22–37.

Hackman, J. Richard, and Greg Oldham. "Development of the Job Diagnostic Survey," *Journal of Applied Psychology* 60 (1975): 159–170.

Hackman, J. Richard, Greg Oldham, Robert Janson, and Kenneth Purdy. "A New Strategy for Job Enrichment," *California Management Review* 17(4) (1975): 57–71.

Hammer, Michael, and James Champy. *Reengineering the Corporation: A Manifesto for Business Revolution.* New York: HarperBusiness, 1993.

Harrison, F. L. *Advanced Project Management: A Structured Approach.* New York: Halsted Press, 1992.

Henkoff, Ronald. "Finding, Training and Keeping the Best Service Workers," *Fortune* (October 3, 1994): 110–122.

Herzberg, Fredrick. "One More Time: How Do You Motivate Employees," *Harvard Business Review* 46 (January–February 1968): 53–62.

House, Ruth Sizemore. *The Human Side of Project Management.* Reading, Mass.: Addison-Wesley, 1988.

Kerzner, Harold. *Project Management: A Systems Approach to Planning, Scheduling, and Controlling* (3rd ed.). New York: Van Nostrand Reinhold, 1989.

Kimmons, Robert L. *Project Management Basics: A Step by Step Approach.* New York: Marcel Dekker, 1990.

Lawler, Edward E., III. *The Ultimate Advantage: Creating the High-Involvement Organization,* San Francisco: Jossey-Bass, 1992.

Meyer, Christopher. *Fast Cycle Time.* New York: Free Press, 1993.

Mohrman, Susan Albers. "Integrating Roles and Structures in the Lateral Organization," in *Organizing for the Future,* Jay R. Galbraith, Edward E. Lawler III, & associates (eds.). San Francisco: Jossey-Bass, 1993.

Parker, Glenn M. *Cross-Functional Teams: Working with Allies, Enemies, and Other Strangers.* San Francisco: Jossey-Bass, 1994.

Peters, Tom. *The Tom Peters Seminar: Crazy Times Call for Crazy Organizations.* New York: Vintage Books, 1994.

Roman, Daniel D. *Managing Projects: A Systems Approach.* New York: Elsevier Science Publishing, 1986.

Rummler, Geary A., and Alan P. Brache. *Improving Performance: How to Manage the White Space on the Organization Chart.* San Francisco: Jossey-Bass, 1990.

Smith, Adam. *The Wealth of Nations* (1776). New York: Random House, 1937.

Spinner, M. Pete. *Improving Project Management Skills and Techniques.* Englewood Cliffs, N. J.: Prentice-Hall, 1989.

Taylor, Frederick W. *The Principles of Scientific Management.* New York: Harper & Row, 1911.

Thornberry, Neal E. "Training the Engineer as Project Manager: How to Turn Technical Types into Top-Notch Project Managers," *Training and Development Journal* (October 1987): 60–62.

The Monitor and Coordinator Roles

As we did at the end of the mentor and facilitator chapters (Chapters 2 and 3), let us now put the monitor and coordinator roles in the context of the full competing values framework before moving on to the next quadrant. As with the other roles, you will find that these roles are more appropriate in some situations and less appropriate in others. It is important for you to think about those situations where you will need to call upon the competencies associated with the monitor and coordinator roles.

A BRIEF REVIEW

The monitor and coordinator roles are part of the internal process model. In this model the desired ends are stability and control and the assumed means to these ends have to do with routinization, measurement, and documentation. In this quadrant we are most concerned with maintaining a smooth workflow and a smooth flow of information, and managerial leaders are expected to monitor the situation that surrounds them and to use analytical tools to control the processes. This model assumes that in generating organizational structures, such as rules, policies, and procedures, the manager can see to it that things stay in equilibrium.

WHEN THE MONITOR AND COORDINATOR ROLES ARE APPROPRIATE

Again, the two axes show us when it is appropriate to draw on the competencies associated with the internal process model. On the horizontal axis the model, like the human relations model is defined by an internal focus, again suggesting less external pressure for action and more internal pressure for communication, coordination, and conformity. On the vertical axis, the internal process model is defined by high control, which suggests that it is most useful when situations are well understood or when there is a need for maintaining consistency in production or delivery of service. When a situation does not require fast action (minimal external pressures) and the basic goals are well defined, things are more easily routinized or standardized.

Moreover, in some situations, we need routinization. For example, imagine a situation where buses, trains, and planes ran according to a different schedule each day, or one where business and government offices felt free to change their hours of operation arbitrarily. What would it be like if organizations did not monitor the quality of their output or if when you arrived at work each day you could not be certain that you would find the materials and supplies you needed to do your job properly? Clearly there are times that call for a standard or routine to be maintained. The monitor and coordinator roles are most applicable when there is a need for stability and continuity.

COMPLEMENTARY ROLES

With each of the organizational effectiveness models, there will be people who most value the effectiveness criteria associated with that model. As a result, they will most likely also feel more comfortable with the managerial leadership roles in that quadrant and so may tend to overuse those roles. Overusing the monitor and coordinator roles would result in maintaining the status quo when it is time to change, creating rules and procedures for the sake of having rules and procedures, and analyzing situations down to the most minute detail when seeing the big picture is more important. The failure to balance and blend the monitor and coordinator roles with the other roles, particularly with the innovator and broker roles in the open systems quadrant, can lead to problems. Indeed, this notion surfaced within the discussions of each role as both made reference to the need to be aware of external issues.

A classic example of the need to blend the coordinator and monitor roles with other roles is seen in the story of Henry Ford. Ford was a determined entrepreneur with a vision. He wanted to build an automobile for the common man. He felt that if he could provide a dependable vehicle and sell it at a low price, he could become rich by selling the car in huge volume. His first big step was to apply the principles of scientific management to the production process, making great strides in efficient production. For example, he reduced the assembly time for the automobile from many hundreds of hours to a little over 90 minutes. This very innovative man became very rich. While he continued to be innovative about production, he became too oriented to routinization and standardization, and allowed no changes in his car. His philosophy, in fact, is reflected in his famous statement, "They can have any color they want, as long as it's black." With hindsight, the outcome was predictable and disastrous: Ford, the unquestioned leader in automobile production soon fell behind General Motors and would never again match them in size. Later the company was forced to close for a year while they moved to the new Model A.

Clearly the roles in the internal process quadrant must be seen in context and must be used appropriately. Stability and continuity are important values in an organization, but there is also value in flexibility and change. When managerial leaders become too focused on the internal processes of the organization (work and information flow), they lose awareness of the organization's environment and are thus not able to help the organization adapt when changes in the external environment require new internal processes. Alternatively, in the recent efforts to keep up with the global economy we have created many internal organizational changes that have, in many cases, encountered resistance from employees who feel that change is occurring for its own sake, rather than as a result of careful analysis of the situation. It is the managerial leader's job, in the roles of the monitor, coordinator, innovator, and broker, to see to it that these orientations are appropriately balanced.

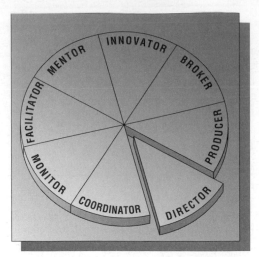

THE DIRECTOR ROLE

6

■ COMPETENCIES

Visioning, Planning, and Goal Setting

Designing and Organizing

Delegating Effectively

The director role in many ways defines the stereotypical "strong" or "great" leader. Leaders who excel in this role provide a vision that others can follow. They are seen as strong or great leaders because they take charge and make things happen. The competencies we have chosen to frame this role include:

Competency 1 Visioning, Planning, and Goal Setting
Competency 2 Designing and Organizing
Competency 3 Delegating Effectively

These three competencies are all very much of the same cloth. Together they constitute the most basic activities of managing and organizing—namely, identifying a clear, motivating, challenging vision and direction; building an architecture to implement that vision and direction; and empowering and enabling organizational members to carry out and implement that vision and catalyzing action. A good example of a strong director is Herb Kelleher, founder and head of Southwest Airlines, who was characterized by *Fortune* magazine in 1994 as "one of a kind," and, perhaps, America's best CEO.

214

HERB KELLEHER, FOUNDER AND HEAD OF SOUTHWEST AIRLINES

The airline industry has proved to be one of the most complex and competitive businesses in the Untied States over the past decade. It has, however, given us several very interesting leaders who are good examples of our director (and producer for that matter) role mode. Three particularly interesting leaders are Robert Crandall of American Airlines, Frank Lorenzo from what was Texas Air, and Southwest Airlines founder and head herb Kelleher. Lorenzo is no longer a part of the industry—one of many casualties in a series of industry traumas. After experiencing great success in capitalizing Texas Air Corporation, Lorenzo was not able to build the internal relationships and coalitions necessary to make it a continuing success. He had a particularly difficult time with a large number of dislocated Eastern Airlines workers: "They loved their work and their airline, but hated Lorenzo" (Quick, 1992, p. 47). Lorenzo perhaps excessively emphasized the rational goal criteria organizationally and individually. Clearly he could not balance his aggressiveness and drive for his company's success with an appropriate concern for the criteria of the human relations model (see Chapters 2 and 3).

Crandall and Kelleher have been more successful during deregulation and both also exhibit strength in the director role. In a study of the role of the founder and the airline organization culture, James Campbell Quick observed the following about Crandall:

> A fierce visionary with competitive anger, Crandall hammered out for himself a position of leadership among the major carriers. Temperamental, obsessive about details, and super aggressive, Crandall has nonetheless managed to meld functional relationships with his many internal stake-holders. While these relationships, as with the pilots in late 1991, may at times be testy and stormy, Crandall directs most of his aggression toward corporate achievement, not toward damaging key internal relationships (Quick, 1992, p. 47).

Herb Kelleher was a New York University Law School graduate. This proved invaluable training for the legal battles that were part and parcel of the airline business over the past several decades. While Southwest was clearly in the midst of legal battles with some of its competitors, it was not engaged in scorched-earth battles with its competitors. In fact, Herb Kelleher is renowned for his robust sense of humor. Although while Kelleher may be more inclined to crack a joke and Crandall to crack a whip, both are seen as quite demanding.

While Delta, United, and American have lost billions over the past four years, Southwest has accomplished the following: winner of the first Triple Crown Award, 1988 (best on-time record, best baggage handling, and fewest customer complaints in a single month)—the first and only airline to win the award; winner of the second Triple Crown Award in 1989; winner of the third and fourth Triple Crown Awards, 1990 and 1991; honored with *Air Transport World's* Airline of the Year Award in 1991; ranked #1 in customer satisfaction among all major U.S. airlines in 1991; winner of the fifth Triple Crown Award, 1991; winner of the sixth and seventh Triple Crown Awards in 1992—and *still* the only airline to have earned the Triple Crown Award.

Southwest Airlines, an operation based on carrying passengers relatively short distances for prices that are very low, has evolved into a business with over a billion dollars in revenues annually and a fleet of over one hundred aircraft. It is the seventh largest airline in the United States by virtue of passengers boarded and potentially the most profitable airline of the last twenty years. From a productivity standpoint, Southwest also shines brightly. The U.S. airline industry average net profits (loss) per

HERB KELLEHER . . . CONTINUED

employee for 1991 was $3,505—Southwest's was $2,753; operating profits (loss) per employee for the industry was $3,230—for Southwest it was $6,436;—industry average passengers/employee, 8438—Southwest, 2318; industry average employees per aircraft 131-Southwest, 79; industry average available seat miles/employee, 1,339,995—Southwest, 1,891,082; and industry average revenue passenger miles/employee, 839,552—Southwest, 1,155,265 (American Transport Association, 1991). The U.S. Department of Transportation concluded in 1993 that Southwest was the "principal driving force for changes occurring in the airline industry" (*Fortune*, May 2, 1994, p. 45).

No matter what one thinks of his sense of humor, his airline's unconventional practice of seating passengers without seat assignments, his no frills policy, his flight attendants dressed in bermuda shorts and flowered shirts, and boarding and safety announcements that would rival many comedy club monologues—Herb Kelleher is a very shrewd managerial leader. Kelleher is able to address both the nitty-gritty aspects of the rational goal model—productivity, efficiency, timeliness, and cost-effectiveness—and the human relations concerns that must be addressed without appearing harsh or patronizing.

Kelleher well exemplifies the three competencies we have chosen to frame the director role—visioning, planning, and goal setting; designing and organizing; and delegating effectively. Kelleher's vision is reflected in core values, beliefs, and assumptions of the company: (1) Work should be fun—it can be play—enjoy it; (2) Work is important—don't spoil it with seriousness; (3) People are important—each one makes a difference. These values are sometimes recast as humor, altruism, and "luv." Most importantly, Kelleher's every word, deed, and act of symbolic leadership clarifies, reinforces, and promotes these core values. The bond between the company and many of the workers is so strong that some have compared Southwest to a religion. Herb Kelleher relishes such observations—he suggests that the operation maintains a "patina of spirituality" . . . "I feel that you have to be with you employees through all their difficulties, that you have to be interested in them personally. They may be disappointed in their country. Even their family might not be working out the way they wish it would. But I want them to know that Southwest will always be there for them" (*Fortune*, May 2, 1994, p. 50).

The Southwest organization is "designed" with goal accomplishment and customer satisfaction (one and the same for Southwest) first and foremost—whatever it takes to get the job done by whomever. Pilots have been known to help with baggage in order to attain an on-time departure. The flexible and loosely defined job responsibilities (only pilots fly the planes, however) at Southwest make delegating effectively almost a nonissue. In many ways the Southwest organization epitomizes the rational goal perspective. Southwest's distribution system is starkly different from all of the competition's. It is not linked up to any of the computer reservation systems travel agents use—hence saving the company almost 30 million dollars per year. The airline also avoids the hub-and spoke systems used by the other carriers, utilizes less congested airports, flies one type of aircraft (Boeing 737s), and does not assign seats, serve food other than peanuts, or check through bags from one destination to the next even on other Southwest flights. The company is severely cost conscious (*Fortune*, May 2, 1994, pp. 46–47). Each of these practices positively affects the bottom line. Kelleher's leadership seems thus far to have successfully managed the tension between the rational goal and human relations quadrants.

Competency 1 Visioning, Planning, and Goal Setting

ASSESSMENT PART I: Understanding the Big Picture

Project yourself into the future—to the age that you would ideally like to live to. Write a two-page article that you would like to appear in the local newspaper the week after you have gone to your eternal reward. How would you like yourself and your life to be characterized in that article? What would you like to have identified as your "legacy"? What would you have liked to have accomplished? What do you want to be most fondly remembered for? What would you like others to most admire you for when you have departed?

Hint: In order to be able to complete this assessment, you must be able to answer the following questions now:

Where will you be in twenty years and what will you be doing?

What are your key success factors?

What are the most important things (what do you value most) in your life?

What are the core values that define you as a unique individual?

ASSESSMENT PART II: Personal and Organizational Goal Setting

Directions The following questions are designed to help you assess how well goal setting processes are working in your personal and work lives. Indicate how much you agree or disagree with each statement. When you finish, review the items that received the lowest scores.

Scale

Strongly disagree	Disagree	Neutral	Agree	Strongly agree
1	2	3	4	5

At School and in My Personal Life

____ 1. I am proactive rather than reactive.

____ 2. I set aside enough time and resources to study and complete projects.

____ 3. I am able to budget money to buy the things I really want without going broke.

____ 4. I have thought through what I want to do in school.

____ 5. I have a plan for completing my major.

____ 6. My goals for the future are realistic.

At Work (complete only if you have work experience)

_____ 1. We are proactive rather than reactive.

_____ 2. Policies, programs, and procedures are developed in an integrated fashion.

_____ 3. Time and resources are committed to set goals and objectives.

_____ 4. We work on forecasting future opportunities and threats.

_____ 5. The overall mission is clear to all.

_____ 6. Goal-setting processes take place at the organizational, unit, and individual level.

_____ 7. There are written goals and objectives.

_____ 8. There are long-range goals and objectives.

_____ 9. There is short-range objective setting.

_____ 10. Goals and objectives are realistic.

_____ 11. Goals and objectives are challenging.

_____ 12. Goals and objectives are reviewed and modified on a regular cycle.

_____ 13. Accomplishment of goals and objectives is tied to a reward system.

_____ 14. Pursuing goals and objectives is a productive activity.

Interpretation

The goal setting assessment helps you focus on basic aspects of goal setting processes in your personal and professional or school life. There are several keys to making *any* goal setting process effective and we discuss those throughout the Learning section below. Our intent with this brief assessment is to get you thinking about goal setting as it relates to you school, personal, and work settings.

In the first part of the assessment, we focus on whether your personal goal setting is *passive* or *active*. Question 1 queries your general tendency around "action" and questions 4 and 5 select a specific example of proaction vs. reaction (i.e., having a plan for completing your major). *Allocating "resources"* for the completion of goals is queried in questions 2 and 3. Question 6 focuses on a cornerstone of effective goal setting: creating goals that are *attainable,* yet *challenging.* If your score on any of these questions is "3" or less, you should pay particular attention to the corresponding material in the Learning section below.

In the second part of the assessment we ask you to focus on the goal setting processes of an organizational unit that you may work in or have knowledge about. Questions 1, 6, and 12 focus on the extent to which goal setting is an *integral part* of a work unit's operation (i.e., proactive, at all organizational levels, predictable, periodic intervals). The extent to which goal setting processes are *supported by other organizational* factors is queried in questions 2, 3, and 139 i.e., consistent policies, procedures; appropriate allocations of time and resources, goal setting linked to reward systems). The *comprehensiveness* of organizational goal setting is the focus of questions 4, 5, and 7–9 (i.e., goal setting proceeds from a clear mission, incldues short- and long-range considerations, formalized or written). Questions 10, 11, and 14 address the *appropriateness* of goals (i.e., attainable, challenging, worthwhile).

If the organizational unit you assessed scored low in any of these areas, you may want to pay special attention to the corresponding discussions in the Learning section below for potential improvement suggestions.

LEARNING   Visioning, Planning, and Goal Setting

The topics of visioning, planning, and goal setting could individually fill several textbooks each. Our approach here is to look at them as constituting an integrated competency that in many ways is the foundation of the director role. Typically, the three topics are viewed hierarchically: Begin with a grand "vision" (often embodied in or by a visionary and charismatic leader), formulate a long-term plan (often referred to as strategy and strategic planning), and identify specific organizational plans and goals (and objectives) to be attained. Organizational goals then (ideally) get translated into various subgoals at the divisional, functional, or other business-unit level and then continue to cascade down throughout the organization to departments, units, teams, and individuals. Again, this is in the ideal state. Reality is often fuzzier, and much less comprehensible.

In this chapter, we will attempt to formulate a practical way of thinking about visioning, planning, and goal setting as an integrated competency that complements designing and organizing and delegating while at the same time discussing some fundamental tools and processes that are essential for effective managerial leadership.

VISION, VISIONARY LEADERS, AND VISIONARY ORGANIZATIONS

There is an aura around the topic of vision that often leads people into believing that it is very much like "charisma"—either you have it or you don't. We often hear of visionary leaders who had an almost magical capacity to see the future and understand perfectly how, when, where, and why the present fits in. Having a vision has in some respects become almost a prerequisite attribute for leaders who have high visibility. Former President George Bush was dogged during the last year of office by charges that either he had no grand vision for the country or that he had not made it clear to the American people. For President Bush it was almost a constant barrage about the "vision thing." As we tried to demonstrate in the first part of the assessment above, if you have ever tried to wrestle with any of those questions you have a fairly good idea what a vision is and have actually had some experience building one. While the assessment focuses on personal vision, organizational vision by and large functions according to the same principles. An organizational vision is "a realistic, credible, attractive future for your organization" (Nanus, 1992, p. 8). It is the articulation of a destination toward which an organization or part of an organization should turn its focus. It is a future that in many ways is more desirable than the present. A vision inspires action and helps shape that future through the effects it has on the people who are involved with the organization or unit.

Vision is not only an attribute of individual managerial leaders, it can also be a characteristic of organizations. Collins and Porras (1994) did a major study of 20 renowned organizations and concluded that visionary companies are the premier companies in their industry, the "crown jewels" so to speak. They have the respect and admiration of their peer organizations and a long history of having a significant impact on the world around them. Visionary companies are truly institutions that have had multiple generations of chief executives, have been through multiple product or service lifecycles, and have been around for at least 50 years. Collins and Porras (1994) suggest that it is the degree to which the organization has been built to be visionary rather than the visionary qualities of an individual leader that determines its long-term success and effectiveness. One of the habits of visionary companies that Collins and Porras focus on is referred to as "big hairy audacious goals (BHAG)": bold missions with superordinate goals that engage individuals. BHAGs "reach out and grab [people] in the gut." They are clear and compelling and serve as a unifying focal point of effort. They are tangible and energizing. People "get it" right away; it takes very little explanation. One example of a BHAG they cite is Henry Ford's pronouncement of 1907:

> *[To] build a motor car for the great multitude. . . . It will be so low in price that no man making a good salary will be unable to own one—and enjoy with his family the blessings of hours of pleasure in God's great open spaces. . . everybody will be able to afford one, and everyone will have one. The horse will have disappeared from our highways, the automobile will be taken for granted (Boortsin, 1974, p. 548).*

There is no denying that this vision of Ford, the founder, was instrumental in making the company what it is today. This was the starting point and catalyst for making Ford the visionary organization it is today. This vision, big, hairy and audacious as it was, cannot be credited solely for Ford's continuing success. The complementary competencies of the director—designing and organizing and delegating—were very much involved in Ford's evolution into the second most successful automobile company in the world.

PLANNING AND GOAL SETTING

Visions, like Henry Ford's cited above, can play a key role in serving as the front end of a strategic planning and goal-setting process. Ford's aim to build a car for the masses that was affordable to all heavily influenced all aspects of the planning and goal setting in the early years of Ford Motor Company. While customer focus is one of Ford's core values and guiding principles today, customers of the Model T could have any color automobile they wanted, as long as it was black. While processes like lean manufacturing (Womack et al., 1990) and mass customization and the "batch of one" often dominate discussions of manufacturing and product planning today, in Ford's early years, its vision of a car for the masses made scientific management's greatest manifestation—the assemble line—the major determiner of organizational strategies, plans, and goals. Another example of how vision serves as the first breath of strategic planning and goal setting can be found in another car company—Toyota. When Toyota first articulated its vision of a totally new line of automobiles that exceeded all currently existing standards for high-performance luxury automobiles, it still needed a strategy and a set of goals for attaining that vision. What turned out to be the Lexus vision provided the direction, but the strategy and goals provided the framework for getting there. Among numerous other things, the strategy and plans undoubtedly included objectives relating to the intended technical quality and performance of the car, marketing and production goals, a reframing of supplier and distribution arrangements, and carefully drawn financial plans and objectives. It in all likelihood also included specific strategies and goals related to vehicle servicing and customer satisfaction (Nanus, 1992).

The critical importance of strategy, plans, and goals cannot be denied—they are indispensable in designing and organizing to implement the strategy and coordinate management decisions and prepare for contingencies. Strategies, plans, and goals, however, serve as catalysts for action and unifying forces in organizations primarily within the context of a clearly articulated and widely shared vision of the future. A strategy is only as powerful as the vision that drives it. When vision, strategy, goals, and organizations are aligned and consistent, visions like Toyota's are more likely to result in realities like the Lexus—the most highly rated vehicle in customer satisfaction every year since its appearance in the showroom.

GOAL SETTING—THE BASIC BUILDING BLOCK

What is goal setting, and why should the manager be concerned about it? The classic response to these questions can be found in Yogi Berra's reported maxim: "If you don't know where you're going, you might end up someplace else." Without knowing where it is you want to go, either as an individual or as an organization, you won't know how to get there and you may wind up somewhere else! If you don't articulate what it is you want to accomplish, you won't be able to determine how best to get it done.

Experts in the planning and goal-setting field tell us that formalized planning and goal-setting processes have been used by managers and supervisors since the turn of the century. Hundreds of research studies on goal setting have been conducted with 90% of them reporting positive results. These results suggest that a median improvement of 16% in performance (with minimum and maximum ranging from 2% to 58% respectively) can be attained through the use of goal-setting techniques (Locke and Latham, 1985, p. 6). Latham and Wexley (1994) cite several research studies that conclude that whenever one group of employees is required to set and pursue specific goals, members of that group invariably increase their productivity substantially over that of groups who do not set goals. They cite studies of employees whose professional diversity varies from engineers and scientists to loggers!

Goal setting takes place at all levels in an organization. The focus, purpose, and kinds of activities that take place as part of the process, however, vary with the level of the organization within which they take place. At the most senior levels of managerial leadership, for example, goal setting tends to be focused primarily around what Latham and Wexley (1994) refer to as the organization's superordinate goal—namely its vision. As we mentioned above, that focus tends to be strategic and directional. It involves an organization's most basic and fundamental decision: the choice of missions, strategies, and major allocations of resources. These strategic/visionary choices, taken together, will generally shape the organization's overall future. At lower managerial and supervisory levels, goal setting tends to be more tactical, with a primary emphasis on *implementing* and carrying out decisions made as part of strategic visioning or directional planning. Here, the process involves:

1. Formulating specific objectives, targets, or quotas that need to be achieved by a certain time.

2. Developing an action plan to be followed and identifying specific steps to be taken in order to meet or exceed those objectives.

3. Creating a schedule showing when specific activities will be started and/or completed.

4. Developing a "budget" (including any type of necessary resources).

5. Estimating or projecting what will have happened at certain points during the life span of the plan.

6. Establishing an organization to implement decisions.

7. Setting standards against which performance will be evaluated.

LESSONS LEARNED FROM GOAL-SETTING RESEARCH AND PRACTICE[1]

Our focus in this section on goal setting will be on that process as it most affects the manager. We will begin by reviewing the lessons learned about that process from research and practice. We will then move to an examination of a set of techniques that have been developed to increase the effectiveness of tactical goal setting—management by objectives (MBO).

1. *Specific, challenging goals tend to result in better performance than vaguely specified, easily attained goals.* Goal setting is more effective when goals are clearly defined in terms of what needs to happen, how often, in what quantity and by when. Clear, specific goals reduce the probability of miscommunication or misunderstanding and provide a clearer "target" to work toward. Generally, more challenging goals result in higher levels of performance—

---

[1]*Adapted from* E.A. Locke and G.P. Latham, *Goal Setting: A Motivational Technique That Works.* Englewood Cliffs, NJ: Prentice-Hall, Inc. 1984. Used with permission.

within certain constraints. Goals should be perceived as attainable given a reasonable "stretch" of effort.

2. *Feedback on goal attainment progress enhances the process.* Feedback on progress toward the desired objective is essential. When individuals are told how well they are performing against some expected standard, they can make changes in their efforts, if necessary, or continue unchanged if their actions have proven to be effective. The source of feedback and its timing are also important variables.

3. *Goals should be prioritized if there are more than one.* Using the relative importance of a goal or objective to rank it enables individuals to direct their actions and efforts in proportion to the importance of each goal. This ranking also serves to verify both the manager's and the subordinates' expectations.

4. *Informal competition among employees produced by goal setting and feedback can enhance the benefits of the process.* Informal competition often arises spontaneously when performance is evaluated and fed back to individuals in quantitative terms. Excitement, challenge, and pride in accomplishment can result from constructive peer pressure. However, too much "formal" competition can lead to unproductive rivalry.

5. *Goal accomplishment and performance should be rewarded.* These incentives cover the gamut from monetary incentives to various forms of nonmonetary reward.

6. *Goal setting can be an important part of performance management.* Performance appraisal processes serve several intended and sometimes unintended functions in organizations. Ideally, appraisals lead to the identification of strengths and weaknesses in individual performance and, consequently, improved individual and hence organizational performance. Some performance appraisal processes, however, lead to a decline in performance when individuals are criticized and respond defensively. One key way to avoid this unintended outcome is to evaluate a person's performance against preset goals.

7. *Individuals need to develop action plans to carry out their goals.* Action plans detail the specific tasks and schedules required to accomplish goals. The development of an effective plan presupposes that the goal or objective has been clearly defined.

8. *Organizational policies need to be reviewed for consistency and complementarity with goal accomplishment.* Organizational policies exert a tremendous influence over the effectiveness of goal accomplishment. Typically, policies related to decision-making processes and speed, communication, and productivity have the greatest impact.

9. *The climate within which goal setting occurs should be a supportive one in which managers help and encourage their employees to succeed.* Results suggest that individuals whose managers behave supportively during goal-setting processes accept or set much higher goals than those whose managers are nonsupportive. Managerial support gives people confidence and trust, which leads to higher levels of performance.

10. *Depending on how they are used, goals can decrease or increase the amount of stress perceived by subordinates.* The goal-setting process generates negative stress when goals are too difficult (have a high risk of failure) or when there is goal overload, goal conflict, or goal ambiguity. The process can reduce or prevent negative stress by making certain expectations are clear.

These 10 lessons on planning and goal setting suggest that the processes involved, although only a part of the manager's function, are tied to and intimately relate to almost *all* aspects of management and organization. They have an *impact on* subordinate understanding and communication, motivation, performance appraisal processes, and reward systems. The 10 lessons cited also suggest that planning and goal-setting processes are *affected by* broader organizational policies and processes, and the specific "climate" within which those processes take place.

Instead of looking at all of these, let's focus on one key management tool: the use of objectives. We'll emphasize developing and articulating clear goals and objectives, and tracing performance against them as a keystone in a management system.

USING OBJECTIVES AS A MANAGEMENT TOOL: MBO-TYPE APPROACHES

Management by objectives (MBO) is a term used to describe a broad array of systems, procedures, and programs. What may be called MBO in one organization may not exactly match what you find in another organization. But, generally speaking, all MBO programs share the following characteristics:

Characteristics of MBO-Type Processes[2]
1. Joint goal setting between members of two consecutive levels of supervision.
   - Managers provide subordinates with a framework reflecting their own purposes and objectives.
   - Subordinates propose objectives for themselves.
   - Managers and subordinates discuss, sometimes modify, and eventually agree upon a set of objectives for the subordinates.

2. Periodic measurement and comparison of actual performance against agreed-upon goals and objectives.
   - Subordinates review their own progress and describe it periodically (as agreed) to their managers.
   - (This sequence is repeated as necessary.)

[2]Filley, House, and Kerr, 1976.

3. Objectives, whenever and wherever possible, are stated in quantifiable terms like units, dollars, percentages, and so on.

WHAT MAKES A GOOD MBO

Well-written and formulated goals and objectives can serve as the cornerstone of an MBO system. There is, however, an art and science to the process. Take New Year's resolutions as an example. Two out of three people you query on January 1 about resolutions or objectives for the coming year will identify the following as one of their top two or three: "I want to lose weight this year." Consider this personal example of an objective for its utility in an MBO-type system. In and of itself, the objective of "losing" weight is not very informative. It gives no indication of *how much weight* (quantity), no sense of how fast the weight is to be lost (time), or any indication of the "processes" to be used in losing the weight (quality). It also gives no indication of attainability (hence, not allowing for any health challenge), or any sense of flexibility to allow for changes or midcourse corrections.

Consider some examples that are work related.

- To work on my interpersonal skills.

- To purchase a computer-based system.

- To improve the file system so that it's easier to find things.

- To reduce the daily entry error rate.

- To make better decisions.

How can we improve these goals and objectives to make them more useful in an MBO-type system? Doran[3] has suggested that meaningful objectives are "smart"—that is:

Specific	A specific area of improvement is targeted.
Measurable	Some indicator of progress is established.
Assignable	Ability to specify an individual or group who will be responsible to accomplish the goal.
Realistic	Given available resources, state what can realistically be achieved.
Time Related	Specification of when the result(s) can be achieved.

WRITING AN MBO

Let's revisit the weight loss example already cited and apply what we have just presented.

[3]"There's a S.M.A.R.T. Way to Write Management's Goals and Objectives" by George T. Doran, Nov. 1981, from *Management Review*. Reprinted, by permission of publisher, from *Management Review*, November/1981 © 1981. American Management Association, New York. All rights reserved.

Old Objective	Lose weight this year.
New Objective	Lose 30 pounds by June 15 so that I can wear a size 39 suit to my twentieth high school reunion.
Action Steps	To accomplish this, I must

1. Cut my calories to 1500 per day.
2. Eliminate beer from my diet beginning immediately.
3. Eat fruit or nothing between meals beginning next week.
4. Reduce consumption of sweets to one serving per week beginning in two weeks.
5. Begin a regular exercise program (alternating jogging and aerobics).

ANALYSIS   MBO Is Not for Me[4]

Directions   Read this case of Don Smith's objection to objectives, and then answer the questions that follow the case.

You are Nancy Stuart, plant personnel manager for Countrywide Manufacturing Company's local plant in Jamestown, Ohio, a city of about 17,000 people. The plant is the principal employer in the area.

During the past two years, the personnel division (see Figure 6.1 for the organization chart) in the central headquarters of Countrywide has been quite successful in helping line managers learn and implement a new management by objectives (MBO) program throughout the company. The vice president for personnel of Countrywide was recently embarrassed when the company president asked him, "If MBO is improving effectiveness in the line divisions throughout all the plants, why haven't you used it more in your own personnel area?" This resulted in a directive to you and all plant personnel officers to come up immediately with a five-year plan applying the MBO approach. You wrote a memorandum to your branch chiefs asking them to submit a first draft of a plan to include objectives and how they are to be implemented and evaluated. This would provide data for a planning conference of your branch chiefs.

Don Smith is the chief of your counseling branch. He was hired two years ago to replace an employee who was retiring. Don was right out of college, having completed a masters in counseling. He has proved himself to be highly successful in getting the line managers in the plant to use counseling services. The quality of his branch's service is recognized throughout the plant. Last year, Don recruited Donna Maire, who had just completed her graduate work. Don has trained her well, and the two of them are a great team.

[4]"Don Smith's Objection to Objectives" from *Behavior in Organizations: An Experiential Approach,* 5th edition, by J.B. Lau and A.B. Shani, 1992, pp. 356–357. Reprinted by permission of Richard D. Irwin Inc. and the authors.

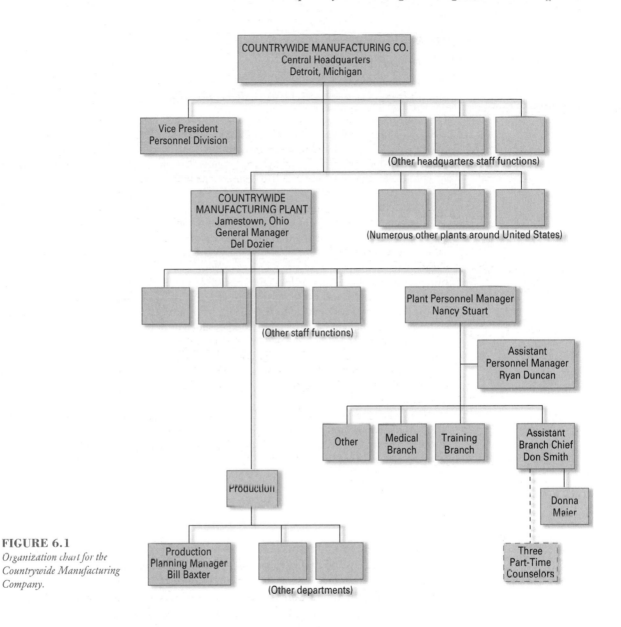

FIGURE 6.1

Organization chart for the Countrywide Manufacturing Company.

In addition, Don employs on a part-time basis three counselors (they work full time for the public health office, but are allowed to work for Countrywide in their free time). Don and Donna are the only regular employees in the branch.

The following is an informal memorandum you received from Don in answer to yours:

MEMORANDUM

TO: Nancy Stuart

From: Don Smith

RE: MBOs

I am scheduled to leave on my two-week vacation tonight, so I am writing you about my views on MBO. I am sure you will understand when I say MBO seems to apply to production areas very well and to areas of personnel such as wage and salary administration, but it really does not apply to counseling services. Last week, Donna and I saw a total of 25 employees for counseling and had 8 interviews with managers about problem people. The three part-time counselors each worked two hours last week, and their caseload was 4 each, for a total of 12. Compare this with the situation two years ago when I came aboard and the one-person counseling service was handling only 4 to 5 cases a week.

   Our business is so pressing that the obvious objective is to get another full-time counselor. We find that more and more we have to book appointments for a week or two ahead. The people who need several sessions with a counselor because of the seriousness of their cases are being assigned whenever possible to the part-timers from Public Health. We are getting more and more calls from managers asking for help in handling nonproductive employees. One has asked us to work with him on a motivation program for his section that would help raise the production of all eight of his people. We have been able to do nothing so far on the program to help alcoholics and problem drinkers, which central headquarters thinks we should be doing. I am really not sure this is a problem here; we have had no referrals. Managers seem more interested in problems of pregnant women than social drinkers. We ought to also get started on a policy guidance statement for work-related stress illness.

   Do you agree with me when I say that in a service area like counseling the main objective is to get enough qualified counselors to handle employee problems that already exist? So the objectives of my branch are (1) more personnel and (2) a bigger budget. If you need anything else on MBO for our branch, ask Donna. She knows our work as well as I do.

See you in two weeks,

Don Smith

Don's answer is the first you receive from your branch chiefs. You are a little taken aback and wonder if the rest of your team is going to be as flippant, and apparently perplexed, in trying to formulate their objectives. The chiefs of your medical training branches were making snide remarks about MBO at lunch yesterday. This could prove embarrassing because the vice president of Personnel is the executive who brought MBO programs into the organization. You become vaguely aware that you are not sure how Don should go about defining his objectives. You decide, in view of Don's vacation, to write his objectives yourself.

Discussion Questions

1. Based on the limited evidence presented, what are the factors you, as Nancy Stuart, will have to consider before working out the objectives for Don Smith's branch? (Use Figure 6.1 to generate ideas.)

2. Prior to sitting down to write, is there any action you could take that would help you get started?

3. How would/could better planning and a clear vision for the organization improve this situation?

PRACTICE   Write Your Own MBO

Directions   Review the vision/legacy statement you completed in the assessment portion of this competency—Part 1.

Restate each of the following in a manner that will allow them to be pursued using an MBO process:

1. Be a better manager.

2. Be a more supportive friend.

3. Be a more successful student.

4. Increase my attractiveness in the job market.

5. Get more organized.

How would/could each of these help you in the attainment of your personal vision/legacy?

APPLICATION   Setting Your Goals

1. Choose a goal for your schoolwork, job, or personal life, and develop an implementation plan. Include.
   Smart objectives.
   Outside factors that might affect the objective.
   Steps necessary to achieve the goal. By when?

2. Evaluate the possible results:
   What would be a good result?
   What would be a satisfactory result?
   What would be a poor (unacceptable) result?

3. Include any other comments or explanations about your goal and plan.

Competency 2   Designing and Organizing

Directions   Recall your last visit to the Postal Service or the Department of Motor Vehicles. Write a one-page description of the organization, the processes that it used, and the people that worked there. Be sure to include your personal experience and your reactions to it as a "customer" or "client."

Suspend disbelief and assume the following scenario:

The Postmaster General or the State Commissioner of Motor Vehicles phones you and asks you to serve as a special consultant/advisor to their respective organization. They would like you to help them remake their organization to be more consistent with their own personal vision for the organization—namely: To be the most customer/client focused and friendly public service organization in the world. They want to begin at the local office level and would like you to design and organize the office you just visited to make it consistent with and reflective of their personal vision.

Prepare a model design and organization for either the local Postal Service office or the local DMV office.

LEARNING   Designing and Organizing

Traditional organization theory focused on the role of an organization's strategy and environment in determining an appropriate structure and design for the organization. Structural contingency theory suggested that organizations be designed and structured along some continuum of mechanistic to organic depending on the complexity and turbulence of the environment within which the existed. The basic rule is that the more complex and turbulent the environment, the greater the need for a more organic structure and design. Organizational designs are often discussed in terms of the overall "structure" of the organization: functional, divisional, and matrix. They are also often discussed in terms of the authority structure that permeates the organization—Richard Walton talks of the control—commitment continuum (Walton, 1985, pp. 76–84). Lawler has written extensively on the "high involvement organization" (Lawler, 1986, 1992). We will discuss the basics of design and organization below, and address such topics as efficiency and organizing principles, traditional structural configurations, the principles of integration and differentiation, and traditional authority schemes. Before that, however, we would like to review some of the recent "revolutions" in designing and organizing and their implications for effectiveness in the director role.

EVOLUTION TOWARD THE LATERAL ORGANIZATION

The last five years have seen organizations subjected to more than the usual trials and tribulations of business life. Globalization has gone from being an interesting conversation at company off-sites to a fundamental reality of many organizations' lives. Cost-effectiveness has moved from the realm of the finance function to the fundamental gospel of all organizational leaders. Pressures for speed—in particular, shorter time to market and reduced cycle times—have increased exponentially. Advances in computer and communications technology have increased the number and types of activities that can take place in real time. Quality and customer focus have ceased being the domain of public relations and advertising firms and have become the bedrock of seriously competitive global firms. Organizations must confront the following in order to survive and grow: Customers demand the best product for the least cost and highest quality—and they want it faster than ever. They also want it serviced better, faster, cheaper, and more attentively than ever before. Fast cycle time (Meyer, 1993) and process management have become design variables of critical importance to organizations. Jan Carlzon got much notoriety when he led a cultural transformation at SAS that literally turned the airline organization upside down. Carlzon put the customer at the top of the organization. He ensured that the employees who had immediate contact with customers had all the power and authority they needed to please and satisfy the customer (Carlzon, 1987). More recently, many have called for more revolutionary design alternatives than merely turning the company upside down. Proponents have recommended bashing the bureaucracy, smashing the hierarchy, and fundamentally reengineering (Hammer and Champy, 1993) the organization (and management). Other organizational design variations see the organization going "molecular" and "virtual." Perhaps the most widespread and long-lasting trend in organization design is movement to variations of what is being referred to as the lateral organization.

THE LATERAL ORGANIZATION

The lateral organization can be defined as all of the horizontal cross-functional processes that cross hierarchical lines. The potential effects of the lateral organization can be great. Organizational systems that were typically functional, vertical, and reflective of the hierarchy—such as information technology, career management, and performance management—will need to be essentially flatter, less hierarchical, and more horizontal. The lateral organization will entail cross-functional teams dedicated to products, services, projects, or customers. The horizontal processes that will be included can be informal (voluntary and spontaneous) or formal (explicit). In a pure state the lateral organization would largely eliminate boundaries of a functional or departmental nature. A core group of very senior executives would concern themselves with traditional support functions. But essentially everyone else in the company would work together in ad hoc multidisciplinary teams that focused on core processes rather than functions.

The clear implication of this type of purely lateral or horizontal organization is that "flattening" will continue—instead of the ten or twelve layers that still separate the CEO from those at the front line of organizations, we would see only three or four layers intervening. Autonomous and semiautonomous work teams would become the fundamental building block of this new organizational form. Key basic indicators of organizational performance would likely shift from singular focus on profitability or shareholder value to increased concern about customer satisfaction and quality. Individuals would be rewarded not only for their personal contributions but also for their contributions to teams and their development of new skills required by the new organizational configurations (Galbraith, 1993).

Some early applications of the notion of the horizontal or lateral organization have been very successful. John F. Welch, Chairman of General Electric Company, speaks of GE's initiatives with lateral organization as building a "boundaryless" company. GE claims their efforts have resulted in reduced costs, shortened cycle times, and increased responsiveness to customers. Specifically, GE's mutibillion-dollar lighting business reframed a more typical and traditional organizational structure for its global technology unit into one in which a high-level team of 9 to 12 people oversees almost 100 processes or programs worldwide, ranging from new-product design to improving the yield on production machinery. In almost all cases, a multidisciplinary team works together to achieve the objectives of the process. The senior leadership team, made up of executives with multiple skills and competencies as opposed to narrow areas of expertise, serves as an allocator of resources and a coordinator of programs and processes. It specifically and intentionally avoids micromanaging everyday activities, which are managed by the teams themselves. This design change spawned many other changes in related systems and processes such as training, appraisal, and compensation. One such secondary change was the move from top-down, boss-only appraisal of individual performance to "360-degree" performance appraisal. This process invites peers and others above and below the employee to evaluate the individual's performance of a process. In some cases, up to 20 people are now involved in evaluating a single individual. The objective is to create greater allegiance to a process as opposed to a single boss or supervisor. The focus is on rewarding employees for the skills they learn rather than merely for the work they perform. Organizations that are in a startup mode are also using aspects of the lateral/horizontal organization to become more effective. Astra/Merck Group is a new stand alone company created to market antiulcer and high-blood-pressure drugs licensed from Sweden's Astra. Rather than choosing a traditional functional structure, Astra/Merck chose to organize around a core of six "market-driven business processes" ranging from drug development to product sourcing and distribution. One of the major drivers of this choice was the company's strategic focus on being "lean, fast, and focused on the customer" ("The Horizontal Organization," *Business Week*, December 20, 1993).

In Chapter 5 (the Coordinator Role), we explored the implications of these revolutions in organizational design for managerial leaders, by examining what the consequences of these changes in structure and design are for day-to-day integration of the organization's activities. Our focus in that chapter is "managing cross-functionally." We would now like to review what we believe are the basic building blocks of organizational design.

DESIGNING AND ORGANIZING: CORE CONCEPTS AND PRINCIPLES

Once organizational and work unit plans are set, a manager must decide how to allocate and coordinate organizational resources in order to accomplish the goals. **Organizing** is the process of dividing the work into manageable components and assigning activities to most effectively achieve the desired results. Said in another way, if planning provides the tools for deciding where "you want to go and how best to get there," organizing provides the tools to actually "get you there."

At the organizational level, organizing involves designing the organizational structure so that the work can be efficiently and effectively allocated across the different departments and work units. At the work-unit level, organizing involves designing jobs and allocating tasks so that the work unit can effectively accomplish its goals in support of the overall organizational mission. In this section we will examine both organizational and job design, focusing on current tools and techniques of organizing that have evolved from ideas first written about by Adam Smith in 1776.

EFFICIENCY AS AN ORGANIZING PRINCIPLE

In his treatise, *The Wealth of Nations*, written in 1776, Adam Smith established two management principles which today still stand as guiding principles of organizations. Writing about the manufacture of straight pins, Smith noted that if (1) the work were divided into its component tasks and (2) workers were specialized so that each individual only had responsibility for completing one of the component tasks, the overall job would be accomplished far more efficiently than if each worker performed all tasks associated with the job.

More than 200 years later, the process of organizing is still very much influenced by the principles of **division of labor** (that work should be divided into component tasks) and **specialization** (that each person should only be assigned a small piece of the total job). Although current management thought on how to design organizations and jobs effectively no longer focuses exclusively on efficiency, it remains an important building block in the process of organizing.

Small organizations often remain informal with respect to rules and procedures. They have little need for standardization of jobs and specialization—when a job needs to be done, people share in the work. Large organizations, however, need rules and procedures. Without standardization and specialization there would be chaos. Organizing, then, serves several important functions.

1. Organizing clarifies who is supposed to perform which jobs and how those jobs should be divided among organizational members.

2. Organizing clarifies the lines of authority, specifying who reports to whom.

3. Organizing creates the mechanisms for coordinating across the different groups and levels of the organization.

DESIGNING ORGANIZATIONS THROUGH DEPARTMENTATION

At the organizational level, dividing jobs among organizational members is called **departmentation**. Here employees are grouped into departments according to some logic. Three pure forms of departmentation are departmentation by function, departmentation by division, and departmentation by matrix.

BY FUNCTION

Departmentation by function creates departments based on the specific functions that people perform. For example, financial management offices, engineering departments, and legal offices are grouped by function. All people in these offices perform similar functions.

Organizing by function increases organizational efficiency by having people with similar expertise working together to perform similar functions. Conversely, it decreases organizational efficiency because the structure creates barriers between departments that generally result in increased time to respond to interfunctional problems.

BY DIVISION

Departmentation by division creates departments based on services, clients, territories, or time differences. For example, AT&T reorganized its computer-oriented division from a functional structure to a divisional structure in order to increase coordination. IBM organizes its marketing by geographic region, both domestic and worldwide. In the United States, IBM has two marketing divisions: North–Central and South–West.

Organizing by division increases organizational efficiency because the departments can be more responsive to specific client or regional needs. Conversely it often leads to duplication of effort and makes it more difficult for people who are doing the same type of work, in different departments, to share their ideas and learn from each other.

BY MATRIX

Departmentation by matrix, or matrix organization, attempts to take the advantages and overcome the disadvantages of functional and divisional organizational forms by combining the two. In matrix organizations, employees are assigned (1) to a functional department and also (2) to a cross-functional team that focuses on specific projects or programs. They report to the heads of both the functional department and cross-functional team. For example, an engineer in a manufacturing firm that is organized in matrix form will report to the head of the engineering department and also to the product manager, who also manages marketing, production, and finance specialists assigned to that project or product. Such diverse service and manufacturing organizations as Prudential Insurance, General Mills, and Caterpillar Tractor are organized in matrix form.

CHOOSING A FORM OF DEPARTMENTATION

As discussed previously, each of the pure forms of departmentation has advantages and disadvantages; they are summarized in Table 6.1. In choosing a form of departmentation, organizations often organize according to a mix of these forms. For example, because of the greater flexibility and ability to respond to client needs, many corporations are organized by division with respect to the specific products or services they provide, but they are organized by function with respect to personnel/human resources management, financial management, and legal offices. Similarly some organizations are organized by division with respect to regions, but they are organized by function within each region. Hospitals and psychiatric institutions may have matrix structures for providing services, but they maintain a functional structure for such activities as records management, building maintenance, and nutrition and dietary services.

TABLE 6.1 Potential Advantages and Disadvantages of Three Pure Forms of Departmentation

Departmentation by Function	
Advantages	*Disadvantages*
Allows task assignments to be consistent with technical training	May reduce accountability for total production or service delivery
Allows greater specialization in technical areas of expertise	Promotes overspecialization
Supports in-depth training and development	Breaks down communication across functions
Promotes high-quality technical problem-solving	Refers too many problems upward in hierarchy
Reduces technical demands on the manager	Promotes narrow, self-centered perspectives within functions
Provides career paths within areas of technical expertise	Allows slow response to interfunctional problems

Departmentation by Division	
Advantages	*Disadvantages*
Allows for flexible response to new developments	May not allow for sufficient depth of technical expertise

TABLE 6.1 Potential Advantages and Disadvantages of Three Pure Forms of Departmentation continued

Departmentation by Division

Advantages	*Disadvantages*
Concentrates functional attention on common tasks	May duplicate efforts as personnel assigned to separate work divisions work on similar problems
Improves coordination across functions	May overemphasize division versus organizational objectives
Facilitates growth by adding new divisions	May result in unhealthy competition among divisions

Departmentation by Matrix

Advantages	*Disadvantages*
Allows for efficient use of resources	Allows for potential power struggles between an employee's two bosses
Allows for flexible response to new developments	Allows for confusion regarding which of two bosses has greater authority
Promotes high-quality technical problem solving	May allow program teams to overemphasize team goals versus organizational goals
Frees top management for long-range planning	May produce prohibitive cost of program manager salaries

Sources: Adapted from John R. Schermerhorn, Jr., *Management for Productivity* (New York: John Wiley and Sons, 1989), pp. 179–185; and John M. Ivancevich and Michael T. Matteson, *Organizational Behavior and Management* (Homewood, IL: Business Publications, Inc., 1993, 3rd ed. Adaptation from pp.518–519). Reprinted by permission of Richard D. Irwin, Inc.

LINES OF AUTHORITY

In addition to defining how the organization's work is to be divided, departmentation defines the organization's authority relationships—who reports to whom. In designing authority relationships, we often rely on three efficiency principles. First, each person should report to one and only one manager. This is referred to as the **unity-of-command principle**. The principle ensures that employees know from whom they should expect job assignments and reduces the potential for conflicting job assignments. Note that, by definition, matrix organizations violate the unity-of-command principle. In fact, the advantages of matrix organizations are considered to be sufficient to warrant this violation. Managers in matrix organizations, however, should monitor job assignments and communication patterns to check that employees are not receiving conflicting messages from their two bosses.

Building on the principle of unity of command, the **scalar principle** states that there should be a clear line of command linking each employee to the next higher level of authority, up to and including the highest level of management. When the lines of authority are clear, it is easier to know who is responsible for the completion of each job.

Finally, the principle of **span of control** states that a person can effectively manage only a limited number of employees. How many, then? The answer is not clear and may vary with the individuals involved. But the principle recognizes that as the number of individuals reporting to a manager increases, the more difficult it is to coordinate and control individual efforts.

The size of the span of control influences the organization's structure. For a given number of employees, as the span of control decreases, the number of levels in the organizational hierarchy will increase. More managers are needed and, hence, the greater the number of layers in the hierarchy. Conversely, the greater the span of control, the fewer the number of managers needed and, hence, the fewer the number of layers in the hierarchy.

Organizations with many levels in the hierarchy are referred to as **tall organizations**; organizations with fewer levels in the hierarchy are referred to as **flat organizations**. In general, tall organizations tend to operation less efficiently than flat ones. Recent trends in both industry and government have been to reduce the number of levels in the hierarchy and to increase the span of control. Here are factors that should be considered in planning any manager's span of control:

Factor	Effect	Recommendation
Variety of functions	The greater the variety of functions to be managed, . . .	The *smaller* the span of control should be
Physical location of functions	The greater the physical distance between functions managed, . . .	The *smaller* the span of control should be
Complexity of functions	The greater the complexity of the tasks being managed, . . .	The *smaller* the span of control should be
Planning required for functions	The greater the planning required for tasks being managed, . . .	The *smaller* the span of control should be
Coordination required among functions	The greater the amount of coordination required, . . .	The *smaller* the span of control should be
Skill level of subordinates	The greater the skill level of subordinates,...	The *greater* the span of control can be
Need for balance between span of control and number of levels of hierarchy	The greater the need for a flatter organization, . . .	The *greater* the span of control should be

CONFLICTS AMONG ORGANIZING PRINCIPLES

The five principles of organizing—specialization, division of labor, unity of command, scalar chain, and span of control—often contradict one another (Simon, 1976). There will always be situations where the adherence to one principle of efficiency will result in violation of a second principle. In these situations, trade-offs will be required across different types of efficiency. To decide which trade-offs to make, return to the overall mission of the organization and determine which principle of efficiency serves this mission most efficiently.

DIFFERENTIATION AND INTEGRATION

When the environments and technologies within a single organization differ, there is greater need for **differentiation** across departments. That is, departments should be structured differently so that they can approach their tasks differently. Departments can be differentiated according to time, goal, and interpersonal orientation.

1. *Time orientation.* Some tasks, such as paper processing, require a shorter time orientation than others, such as planning or research.

2. *Goal orientation.* Even when organizations have a single organizational mission, the goals of the individual work units will differ to some degree. For example, organizational units closely associated with the organization's mission pursue different goals than organizational units associated with maintaining the organization's structure (personnel, financial management, etc.).

3. *Interpersonal orientation.* To the extent that the degree of interdependency among employees varies across organizational tasks, patterns and styles of interaction will differ across work units.

Thus, organizational subsystems that must be more responsive to their environments should be organized to allow for greater response. Organizational subsystems that have more uncertain environments must be organized to allow for greater flexibility and adaptability to sudden changes. And organizational subsystems that have more uncertain technologies should be organized to accommodate the greater need for interaction among people.

Returning for a moment to the organizational level, think about the organizational implications of maintaining a highly differentiated organization. If each subsystem is structured differently, the potential exists for the organization to become a "dis-organization." In fact, the greater the differentiation across units, the greater the need for **integration**, or coordination across units (Lawrence and Lorsch, 1967). Various mechanisms are available to the organization to achieve effective integration, ranging from basic tools (such as rules and procedures, referral of problems up the hierarchy, and planning) to more complex tools (such as liaison roles, task forces and interunit teams, and matrix organization designs). An in-depth discussion of these mechanisms is beyond the scope of this chapter. Suffice it to say that rules, procedures, and the referral of problems up the hierarchy tend to work best when the need for integration is low. Alternatively, when departments that are highly differentiated have high needs for integration, task forces, teams, and matrix structures are most effective.

ANALYSIS Understanding the Impact of Organization Design on Effectiveness

Directions   Think again about the activity you chose as the focus of your assessment at the beginning of this competency—a proposed redesign of either your local Department of Motor Vehicles or Postal Service office. Review and analyze the design/structure you proposed, considering the following:

1. Focusing on the original design of the organization you chose, what role did *efficiency* as an organizing principle play? Was there any evidence of division of labor and or specialization?

2. What form of *departmentation* seemed to be present in the organization? Did it seem to have properties of a functional, divisional, or matrix type of structure?

3. What lines of authority were evident? How would you describe the span of control? Was the organization "tall" or "flat" in terms of hierarchy? What about the degree of differentiation and integration?

4. Reconsider your proposed redesign and incorporate one or two elements of lateral/horizontal organization. What impact will these elements have on the effectiveness of the organization? Why?

PRACTICE Redesigning Organizations

Directions   For this exercise, work in groups of two. If the organization you chose to redesign was the local motor vehicle office, find an individual to work with who chose the Postal Service. Conduct a diagnostic interview with that person in order to come to a full understanding of the existing design and structure of the organization he or she chose. Be sure your interview protocol includes the following questions:

1. Why did you choose to redesign the local Postal Service office (or local Department of Motor Vehicles)? What was it about the organization or its operation that troubled you to begin with?

2. What other data did you have in considering your redesign? What other evidence convinced you of the need for redesign?

3. What conclusions did you draw about the existing organization's:
   - Use of efficiency as an organizing principle
     - Division of labor
     - Specialization
   - Structural properties
     - Functional
     - Divisional

- Matrix
- Other

- Lines of authority
  - Span of control: tall or flat or other?
  - Degree of differentiation and integration
4. What aspects of lateral/horizontal organization did you choose to incorporate in the redesign? Why? What outcomes did you expect to result?

APPLICATION Understanding the Design and Organization of Your Company

Select an organization that you have extensive knowledge of. Ideally, this would be the organization you currently work in or very recently worked in. It could be a school-related organization or some other one that you have been extensively involved with. Using that organization as a focal point, complete the following:

1. Secure the formal organization chart (if available) of that organization. Review it and conduct an analysis of its use of efficiency as an organizing principle, its intended structural configuration, its line of authority, and any available information on the nature of differentiation and integration.

2. Review the notions of lateral/horizontal organization discussed in this chapter as well as your responses to the practice and analysis exercises. Incorporate one or two elements of these concepts into a redesign of your organization. Speculate on what results you would like to see and why.

3. Interview the leader of the organization and query that person as to his or her perceptions of the effectiveness of the organization relative to its current design. Inquire what might make the organization more effective. Propose your lateral/horizontal redesign ideas for discussion.

Competency 3 Delegating Effectively

ASSESSMENT To Delegate or Not to Delegate[5]

Directions Record how you feel about the following statements by using the scale shown.

---

[5] From *First Line Management*, 5th edition, by L. Steinmetz and R. Todd, Homewood, IL: Business Publications, 1992, pp. 82–83. Reprinted by permission of Richard D. Irwin, Inc.

Scale	Strongly disagree	Disagree	Neutral	Agree	Strongly agree
	1	2	3	4	5

_____ 1. Most of the time subordinates are too inexperienced to do a job, so I prefer to do it myself.

_____ 2. It takes more time to explain the job than to do the job myself.

_____ 3. Mistakes by subordinates are too costly, so I don't assign work to them.

_____ 4. In my position, I get quicker action by doing a job myself rather than having a subordinate do it.

_____ 5. Some things simply should not be delegated.

_____ 6. Many subordinates are detail specialists and lack the overall knowledge required for a job out of their specialty; thus, they cannot be assigned additional job responsibilities.

_____ 7. Subordinates are usually too busy to take on any more work.

_____ 8. Most subordinates just aren't ready to handle additional responsibilities.

_____ 9. As a manager, I should be entitled to make my own decisions about my doing detail work rather than administrative work.

_____ TOTAL

Scoring and Interpretation

Your responses to the nine items above, when totalled, will result in a score that ranges between 9 and 45. Each of the questions represents one of the commonly used reasons or "excuses" for not delegating. Those reasons include lack of subordinate experience, amount of time delegation takes, costliness of errors, and the appropriateness of delegating in general. The more strongly *you personally* agree with each of these, the less likely you are to delegate (i.e., the larger your score, the less likely you are to delegate).

In the learning section below, we suggest some ways that these arguments against delegation can be turned into reasons for delegating.

LEARNING   Delegating Effectively

Managers who are most strongly opposed to delegation often use variations of arguments included in the assessment above. Frequent responses by these managers to the topic of delegation include: "Delegation, I tried that once and the employee fouled things up royally"; or "Delegate my authority? Why? I'm the manager—that's my job—I can do it better myself." Given our above discussion about the emergence of lateral organizational forms these responses to delegation (and those discussed below in Table 6.2) can be especially detrimental to effectiveness in the director role. Delegation is typically defined as a rather simple process of giving assignments to subordinates. It is touted for its significant payoffs in providing a manager with more time and allowing him or her to focus attention on more rather than less significant issues. It is also viewed as a key to the training and development of subordinates as well as the wise allocation of organizational resources. These attributes make effective delegation even more critical to the success of lateral forms of organization. If this conception of delegation is accurate, why, then, are managers so reluctant to delegate? Why does delegation tend to be a misunderstood, inappropriately used, or underutilized tool? As you consider these questions and review the most commonly cited reasons for *not* delegating listed in Table 6.2, consider your own responses to the assessment above. What are your top three reasons for not delegating or not delegating more?

Traditional definitions of delegation, while often highlighting the rational reasons and advantages of it, often imply some negative connotations. Among the most negative are "abdicating responsibility for a task and", "letting someone else do the dirty work,"—typically those "lower" in the organization. These traditional definitions need to be rethought in the light of the rapidly changing nature of organizational designs. Delegation should be reconceptualized from merely a vertical process (i.e., from a manager to a staff member) to an omnidirectional one— delegation occuring downward, laterally (from one manager to another), and upward (from a staff member to a manager). Delegation then becomes the entrusting of a particular assignment, project, task, or process by one individual to another (Schwartz, 1992). The three core aspects of delegation, however, should remain the same: responsibility, authority, and accountability. The individual who delegates the assignment, project, task, or process is ultimately responsible for the successful execution of the task. That individual has final say—supervising and monitoring as is appropriate. The individual to whom the assignment is delegated is responsible for achieving intermediate and specific goals and milestones along the way. Sufficient authority must be transferred to individuals to whom assignments are delegated in order for them to obtain the resources and cooperation required for successful completion. Individuals who are delegated assignments are accountable for meeting their established goals and objectives. Periodic reports and evaluations are critical here. Time is an essential and scarce resource in the delegation process. The time invested up front in appropriately delegating an assignment should not be squandered by letting too much time pass between the initial act of delegation and the deadline for its completion. Also crucial are letting individuals know that you trust them within the sphere of delegated goals and objectives.

TABLE 6.2 Delegation: Point–Counterpoint

Reasons for Not Delegating	*Counterarguments*
1. I feel uncomfortable asking subordinates to do my task.	1. Effective managers tend to delegate everything they do not absolutely have to do themselves. If subordinates understand this principle, they will not be offended by your requests.
2. My subordinates lack the appropriate knowledge.	2. If subordinates lack the appropriate knowledge, you are failing in at least one important responsibility you have to them.

TABLE 6.2 Delegation: Point—Counterpoint continued

Reasons for Not Delegating	*Counterarguments*
3. I can do some tasks quicker than it would take to explain them.	3. This may be true and even a wise strategy, but how many tasks fall in this category?
4. My subordinates lack the appropriate skills and experience. I can do it better than they can.	4. If they lack the knowledge and skills, are they getting appropriate training and development?
5. My subordinates are too busy already.	5. Delegating to busy subordinates will force them to learn to delegate or better manage time.
6. If someone else does it, it may weaken my control.	6. Your control may weaken, but you are free to do more strategic and more influential things in the organization, which is what you should be doing.
7. If someone makes a mistake, I am responsible.	7. Learning to live with risk and to allow failure and learning in others is an ability you need in order to move to higher levels where the ability is even more needed.
8. I feel better if people see me as an extraordinarily hard worker.	8. You are working hard but ineffectively. People will eventually see your overcommitment as a weakness.
9. I am uneasy relying on the judgment of subordinates around delegated tasks. I no longer know what is going on.	9. Trusting subordinates is a skill that is increasingly necessary as you move up. In the meantime, you are undermining their development.
10. I do not understand some tasks well enough to delegate them.	10. This may be a legitimate argument. How many of your tasks does it really apply to?
11. It is not appropriate for subordinates to do some of my tasks.	11. This is sometimes true, but usually it is greatly exaggerated. Why is it inappropriate?

Keys to Effective Delegation

1. In your own mind, clarify what it is that you want done. Writing it down can be helpful.

2. Match the desired task with the most appropriate employee.

3. In assigning the task, be sure you communicate clearly. Ask questions to see

if the task is fully understood. Be sure that deadlines and time horizons are clear.

4. Keep the communication channels open. Make it clear you are available for consultation and discussion.

5. Allow employees to do the task the way they feel comfortable doing it. Show some trust in their abilities. Do not hold such high expectations that they can only fail.

6. Check on the progress of the assignment, but do not rush to the rescue at the first sign of failure.

7. Hold the person responsible for the work and any difficulties that may emerge, but do this as a teacher, not a police officer. Explore what is going wrong, and help them to develop their own solutions.

8. Ignoring an employee's efforts can be devastating to motivation. Recognize what has been done, and show appropriate appreciation.

POTENTIAL "PITFALLS" OF DELEGATION

The eight keys to effective delegation will not always result in a successful outcome, even if followed to the letter. Occassionally, a subordinate will receive an assignment and then fail to perform it properly. This can be frustrating to both a manager and the subordinate. Before taking action, it might be useful to try to discover *why* the subordinate has failed to perform the delegated task.

One of the most common explanations for failed delegation is misunderstanding the assignment and the manager's expectations. Both the manager and the subordinate must examine their roles in the communication "breakdown." The manager can reduce the frequency of miscommunication by asking the subordinate to repeat or feed back his or her understanding of the delegated assignment.

A related cause of delegation failure is also based in the communications process. Subordinates may feel that the assignment surpasses their ability, and they fear being embarrassed by failure. This, however, is not communicated to the manager at the time of the initial delegation. The manager may be able to avoid this problem by asking subordinates about how confident they are in their ability to complete the assigned task.

A classic reason for failed delegation is being given the responsibility for an assignment without being given the authority to complete the assignment or the appropriate discretion in choosing the manner of completion. Another simple, but often overlooked, course of delegation failures is the lack of time for subordinates to complete the task. Some subordinates just can't say "no," even when they should (i.e., when they just don't have enough time). Still another reason might be the subordinate's giving the assignment a lower priority than the one assigned to it by the manager. Again, these can be avoided by proactive communication by the manager from the start.

The causes for failure of delegation cited above by and large are a function of the subordinate's *ability* to complete an assigned task or the manner in which the task was communicated. There is a second type of reason that generally is a function of the subordinate's *motivation* to complete the assigned task. Failure to complete the task may reflect rebelliousness, seeing the delegated task as inappropriate to their "status," or no perceived "pay off" in completing the task. These and countless other motivational causes for failed delegation should be treated as motivational problems. (Please see Chapter 7 for a discussion of motivation.)

ANALYSIS The Storm Window Assignment[6]

Directions Read the instructions for George Brown. Assume that you are George Brown and that you have the conversation with Jack that appears in the Script II. Script I is a conversation among the work crew that is going on when you arrive.

Instructions for George Brown You are a manager in the plant department in the telephone company and have your headquarters in a small town. The department is located in a two-story frame building that contains the operation equipment. Your crew is required to maintain the central office equipment, repair lines, install phones, and so on. A total of four people report to you, and this number is entirely adequate. There is no maintenance worker or janitor in the group because there are practically no upkeep problems. When a door lock needs repairing, someone fixes it when he or she has a spare moment. Often you fix little things if everyone is busy. However, now and then certain jobs have to be assigned. The accepted practice you have followed is to give these assignments to the person with least seniority. This procedure is followed quite generally in the company, and no one has even questioned it as far as you know. You put in your share of dirty work when you were new. One of the special jobs that comes up periodically is the washing and putting up of storm windows in the fall and taking them down in the spring. There are 12 windows on the first floor and 12 windows on the second. The windows are stored in the basement. There is a new aluminum ladder that you just got. That ought to make the job easier.

The time is late October. It's getting chilly, but today is a nice day. It is a good day to put up the storm windows. Jack, Steve, Dave, and Bill are in the other room having lunch. They bring their lunches and have coffee in thermos bottles. You got them this table, and they seem to like eating together. It's time for everybody to get back to work, so it's a good time to assign the job. Steve, Dave, and Bill have just left for work, so Jack is now available.

Jack has the least seniority, so you are going to ask him to do the job. Since you have had no replacements for some time, Jack has done this job for several years and knows the ropes. He is a good fellow and cooperates nicely:

Scene   Telephone crew work out of a small building which contains central office equipment serving the community.

Although Jack has been on his job five years, he has the least seniority of anyone in his group. Many of the unpleasant jobs around the place fall to him because he is the newest man. One of these is washing and putting up the storm windows each year. There are 12 windows on the first floor and 12 on the second. Jack has never complained about this assignment.

However, after lunch one day when he is sitting around with other members of the group, the conversation takes an interesting turn. Let's listen in.

Script: Part 1

Jack: Boy, that hot coffee really tastes good.

Steve: Yeah, it's getting chilly outside. Almost had a frost last night.

Dave: Yeah! Time to finish my fall plowing in the south forty.

Bill: *(reading from the paper)* There's a special on storm windows that looks good. It's time to start thinking of them. By the way, Jack, it seems to me that we ought to be getting them put up here, too, shouldn't we?

Steve: Sure, Jack. Get out the Glasswax and shine 'em up.

Jack: Aw, quiet—you guys are always riding somebody.

Dave: What's the matter, don't you like the job?

Bill: Takes all your brains to do it, doesn't it, Jack?

Steve: That's a real stiff job! You have to figure which one to wash first and which end is up.

Jack: Why don't you dry up?

Dave: What's the matter, Jack? Don't you like the job?

Bill: Aw, it can't be that! He's been doing it for years. He must like it.

Jack: You know well enough I don't like it.

Steve: Well, you keep doing it, don't you?

Jack: I'm going to get out of it, though.

Dave: This I must see!

Bill: What are you gonna do—jump the seniority list?

Jack: I don't know, but I think it's time somebody else did it.

Steve: Not me!

Dave: You don't hook me on it either. I had my turn.

Jack: For how long? One time, that's all you ever did it.

Bill: And that was enough, too, wasn't it, Dave?

Steve: What's the matter, Jack, can't you take it?

Jack: Sure I can take it. I have for five years.

Dave: Looks like you're gonna make it six years now.

Jack: Not me—I'm through doing all the dirty work around here.

Bill: What do you mean dirty? You get your hands clean, don't you?

Steve:	Who do you think's gonna put 'em up–Brownie himself?
Jack:	I don't care who does it, but it's not me any more.
Dave:	Aw, you talk big but you can't make it stick.
Bill:	Yeah, Jackie, you're just asking for trouble.

Script: Part II

Mr. Brown, the manager, enters.

Brown:	Hello, fellows. *(Greetings from the group.)* Say, Jack, could I see you a minute? I don't want to break up the lunch session. *(Looks at some papers in his hand.)*
Dave:	Oh no—it's time we were getting back on the job, anyway.
Jack:	Yes, sure, Mr. Brown. *(Picks up the paper bag and waxed paper and throws them in the basket.)* Anything wrong?
Brown:	No, Jack, not at all. I just wanted to remind you about the storm windows. *(Laugh from group at the table.)*
Jack:	What about 'em?
Brown:	It's starting to turn cold, Jack—I think we ought to get 'em up. Don't you think so?
Dave:	This is where we came in, fellows, let's go. *(All but Jack leave.)*
Jack:	Yeah, I guess *somebody* ought to put 'em up.
Brown:	Will you take care of that, Jack—anytime this week you can manage it.
Jack:	I wanted to talk to you about that, Mr. Brown. I'd rather not do it this year.
Brown:	Do what–put up the storm windows?
Jack:	Yes, Mr. Brown, I'd rather not do it.
Brown:	Well, Jack, it won't take you any time at all. I'll get you some help to get 'em out when you're ready.
Jack:	It isn't that—I just don't want to do it again. I've had it for five years. It's not fair!
Brown:	Well, now—I know how you feel, Jack. I know it's a chore, but somebody has to do it.
Jack:	If you don't mind—count me out this time.
Brown:	But I do mind, Jack—We've got to do what's part of our job. And you're the newest one here. Be a good fellow.
Jack:	I've been the goat around here for five years. Let somebody else do it for a change.
Brown:	Now, Jack, the others had their turn.
Jack:	For how long? Dave did it once and so did Bill. I don't think Steve ever had to put 'em up. Why pick on me?
Brown:	Nobody's picking on you. We just have to do our jobs, that's all.
Jack:	Well, it's not part of my job—it's not in my job description.
Brown:	It is part of your job, and I think we have a right to expect you to do it.
Jack:	Count me out.
Brown:	Now, be yourself, Jack. I don't want to be unreasonable about this thing, but after all. . . .
Jack:	Well, I think I've done my share.
Brown:	We can try to work something out on this next year, but suppose you take care of it this time.
Jack:	No, Mr. Brown, I just don't feel I ought to do it.
Brown:	Jack, I think I'll have to say you've got to do it.
Jack:	I'm sorry, but I'm not going to do it this time.
Brown:	It's an order.

Jack:	Not to me it's not.
Brown:	You'll take an order, Jack, or get out.
Jack:	You're not firing me. I quit, and you can give your dirty job to some of those other guys. I'm through.

Discussion Questions

1. How did George Brown use the eight keys to effective delegation discussed previously?

2. Which keys did he use effectively?

3. Did he neglect any of the keys?

4. How do you account for Jack's reactions and behavior? Can any of the pitfalls of delegation be used to explain the situation?

PRACTICE Improvising a Delegation Problem

Directions

In groups formed by your instructor, select half the members to enact the role of George and half to enact the role of Jack.

Each subset of role players should brainstorm how they would carry out their respective role. George Brown role players: Use the keys to effective delegation and your knowledge of the potential pitfalls to change the outcome of the preceding conversation.

APPLICATION Interviewing a Delegator

1. Conduct a 45-minute interview with a parent, a manager, and a friend who is not taking this course. Pose the storm windows situation (in brief form) to the interviewees and ask for *their* explanation and solution.

2. Ask the interviewees to identify three tasks that they do not currently, but could, delegate to someone else. Each task should be defined in terms of:

    ■ Nature of the task.

    ■ Qualities the task requires.

    ■ Individual selected.

    ■ Influence strategy to be used.

REFERENCES

Boorstin, Daniel J. *The Americans: The Democratic Experience.* New York: Vintage Books, 1974, p. 548.

Carlzon, Jan. *Moments of Truth.* New York: Harper & Row, 1987.

Collins, James C. and Jerry I. Porras. *Built to Last.* New York: Harper Collins, 1994.

Doran, George. "There's a S.M.A.R.T. Way to Write Management's Goals and Objectives," *Mangement Review* (November 1981).

Filley, A.C., R.J. House, and S. Kerr. *Managerial Process and Organizational Behavior* (2nd ed.). Glenview, Ill.: Scott, Foresman, 1976.

Fortune, May 2, 1994. p. 45.

Galbraith, Jay R. "The Business Unit of the Future," in *Organizing for the Future,* Jay R. Galbraith, E.F. Lawler III and Associates. San Francisco: Jossey-Bass, 1993.

Hammer, Michael, and James Champy. *Reengineering the Corporation.* New York: Harper Business, 1993.

"The Horizontal Organization," *Business Week,* Dec. 20, 1993, pp. 76–81.

Ivancevich, John M., and Michael T. Matteson. *Organizational Behavior and Management.* Plano, Tex.: Business Publications, Inc., 1993.

Labich, Kenneth. "Is Herb Kelleher America's Best CEO?" *Fortune,* May 2, 1994, pp. 44–52.

Latham, Gary P., and Ken N. Wexley. *Increasing Productivity Through Performance Appraisal* (2nd ed.). Reading, Mass.: Addison-Wesley, 1994.

Lau, J.B., and A.B. Shani. *Behavior in Organizations: An Experiential Approach* (5th ed.). Homewood, Ill.: Irwin, 1992.

Lawler, Edward E. *High Involvement Management.* San Francisco: Jossey-Bass, 1986.

———. *The Ultimate Advantage.* San Francisco: Jossey-Bass, 1992.

Lawrence, Paul R., and Jay W. Lorsch. *Organization and Environment. Managing Differentiation and Integration.* Boston: Division of Research, Graduate School of Business Administration, Harvard University, 1967.

Locke, E.A., and G.P. latham. *Goal Setting: A Motivational Technique That Works.* Englewood Cliffs, N.J.: Prentice-Hall, 1984.

———."Organizational Goal Setting Questionnaire Interpretive Guide," Organization Design and Development, Inc. Copyright 1985.

Maier, N.R.F., A.R. Solem, and A.A. Maier. *Supervisory and Executive Development.* New York: John Wiley & Sons, 1957.

Meyer, Christopher, *Fast Cycle Time.* New York: Free Press, 1993.

Nanus, B. *Visionary Leadership.* San Francisco: Jossey-Bass, 1992.

Peters, Tom, *Thriving on Chaos.* New York: Harper & Row, 1987.

Quick, James Campbell. "Crafting an Organizational Culture: Herb's Hand at Southwest Airlines." *Organizational Dynamics,* Autumn, 1992, Vol. 21, no.2, pp. 45–56.

Schermerhorn, John R., Jr. *Management for Productivity.* New York: John Wiley & Sons, 1989.

Schwartz, Andrew, E. *Delegating Authority.* Hauppauge, N.Y.: Barron's Educational Series, 1992.

Simon, Herbert A. *Administrative Behavior.* New York: Free Press, 1976.

Smith, Adam. *The Wealth of Nations* (1776), New York: Random House, 1937.

Steinmetz, L., and R. Todd, Jr. *First Line Management* (rev. ed.). Dallas, Tex.: Business Publications, 1979.

Walton, R.E. "From Control to Commitment in the Workplace." *Harvard Business Review* 63 (2) (1985): 76–84.

Womack, J.P., D.T. Jones and D. Roos. *The Machine that Changed the World.* New York: Rawsan Associates, 1990.

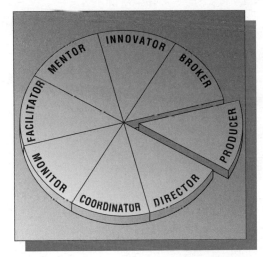

THE PRODUCER ROLE

7

■ COMPETENCIES

Working Productively

Fostering a Productive Work Environment

Managing Time and Stress

The rational goal's complement to the director role is that of the producer. Effectively enacting the producer role implies that the individual managerial leader is personally productive—motivated, empowered, and committed. It also implies that the individual managerial leader creates an environment within which his or her employees and associates can become motivated, empowered, and committed—one within which they can work productively. Effective execution of the producer role also requires individual managerial leaders to achieve and maintain a balance between push for effort and productivity and maintenance of overall health and effectiveness for themselves individually and for their people. In this chapter we frame the producer role with the competencies:

Competency 1 Working Productively
Competency 2 Fostering a Productive Work Environment
Competency 3 Managing Time and Stress

251

ROLE PERFORMANCE—THE PRODUCER ROLE: GE's JACK WELCH

As CEO of one of the most successful companies in the world, Jack Welch has enacted the producer role in his attempt to create a "values-based organization." Since the early 1980s, General Electric and Welch have evolved and refined their statement of values to include the creation of a practical and simple customer-driven vision and the ability to communicate it widely, the importance of accountability and commitment, decisiveness, aggressive goal-setting, and uncompromising integrity. Core GE values also reflect a passion for excellence, the need for empowerment and the hatred of bureaucracy, and global sensitivity and diversity. Underlying all of the values is the belief that change is an opportunity to be relished and a source of energy to invigorate the organization (Tichy and Sherman, 1993, pp. 343–344).

This statement of values conjures up the very essence of the producer role. Targets are to be "aggressive" and pursued with "unyielding integrity," excellence must be a "passion" and bureaucracy must be "hated." Self-confidence, "enormous energy," and the ability to "empower" and invigorate oneself and others are also essential. These values illustrate the importance of individual productivity at GE as well as the responsibility to make the working environment of others productive. A letter that Welch wrote to accompany GE's 1991 annual report in which he defines *four types of executives* conveys even more vividly the demands of the producer role to be personally productive, fostering a work environment that is appropriately productive for others, and maintaining both an individual and work unit balance between pressures for production and overall effectiveness:

The first is one who delivers on commitments—financial or otherwise—and shares the values of our Company. His or her future is an easy call. Onward and upward.

The second type of leader is one who does not meet commitments and does not share our values. Not as pleasant a call, but equally easy.

The third is one who misses commitments but shares the values. He or she usually gets a second chance, preferably in a different environment.

Then there's the fourth type—the most difficult for many of us to deal with. That leader delivers on commitments, makes all the numbers, but doesn't share the values we must have. This is the individual who typically forces performance out of people rather than inspires it: the autocrat, the big shot, the tyrant. Too often all of us have looked the other way—tolerated these "type 4" managers because "they always deliver"—at least in the short term (Tichy and Sherman, 1993, p. 230).

Welch suggests that while type 4 executives were more palatable in less competitive times, their intimidating styles are a liability in an environment where the organization needs optimal contributions from everyone. Welch identified changing the style of type 4 executives (or parting company with them) as the ultimate test of the company's transformation into the kind of organization its values aspire to. "We know now that without leaders who "walk the talk," all of our plans, promises, and dreams for the future are just that–talk (Tichy and Sherman, 1993, p. 231).

This statement from Welch emphasizes the tension between aggressively "pushing" for results and productivity as an individual managerial leader and creating an environment that draws or "pulls" people into working productively without a so-called "push" (i.e. shove!). It also illustrates Welch and GE's recognition of an inescapable fact of organizational life in the shadow of the year 2000—namely, that you are not going to push, force, cajole, order, batter, or coerce your workforce into commitment—people will not give 150% because they have to—they will because they choose to and want to!

Competency 1 Working Productively

Directions   Take five minutes to think about a situation during the last few months when you felt you worked very productively and were very motivated. Write a short, one-paragraph description of that situation. In it be sure to explain *why* you were able to work so productively. Also, as part of your paragraph, identify which of your reasons were under your *direct and personal* control and which were not. Conclude your paragraph with a statement about whether the situation you described is an exceptional one or a typical one.

Interpretation   In the situation you described, your high level of productivity and motivation was very likely a consequence of a large number of factors. The ones you identified as being under your direct and personal control likely reflect your own underlying sources or catalysts for working productively. While these factors vary from person to person, there is a growing body of literature and research on what helps individuals work productively and with a high degree of motivation. We discuss that in the following section.

Productivity is a key measure of individual, group, organizational, and societal effectiveness. The nature of organizations and the competitive environment within which they operate have made high productivity and superior performance at all levels of endeavor imperative. We will examine several perspectives on what contributes to a high level of performance at the individual and organizational levels and examine the construct and process of "empowerment" as a unifying theme.

At the individual level of analysis, superior productivity or performance has often been examined from the perspective of "personal peak performance" (PPP). Garfield's (1986) research on PPP studied individual high achievement in a wide array of endeavors. The results were truly encouraging for all individuals because the conclusions reached suggest that PPP does not result from a specific innate talent or trait. Nor does it result from a particular set of behaviors. Rather, PPP seems to result from an overall pattern of traits or attributes. A peak performer possessing this pattern of attributes will most likely be (pp. 16–17):

1. *Results-oriented* because of a sense of personal mission.

2. Able to display the dual capacities of *self-management and team mastery*.

3. Capable of making course corrections and managing *change*.

TABLE 7.1 Conditions that Stimulate Personal Peak Performance

1. Commitment	4. Control
2. Challenge	5. Transcendence
3. Purpose	6. Balance

Table 7.1 presents six "conditions" that stimulate personal peak performance (Adams, 1984). Let's take a closer look at each. Several PPP researchers found a strong sense of commitment evident. Pines (1980) determined that a high level of commitment shields people from the adverse effects of stress load and work loads. Vaill (1982) concluded that significant investments of time and feeling are required if you want to generate high levels of performance in a work group. Garfield (1986) discovered that peak performers value internal goals and intrinsic rewards most, and care a great deal about the tasks they perform. A second characteristic identified in peak performers was a need or desire for an appropriate level of challenge—a consistent search for reasonable risks and opportunities to pursue "stretch" goals. Peak performers respond to challenge by emphasizing outcomes, results, and solutions, rather than ruminating about perfection (Garfield, 1986). A third condition associated with peak performance is a clear vision or purpose (Vaill, 1982). Managers need not only to know the answers to the *what* and *why* questions, but also to agree with the answers. Control was also a factor in understanding personal peal performance. Peak performers require a delicate balance between acting autonomously and responding to clear and specific goals. They need to have enough discretion to exercise their judgment while not being left without guidance or standards. A fifth condition found to be common among peak performers is a drive to transcend previous performance levels. This drive for "continuous improvement" is very similar to the Japanese notion of "Kaizen" (Imai, 1986). The sixth condition was a sense of overall balance, of perception about the "health" of the total being. Peak performers were able to enjoy and manage work, home, family, friends, and play.

What does the individual require from an organization in order to be able to work productively—and to potentially perform at a peak performance level? Mink, Owen, and Mink (1993) borrow the notion of "workscape" from anthropologists and conclude that workscapes can be either productive or unproductive. When unwritten rules and norms (i.e., culture) encourage and support high performance rather than inferior performance, productivity usually results. Mink et al. (1993) are somewhat pessimistic about the potential of more traditional organizational forms to be productive: "Because few existing bureaucracies emphasize competence and individual development, most organizations produce mediocrity" (1993, p. 56).

The authors' definition of a high-performance workspace (i.e., environment) is one that includes leadership reflected in vision, shared purpose and values and teamwork; a work unit climate that fosters individual autonomy and freedom, positive interpersonal relationships with appropriate feedback and problem solving, and management attention and focus on requisite resources and unit structure (Mink, Owen and Mink, 1993, pp. 56–57).

There is a striking similarity between what the experts on peak individual performance identify as conditions that stimulate such productivity and what Mink et al. (1993) delineate as the nature of a high-performance work context. The commitment aspect of PPP is reflected in the "why we exist" component of vision, shared purpose, and leadership and in the trust component of shared values and teamwork. The challenge piece of PPP is reflected in the performance aspect of positive relationships characterized by feedback and problem solving and the goal accomplishment aspect of management of focus. The role of purpose in PPP is similarly reflected in the productive workscape's vision, shared purpose, and leadership. The control aspect of PPP is similar to the individual autonomy and freedom component of the productive workscape. Transcendence in PPP is very much like the trust aspect of shared values and teamwork, and balance (from a PPP perspective) is reflected in the expectations aspect of work structure and management of focus in the productive workscape. These similarities between what makes individuals work productively and the characteristics of work settings that lead to productive work leads us to the notion of empowerment as a potential unifying theme.

EMPOWERMENT—A KEY TO WORKING PRODUCTIVELY

Perhaps no concept has garnered more attention or caused more contention than empowerment. Used and misused to describe myriad personal managerial styles and philosophies as well a series of organizational practices and programs, the term *empowerment* often generates as much cynicism as potential enlightenment in the minds of organizational members. What is empowerment? How docs one become empowered? What is the role of the managerial leader in empowerment? Does my boss empower me? Does the organization empower me? Is empowerment a program? A process? Can I be empowered without the help or support of my boss or organization? More importantly for us, what does empowerment have to do with working productively, the competency at hand, and how does it relate to the next competency of the producer role—fostering a productive work environment?

Bowen and Lawler (1992, p. 32) have defined empowerment as:

> . . . *sharing with frontline employees four organizational ingredients: (1) information about the organization's performance, (2) rewards based on the organization's performance, (3) knowledge that enables employees to understand and contribute to organizational performance, and (94) power to make decisions that influence organizational direction and performance.*

Bowen and Lawler, like many other organizational researchers, have focused their definition of empowerment on management practices—factors in the situation or context that may empower employees. Spreitzer (1994) has examined the internal process of empowerment as it occurs in the individual—psychological empowerment if you will. Spreitzer, de Janasz, and Quinn (1994, p. 3) have suggested that empowerment is defined as a "motivational construct" manifest in four cognitions. Those cognitions or perceptions are meaning, competence, self-determination, and impact. Meaning is the perception of fit between one's work or job and one's deeply held personal beliefs and values (Thomas and Velthouse, 1990). Competence (i.e., self-efficacy) is the notion that one has all the required abilities and skills to perform one's work or job well (Bandura, 1977). Self-determination is the belief that one has control (i.e., autonomy) over how one does one's work or job (Hackman and Oldham, 1989). Impact is the belief that one can affect outcomes that make a difference in the work setting (Ashforth, 1989). Conger and Kanungo (1988) also focus on the psychological aspect of empowerment and define it as the motivational concept of self-efficacy. But they also point out that management practices like the ones identified by Bowen and Lawler (1992) may be one set of conditions that may or may not empower employees.

We believe that understanding both the individual psychological aspects of empowerment as well as the various management practices that contribute to an individual's sense of empowerment, as well as the conditions that stimulate individual peak performance and productive workplaces, are critical for effective execution of the "working productively" competency in the producer role. As an individual managerial leader you must understand what it is that leads to productive (maybe even "peak") performance for yourself personally as well as for all of the individuals you are responsible for. You must understand what contributes to your sense of "meaning, competence, self-determination, and impact" as well as what contributes to that sense in your employees. You must feel personally empowered before you can be effective at helping your people to feel empowered. You have an especially burdensome responsibility when it comes to understanding the situation and context (e.g., management practices) of personal productivity and empowerment since, as a managerial leader in the organization, you help create and control them. In the next competency, "fostering a productive work environment," we will concentrate on two management practices that are very relevant to helping our people work productively: motivating others and understanding the importance of the role of coaching.

ANALYSIS   When Are You the Most Productive and Motivated?

Directions   Refer back to your description of the situation when you were most motivated and productive. In groups formed by your instructor, consider and respond to the questions that follow. Appoint a spokesperson in your group to present a five-minute summary of your work.

1. What common factors exist across your group members' descriptions of personal productivity and motivation?

2. What factors seem most unique to individual members? Are these under the direct control of individual members?

3. Do any of the psychological aspects of empowerment (meaning, competence, self-determination, and impact) help explain the productivity and motivation in your examples?

4. Were the conditions that stimulate personal peak performance a factor in any of the examples?

5. What key lessons can you generate from the experiences of the group?

PRACTICE   "Feeling Dead-Ended"[1]

Directions   Read the following case study and individually answer the questions that follow. Discuss your responses with the other members of your small group. Choose a group spokesperson to present responses to questions 2, 4, and 6 to the larger group.

Margaret Jardine was sure when she completed her associate's degree in business at Wagner Community College more than eight years ago, that she would go places in her career in the public sector. She had graduated with honors from WCC with an emphasis in Finance and Accounting. She passed the Audit Clerk exam the first time with a grade of 92; she was second on the list, and hired within six months. Within the next 14 months she had taken and passed the Senior Audit Clerk exam. It took two years to be selected from the list.

She felt she had truly made the right decision because she moved so quickly within the first four years. She felt that the Civil Service system was large enough to allow for movement into a variety of areas considering her two year degree, her good work performance and her ability to do well, it seemed, on exams.

She felt that she had been successful in her first four years because she had been able to work closely with good people. She was a hard worker and a fast learner.

Margaret waited almost two years to take the Principal Audit Clerk (grade 11) exam and failed it with a grade of 68. She couldn't believe it. She went to the review to determine what she had done wrong. The answers, though tricky, seemed so clear when the monitor explained them. Now she had to wait between two and three years for the next exam, depending on the need to fill positions. She felt thoroughly discouraged.

What distressed her even more was that she worked with a grade 11 Principal Clerk who "didn't know beans about the work." Margaret was the one who got all the difficult assignments because her accuracy rate was so high and she always met her deadlines.

Margaret felt that given her ability and recent responsibility she should really be in charge of the unit, regardless of her grade on the test. Recently, she began to wonder about her future in the Tax and Finance Department. She even wondered

[1]*Adapted from* an exercise used in *Getting Work Done Through Others: The Supervisor's Main Job,* Advanced Human Resources Development Program, New York State Govenor's Office of Employee Relations and CSEA, Inc., 1987.

about staying with government service. She was feeling almost dead-ended and didn't know how or where to move. It seemed, suddenly almost, that there was little or no movement within her area of expertise.

In her years with state government, she felt that she had done well with fairly regular pay increases, promotions, the degree of responsibility held and the expertise gained. Now, however, she felt that she had lost some of her motivation. Now if she put in extra time, it was only out of necessity of getting something done that *had* to be done. It certainly was not voluntary.

Margaret felt trapped, pigeon-holed in some way. She felt like she had no idea where she was going in the state. Others who had come when she did all seemed to be on their way to their goal, so to speak. She thought that perhaps they had chosen a broader, more diversified career path, situations that were easier to promote from. She felt that her work was very good and highly valued, but her salary increases were getting smaller and her options were becoming more limited. Recently, Margaret had turned down a very attractive offer from Northwestern Security and Exchange, a small finance company in Salem, near Albany, New York because she thought there would be too little opportunity for advancement. Now she wondered if it would have been better to take the opportunity.

Still, Margaret was confused about her feelings about the State. She felt that a move elsewhere might not be wise because she'd lose what seniority she had, her retirement benefits, and so on.

After dialing Northwestern's number, only to hang up before it rang, Margaret decided that she would put off any decision for at least a month so she could have plenty of time to think over her situation.

Discussion Questions

1. How would you describe Margaret's personal productivity and motivational level at the present time?

   (a) Are any of the conditions that stimulate personal peak performance present?

   (b) Are any of the psychological aspects (meaning, competence, self-determination, and impact) of empowerment present?

2. What factors contributed to this present situation?

3. What can Margaret do to clarify her options and choices?

4. What specific steps would you suggest to her?

5. Do you see any similarities between Margaret's situation and situations you have gone through? Explain.

6. With your answers to question 5 in mind, what actions can you identify that help renew enthusiasm, increase productivity, and boost motivation?

(a) Does Margaret's work situation have any of the characteristics of the productive workscape discussed above?

7. In a structured system like this one seems to be, how can you feel empowered, stay productive, and "fit in" while fulfilling your projected goals?

APPLICATION Creating Your Own Strategy for Increasing Personal Productivity and Motivation

Throughout this section you have had the opportunity to assess and explore your personal productivity and motivation level and the factors that influence and affect them. In this application activity, you will have a chance to plan ways to maintain or increase your personal productivity and motivation using those ideas and skills discussed so far. Please answer the following questions as specifically as you can. Although some responses (e.g., questions 1, 4, and 5) may be voluntarily shared, this information will be seen only by you.

1. What are the major forces contributing to productivity and motivation in your life? (Please consider your work at school, or at a job, or any extracurricular activity in which you're involved.)

2. What are the principle blocks or impediments to these forces?

3. Are any of these forces related to personal peak performance or the psychological aspects of empowerment?

4. What can you do to enhance the positive forces contributing to your productivity and motivation?

5. How can you neutralize the blocks or impediments to these forces?

6. How will you know you are successful?

Competency 2   Fostering a Productive Work Environment

ASSESSMENT Your "Motivating" Potential

Directions   A critical component of fostering a productive work environment is the ability to understand that *what* and *how* of others' motivation. Motivation often wanes when people cannot satisfy the needs they have. Here are eight sets of needs that might be considered. Indicate, in the first column, how important you think each need is to employees, and in the second column, how much opportunity employees have to satisfy that need.

Scale	Very Low	1	2	3	4	5	Very High

Importance	*Opportunity*	
_____	_____	1. Direction, purpose, role clarity.
_____	_____	2. Belonging, teamwork, affiliation.
_____	_____	3. Compensation, recognition, rewards.
_____	_____	4. Productivity impact, achievement.
_____	_____	5. Standardization, measurement, objectivity.
_____	_____	6. Sensitivity, consideration, support.
_____	_____	7. Challenge, variety, stimulation.
_____	_____	8. Coordination, predictability, control.

Interpretation   Now consider the following in small groups formed by your instructor. Prepare a five-minute summary presentation for the larger group.

1. How do you account for the magnitude of the *difference* between importance and opportunity in each of the eight?

2. Who has more control over (i.e., responsibility for) each, you or your subordinates?

3. What could you, as a manager, do to address these *differences?*

LEARNING   Fostering a Productive Work Environment

As we have indicated many times previously in this book, the competitive challenges confronting our organizations are unlike any that have preceded them. Customers are more demanding than ever. Our competitors have never been better and our employees have never expected more from their organizations and their "bosses." The upshot of all this is that it has never been more critical or more difficult to maintain a productive work environment with motivated people in it. One management consultant and trainer routinely asks two questions of his students: "How many of you think your boss would notice if you put 15 percent *more* effort into your jobs?" and "How many of you think your boss would notice if you put 15 percent *less* effort into your jobs?" With a sample of over 1,500 respondents the results were almost unanimous in replying that their bosses would not notice if their performance differed 15 percent in either direction (Kinlaw, 1993, p. 2). The point is all organizational members control much discretionary time, effort, and energy when it comes to doing their jobs. Individuals could give a fair amount more to it or a fair amount less. The challenge is to create an environment within which employees will give a fair amount more, and then some—not because they have to but because they really want to.

In this section, we will review two critical aspects of fostering a productive work environment. First we will examine motivating others specifically—the application of motivation theory to understanding the needs of our employees. We will then turn our attention to the importance of the role of coaching in maintaining a productive work environment.

MOTIVATING OTHERS: APPLYING MOTIVATION THEORY

The extent and depth of motivation theory fills literally thousands of books and journal articles. Again, it is our concern to only discuss theory as it informs practice. One of the most comprehensive theories of motivation in use today is **expectancy theory**, which is a motivational theory based on the relationships among job effort, performance, and outcomes of performance. The expectancy framework incorporates the central elements of need and process approaches. Victor Vroom (1964) was the first to conceptualize expectancy theory with the following "equation":

$$Motivation = Expectancy \times Valence \times Instrumentality$$
$$or$$
$$M = E \times V \times I$$

Figure 7.1 graphically depicts expectancy theory.

Vroom's formulation of the theory has been expanded to take into account multiple outcomes (Nadler and Lawler, 1977). The expanded equation becomes:

$$Motivation = E \rightarrow P \times \Sigma[(P \rightarrow O) \times (v)]$$
$$or$$
$$Motivation = Effort\ to\ Performance \times the\ sum\ of$$
$$[(Performance\ to\ Outcomes) \times (Valence)]$$

Note that the fundamental linkages are the same, but the expanded equation allows the consideration of multiple outcomes. Consider the following example: Anne Johnson is the project leader of a group of computer programmers and systems analysts who have been charged with the task of creating a new MIS for one of her company's largest divisions. Johnson is a little disappointed at the rate at which progress has been made. She is considering working on the project during the entire holiday weekend that is coming up.

Applying the multiple outcomes version of the expectancy theory, we can analyze Anne's level of motivation regarding working the holiday weekend. Let's begin with the effort to performance linkage (i.e., expectancy). Here, the consideration is whether or not working the holiday weekend (the "effort" to be expended) will

FIGURE 7.1
Elements in the expectancy theory of motivation.

Source: John R. Schermerhorn, Jr., Management for Productivity, *3rd ed., New York: John Wiley & Sons, 1989, p. 365. Used with permission.*

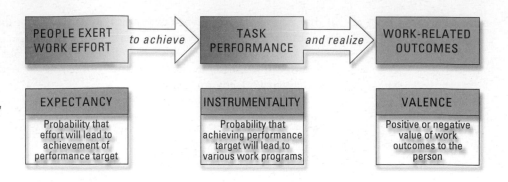

result in her completing the new MIS more quickly. Anne can estimate the probability of this using a number between 0 and 1. If she believes that she personally can be productive and move the project along over the holiday weekend, then she will likely estimate this probability as being relatively high—say 0.9.

Let us now turn to the instrumentality or performance to outcome linkage. Here, the concern is what the probability is that if she does indeed complete the project more quickly, it will lead to certain outcomes. Those outcomes could include a promotion, increased responsibility, a special recognition award, a spat with her husband and family about not being at home over the holiday, exhaustion, fatigue, and so on. Johnson could estimate a probability for *each* of these (e.g., what is the probability that if I complete this project quickly, I will get a promotion?). Johnson must then determine the valence (attractiveness, value) each of these has to her and then include those valences into the equation (using a–1 . . . 0 . . . + 1 scale for each outcome, with –1 being extremely undesirable and + 1 being extremely desirable.

With the multiple outcomes version of the expectancy formulation, Johnson can weigh, balance, and make trade-offs among the various outcomes and their valences.

SUMMARY GUIDE FOR APPLYING THE EXPECTANCY THEORY

How can you, as a manager, apply the expectancy theory? There are three ways for you to tie directly to the three components of the expectancy theory:

1. Tie effort to performance.

2. Link performance to outcomes.

3. Understand valences for desired employee outcomes.

TIE EFFORT TO PERFORMANCE

An employee will ask himself or herself: "If I work hard (exert a certain level of effort), can I attain the level of performance expected by my manager?"

Managers can respond in two ways to tie an employee's effort to performance:

1. They can increase the employee's estimate of the effort to performance probability by involving the subordinate in defining what "performance" is. This implies the existence and use of MBO-type processes and performance evaluation systems (see Chapter 6's discussion of goal setting).

2. They can utilize the power of positive expectations with subordinates (see "Be a Positive Pygmalion").

BE A *POSITIVE* PYGMALION

Pygmalion was a sculptor in Greek mythology who created a gorgeous woman who was subsequently brought to life. George Bernard Shaw's play of the same name and the musical "My Fair Lady" are built on the same theme—that through the power of sheer self-effort and will, an individual can transform another person. J. Sterling Livingston, a professor at the Harvard School of Business, believes that supervisors, managers, and executives at all levels in organizations can also play Pygmalion-type roles. He bases this belief on research of his own that suggests:

1. What managers expect of their subordinates and the way they treat them largely determine subordinates' performance and career progress.

2 A unique characteristic of superior managers is their ability to create high performance expectations that their subordinates fill.

3. Less effective managers fail to develop similar expectations, so, as a consequence, the productivity of their subordinates suffers.

4. Subordinates, more often than not, appear to do what they believe they are expected to do.

Source: Reprinted by permission of *Harvard Business Review.* An excerpt from "Pygmalion in Management" by J.S. Livingston, 47:4 (July/August 1969). Copyright ©1969 by the President and Fellows of Harvard College; all rights reserved.

Being a positive Pygmalion is probably the single most important way a manager can motivate his or her subordinates. It does not require large amounts of money or other types of rewards. It does not require dealing with the complexities and contingencies of job design. It is under the complete control of the manager. But it is not easy. Being a positive Pygmalion for your subordinates goes to the very heart of your assumption about people and your own managerial style. It also requires that you be a positive Pygmalion for yourself—that is, believing that you are capable of being a peak performer as we discussed in Competency 1.

LINK PERFORMANCE TO OUTCOME(S)

Employees will ask themselves: "If I, in fact, perform at the level expected by my manager, what is the likelihood that certain outcomes will result?"

The manager can address this concern by making certain that employees are aware of all the possible outcomes that will result from performance. Regular and consistent use of performance appraisals and MBO-type discussions like those discussed earlier are again the most effective means of accomplishing this.

UNDERSTAND VALENCE FOR DESIRED EMPLOYEE OUTCOMES

Employees can evaluate all possible outcomes and the attractiveness or value (i.e., positive or negative) each has to them.

Managers can address this component by making certain that they know what "outcomes" are important to their employees. There's no substitute for knowing your employees. Depending on the size of your group, you can obtain this information either through one-on-one conversations or, if the group is too large, through employee attitude survey processes.

THE ROLE OF COACHING IN FOSTERING A PRODUCTIVE WORK ENVIRONMENT

In our discussion of the mentor role (Chapter 2), we literally define mentor as a type of coach—a counselor or guide. We also discuss some of the core skill components of coaching, like giving and receiving feedback. Additionally, we focus on performance appraisal as a critical role we play as coaches. We would like to expand on our concept of coaching here and propose it as a key method for creating and communicating the core components of a high performance and productive workplace.

Kinlaw (1993) has acknowledged the many uses and definitions of the word *coach*. We find his description of the four "functions" of coaching as counseling, mentoring, tutoring, and confronting useful here in our attempt to broaden its definition and expand its role. Kinlaw (1993) suggests that each function of coaching generates different potential outcomes. Counseling helps others accurately describe problems and their potential causes as well as gain deeper personal insights about their feelings and behavior. Mentoring typically helps individuals develop their own "political savvy," get more proactive about their own career, and increase their commitment to the organization's goals and values. Tutoring typically results in increased technical competence and faster movement to expert status. Confronting typically results in clarification of performance expectations and strategies to improve performance. While each of the functions of coaching can result in different outcomes, the core skills required to perform each are quite similar. As mentioned earlier, we cover those core skills in Chapter 2 (the mentor role) with our discussion of giving and receiving feedback and developing others. Kinlaw (1993) also identifies four very useful criteria for determining whether or not coaching (no matter what the function) was effective: positive change in actual performance or a renewed commitment to self-sufficiency and the values and goals of the organization, continuous learning, and a consistent high level of performance occurs; a positive work relationship is achieved or maintained; the coaching session was two-way, problem-focused, change-oriented, and respectful; and the session followed an identifiable sequence or flow (e.g., our discussion of rules for effective feedback in Chapter 2).

In our discussion of working productively (preceding competency in this chapter), we referred to characteristics of high-performance work environments as including leadership reflected in vision, shared purpose and values, and teamwork, a work unit climate that fosters individual autonomy and freedom, positive interpersonal relationships with appropriate feedback and problem solving, and management attention and focus on requisite resources and unit structure (Mink, Owen and Mink, 1993, pp. 56–57). We believe that the process of coaching, no matter which of the four functions it might be used for, can be an opportunity to create, contribute to, or reinforce one or more of the above dimensions. Kinlaw's (1993, p. 19) observation about coaching makes our point:

> *Coaching is the process by which managers stay in touch with their subordinates. All the walking around in the world will not help managers to get the best from their employees unless they are walking around as coaches.* Coaching is eyeball-to-eyeball management. *Every conversation between managers and employees is potentially a coaching conversation. It is a chance to clarify goals, priorities, and standards of performance. It is a chance to reaffirm and reinforce the group's core values. It is a chance to hear ideas and to involve employees in the processes of planning and problem solving. More important than all the rest, it is a chance to say "thank you."*

ANALYSIS   The Case of Michael Simpson[2]

Directions   Read the case of Michael Simpson, and answer the questions that follow.

Michael Simpson is one of the most outstanding managers in the management consulting division of Avery McNeil and Co. He is a highly qualified individual with a deep sense of responsibility.

Simpson obtained his MBA two years ago from one of the leading northeastern schools. Before being graduated from business school, Simpson had interviewed with a number of consulting firms and decided that the consulting division of Avery McNeil offered the greatest potential for rapid advancement.

[2]*From* David Nadler, M. Tushman, and N. Hatvany (eds.), *Managing Organizations* (Boston: Little, Brown 1982). Used with permission from the authors.

Simpson was recently promoted to manager, making him the youngest manager at the consulting group. Two years with the firm was an exceptionally short period of time in which to achieve this promotion. Although the promotion was announced, Simpson had not yet been informed of his new salary. Despite the fact that his career had progressed well, he was concerned that his salary would be somewhat lower than the current market value that a headhunter had recently quoted him.

Simpson's wife, Diane, soon would be receiving her MBA. One night over dinner Simpson was amazed to hear the salaries being offered to new MBAs. Simpson commented to Diane, "I certainly hope I get a substantial raise this time. I mean, it just wouldn't be fair to be making the same amount as recent graduates when I've been at the company now for over two years! I'd like to buy a house soon, but with housing costs rising and inflation following, that will depend on my pay raise."

Several days later, Simpson was working at his desk when Dave Barton, a friend and a colleague, came across to Simpson's office. Barton was hired at the same time as Simpson, and had also been promoted recently. Barton told Simpson, "Hey, Mike, look at this! I was walking past Jane's desk and saw this memo from the personnel manager lying there. She obviously forgot to put it away. Her boss would kill her if he found out!"

The memo showed the proposed salaries for all the individuals in the consulting group that year. Simpson looked at the list and was amazed by what he saw. He said, "I can't believe this, Dave! Walt and Rich are getting $2000 more than I am."

Walt Gresham and Rich Watson had been hired within the past year. Before coming to Avery McNeil, they had both worked one year at another consulting firm.

Barton spoke angrily, "Mike, I knew the firm had to pay them an awful lot to attract them, but to pay them more than people above them is ridiculous!"

"You know," replied Simpson, "if I hadn't seen Walt and Rich's salaries, I would think I was getting a reasonable raise. Hey listen, Dave, let's get out of here. I've had enough of this place for one day."

"Okay, Mike, just let me return this memo. Look, it's not that bad; after all, you are getting the largest raise."

On his way home, Simpson tried to think about the situation more objectively. He knew that there were a number of pressures on the compensation structure in the consulting division. If the division wished to continue attracting MBAs from top schools, it would have to offer competitive salaries. Starting salaries had increased about $3500 during the last two years. As a result, some of the less-experienced MBAs were earning nearly the same amounts as others who had been with the firm several years but who had come in at lower starting salaries, even though their pay had been gradually increased over time.

Furthermore, because of expanding business, the division had found it necessary to hire consultants from other firms. In order to do so effectively, Avery McNeil found it necessary to upgrade the salaries they offered.

The firm as a whole was having problems meeting the federally regulated Equal Opportunity Employment goals and was trying especially hard to recruit women and minorities.

One of Simpson's colleagues, Martha Lohman, had been working in the consulting division of Avery McNeil until three months ago, when she was offered a job at another consulting firm. She had become disappointed with her new job and, on returning to her previous position at Avery McNeil, was rehired at a salary considerably higher than her former level. Simpson had noticed on the memo that she was earning more than he was, even though she was not given nearly the same level of responsibility. Simpson also realized that the firm attempted to maintain some parity between salaries in the auditing and consulting divisions.

When Simpson arrived home, he discussed the situation with his wife. "Diane, I know I'm getting a good raise, but I am still earning below my market value—$3000 less than the headhunter told me last week. And the fact that those two guys from the other consulting firm are getting more than me shows that the firm is prepared to pay competitive rates."

"I know it's unfair, Mike," Diane replied, "but what can you do? You know your boss won't negotiate salaries after they have been approved by the compensation committee, but it wouldn't hurt to at least talk to him about your dissatisfaction. I don't think you should let a few thousand dollars a year bother you. You will catch up eventually, and the main thing is that you really enjoy what you are doing."

"Yes, I do enjoy what I'm doing, but that is not to say that I wouldn't enjoy it elsewhere. I really just have to sit down and think about all the pros and cons in my working for Avery McNeil. First of all, I took this job because I felt that I could work my way up quickly. I think that I have demonstrated this, and the firm has also shown that they are willing to help me achieve this goal. If I left this job for a better paying one, I might not get the opportunity to work on the exciting jobs that I am currently working on. Furthermore, this company has time and money invested in me. I'm the only one at Avery that can work on certain jobs, and the company has several lined up. If I left the company now, they would not only lose me, but they would probably lose some of their billings as well. I really don't know what to do at this point, Diane. I can either stay with Avery McNeil or look for a higher paying job elsewhere; however, there is no guarantee that my new job would be a fast track one like it is at Avery. One big plus at Avery is that the people there already know me and the kind of work I produce. If I went elsewhere, I'd essentially have to start all over again. What do you think I should do, Diane?"

Discussion Questions

1. What are the motivational drivers of Simpson's dilemma?

2. Using the expectancy theory, define the dilemmas.

3. If you were Simpson's manager, and he approached you with this problem, how would you respond? Could you use this opportunity to "coach" Simpson? What would be the primary function(s) of the coaching?

PRACTICE   The Same Old Job[3]

Directions

Read the following case study and answer the questions that follow. When each person has finished answering the questions individually, discuss your answers in your small group. Choose a recorder/reporter to present the small group's findings to the large group.

Helen Ames awoke this morning with another headache. This was the second time in three days. She hadn't been sleeping well for the past four months or so either. When she awoke, a feeling of dread overpowered her again; she thought about going to work. As she sat on the edge of the bed, she thought about the good working conditions, decent pay, and the people with whom she worked. But it didn't seem to matter.

She'd been thinking a great deal recently about how tired and bored she'd become. She'd been on the job now three and a half years, and all the excitement was gone. There was plenty of work to do, but it all seemed routine now. She didn't even get upset or excited about the problems that arose because she felt like "she'd heard it all before."

She was tired of doing "the same old thing, day in and day out." Even though the assignments were different, the tasks seemed almost identical—writing reports, checking quotas, giving the same directions over and over again to the same people—the same problems in the same areas. She could almost describe what would happen every day for each situation.

Helen's friends and family told her how lucky she was to have a job at which she did well, and one that offered security. Some had begun to ask her what it was that she would really like to do or what it was that would make her happy. They suggested that she take some time to think about what was wrong and what she could do about it.

She decided to request three days off.

[3] *Adapted from* an exercise used in *Getting Work Done Through Others: The Supervisor's Main Job*, Advanced Human Resources Development Program, New York State Governor's Office of Employee Relations and CSEA, Inc., 1987.

Discussion Questions

1. How would you describe Helen's personal motivation level?

2. What personal conflicts exist for her?

3. What do you think Helen might do during her time off?

4. Do you see any similarities between any of the following? Explain.
   Helen Ames and you, now or at some other time?
   Helen Ames and people you've known?
   Helen Ames and workers you've known or dealt with?

5. If you were supervising Helen Ames and had all this information, how would you try to motivate her?

6. Which of the conditions for PPP presented to you earlier could be used to increase Helen's personal motivation?

APPLICATION   Understanding Organizational Reward Systems

The diagnostic framework that follows will be helpful to you in assessing the overall motivation potential and reward systems in potential job areas. Using the questions as a starting point, interview three potential employers about how they motivate their employees and what their reward systems are.

Motivation and Reward Systems: A Diagnostic [4]

1. What are the rewards offered by your organization that are useful in getting individuals to pursue organizational objectives?

   - Consider economic incentives such as pay and benefits.

   - Consider symbols of prestige and status.

   - Consider informal job content incentives such as freedom, recognition, and interesting work.

2. How is each reward listed in question 1 obtained? Is it for:

   - Individual performance.

   - Group performance.

   - Attendance.

   - Fixed membership (the reward is automatically awarded to all organization members).

[4] *Adapted from* "On the Folly of Rewarding A While Hoping for B," by Steve Kerr, *Academy of Management Journal* 18 (1975): 769–783. Used with permission.

- Variable membership (the reward is given to long-service members only, or is given in proportion to time on job or years with the company).

- Level (the reward is given automatically to all those who are at a particular organization level).

- Don't know (the reward is given, but it is not clear what recipients do to get it).

3. Which organization unit or level is primarily responsible for the distribution of each reward listed in question 1?

- Top management/company policy.

- Personnel.

- The union.

- Level of management immediately above your own.

- Yourself.

- Your subordinates.

Competency 3 Managing Time and Stress

ASSESSMENT Stress in Your Organization

Directions
Listed below are ten stressors that often surface in work organizations. They also sometimes occur in other types of organizations, such as voluntary or community organizations, athletic teams, or social organizations. Most can occur whenever there is work to be done and people must interact with others in deciding how the tasks are to be carried out. Choose an organization in which you spend a good deal of time, preferably a work organization. If you are not currently actively involved in such an organization, think back to a previous job.

Think for a moment about each of the potential stressors and ask yourself the following questions:

1. On a scale from 1 to 10, to what extent do you experience this type of stress (1 = not a stressor; 10 = creates much stress)?

2. On a scale of 1 to 5, to what extent do you feel you have control over this stressor (1 = no control; 5 = full control)?

3. When faced with this type of stressor, what do you do to cope with it?

Note: There is room for you to add additional stressors that you may have experienced.

Potential Stressor	Extent of stress (1–10)	Extent of control (1–5)	Methods of coping
1. Lack of clarity regarding your role in the organization	_____	_____	_____
2. Feeling that you are overqualified or underqualified for the job	_____	_____	_____
3. Too much work to do in the time you have	_____	_____	_____
4. Too much responsibility for task completion	_____	_____	_____
5. Not enough information to make necessary decisions	_____	_____	_____
6. Too much responsibility for others' actions	_____	_____	_____
7. Not enough authority to make decisions	_____	_____	_____
8. Poor interpersonal relationships with others	_____	_____	_____
9. Organizational politics	_____	_____	_____
10. Conflict between organizational needs and personal needs	_____	_____	_____
11.	_____	_____	_____
12.	_____	_____	_____
13.	_____	_____	_____

Discussion Questions

1. Which of these stressors are you experiencing? What is your total level of stress in this organization?

2. Of the stressors you experience, over which do you feel you have the most control? the least control? What influences the level of control you have?

3. When you have experienced stress in an organization, what have been your most effective coping strategies? your least effective coping strategies?

4. Have you ever helped others (e.g., friends, employees, peers) cope with organizational stress? If so, what differences are there in coping with stress yourself and helping others cope with stress?

LEARNING   Managing Time and Stress

The topics of time and stress management are often discussed together because they are both key skills in helping people become more productive. For many people this means "doing more in less time." In this chapter, however, we do not make the assumption that being more productive simply means packing more activities into your day. Rather, we assume that measures of productivity should also focus on the quality of your activities. In this sense, we see personal productivity, as Stephen Covey and his associates (1994, p. 16) suggest, as "more than doing things right, it's . . . doing the right things." In their book, *First Things First,* Covey, Merrill, and Merrill (1994) suggest that one of the problems with traditional approaches to time management is that they focus on speed, rather than direction. They argue that when you are making decisions regarding how to spend your time you should focus more on where you are headed than on how fast you are going.

Including quality in our definition of productivity makes evident the strong relationship between time management and stress management, and so it is easy to see that good time management can help reduce your stress and that healthy stress management can allow you to use your time more effectively. In this chapter we will treat time and stress management as two complementary tools that can help you find an appropriate balance across the various demands on your time. It then becomes clear that the purpose of time management is not simply to "do more in less time," because this would more likely increase your stress than reduce it. Similarly, the purpose of stress management is not simply "Don't worry, be happy," because this would more likely reduce your effective use of time than increase it. Rather, the purpose of both is to learn how to live your life so that your most important goals are accomplished.

We will begin this section of the chapter with a discussion of stress management, briefly examining the sources and organizational consequences of stress. We will then present several stress management methods, some that you can do easily, some that will take practice. We will then turn to time management, examining some of the current thinking about time management and suggesting some techniques to help you manage your time better.

STRESS IN ORGANIZATIONS

The topic of stress (and stress management) has become an increasingly important area of concern for organizations and their managers. Research over the past three decades has linked stress to a vast array of illnesses, including tension headaches, various forms of heart disease, cancer, ulcers, and even arthritis (Dossey, 1982, McGee-Cooper,1994). Beyond affecting their physical health, stress can affect employees' ability and willingness to do their jobs by reducing their cognitive abilities, level of energy, and motivation, as well as their ability to relate interpersonally with co-workers. The costs of individual stress to organizations can be measured in terms of increased absenteeism, turnover, and accident rates; low quality of performance and low rate of performance; and stress-related disability claims. Estimates of the annual cost of individual stress to organizations in the United States exceed $100 billion. And the trend is likely to increase. A survey of a random sample of 600 U.S. workers conducted by Northwestern Life Insurance in 1990 found that 46 percent described their jobs as highly stressful and 34 percent indicated that they considered leaving their jobs because of the stress they were feeling (Metcalf and Felible, 1992).

While we may be tempted to think about stress as a uniquely American phenomenon, it is important to note that stress-related diseases are found wherever organizations value long work hours over workers' and managers' physical and mental health. In Japan, medical expert Tetsunojo Uehata coined the term *karoshi,* which literally means death from overwork, to refer to a "condition in which psychologically unsound work practices are allowed to continue in a way that disrupts the worker's normal work and life rhythms, leading to a buildup of fatigue in the body and a chronic condition of overwork accompanied by a worsening of pre-existent high blood pressure and a hardening of the arteries and finally resulting in fatal breakdown" (cited in Metcalf and Felible, 1992, pp. 151–152). In 1987, karoshi was blamed for the deaths (from stress-related illnesses) of the presidents of ten major Japanese companies within an eight-month period.

Given the potential impact of stress on individuals' physical and mental health, as well as on individual and organizational performance, it is important for the manager to be aware of how the work environment creates stress for individuals. Dr. Hans Selye, often considered the father of current research on the health effects of stress on human beings, argued that stress is a nonspecific response to demands placed on the body (1976). Here, the term *nonspecific response* is used to differentiate reactions to specific stimuli, for example, changes in temperature that cause the body to shiver or sweat in order to restore equilibrium, from the more generalized reaction to a stimulus that forces the body out of equilibrium. Thus stress is within the person; it is the person's response to a change in the external environment.

Selye further posited a *general adaptation system* to describe how the body responds to a stressor. This theory identifies three stages of reaction to environmental demands. In the first stage, the *alarm stage,* the body's defense mechanisms are triggered. Often referred to as the "fight-or-flight" reaction, when the body senses a threat, it releases adrenaline, cortisone, and other hormones, thus raising both heart rate and blood pressure. If the situation allows the stress to subside, the body will return to equilibrium. Alternatively, if the demand continues, the person enters the *resistance stage.* In this stage, the body attempts to return to equilibrium, and essentially focuses full attention on the stressor. By definition, this results in decreased attention to any other stressors. Thus, an individual who is experiencing large amounts of stress over workload, financial, or personal concerns may be more susceptible to colds or other illnesses than one who is experiencing less stress. The final stage is the *exhaustion stage.* In this stage, the person has experienced intense and/or prolonged stress, and the body is no longer able to resist. In this stage, the physiological reactions that occurred during the alarm stage may likely reappear and the body is not able to return to its normal state. The result may be psychological, as with depression or other mental illness, or physiological, as with heart disease, ulcers, and so forth.

It should be noted that not all stress is negative in its source or in its consequences. Selye distinguishes *distress* from *eustress,* the latter being the type of stress the body experiences during very positive or joyous circumstances, noting that both cause the physiological fight-or-flight reaction and that, in both circumstances, the body will naturally attempt to return to its equilibrium state. Eustress, however, is seldom maintained over long periods of time. In addition, medical experts agree that a certain amount of stress is natural and even healthy. Indeed, Selye argued that "complete freedom from stress is death" (1974, p. 20). The key is to keep the body from entering the exhaustion stage of the general adaptation system. A useful analogy is the tension on the strings of a tennis racket; if they are either too loose or too taut, they will keep the player from playing at peak performance.

SOURCES OF STRESS

While the discussion about the relationship between stress and illness raises issues about the nature of the work environment and its influence on people's stress, you are probably aware that different people react differently to different situations. Some people like to work under tight time pressures and would argue that they become most efficient and even creative as the deadline approaches. Others find working under tight deadlines to be too stressful and prefer to pace themselves so that everything is completed ahead of time. Similarly, when traveling, some managers like to plan to get to the airport early. In order to avoid the stress associated with getting caught in traffic on the way to the airport, they schedule enough slack into their schedule so that they will still catch the plane, even if delayed by traffic. Other managers find the waiting time to be stressful and prefer to time their arrival at the airport so that they avoid the crowded waiting area. Are deadlines and traffic inherently stressful? Why do some people react to certain situations in a very intense manner while others seem to take these situations in stride? Are there stressors that affect all people consistently?

Psychologists have identified two major categories of sources of stress related to illness and disease: stressful life situations and personality characteristics (Cohen, 1979). Stressful life situations are those events that cause major changes in (daily) life patterns, thereby creating strain or atypical emotional states. Much research during the late 1960s and early to mid-1970s focused on these stressful life situations. Perhaps the best known work in this area is built around the Holmes and Rahe (1967) *Social Readjustment Rating Scale.* Based on a series of research studies that examined the relationship between stressful life events and the onset of illnesses of all types, this scale assigns a "life change unit" score to a number of major life changes, both positive and negative, such as death of a spouse (100 points), divorce (73 points), marriage (50 points), retirement (45 points), and gaining a new family member (e.g., through birth, adoption, older relative moving in) (39 points). Individuals identify which events they have experienced within the previous two years and add up their scores. Those who score very high on this scale are said to have an increased likelihood of becoming ill or injured. While the scale has become quite popular, it is somewhat controversial and has been criticized on both methodological and theoretical grounds. In particular, a number of researchers have argued that the relationship between stressful life events and illness is not a direct one; rather it is mediated by other variables such as biological predispositions to illness, the person's appraisal of the situation, the person's resources for dealing with the situation, the degree of social support from others, and the degree of change in daily activities (Cohen, 1979).

The second category of sources of stress, personality characteristics, comprises those characteristics that predispose individuals to appraise and react to similar situations in different ways. The best known research in this area is probably Friedman and Rosenmann's (1974) work on the Type A behavior pattern, described as "a particular complex of personality traits, including excessive competitive drive, aggressiveness, impatience, and a harrying sense of time urgency. Individuals displaying this pattern seem to be engaged in a chronic, ceaseless, and often fruitless struggle—with themselves, with others, with circumstances, with time, sometimes with life itself. They also frequently exhibit a free-floating but well-rationalized form of hostility, and almost always a deep-seated insecurity" (p. 4). In contrast, individuals who are categorized as exhibiting Type B behavior have a more relaxed approach and are not as driven by time. Research in this area has shown a strong link between Type A behavior and coronary heart disease (CHD), even after controlling for such factors as parental history of CHD, smoking behavior, blood pressure, and cholesterol levels. This work is particularly important in the context of this chapter because it provides evidence that trying to do more in less time is not effective time management. People who exhibit Type A behavior build their lives around goals, objectives, and deadlines, but "are unable to approach a task in a healthy, balanced way" (Dossey, 1982, p. 50).

As noted above, organizational researchers have added work-related stressors to the list of sources of stress. Work overload and time pressures, role conflict (see Chapter 3), work relationships, and office politics are, to a large degree, external factors that can lead to stress, regardless of an individual's personality or predispositions. On the other hand, there are a variety of stressors in the work environment that individuals can learn to manage in an effective way. In the producer role, managers must be proactive in assisting their units and departments to maximize positive stress (without physical, psychological, or emotional strain), minimize negative stress, and effectively manage those situations where negative stress cannot be minimized. But first, managers must be effective in managing their own stress. In the next section we provide several tools and techniques for managing individual stress.

STRATEGIES FOR MANAGING STRESS

As noted above, stress is not an event; rather stress is a reaction based on one's perception of the event. Although some situations are arguably more inherently stress provoking than others, many day-to-day experiences are more subjective in nature. Thus two people can experience the same objective situation and have two different reactions—one will feel stressed and out of control while the other will approach the situation with a sense of composure, and perhaps even with a sense of humor. For example, when the boss calls and says that the report you took all of last week to prepare for upper management needs to be expanded and delivered by the end of the day, you can expect the adrenaline to start flowing. The big issue is: What happens next?

In order to reduce or eliminate the negative effects of the resistance and exhaustion stages of stress, you have three options. First, remove yourself from the situation. Second, alter the situation or environment that is causing the stress. Third, teach yourself to respond differently to the situation by altering your evaluation of the situation. Given that you cannot expect to avoid or alter all situations you find stressful (and indeed, as noted above, this is not a recommended strategy), this third strategy, which focuses on altering your reactions to situations in order to reduce the negative effects of stress, is considered to be the most effective. Below we focus on five strategies for managing stress. Note that, in general, these are *long-term* strategies that focus on building your personal resources for approaching potentially stress-provoking situations, rather than instantaneous strategies that will help you reduce the stress at the moment the boss calls to ask you to expand the report. The strategies can be seen as investments that require regular attention. Just as you would not expect to be able to go out and run a marathon if you have not been training for this activity, you cannot maintain a Type A behavior pattern approach to work, and expect that with a few deep breaths you will be ready to face a difficult task with a sense of calmness. The strategies that work best for managing stress are those that focus on how you approach life in general.

CLARIFY YOUR VALUES

The first step in learning to manage stress is to figure out what is important to you in life and then to empower yourself to follow these beliefs. As noted earlier in this chapter, we agree with Stephen Covey's suggestion that it is more important to focus on where you are going than on how fast you can get there. In Chapter 2, we discussed the importance of self-awareness as a managerial competency. Here we suggest that self-awareness also includes being aware of your goals, needs, and expectations. As Marlene Wilson notes, "It is essential to develop a keen self-awareness regarding your own goals, needs, and expectations (instead of responding only to the 'oughts and shoulds' of other people). Your personal value system should serve as the basis for all of the major life choices you make. It is important that your expenditure of time and energy be congruent with these values or stress is inevitable. It does not work for long to put first things last" (1981, p. 212).

Wilson suggests two exercises to help you clarify your values. First, assume that you are about to be given $1 million, tax-free. Make a list of five to ten things you will buy in the next six months with the money. Next, imagine that you will be fatally struck by lightning in six months. Assuming that all matters pertaining to your death have been taken care of, make a list of five to ten things you would like to accomplish over the next six months. Now, go back to your lists and identify those items on the list that have nothing to do with money or time pressures and establish one or more goals for the next six months. Be realistic! You might even want to write a brief action plan for yourself and review it periodically over the six-month period. Imagine how good you will feel in six months for having accomplished at least one of the goals.

PAY ATTENTION TO YOUR PHYSICAL HEALTH

There is considerable research that shows that individuals who are in good physical condition are better able to deal with stressful situations than are those who are in poor physical condition. There are a number of key elements that contribute to your physical health. Here we focus on three: diet, exercise, and rest. Maintaining a healthy diet and nutrition habits is vital to maintaining your physical health. McGee-Cooper, who gives *Energy Engineering* seminars on maintaining and maximizing one's energy, productivity, and zest for life, writes, "too much salt, sugar, fat, cholesterol, and caffeine will lower performance levels. They interfere with the chemistry of your brain and impede optimum performance, and they can plug up your cardiovascular system, causing your heart to pump harder, your body to get less oxygen, and toxins in your blood to be less effectively filtered out" (McGee-Cooper, 1992, p. 165). Healthy nutrition also means avoiding fad diets and not skipping meals on a regular basis. Indeed, some nutritionists recommend eating several small meals, instead of three big ones.

A second key to maintaining physical health is regular aerobic exercise, such as running, swimming, rowing, rope skipping, bicycling, and dancing. Aerobic exercise inoculates the body against stress in a manner similar to medical vaccinations. By exposing the cardiovascular system to a small amount of stress on a regular basis, it can better cope with other stresses it encounters. In addition, during exercise the body releases endorphins, a natural (internal) pain-killer, that has also been shown to stimulate the body's immune system to increase its ability to fight disease. To be considered aerobic, the exercise should raise your heart beat to a certain level, depending on your age, for a sustained period of time. To calculate the level, subtract your age from 190. This is an upper limit, above which your heart rate should not go. Subtract 20 from the upper limit to get the lower limit. Aerobic exercise should maintain your heart beat between these two limits for at least twenty minutes (Fontana, 1989). For maximum benefit, you should exercise at least three times a week. Besides being aerobic, the exercise should be enjoyable. If you are spending the entire time you are running thinking about how much you hate running, you will create stress for yourself and diminish the positive effects of the exercise (Jette, 1984, McGee-Cooper, 1992).

A third key to maintaining good physical health is to get enough rest. While on average, people tend to feel best with six to eight hours per night, what is enough rest varies by individual. Some people require eight hours of sleep a night; others do quite well with less. In addition, while most people tend to get their sleep at night, others prefer to take short, 15- to 30-minute catnaps during the day and sleep fewer hours during the night. Research has also shown that people who engage in daily aerobic exercise need less sleep. A good way to figure out how much sleep you need is to listen to your body.

TRY USING A RELAXATION TECHNIQUE

The term "relaxation technique" is used here to include a wide variety of stress management approaches that involve using mental exercises to help you gain greater control over your physiological functioning, and therefore over your stress reaction. Relaxation techniques, like aerobic exercise, should be practiced on a regular basis, usually once or twice a day. Most of these techniques involve increasing one's self-awareness by training the mind to focus attention on a single object or experience, and thus allowing both the mind and body to relax. As David Fontana notes, "The mind has got into the habit of flitting from one thought to another, of following first this chain of associations then that, of existing in a state of almost constant distraction while our thoughts chatter away at us like a cartload of monkeys" (1989, p. 89). Relaxation techniques make you more aware of your body's internal processes and your feelings, and increase your ability to reproduce these feelings so that you can alter your reaction to a stress-provoking situation. Here we will discuss three types of relaxation: meditation, muscle (or progressive) relaxation, and imaging (or visualization).

Meditation techniques commonly focus on mental relaxation through breathing exercises. Like relaxation techniques in general, there are many different types of meditation. Many of these, such as transcendental meditation, Zen meditation, and Sikh meditation, are associated with a religion or spiritual lifestyle, but this is not always the case. Perhaps the most well known of the secular approaches is Benson's (1975) *Relaxation Response,* which was developed by incorporating those elements that are common to the different meditation techniques. Fontana (1989) suggests the following approach to meditation:

1. Find a quiet location and a time when you will not be disturbed. It is best to meditate at the same time every day.

2. Sit in a comfortable position, either in an upright chair or in a cross-legged position. Sit upright, with your hands resting lightly in your lap.

3. Close your eyes and begin to focus on your breathing. Do not strain.

4. Breathe through your nose, and focus either on the nostrils, where cool air is being taken in and warm air let out, or on the rise and fall of the abdomen. Maintain one point of focus; do not allow your attention to switch from one point to the other.

5. You can count silently on the out-breath, counting to ten and then backwards to one. (Other meditation techniques suggest using repetitive words or phrases, or suggest focusing on a particular visual image.) Continue the pattern, breathing easily and naturally for about 10 to 20 minutes. (You may open your eyes to check the time; do not use an alarm clock.) If other thoughts enter your head, do not try to follow them or push them out; simply bring your attention back to your breathing and let the other thoughts pass out of your head.

6. When you are finished, sit quietly for a few moments. When you rise from your seat, rise slowly and try to maintain the calmness for as long as you can. Also try to be aware of your surroundings as you were aware of your breathing.

Muscle relaxation techniques, like meditation, emphasize self-awareness. Unlike meditation, muscle relaxation exercises focus on gaining an awareness of the whole body. Muscle relaxation exercises are designed to allow you to gain a better sense of your internal processes, so that you can be aware of and then release the tension when it arises. Fontana (1989) suggests the following approach to muscle relaxation.

1. Find a quiet location and a time when you will not be disturbed.

2. Wear lightweight clothes.

3. Lie on your back on the floor.

4. Tense the muscles in your right foot and ankle for several seconds and then relax your foot and wiggle your toes. Notice how it feels. Tighten the muscles and release them several times. Focus on the difference between the two states and try to remember the feelings.

5. Do the same with your left foot and ankle.

6. Repeat with your calf muscles, and then your thigh muscles. Again, as you tense and relax the muscles each time, focus on the difference in sensation between the two states and try to remember the feelings.

7. Continue moving upward through the muscle groups, to the groin, the abdomen, the chest, and the back and shoulders. Then move down the arms, to the biceps, the forearms, and then the hands. Finally, repeat with the neck, the jaw, the face and forehead, and the scalp. With each muscle group, tense and relax the muscles, and notice the difference in sensations.

8. If you have trouble relaxing some of the muscle groups, do not be discouraged. Also do not try too hard, as this can increase the tension. If you practice daily, you will increase your ability to control each muscle group.

Finally, imaging is a technique that takes advantage of the brain's ability to create images that are real to the body, in the sense that it will release hormones and other chemicals as if the body were actually having the experience. In recent years, imaging has become popular among athletes as a way to help them visualize winning performances (McGee-Cooper, 1992). Research in the field of psychoneuroimmunology (Borysenko, 1987) has shown how the connections among the mind, the nervous system, and the immune system can explain the incidence of illness and disease among people who are feeling stress. It also shows how imaging can be used to imprint positive images that can help you relax and release tension, as well as improve performance. McGee-Cooper (1992) suggests the following approach to imaging:

1. Prepare your body through relaxation. (You can use the first few steps of meditation discussed above to help you relax.) You may also want to listen to calming music. As you focus on your breathing, visualize the fresh, oxygen-rich air coming into your lungs and the toxins or stress and pressure leaving.

2. Prepare your mind by releasing anxieties. Picture a favorite place in all its detail. Imagine the colors, textures, emotions, tastes, smells, and sounds; experience the positive feelings you had when you were there.

3. Imprint scenes of success in your mind. Picture yourself performing at your peak. You can either take yourself through your whole day or you can picture a particular area of performance. Visualize what it feels like to perform at this optimal level. Feel the emotions you will experience when you have accomplished your goal.

4. Reward yourself with a mental vacation. Once you have a good sense of what it feels like to perform at an optimal level, visualize yourself playing or relaxing.

CREATE A PERSONAL SUPPORT SYSTEM

Humans are social animals. We thrive on positive relationships with others. When we are experiencing stress, the need for personal relationships becomes even more important. Several research studies point to social support as among the most important factors in stress management (Farnham, 1991, Quick, Nelson and Quick, 1990). Indeed, Dr. David Marlowe, chief of the department of military psychiatry at the Walter Reed Army Institute of Research, indicates that the small, primary work group is considered to be the soldiers' primary protection against stress (Farnham, 1991).

In considering your own social support system, think about your friends and decide who you can count on, who will listen to you when you need to let off steam, who will both respect you and challenge you. Let these people know that you are also available to support them when they need it. Nurture the relationship by sharing positive, as well as negative, feelings. Keep in mind that while having a personal support system has been shown to be one of the most important elements in coping with stressful life events, you do not want to be seen by your friends as a negative stressor. McGee-Cooper (1992) cautions against what she calls chain-dumping, dumping your problems on one person and then the next, with little attention to finding solutions. There is no doubt that talking about the stress can help you to decrease it, but then you have to move on and look for positive solutions.

TAKE ENERGY BREAKS TO HELP YOU RESTORE YOUR ENERGY

You may not want to think of your body or mind as a machine, but the fact is, they need to be refueled regularly. In general, you can only work for about five hours before your performance starts to deteriorate, you have trouble concentrating, your level of creativity diminishes, and/or you feel less motivated. While you can certainly occasionally maintain performance for longer periods of time, if you consistently exceed your limit, you will feel stressed. If, however, you find time during the day for relaxation and/or play, you give your body and mind a chance to rejuvenate. McGee-Cooper states that "a good general tip when deciding what type of break to take at a given moment is to choose an activity, and possibly a location, that is different from your current task and site" (1992, p. 71). For example, if you have been sitting for a long period of time, it may help you to stand up, stretch, take a walk, use your muscles. If you have been doing close, detail work, try to sit back and stare out the window or close your eyes and do an imaging exercise. If you have been working intensely for an extended period of time on something that requires a great deal of mental energy and creativity, do something that allows your brain to relax. If you have been working alone, find someone who also needs an energy break and enjoy each other's company for ten minutes.

TIME MANAGEMENT

We now turn to the topic of time management. As discussed earlier, we approach time management from the perspective that managing your time should focus on the quality, rather than the quantity, of your work. Hyrum W. Smith, CEO of Franklin Quest Co., a company that each week trains 4,000 to 6,000 people in time management techniques, talks about the productivity pyramid. At the base of the pyramid are personal governing values, those things in our life that are most important to us. Next are long-range goals, those things we want to accomplish over time. Above the long-range goals are the intermediate goals, those goals that help us reach the long-range goals. Finally, at the apex of the pyramid are daily tasks. Smith argues "that everything starts with governing values. If you set goals that aren't aligned with your values, you may accomplish a great deal, but you won't ever be satisfied, because you'll be neglecting the things that matter most to you. By the same token, if you create a daily task list that doesn't reflect your long-range and intermediate goals, you'll be *busy* but not *productive*" (Smith, 1994, p. 67, emphasis in original).

Many traditional tips, tools, and techniques of time management assume that managers function in a rational, logical, mundane, orderly world in which the only thing about which they must be concerned is doing their own work for eight hours each day. Thus they focus on monitoring activities and keeping track of appointments, on "getting the job done," and on avoiding interruptions. Managers do not, however, live in a rational, logical, mundane, orderly world.

Rather, they are usually in the midst of transactions and operations. They need to be able to use their time efficiently, but they also need to allow time for unscheduled encounters and, as noted above, they need to be able to stop for an energy break. Most managers listen and talk far more than they read; and they share far more information through the spoken word, via plant tours, telephone and doorway conversations, and meetings, than they do through written reports. Managers need to keep in touch with colleagues and customers so that they know what is going on within their organization, their industry, and the world. Much of their important work is accomplished in bursts of collaborative encounters with others, the average duration of which is about 11 minutes (Alesandrini, 1992). This suggests that time management techniques need to accommodate managers' need for a more fluid approach to time (Deutschman, 1992), one that focuses more on identifying priorities and concentrating on the critical tasks than on mapping out each minute of the day.

In the next section, we present four strategies for managing your time. They reflect the notion that, ultimately, managing your time means managing yourself. Thus, like the strategies for managing stress, the strategies presented for managing time tend to be for the long-term. They build on the notion that what you want to accomplish in life should determine how you use your time each day, rather than vice versa. As a result, most of the advice presented here is relevant whether you are a CEO, a middle-level manager, or a front-line employee.

CLARIFY YOUR VALUES

You are probably not surprised to see this advice again; by now it should be apparent to you that the number-one strategy for managing stress should also be the number-one strategy for managing time. We will, however, add a slightly new perspective as we focus on practical advice for using the time available to you each day. Keep in mind that virtually no one has the time or resources to do everything that he or she wants to. That limitation requires us to set priorities. While priorities may change (indeed they must change to adapt to changing conditions), without priorities, any task is as important as any other. Without priorities, we do things because we are confronted with them, not necessarily because they will bring us the greatest results. When Rod Canion started Compaq Computer he was always aware of everyone's activities. But as the company grew to over 9,000 employees, he realized that he could no longer keep track of everything. "In the past eight years I've had to reassess repeatedly what I felt was the most important area for me to spend my time in. You have to prioritize your activities again and again—otherwise something is going to snap" (quoted in Calonius, 1990, p. 250).

The challenge is to prevent the urgent, but less important, tasks from diverting us from important, but less urgent, ones. How do we decide what is important? Important tasks are those that are driven by long-term goals and values. Covey, Merrill, and Merrill (1994) present a *Time Management Matrix* that can help you think about your tasks. The matrix is divided into two dimensions—importance and urgency—and includes four boxes (quadrants): important and urgent, important but not urgent, urgent but not important, neither important nor urgent. In

Quadrant I, urgent and important, are crises, pressing problems, and projects with deadlines. You could also include interpersonal crises with close friends, relatives, or co-workers in this quadrant. Quadrant II, important but not urgent, includes long-term planning and prioritizing, professional development, relationship building, taking care of yourself (physical health, relaxation, energy breaks, etc.), and working on long-term projects that do not have imminent deadlines. Covey refers to this quadrant as the Quadrant of Quality. These two quadrants are where you should spend most of the time, with Quadrant I taking precedence over Quadrant II of necessity. Note though, that the more time you spend on the activities in Quadrant II, the less time you are likely to have for dealing with the crises and imminent deadlines in Quadrant I.

Quadrant III includes those items that are urgent but not important. These are some of the phone calls, mail, meetings, and drop-in visitors you respond to. This is where you spend a lot of time meeting other people's expectations and demands, rather than your own. A corollary to the strategy of clarifying your values is: Learn to say no! This does not mean that you are never available to help others; but keep in mind that saying yes to others means that you are saying no to yourself. Ask yourself: Is this request as important as the items in my own Quadrants I and II? Finally, Quadrant IV includes those items that are neither important nor urgent. These are the real time wasters—junkmail, busywork, some "escape" activities that do not help to reenergize you. In the practice exercise you will get a chance to look more closely at how you spend your time.

PLAN AND PRIORITIZE ON A REGULAR BASIS

In line with the first strategy, it is important that you plan your time to maximize the amount of time you can spend in Quadrants I and II. Hyrum Smith (1994) suggests that you should spend 10 to 15 minutes each morning planning your day. This does not mean that you plan out every minute. Rather, it means that you examine the list of all the things you could do, decide which have the biggest payoffs, and schedule your time accordingly. In addition, try to keep in mind your own personal rhythms. No doubt you are aware of which times during the day you have the most creative energy and which times you are at a low ebb. Wherever possible, work on the items that are most important during the times when you have the most energy. Also, remember that most top managers leave time on their calendars for the unexpected. If you schedule yourself for back-to-back meetings, and one of the meetings runs longer that expected, there is no slack. If, on the other hand, you have extra time between appointments, you can always fill in that time with activities from the first three quadrants. For example, Robert Dilenschneider, CEO of Hill & Knowlton, uses that time to make phone calls or to do something else that keeps him in touch with people (Calonius, 1990). If you have too much to do in a day, McGee-Cooper (1994) suggests that you choose one or more items that you can do imperfectly. She argues that it is better to plan this than to let it happen by default.

Note that this all assumes two key elements of time management. First, you need to keep a calendar, preferably one calendar so that you don't lose appointments from one calendar to the other. Second, you need to keep a master list of things you need to do. From this list, you can make your daily to-do list or schedule, based on your priorities.

MAINTAIN YOUR WORKSPACE SO THAT YOU CAN WORK MOST EFFECTIVELY

Many people would translate this strategy into two words: avoid clutter. But the fact is, different people have different approaches to organizing. In her books, *Time Management for Unmanageable People* (1994) and *You Don't Have to Go Home From Work Exhausted* (1992), Ann McGee-Cooper discusses the notion of brain hemisphericity—that the two sides of the brain have different functions and two different ways of processing information, sometimes labeled convergent and divergent thinking. Research has shown that by the time we reach our twenties, we have established a preferred thinking style that influences the way we organize ourselves, including how we organize our time and our workspace. (This is another reason why traditional time management techniques do not work for some people.) Convergent thinkers tend to be logical and orderly in their thinking, work in a step-by-step fashion, focus on details, and keep their desks free from clutter. Alternatively, divergent thinkers tend to be more intuitive in their thinking, skip around from one task or issue to another, look at the big picture, and have workspaces that are covered with papers and files.

McGee-Cooper argues that divergent thinkers are more visual, and so find it easier to locate a file folder if they can picture where it is. Putting a folder that is currently being used in a file cabinet can be inefficient if you can justify filing that folder in several different places, based on the substantive topic, and are not likely to remember which place you chose when the time comes to retrieve the file. Alternatively, convergent thinkers are more abstract in their thinking, know exactly where to file the folder, and have no problem remembering where the folder was filed. The bottom line is: A messy desk is only a problem if you cannot find things when you need them. While knowing how to keep a well-ordered filing system is certainly a skill that can be helpful when trying to find things that are not currently being used, you may find that you prefer to have all your current work within easy reach. The key here is you need to figure out what type of workspace works for you. If you cannot find things easily, if you miss deadlines and commitments, you have a problem! If you are able to locate what you need easily, do not try to make yourself use a system that you find uncomfortable. Remember, the most effective workspace is one where you feel comfortable working.

REGULARLY REVIEW HOW YOU ARE SPENDING YOUR TIME

The first two strategies focused on looking forward in time. This last strategy suggests that every few months you need to take a look backward and assess how well you are doing in maintaining your time management system. Many time management experts suggest that you should keep a log for a week. Note how you spend your time. Are you working on those things that are important, or just on those things that are urgent? Are you making progress toward meeting your intermediate and long-term goals? As we indicated at the beginning of this section, managing your time essentially means you are managing yourself. You may want to review the first competency in Chapter 4 (the monitor role), Monitoring Personal Performance, to see if you can identify additional ways to become more aware of your work habits. Remember that you are the only person who is responsible for how you manage your time; you must make the commitment to manage yourself in a way that allows you to focus on those activities that are important to you.

ANALYSIS   Wasting Time[5]

Directions   Read the case of Frank Fernandez. In your small group discuss the case, using the questions below as a guide. A large group discussion will follow.

Wednesday morning Frank Fernandez, a unit manager in the Human Resources Management Department, reported to the office promptly at 8:30 A.M. After washing out his coffee cup, Frank poured a fresh cup and walked over to Bonnie Wiczarowski's desk. As one of the new employees, Bonnie had been at a training session the last few days, and they spent about fifteen minutes reviewing how the course had gone and what had gone on at the office while Bonnie was away.

Leaving Bonnie's desk, Frank stopped by the washroom before heading to his desk. Back at his desk was a memo detailing new policies concerning personal use of state vehicles while on state business. The policy basically stated that state vehicles should be used only for official state business and that employees using these vehicles could not provide transportation for friends or relatives while driving the state vehicle for official state business. Frank was surprised by this news, and he went to ask Ralph Larrowe if he had read the memo. Although Ralph was a good colleague and well liked in the office, he did have a reputation for talking; once he started it was hard to get him to stop. It was 9:30 before Frank finally told Ralph he had other work to do and would have to return to his desk. In fact, Frank needed to get started on his section of the quarterly progress report. The branch chief wanted the first draft to be completed by close of business on Friday.

When Frank got back to his desk, he found a note from Bonnie. She had wanted to ask him about one of the issues that had come up while she had been out of the office at the training session. Frank went to answer Bonnie's question, but she was away from her desk.

[5]*Adapted from* training material for *Getting Work Done Through Others: The Supervisor's Main Job,* Advanced Human Resources Development Program, New York State Governor's Office of Employee Relations and CSEA, Inc., 1987. Adapted with permission of the New York State Governor's Office of Employee Relations.

At 10:30 the branch chief telephoned and asked Frank to find a report detailing program expenditures over the last three years. The branch chief also expressed her disgust with the new vehicle policy and discussed (at length) the absurdity of the policy, given its low potential for saving money or improving image and its likely negative impact on employee morale. Clint Thompson, the administrative assistant, would usually be the one to locate the report, but he was upstairs attending a meeting of the Employee Assistance Program's peer counselors. Frank decided he would try to locate the report himself, but trying to understand Clint's filing system confused him, and after 20 minutes he decided to wait until Clint returned to the office. It was now almost 11:00, and there was not enough time to begin any major project before lunch. Frank cleaned up his desk instead, preparing himself for an efficient afternoon.

Returning to work at 1:00, Frank took a few minutes to glance over the departmental newsletter and then started to take out the material he would need to work on the quarterly report. As he was taking out the material, he remembered he had a few telephone calls to make regarding the survey that the interagency task force subcommittee on which he served was planning on conducting. He decided he would take care of the telephone calls and then begin working on the quarterly report promptly at 2:00. It was 1:30 before Frank remembered to ask Clint to find that report. About 15 minutes later Clint came back with two reports. One report listed program expenditures over the past two years; the other report listed expenditures over the past five years. There was no three-year report, and Clint said he was pretty sure there had never been one. Frank did not want to question the branch chief's authority and so asked Clint to look again.

At 2:00, Clint returned and this time insisted that there was no three-year report. When Frank called the branch chief, her secretary said she was in a meeting and didn't know when she would return. After Frank left a message, he and Clint returned to what they were doing.

When Frank looked at his watch, he noticed it was almost 3:00 (actually it was 2:45). He felt that he needed to get to the quarterly report, but then had second thoughts. He had barely gotten half-way through his telephone calls and he felt that two hours would probably not be enough time to really get a good start. The quarterly report is the type of project that is best accomplished when a large block of time is available. Frank knew that by the time he gathered up the materials he needed and laid them out on the desk in a way that he could look them over all at once, it would be time to put them away. Frank decided he would take some of the material home and work on it in the evening so that he would be ready to start first thing in the morning. Then he turned to his master to-do list and looked it over to see what other tasks he could work on until the end of the day.

"Wasting Time"

Discussion Questions

1. What are some of the problems Frank has in managing his time? To what extent is he accomplishing what is important as opposed to what is urgent?

2. If his productivity today is typical, what may happen to his level of stress in the coming months?

3. What could Frank do to improve his use of time? What specific steps would he need to take?

PRACTICE Clarify Your Values

Directions   The first strategy for managing both time and stress is to clarify your values. This is generally an activity that could take you days or even weeks to fully complete. This exercise gives you an opportunity to get started.

1. Make a short list (no more than five items) of those things that are most important to you in life. Try to stay focused on the end state. For example, if you think it is important for you to get a good education, think about why you want to have a good education. What could you accomplish or what would you have if you were well-educated?

2. Take one or two of the items from your list and identify one or two long-term goals that derive from your governing values. Next, take one or two of your long-term goals and identify one or two intermediate goals that derive from the long-term goals.

3. Review your activities over the past week and think about how much time you spent on these goals.

4. Decide on how you can devote a little more time to accomplishing a goal that is derived from your governing values.

APPLICATION Improving Your Stress and Time Management

1. Review the strategies for stress and time management.

2. Pick one key thing you could do over the next week to improve your productivity. For example, you may want to watch your diet, try a relaxation technique, or start keeping a master to-do list and beginning each day with a planning session. Keep track of what you do each day to implement this strategy.

3. Write a three- to five-page paper describing what change you made and the effect it had on your productivity. In your paper, discuss why you chose the particular strategy, what you did and the effect it had on you, and what are your next steps (ways to maintain this new "habit," or thoughts you have about trying an additional strategy). Based on your experience, you might also want to provide suggestions to others who are planning to implement this strategy.

REFERENCES

Adams, J. D. "Achieving and Maintaining Personal Peak Performance," in *Transforming Work.* J. D. Adams (general ed.). Alexandria, Va.: Miles River Press, 1984.

Alesandrini, Kathryn. *Survive Information Overload: The 7 Best Ways to Manage Your Workload by Seeing the Big Picture.* Homewood, Ill: Business One Irwin, 1992.

Ashforth, B.E., "The Experience of Powerlessness in Organizations." *Organizational Behavior and Human Decision Processes,* 43 (1989): 207–242.

Bandura, A. "Self-Efficacy: Toward a Unifying Theory of Behavioral Change." *Psychological Review* 84 (1977): 191–215.

Benson, Herbert. *The Relaxation Response.* New York: Avon Books, 1975.

Borysenko, Joan. *Minding the Body, Mending the Mind.* Reading, Mass: Addison Wesley, 1987.

Bowen, David E., and Edward E. Lawler. "The Empowerment of Service Workers: What, Why, How, and When." *Sloan Management Review* (Spring 1991): 31–39.

Calonius, Erik. "How Top Managers Manage Their Time." *Fortune* (June 4, 1990): 250–262.

Cohen, Frances. "Personality, Stress, and the Development of Physical Illness," in *Health Psychology,* George C. Stone, Frances Cohen, Nancy E. Adler & Associates, (eds.). San Francisco: Jossey-Bass, 1979.

Conger, J.A., and R.N. Kanungo. "The Empowerment Process: Integrating Theory and Practice." *Academy of Management Review* 31 (1988): 471–482.

Covey, Stephen R., A. Roger Merrill, and Rebecca R. Merrill. *First Things First: To Live, to Love, to Learn, to Leave a Legacy.* New York: Simon and Schuster, 1994.

Deutschman, Alan. "The CEO's Secret of Managing Time." *Fortune* (June 1, 1992): 135–146.

Dossey, Larry. *Space, Time & Medicine.* Boulder, Col.: Shambhala Publications, 1982.

Farnham, Alan. "Who Beats Stress Best—And How." *Fortune* (October 7, 1991): 71–86.

Fontana, David. *Managing Stress.* Leicester, England: British Psychological Society, 1989.

Friedman, Meyer, and Ray H. Rosenmann. *Type A Behavior and Your Heart.* New York: Alfred A. Knopf, 1974.

Garfield, Charles S. *Peak Performers.* New York: Avon Books, 1986.

Getting Work Done Through Others: The Supervisor's Main Job, Advanced Human Resources Development Program, NYS Governor's Office of Employee Relations and CSEA, Inc., 1987.

Hackman, J.R., and G.R. Oldham. *Work Redesign,* Reading, Mass.: Addison-Wesley, 1980.

Holmes, Thomas H., and Richard H. Rahe, "The Social Readjustment Rating Scale." *Journal of Psychosomatic Research* 11 (1967): 213–218.

Imai, M. *Kaizen.* New York: Random House, 1985.

Jette, Maurice. "Stress Coping Through Physical Activity," in *Handbook of Organizational Stress Coping Strategies,* Amarjit Singh Sethi and Randall S. Schuler (eds.). Cambridge, Mass: Ballinger Publishing, 1984.

Kerr, Steve. "On the Folly of Rewarding A, While Hoping for B." *Academy of Management Journal* 18 (1975): 769–783.

Kinlaw, Dennis C. *Coaching for Commitment.* Sand Diego, Calif.: Pfeiffer & Co., 1993.

Livingston, J.S. "Pygmalion in Management." *Harvard Business Review* (July–August, 1969).

McGee-Cooper, Ann, with Duane Trammell. *Time Management for Unmanageable People.* New York: Bantam Books, 1994.

McGee-Cooper, Ann, with Duane Trammell and Barbara Lau. *You Don't Have to Go Home From Work Exhausted.* New York: Bantam Books, 1992.

Metcalf, C.W., and Roma Felible. *Lighten Up: Survival Skills for People Under Pressure.* Reading, Mass: Addison Wesley, 1992.

Mink, Oscar G., Keith Q. Owen, and Barbara P. Mink. *Developing High-Performance People.* Reading, Mass.: Addison-Wesley, 1993.

Nadler, David A. and Edward E. Lawler (eds.) "Motivation: A Diagnostic Approach." Hackman, J.R., and E.E. Lawler, *Perspectives in Behavior in Organizations,* New York: McGraw Hill, 1977.

Nadler, D., M. Tushman, and N. Hatvany (eds.). *Managing Organizations.* Boston: Little Brown, 1982.

Pines, M. "Psychological Hardiness: The Role of Challenge and Health." *Psychology Today* (December 1980): 34–44.

Quick, James Campbell, Debra L. Nelson, and Jonathan D. Quick. *Stress and Challenge at the Top: The Paradox of the Successful Executive.* Chichester: England: John Wiley & Sons, 1990.

Quinn, Robert E. *Beyond Rational Management.* San Francisco: Jossey-Bass, 1988.

Schermerhorn, R. *Management for Productivity,* 3rd ed. New York: John Wiley & Sons, 1989.

Selye, Hans. *Stress Without Distress.* Philadelphia: Lippincott, 1974.

———. *The Stress of Life* (rev. ed.). New York: McGraw-Hill, 1976.

Smith, Hyrum W. *The 10 Natural Laws of Successful Time and Life Management: Proven Strategies for Increased Productivity and Inner Peace.* New York: Warner Books, 1994.

Spreitzer, Gretchen M. "Psychological Empowerment in the Workplace: Dimensions, Measurement, and Validation." Unpublished Manuscript, University of Southern California, October 1994.

Spreitzer, Gretchen M., Suzanne C. de Janasz, and Robert E. Quinn. "The Transformational Capacitites of Empowered Managers." Unpublished Manuscript, University of Southern California, Sept. 1994.

Thomas, K.W., and B.A. Velthouse. "Cognitive Elements of Empowerment: An Interpretive Model of Intrinsic Task Motivation." *Academy of Management Review,* 15 (1990): 666–681.

Tichy, Noel M., and Stratford Sherman. *Control Your Destiny or Someone Else Will.* New York: Doubleday, 1993.

The Director and Producer Roles

As we did at the end of the previous sets of chapters, let us now put the director and producer roles in the context of the competing values framework before moving on to the next quadrant. Again, as with the other roles, you will find that these roles are more appropriate in some situations and less appropriate in others. It is important for you to think about those situations where you will need to call upon the competencies associated with the director and producer roles.

A BRIEF REVIEW

The director and producer roles are part of the rational goal model. In this model the desired ends are productivity, accomplishment, and general goal attainment, and the assumed means to these ends have to do with goal clarification and direction. In this quadrant we are most concerned with maximizing (or optimizing) output. In the director role, managerial leaders are expected to take charge and clarify expectations by defining problems, establishing objectives, designing the organizational structure, and generating policies; in the producer role the managerial leader is task-oriented and expects high levels of output from self and others. This model assumes a strong action orientation. To be an effective leader in this quadrant one needs to be independent and strong-willed, and to have a vision that others are willing to follow.

WHEN THE DIRECTOR AND PRODUCER ROLES ARE APPROPRIATE

The two axes that define the rational goal model are external focus and high control. Thus, the director and producer roles are similar to the monitor and coordinator roles in their emphasis on control; both sets of roles assume that organizational processes need to be centralized and integrated. Here again, we can assume that the director and producer roles are most applicable when the situation is well understood, when goals can be well defined, and/or when there is a need for maintaining consistency in production or delivery of service. The horizontal axis, however, is defined by a greater emphasis on external pressures and shorter timelines. Thus, when a situation is pressing and there is need for centralization of effort, it is appropriate for the leader to take charge, specify a direction, and push for action. Indeed, others look to the leader to be decisive in this type of situation and criticize leaders who vacillate or waver in their opinions.

COMPLEMENTARY ROLES

Because the rational goal model is the oldest paradigm of effectiveness, it is seen by some as inherently good. When asked "How do you know if an organization is effective?" the vast majority of people will first respond by saying "If it meets its goals," or "If it makes a good profit." The notion of leaders being in charge of followers is a strong image that is difficult to put aside; in our culture it is almost natural to feel that one needs to take charge in order to be seen as an effective leader. And so the leadership roles in this model are easy to overuse. At times, though, acting as a director or producer is not the best course that a manager can take. Indeed, as you saw in the producer role, an overemphasis on productivity can lead to high levels of stress and heart disease. Thus, as with the previous roles, a failure to balance and blend the director and producer roles with the other roles, particularly the mentor and facilitator roles in the human relations quadrant, can lead to both personal and professional problems.

Consider, for example, Roger Smith's tenure as CEO of General Motors. Smith took over in 1981 and made huge technical changes as he set out to "reindustrialize" the company. Initially, he was seen as a man of vision, a true leader. But then things started to go wrong. Ford out-earned GM for the first time since the 1920s. GM's market share slipped from 45% to 36%. Where there had been praise for Roger Smith, the evaluation began to turn negative and eventually it became vicious. In 1989, when he reviewed his efforts to rebuild GM, he wrote about the most important lesson he had learned.

> But I sure wish I'd done a better job of communicating with GM people. I'd do that differently a second time around and make sure they understood and shared my vision for the company. Then they would have known why I was tearing the place up, taking out whole divisions, changing our whole production structure. If people understand the why, they'll work at it. Like I say, I never got all this across. There we were, charging up the hill right on schedule, and I never looked behind me and saw that many people were still at the bottom, trying to decide whether they wanted to come along.[1]

Clearly the roles in the rational goal quadrant must be seen in context and must be used appropriately. Productivity and clarity of direction are important values in an organization, but there is also value in having people participate in the decisions that set the direction. When managerial leaders become too focused on the goals and the output of the organization they lose awareness of the people who actually do the work, and create an oppressive sweatshop atmosphere rather than one where people are committed to the work. Alternatively, there are times when leaders must take charge and make decisions they believe to be in the best interest of the organization as a whole, even if individual units are hurt in the short term. It is the managerial leader's job, in the roles of the director, producer, mentor, and facilitator, to see to it that these orientations are appropriately balanced.

[1]"Roger Smith: The U.S. Must Do as GM Has Done," *Fortune,* February 13, 1989, p. 71.

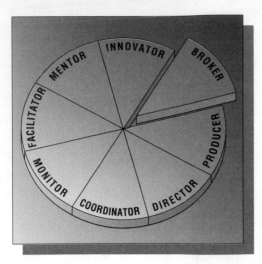

THE BROKER ROLE

8

■ COMPETENCIES

Building and Maintaining a Power Base

Negotiating Agreement and Commitment

Presenting Ideas: Effective Oral Presentations

The competing values framework helps us see that leadership at any level is a social activity as well as a technical one. It is a job that requires the human relations competencies of the coach and mentor as well as the analytic and take-charge competencies of the monitor and director. This chapter focuses on the broker role. With the innovator, the broker occupies the upper-right quadrant of the competing values framework. While the innovator envisions change and a better way of doing things, the broker presents and negotiates those ideas effectively. In organizations, good ideas work only if people can see a benefit to adopting them.

This chapter will focus on the broker role and the core competencies associated with it.

Competency 1   Building and Maintaining a Power Base
Competency 2   Negotiating Agreement and Commitment
Competency 3   Presenting Ideas: Effective Oral Presentations

292

Competency 1 Building and Maintaining a Power Base

Some sources of power and influence in your personal life, or in an organization with which you are affiliated, may have little direct impact on you. Others affect you a great deal. A good way to start mapping the complex network of power and influence that most affects you is to draw a diagram of the people and positions upon which you depend. On the surface, the network of dependencies may be quite simple, but it will probably become more complex the more you think about it.

Directions   Look at Figure 8.1. The case in point is a hospital manager. You'll notice that the degree to which this manager (in the center of the diagram) depends upon other people and positions has been indicated.

Now draw a diagram of your organization on a separate sheet of paper. You may choose to analyze your position as a student or a member of your family, or you may choose a position in an organization with which you have experience. When you have your diagram completed, answer the following questions, first to yourself, and then, if time permits, in small groups.

FIGURE 8.1

A power/dependency diagram.

Reprinted from "Power, Success and Organizational Effectiveness," by John P. Kotter, Organizational Dynamics *(Winter 1978) p.29. Copyright© AMACOM, a division of American Management Association, New York. All rights Reserved.*

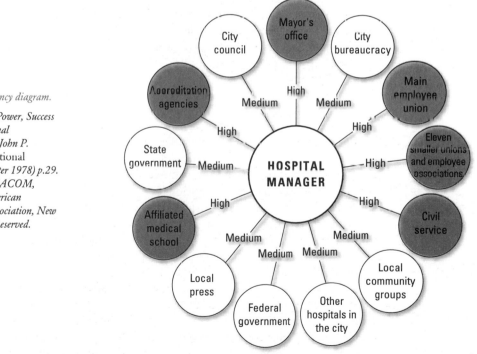

Interpretation

1. Whom do you really depend on in the position you're analyzing? How important is each dependency? What is the basis of each dependency? Do people on whom you depend also depend upon you? In what ways?

2. Are any of these dependencies inappropriate or dysfunctional? What can you do about that?

3. How do you maintain your own base of influence in each of these dependencies? Do you feel you have a base of influence in each of them?

4. What kind of power and influence do you think you need to develop further? What resources can help you? What people or positions are missing in the network you have sketched?

LEARNING Building and Maintaining a Power Base

POWER: WHY ARE WE AMBIVALENT?

Our perceptions of power are very revealing. They tell us as much about ourselves as they do about power. How do you feel about the role power plays in the organizations you have observed? When you think of power, what people, experiences and memories are called to mind? Refer to Box 8.1 and ask yourself whether you share these misconceptions.

All of us have power, and all of us are influenced by others who have power. Some of our most painful memories revolve around someone else's misuse of the power and influence they held over us. As children, school may have brought us enough boredom, confusion, and fear to last a lifetime. As teenagers, the authority of our parents may have collided with our need for freedom. To handle power is to make mistakes, often at the expense of others. But to be powerless is to be frustrated and defensive. Thus, most of us have mixed feelings about power. We need it and want it, but we know we can easily abuse it, or create the impression that we are abusing it.

In an organization setting, the term *power* is most often defined as essentially "the ability to produce; the capacity to mobilize people and resources to get things done" (Kanter, 1983, p. 213). People often say power is a "necessary evil" in organizations. That statement assumes that power, in all its manifestations, is evil in itself. Power in organizational life is inescapable, but is it inherently bad? Organizations exist in order to get things done. Power clusters around the most important things an organization has to do, and around the people who have the greatest access to the resources required to do those things. Working for a weak leader can be a liability. Leaders with little influence cannot represent the needs of their people, promote their ideas, or acquire the resources they need to do their jobs. (Handy, 1993, pp. 123-127).

BOX 8.1 MISCONCEPTIONS ABOUT POWER

1. *I am the manager. I can do what I want.* Authority and power are not the same thing. People do not do what you want simply because of the position you hold. It takes more than position to effectively influence people.

2. *Power is something people in higher positions exercise upon people in lower positions.* Managers exercise power and influence on subordinates, but subordinates also exercise power and influence on managers. Power is something that exists when people are dependent on each other. Think of your peers. Do they ever influence your managers? Do some influence your manager more than others? Why is this so?

3. *Supervisors and middle managers are powerless.* This statement is partially true. Some are powerless. However, supervisors and managers are never powerless unless they choose to be. Claims of powerlessness are often a flight from responsibility. Because the organization is dependent on supervisors and managers, they do, in fact, have latent power. If you use power effectively, it increases; if you use it ineffectively, it decreases. The more you have to use it the less you will have.

POWER AT THE INDIVIDUAL LEVEL

There are three levels from which to study power: first, the macro, or organizational level; second, the group or team level; and finally, the individual, or personal level. On the organizational level, power can be viewed as the ability to influence the flow of available energy and resources toward certain goals. This kind of power shows up in activities such as legislating policies and laws, setting rules and procedures, bestowing rewards and punishments, and making goals and plans. On the group or team level, power can be seen as the ability to influence your peers through the strength of expertise and experience, and the ability to build coalitions of those who share your views and goals. On the third, or personal level, power can be seen as person *A*'s capacity to influence person *B*'s behavior so that *B* does something he or she would not do otherwise. This focus on power and influence stresses interpersonal relationships and the resources we bring to bear in those relationships. In this chapter we will deal primarily with power and influence at the individual level, because it's the level we can influence the most.

THE MYTH OF THE SOLITARY ENTREPRENEUR

In U.S. culture we value individualism and self-reliance. But we have become, particularly since the second world war, a society that does most of its work and play through formal organizations. That means we are much more interdependent than ever in our history. It also means that most power and influence must be channeled through interconnecting groups. Nearly all of the work of our society is now done through organizations. Even very specialized and creative work such as composing music, performing cosmetic surgery, or practicing trial law, is coordinated through some kind of organization or interdependent team. So, no matter how much we seek to work alone inevitably we end up working with people.

GOOD POWER, BAD POWER, AND NO POWER

Power can be manipulative and coercive. Power can and has corrupted many people who could not resist using it for personal gain at others' expense. People can use the power contained in their professional positions to get personal gain beyond their entitlement; people can use their access to information to extort or blackmail others; they can use their ability to reward or punish others unfairly, to escape blame, or receive undeserved credit. Power, like energy, is neither good nor bad. It is tempting. But the moral or immoral use of power is the product of motives, decisions, and thinking—not the fault of power itself.

Power is necessary in using resources to meet goals and to get things done. Not using power when you need to can be as bad as abusing it. For every person who has dealt in bad faith, broken the law, and played fast and loose with influence, there may be three people who are guilty of not pushing hard enough, not exerting enough influence and gumption to gain the power necessary to accomplish a worthwhile goal.

When we commit ourselves to a cause or a project, we want strong, solid people in our corner. We don't want to entrust the things we cherish to weak and passive leaders. Managers who have no power base are not doing their jobs. Part of their job is to effectively and appropriately build a base of legitimacy, information, and influence from which to serve the needs of their unit and their organization. Increasingly, the work of organizations is being done by cross-functional teams and special project groups. These people are usually peers, with a lot of responsibility, with no one person having all the sign-off authority to make the decisions. In these situations, influence, not formal authority is the essential resource (Cohen and Bradford, 1990).

FIVE SOURCES OF POWER

Where does power come from? First, and perhaps most obvious, is position. If you are director of finance for a large firm, you have power by virtue of that position. That position carries a good deal of legitimacy and influence. **Position power** is also known as "legitimate power."

Personal power comes from the shape and impact your presentation of self has on others—the personal characteristics that people find attractive or influential or persuasive. These resources include attributes such as articulateness, physical stature and appearance, dynamism and spontaneity, intelligence, humor, and the ability to empathize with others. Your personal power is also rooted in the overall impressions you generate in other people—impressions of being trustworthy, reasonable, modest, or courageous. Personal power is sometimes called "social capital."

Expert power is based on the expertise that you may have in a special field or knowledge area. Notice that expert power is not the same as the personal resource of intelligence. It is tied to valuable, specialized skills or abilities. The in-house computer expert may have more power when the computer system crashes and his expertise is invaluable, than when the system is working. When the United States suddenly has vital interests at stake in a certain region of the globe, people who speak the languages of that region have more power and influence than they had before.

Opportunity power is related to expert power, but it deals more with being in the right place at the right time. One of the rules of success, as some cynics have pointed out, is to be lucky— and lucky people are around when opportunities and resources are being handed out. However, not everyone recognizes an opportunity when it surfaces. In written Chinese, the word *crisis* is expressed with two characters, one meaning "opportunity" and the other "danger." Most people don't see opportunities in crises or the potential benefits offered by problems. Too often we see only the dangers.

Information power depends upon access to information and is, of course, tied directly to expert power. But information power is related, not only to what you know, but to what is known by all the people you know. This grand total of all the knowledge and influence wielded by the people you know who are willing to make their knowledge and influence available to you is your social network.

In this description by Ford Harding, an international expert on sales training, we see a person who understood instinctively how to build a network. It was a natural process for him because he saw himself as a helpful broker, a person who could match one set of needs with another.

Osgar Megerdichian grew up in the rough and tumble moving industry in New York City and never went to college. Combining social skill with business acumen, he built a consulting firm specializing in move management. A self educated, intelligent man, he liked people. He liked talking and was always on the phone. He honestly cared about his business friends and tried to help them whenever he could. He knew thousands of people. I once introduced him to a client. As we toured the building we met five different people. During five minute conversations, he identified mutual friends with each. "What a small world" he would say each time with a quizzical smile. When this happened a month later at another company, I knew I was dealing with something special.

Once you met Osgar, he didn't forget you. He would call periodically to see how you were doing. Better still, he often offered useful pieces of information. His real help came from introductions. He was always introducing people who could help each other. He introduced me to several people who later gave me large consulting assignments. His calls, needless to say, were always welcome, though they did sometimes make me a little uncomfortable that I had not done enough for this nice man who was working so hard for my benefit. I sought ways to return his help in kind.

By the time Osgar died, he had built a substantial firm. More importantly, his life had been warmed by many friendships, and those of us who knew him reflect on him often with affection. (Harding, 1994, p. 43)

When we think of networking, we often think of social activities and gestures engaged in for self-serving reasons—and we assume that these activities are contrived and "phony." We may believe networking is trying to get a job through friends, or doing lunch to get someone's attention, or asking for leads on new business. But effective networking is a process of helping other people who, over the long term, can also be a resource to you. The help takes many forms, but the help is genuine and timely. Networking is enjoyable and satisfying because it makes you a more effective resource in your career and personal life. Networking is a crucial subskill of brokering. Brokering includes the ability to persuade people that your ideas, projects, values, and assumptions are valid and urgent. But the information and talent necessary to put your ideas into motion are usually delivered by good networking. A good broker knows where to go for answers and whose support is necessary to carry the day. If you have a mission in life, you'll need help fulfilling it. Ford Harding says that networking usually involves these core activities (adapted from Harding, 1994, pp. 45–47).

- **Sharing information.** This is the information age. We can share ideas, tips, names of helpful experts, suggestions on places to look for something. The list is infinite. Brokers spend most of their time brokering information.

- **Introductions, referrals and references.** Brokers put one person in contact with another person. Good brokers are great matchmakers: They match the needs of one person with the needs and abilities of another. If you can't actually introduce one person to another, you can at least "refer" one to another, and allow the person who has the need to use your name in making the contact.

- **Ideas and advice.** When people call you frequently for advice or just a listening ear, you know you're well on your way to having a solid network. What if most of the information seems to flow from you rather than toward you? That's fine. When you need help or information, you'll know where to find it. The best networkers are great listeners. They know that someone's need is often someone else's opportunity.

- **Personal support.** Don't worry about giving people a "What have you done for me lately" speech. If a person is making unreasonable demands on your time and energy, you need to talk about that. But life is not so venal and self-serving that we can't be there for other people. Often the support people need is really easy to give. A little time and a little empathy usually fill the bill. Inevitably, you will be the one who needs some support: "Who you gonna call" if you have not been a support to others?

Here are some questions to consider as you think about your own brokering skills.

- Are you making an effort to get to know instructors in your classes as well as other people you interact with at work? Are these people aware of your interests and abilities? Would you feel comfortable asking some of them to write letters of recommendation for you?

- Think about the network you are building as a current or future job applicant. Is the network broad enough? Do the people you know seem to know the same group of people, or do some of your contacts link into other networks that can provide information and resources you may need?

- Are you a helpful resource to your friends and acquaintances? Do you make a deliberate effort to meet new people and understand their needs and interests? Do you understand what people really do with the major you've chosen once they graduate?

Networking is not just playing political games. It can make a dramatic difference in your ability to contribute to the organizations you work for. At the executive level, people are often hired because of the strength of their network. Of two candidates with comparable talent, experience, and ability, the one with the most powerful information and influence network will probably be offered the position.

INFLUENCE STRATEGIES

In Chapter 1 we talked about the importance of "cognitive complexity," the ability to see things in more than one way or solve a problem in more than one way. But we also pointed out that cognitive complexity is not enough. Managers need a broad repertoire of behavior—ways of influencing people. The master broker knows that effective leadership requires a broad base of approaches and strategies. Too many leaders are assertive or insistent when they need to be open and flexible. Others are passive and deferential when they need to be confrontational and firm.

Read the following list of influence strategies, and make note of how many you use. Which do you seldom or never use? Which strategies are practical in your work environment? Are there any you would feel uncomfortable using? Why?

Eight Influence Strategies

Influence Strategies	*Outcome*
1. Involve the person in the decision process.	Identifies with and accepts the decision.
2. Control the information. Be the expert.	Needs you for direction.
3. Engineer the situation. Control tasks, schedules, where people work, and so on.	Does what you want without knowing you want it.
4. Rely on your position. Make formal requests within your realm of authority.	Complies with your request if it is seen as legitimate.
5. Use rational persuasion. Show people that it is in their best interest.	Complies because the request leads to accomplishment.
6. Offer desired rewards.	Complies to get a particular resource.
7. Generate hope of a better future; show a higher good is being accomplished.	Complies because it is "morally right."
8. Increase your dependence on the other person.	Responds to informal expectations because of growing trust.

INFLUENCE VERSUS MANIPULATION

Of course, the column labeled "outcome" may look simplistic, or naive. When you choose to appeal to a higher good, people don't always comply "because it is right." They may think your approach is ridiculous, or they may suspect that you have an ulterior motive. You have to decide what your motives are and have the integrity and authenticity that make your strategies genuine. And, as you have probably learned from your own experience, you'll have to brace yourself to be misunderstood in spite of good intentions. The people who work with you daily usually know where your values and interests are, and they watch what you do at least as much as what you say. We think it's helpful to conceive of influence as separate from the power and authority that come from position. A good definition of influence is "The capability a person has to motivate someone to do something without using authority or power" (Adizes, 1988, p. 152).

These eight strategies listed are not designed to encourage you to manipulate people. They suggest that there are avenues of influence which habits or cultural norms may have kept you from considering. If you consistently appeal, even in subtle ways, to the authority of your position in order to get people's cooperation, you should probably try strategies that will increase your dependence on your subordinates or offer them more personal support by expressing appreciation or taking time to listen carefully to how things are really going for them. A common belief in U.S. management philosophy is that learning from subordinates is a sign of weakness. But learning from others is really a sign of being secure and authentic, and so is the habit of listening carefully. The master broker knows what other people need and how they feel. Most of that information comes from listening and observing, not from talking.

When we work as consultants with managers who are accused by peers and subordinates of being "overcontrolling," these managers often defend their style by saying, "I'm results oriented more than people oriented." But that response assumes that there is only one way to get results: my way. Many of these managers are not "results oriented" as much as they are control oriented (Fisher, 1993, p. 249). They feel a great need to be in charge, and they assume that if they are not in control, the work unit is "out of control." Not surprisingly, they encounter immense resistance from the people they work with.

INCREASING INFLUENCE WITH SUPERIORS, PEERS, AND SUBORDINATES

Here is an additional list of specific modes of influence tailored to the role and level of the person you are trying to influence. These methods of influence must, of course, be adapted to your situation.

SUPERIORS

- Look for ways to solve problems that your superiors are facing.

- Show appreciation to superiors for things they do to help.

- Encourage superiors to discuss their problems. Listen carefully. Give understanding and support.

- Provide constructive feedback on things superiors do.

- Point out new ways superiors can use your skills.

- Be loyal, even when it's difficult (unless some ethical principle or legal issue is at stake).

- Take the initiative if you feel you are being used or exploited in any way. Try bargaining and negotiating. If this does not help, look for another manager.

These are powerful and practical modes of influence. However, there are roadblocks to using them. A major roadblock is the norms of the organization. Norms are unwritten expectations about how work will be done, how people will act, and so on. Your work unit may have a "them and us" norm about relating to superiors. It may not be socially acceptable to show appreciation to your manager, or to be loyal, or to give encouragement to the people you manage. Suggesting new methods or solutions may be taboo. If so, you may want to consider how much these norms are costing you in your professional and personal development. You may not only need a new manager, but you may also need a more positive work climate. Moreover, as a leader in your work unit, you may have to address those norms specifically and try to change them for everyone's benefit. Think about what modes of influence you could use in that effort.

PEERS

- Find ways to help peers reach their goals and look and feel successful.

- Try to understand their problems and share useful information.

- Look for common goals you can mutually pursue.

- Form informal problem-solving groups between units.

- When a peer becomes a problem, get others to exert pressure to get the person back in line.

Influencing peers is a tremendous challenge. Often organizations have norms that prohibit rocking the boat or going beyond the job description. Efforts to become more influential can be mistaken for power plays or a vote of nonconfidence toward your colleagues. Building influence with peers takes a long time, and a lot of patience. But people ultimately respond when they see that you are determined to do good work and want to share the credit and stimulation with them. Remember, credit is not a zero-sum commodity. Stephen Covey, an author and management consultant, encourages people to create a "mentality of abundance," an attitude that there is plenty of credit and opportunity to go around (Covey, 1990, pp. 289–290).This attitude is often self-fulfilling. When people are generous and encouraging, opportunities increase in an organization. The paradox of selfishness is that it usually results in a net loss of resources. When people start hoarding and hiding information, recognition, physical resources, and their own energy, the work unit begins to wither.

SUBORDINATES

- Consciously try to increase their trust in you.

- Give them recognition for good performance.

- Give them credit for their ideas when talking to your superiors.

- Help them solve problems that may be beyond their ability or experience.

- Keep current on new information and trends in your field.

- Provide training. Champion the cause of professional development even if resources are scarce. You can do a lot informally.

- Never pretend to know something you don't know.

- Hold regular performance appraisals, but go beyond the formal "rating sheet" that so many organizations require once a year. Hold candid, detailed conversations with your people on how they are doing, and what they need. Focused conversations are powerful.

- Do not be afraid to talk about the ways you depend upon each other.

- Clarify your responsibilities to them and theirs to you.

ANALYSIS "I Hope You Can Help Me Out": Don Lowell Case Study

Directions　In your small groups, read the following case study and answer the discussion questions individually. Record your answers on a flip chart, and be prepared to report on your discussion in the large group.

Don Lowell is a mental hygiene therapy aide in a psychiatric center. He has been in his present position for 13 years, having worked his way up from the bottom. He thoroughly enjoys his job, but he missed being chosen for a promotion twice in the last two years. He was one of the top three on the list but was not able to get the promotions he wanted. He has been working very hard to make himself known in the right circles and has volunteered to serve on various county and private committees, boards, and task forces over the past few years.

Don also works three nights a week and weekends at the Rosewood Home, a well-known, highly rated nursing facility. Don serves as one of the two part-time activity coordinators. With his oldest daughter about to enter college, he can certainly use the money. He also enjoys the work and gets to meet a number of people in the community. He's been thinking for some time now that at some point in the future he would like to return to school and complete the degree which he began years ago. Right now, however, he enjoys working with the patients and feels the added experience will help him in the future.

Last week Don received a phone call from Frank Calvin, the chief of service in his division at the development center. Frank's 69-year-old mother is in the hospital recovering from a broken hip. Frank has applied to the Rosewood Home primarily because of its reputation in the area of physical therapy and rehabilitation. The home, however, has a very long waiting list (from six months to a year) and Frank understands that unless his mother receives physical therapy immediately upon release from the hospital, her chances of returning to her former mobility level are quite low. Moreover, Frank's sense of the situation, after meeting with the home's intake social worker, was that his mother was not going to be given priority consideration.

In discussing the situation with Sarah Anderson, Frank's assistant, he was reminded of Don Lowell. Sarah told Frank that Don is working as a part-time activity director at the home. He remembered Don's name from some paperwork that came across his desk. Frank decides to call Don to see if there was any way around normal procedures and asks if Don can help.

During the conversation, Frank mentions that if Don were able to assist him with this, he (Frank) would try to help him when he could. In addition, Frank said that he would put a note in Don's file stating the cooperation he received from Don in placing his mother in the appropriate health facility. "I just don't know where to turn with this problem," said Frank, "and I really hope you can help me."

Don told Frank that he would see what he could do. He told Frank that he didn't know all that much about the admissions process and really didn't have that kind of "pull" at the facility, but he would give it his best shot.

Don made some informal inquiries around the home concerning the admissions procedures (of which he knew very little). He found out that the director of the intake department, Sheila Hogan, is someone he knows slightly, because he worked with her on a couple of committees. He remembered her as being very focused and knowledgeable, and one who usually plays everything by the book. However, he had found her to be accommodating when necessary.

He also remembered an item in the Rosewood newsletter stating that the intake department was severely short staffed and was looking for volunteers or other staff coverage. Don had some ideas that he thought would work very well at providing coverage at no additional cost to the home. He decided to arrange a meeting.

Discussion Questions

1. What influence strategies does Don have available to him?

2. If you were Don, what action would you take?

   a. Would you decide not to try to influence the admission process? If not, why?
   b. Would you decide to help only by clarifying the mother's need for admission?
   c. Would you decide to do everything within your power to get the mother admitted?

3. Using the concepts and skills presented in the learning activity, describe the consequences of how you would handle this situation. What do you think would happen?

4. What strategy and techniques is Frank using on Don?

5. What options or strategies should Don use with Frank?

6. What should Don's next steps be?

7. What positive and negative role does power and influence play in a situation like this? Do you believe power and influence can be used effectively in a positive, ethical way? Explain.

8. Have you ever encountered a similar situation? What strategies, if any, did you use? What steps did you take?

PRACTICE I: The Big Move

Directions

In small groups of six participants, role play a task force in a financial services unit of a large firm. First read the background and instructions, and choose one of the roles indicated. Then prepare yourself by reading only your own role description sheet (not those of the other people in your group). Put on the name tag describing the role you are going to play. Start the role play and discuss the issue at hand for about 45 minutes. Further instructions will follow.

Background

Department X, a financial services unit of a large health care system, is currently located in Albany, New York. The department has come under pressure to move its headquarters from Albany to Westchester County, an area closer to New York City. Many of the hospitals and clients served by the unit are located around Westchester County, and the system has recently acquired a building large enough to house the entire financial services unit under one roof. The relocation would allow the system to cancel a very expensive building lease in Albany. The current offices in Albany are now inadequate, and expansion would be very expensive and pose some legal difficulties with zoning. The board of directors has created an interunit task force to discuss the possibility of the move. This task force has to come up with a recommendation to the board. The department must move as a whole or not at all.

The task force consists of managers from the following areas:

1. Client Financial Services

2. Accounting

3. Purchasing

4. Stock and Bond Transfer

5. Personnel

Each role description sheet outlines an initial position or opinion as to the advisability of the move: for, against, neutral. This is only an initial position, however, and you should feel free to switch sides and/or be influenced by the others. Assume and display the power-personality characteristics outlined in your role description.

A secret ballot vote will be taken at the end of the meeting, and the results will be announced. The board has asked for a recommendation from a task force of managers. You should assume that the recommendation of the group will strongly influence the final decision of whether or not to relocate. At the conclusion of the role play, you will all be asked to complete a questionnaire on your assessment of each character's effectiveness.

Role Description Sheets

Manager: Client Financial Services

You have been with the department since its founding and have worked your way up from your original job. During the 10 years that you have been a manager, you have been committed to the success of the department, have carried it through the lean years, and have contributed enormous energy toward making it the success it is today. You understand the possibilities for expansion and growth that the move to a new location could offer the department; however, you are getting older and definitely feel reluctant to undertake the relocation of your family, the sale of your beautiful home, and the separation from friends that the move would require. Also, although you have not announced it yet, you intend to retire in a couple of years, and the department's move could force you to retire before you had intended.

Your Power Personality. Past experience has shown that your positional power and the weight of your seniority can be used effectively to influence and control others. Your long years of experience make you a credible authority on a variety of matters. You know the workings of the department inside and out.

You use occasional unpredictability as your ace in the hole, catching others off guard by either saying or doing what they least expect. You tend to be calm and soft-spoken most of the time but have found that occasional outbursts of simulated anger (and a penchant for spicy language) can often shock people into compliance.

Manager: Accounting

You have been with the department for several years, and you are in favor of the move because of the positive effect it will have on the distribution of services. Going to a new office space will be much less expensive than trying to expand, even if you could find the available land. The operating budget has increased in the past few years, but lack of expansion space will put a ceiling on the provision of services within a very short time. The strength of the department's financial position and the growth potential of the relocation would really be a boost to the department.

Your Power Personality. You are very careful to have the hard facts about any question before you enter a discussion. You are willing and able to research those facts to enable you to use them to counter emotional arguments. You have a great deal of financial information at your disposal. Since almost every activity in the department affects the bottom line, your auditor's examination of every unit has given you a great deal of information about the efficiency of these units as well as an awareness of a number of skeletons in various closets.

You are soft-spoken, which requires others to listen carefully when you speak. Your power tactic consists largely of strategic use of information, both financial and your own personal experience. Typically, you will let an opponent expound his or her views, then submit your information, pointing out that his or her argument is based on opinion whereas yours is based on hard facts.

Manager: Purchasing

You have been with the department for 25 years and are reluctant to leave the Albany area where you have family and social ties. You think that many others in the department feel the same way you do about leaving Albany. With only a few years left until retirement, you do not want to make any drastic changes in your life.

In terms of logistics, a new location could lack easy access and efficient facilities for shipping equipment and materials. You think that these increased transportation costs are a legitimate argument against moving to the new location.

Your Power Personality. You are personally very suspicious of change. You like the feeling of power you get by, at least initially, saying "no" to any proposal that involves making changes from the traditional way of doing things, regardless of well-supported arguments for the change. You have found that intransigence on your part can produce the desired effect of stopping the proceedings and can prompt others to placate you. When others demand reasons for your refusal, you know you can always blow up any small legitimate objection to defend your position. You are not afraid to let your tone of voice and bodily posture convey that you think people are picking on you unduly. You have often found that if you complain long enough and persistently enough, you will get your way.

Manager: Stock and Bond Transfer

You joined the department eighteen months ago, and the relocation plan is your brainchild. You feel strongly that the move will be good for the department and that services can be expanded only if some kind of move is made soon. You would like to start influencing the department's future in the most obvious way possible: by ushering in a new era of expansion. The move is bound to force some early retirements and resignations among management personnel who want to remain in the Albany area. You feel that this will revitalize the organization, especially with some of the go-getter replacements you have in mind.

Your Power Personality. You have found that few opponents can withstand the force and high energy level of your arguments. You are not afraid to criticize someone or to interrupt at strategic points in a discussion. In fact, you are rather rude. You are not above instilling a little fear in others by reminding them that you control one of the important units of the department and have access to all evaluation data that point toward the need for expansion.

You are quick to pick out another's weakness and capitalize on it. Emotional arguments or personal considerations are very easy to attack. You single mindedly intend to get your way.

Manager: Personnel

The department created a personnel unit some years ago, and you became its manager eight months ago. You are in favor of the move because there could be a wealth of semiskilled and trainable people in the area surrounding the new location. You know that restaffing will be an enormous job, but this very requirement could be an opportunity for you to increase your somewhat tentative power position in the department by demanding that you unit's staff be increased to handle the big job of hiring and firing caused by the move. You personally look forward to moving away from Albany.

Your Power Personality. You try to appear calm, cool, and level-headed. One way to get your point across in a debate is to repeat your statement or position over and over, never raising your voice, and looking your opponent straight in the eye. You counter the arguments of others by an appeal to logic: The most rational alternative must be the best one. You do not attack your opponents directly but, rather, attack the logic of their arguments by questioning their research methods and basic assumptions. You are open-minded to the extent that a more logical solution than your own may sway you.

Improving Power-Oriented Behaviors

Observation Sheet

Directions Make notes on the power-oriented behaviors used by the different people in the role play.

Manager: Client Financial Services
Manager: Accounting
Manager: Purchasing
Manager: Stock and Bond Transfer
Manager: Personnel

Assessing Power-Oriented Behaviors

Questionnaire Sheet

Directions In the two spaces provided on the power scale that follows, first write the number that best represents your perception of the degree of power each of the department managers had in this meeting. Second, indicate the source of each manager's power, that is:

Position (POS)   Personal (P)   Expert (E)   Opportunity (O)   Information (I)

Scale

No power		1 2 3 4 5 6 7 8 9 10		Very powerful

Power Scale   *Power Source*

____ ____ 1. Manager: Client Financial Services

____ ____ 2. Manager: Accounting

____ ____ 3. Manager: Purchasing

____ ____ 4. Manager: Stock and Bond Transfer

____ ____ 5. Manager: Personnel

PRACTICE II: It's About Your Smoking

Directions You have the task of convincing a close friend, spouse, or roommate to stop smoking. Use whatever approaches and strategies you think would be effective. Work in groups of four, and pair off among the group. Each person should take the role of convincing his or her partner to make a commitment to stop smoking. Talk about how effective you think you were and why. Be prepared to respond to the following questions.

1. Did any strategies or approaches seem to be more effective than others?

2. How do you account for the differences in effectiveness?

3. Why is this task so difficult? (If you were working with a real smoker, you may have encountered more resistance than with someone who was pretending to be a smoker.)

APPLICATION Changing Your Power Base by Changing Your Influence Strategy

This activity is designed to help you further develop and maintain your own power base with your subordinates, colleagues, and superiors, if applicable, in your organization.

Think about the power/dependency analysis you did in the assessment exercise at the beginning of this chapter. Using that example, or another one that has occurred to you since, determine which relationships would benefit from an increase (or decrease) in influence from you. For each dependency, identify some of the issues in which you could become more involved right now and, using the ideas and skills discussed in this unit, take some definite action in those areas. You might need to consider how you can use more influence and less power of authority. Or, you might want to work on how to confront some of the frustrations of a relationship in which you feel taken advantage of, misunderstood, or in which your abilities and potential are not recognized.

Competency 2 Negotiating Agreement and Commitment

ASSESSMENT Are You a Novice or Expert Negotiator?

Directions Think about some experiences you've had with negotiating—as a consumer, an employee, or a partner in a relationship you value. Ask yourself questions such as those listed, and add any you think are significant.

After answering the questions to your own satisfaction, discuss those you feel comfortable discussing in small groups (of about six people). Take 30 minutes for the discussion, and be prepared to report to the rest of the class on any themes or insights that surfaced in your group.

1. Have you ever returned a damaged product and negotiated for a refund, even though, technically, the warranty had lapsed, or was somehow invalid?

2. Have you ever bargained for a shift change, a raise, or an adjustment in working conditions with a manager or employer?

3. Have you ever gone around normal channels to secure items such as season

tickets, or a discount, or passes to a concert or play, after initially being told they were unavailable?

4. Do you press for more information or clarification when listening to a sales pitch, or do you hesitate to ask questions for fear of appearing uninformed or unsophisticated?

5. In a personal relationship, do you ever tolerate negative behavior in the other person because (a) you feel incapable of broaching the issue effectively, (b) you fear being misunderstood, or (c) you don't want to hurt the other person's feelings, even though the behavior is causing you serious problems?

6. As a rule, do you feel you have a reputation among your peers and members of your family for being a tough bargainer or as someone who is easy going and deferential in presenting his or her needs and conditions?

LEARNING   Negotiating Agreement and Commitment

HOW IS YOUR CREDIT RATING?

The first competency in this chapter dealt with building and maintaining a power base. However, we can't exert influence in an organization or a group without knowing what kinds of influence people are ready to accept. The rest of this chapter will deal with negotiating agreements and selling ideas.

All members of an organization or group have a credit rating. That rating goes up or down depending on how supportive, cooperative, and competent people perceive us to be. We do a balancing act. We have to be concerned about the needs of others, and we have to get our jobs done as well. Support is not automatic. Amateur brokers believe that their assigned duties guarantee them support. The expert broker never takes such support for granted.

The balancing act between looking after the needs of others and getting the things we need leads us to the topic of negotiation. Negotiation is not limited to formal sessions across the desk with "the other party." We negotiate anytime we need something from someone else. William Ury, an associate at Harvard Law School's Program on Negotiation, reminds us that most of the important decisions we make in life are not made unilaterally. Most are negotiated. "Negotiation," says Ury, "is the pre-eminent form of decision making in personal and professional life" (Ury, 1993, p. 5).

Another way to describe effective negotiations is "dialogue." The word *dialogue* implies a process of working things out through careful reasoning. Our colleagues at the Praxis Group, a consulting firm that specializes in building communication effectiveness, define dialogue as "the free flow of meaning in an atmosphere of mutual trust and respect." We don't learn from people we don't respect, and we seldom make commitments to people we don't trust. The Praxis Group focuses on improving the ability of clients to establish and maintain the conditions of dialogue. For Praxis, these conditions include three elements: mutual meaning, respect, and purpose. If one or more of these elements are not present, dialogue will elude us.

Mutual meaning involves each party knowing what the other is actually saying. Do we share the same definitions of terms, words, and expressions? Establishing mutual meaning is sometimes more difficult than we might think, especially among people who come from different cultures or backgrounds. In some cultures, the concept of intellectual property is a very "foreign" notion. In their experience ideas are meant to be shared and communicated, not patented, stamped, and used only by written permission or for a fee. A student from such a culture may struggle to understand the concept of plagiarism. We can easily label such students dishonest, but this is not only unfair but inaccurate.

Mutual respect is also essential, but fragile, especially if two parties have already had a disagreement or conflict. At least one party has to have the courage and wisdom to not resort to name calling and blaming, or the two parties will never reach dialogue. When you watch two people in a heated argument, you're usually seeing a game of "tit for tat." I call you a name, you call me one; I threaten you, you threaten me. To create and maintain mutual respect, someone has to swallow hard and break the cycle of tit for tat.

William Peace is a former executive with Westinghouse and United Technologies. He is currently director of Doctus Management Consultancy in Great Britain. Peace does not apologize for being a tough minded, soft hearted leader. For Peace, soft leadership does not imply weak leadership, and a desire to consider many sides of an issue and listen to the recommendations of others does not imply indecisiveness. He learned a lot about establishing mutual respect from a manager named Gene Cattabiani, a vice president in the Steam Turbine Division of Westinghouse. Cattabiani faced a huge challenge with labor–management relations. The hourly employees in the division were fiercely loyal to their union leaders, and convinced that management was out to get them. Managers, on the other hand, were equally convinced that the union leaders were turning employees against management at the expense of the company, and even the employees themselves. "Most of these people are just plain damn lazy," was a comment often heard in management team meetings. "We need discipline more than we need negotiation," was another popular comment.

Cattabiani knew things had to change. The division was losing money, costs were climbing, and other companies were eating up market share. But how could he push for improvements and better performance when there was so much anger in the air? He came to the conclusion that he had to communicate with everyone in the plant. If dialogue was going to begin, he would have to step out and make the first move. This would require giving the same presentation several times on the huge shop floor to a hostile audience. His management team tried to dissuade him. "You don't have to submit to bad treatment," they said. "We'll give people the news in smaller groups." Another, stronger argument was that the risk was too great. "This will become a massive gripe session that may get out of control." But Cattabiani insisted and the meetings were held. Here's how Bill Peace describes what happened.

> *The initial presentation was a nightmare. Gene wanted the workforce to see that the business was in trouble, real trouble, and that their jobs depended on a different kind of relationship with management. But the workers assumed that management was up to its usual self-serving tricks, and there, on stage, for the first time, they had the enemy in person. They heckled him mercilessly all through the sideshow. Then, during the question-and-answer period, they shouted abuse and threats.*

At this point, Peace was convinced that Cattabiani had made a serious strategic error. The management team worried that this "weakened" leader had lost all credibility and would now be bulldozed by employees who were really flexing their muscles. But Peace and others began to notice some subtle changes in the days that followed the meetings.

> *When Gene went out on the factory floor for a look around (which his predecessors never did unless they were giving customers a tour) people began to offer a nod of recognition—a radical change from the way they used to spit on the floor as he walked by. Even more remarkable was his interaction with the people who had heckled him at the meetings. Whenever he spotted one, he would walk over and say something like, "You really gave me a hard time last week," to which the response was usually something like, "Well, you deserved it, trying to pass off all that bullshit." Such exchanges usually led to brief but very open dialogues, and I noticed that the lathe operators and blading mechanics he talked to would listen to what Gene said, really listen. (Peace, 1991, p. 46)*

This division made steady progress over the months and years that passed, and Gene Cattabiani was largely responsible for it. He had a purpose greater than protecting his ego. He knew that people needed some opportunity to ventilate, and they needed to be convinced that he meant what he said about wanting their input and suggestions. He was willing to put himself on the line and not return insult for insult. With mutual respect in place, people could build the other conditions of dialogue, mutual meaning, and purpose. Without respect, meaning and purpose don't really matter. But Cattabiani also understood that leadership can be a lonely spot. He did not expect the plant employees to love him or admire him. He knew that his position required tough choices at times. His goal was to build the overall capability of the organization, not to gain the personal approval of everyone in it. He eventually gained the approval of most people, and the organization's performance improved significantly, but that gain was a byproduct of being a reasonable, consistent leader who was willing to listen and learn as well as teach.

The final condition of dialogue, mutual purpose, is sharing a goal or value that the parties can build on. We once saw a group of environmentalists and developers (two groups who often fail to come to dialogue) come together effectively because they had found a common purpose. Several people in each group had mentioned that as children they had learned to fish with parents and friends in the area whose future was now being hotly debated. They wanted to maintain that possibility for their own children. With that common purpose established, the group effectively moved to a constructive dialogue on how to achieve it while still meeting other needs.

In many cases trust is destroyed, not by bad motives, but by ineffective strategies. We may have needs and goals very similar to those of a roommate, spouse, colleague, or team member; however, an ineffective strategy in working through those needs can trigger distrust in the other person. Once distrust sets in, confrontation follows. Once we're in the confrontation box, it's very tough to get out.

In the next few pages we will present some principles that we have found very helpful in avoiding the traps of confrontation.

Just as we are ambivalent about power, most of us have mixed feelings about negotiation. Expert brokers are solid negotiators. They have a clear sense of what their needs are, but they also know that the people they deal with have needs as well. Good brokers take these needs into account early in the process. The salesperson to whom you return your broken stereo, the ticket seller at the box office, the partner in a significant relationship—all these people bring to the situation a set of needs, values, procedures, rewards, and goals they are trying to meet.

The negotiation style recommended in this book is somewhat on the soft and "reasonable" side, but it also recognizes the need for toughmindedness, particularly around the issues you're trying to champion. This reasonable approach tries to be tough on principles and gentle on people.

FOUR PRINCIPLES FOR GETTING TO "YES"

Roger Fisher and William Ury, in their influential book *Getting to Yes* (1986), offer four basic principles they believe should guide any negotiation. These are:

1. Separate the people from the problem.

2. Focus on interests, not positions.

3. Generate a variety of possibilities before deciding what to do.

4. Insist that the result be based upon some objective standard.

SEPARATE THE PEOPLE FROM THE PROBLEM

The natural tendency, when there are misunderstandings or bruised egos, or struggles over credit or blame, is to make personalities the focus. This is a mistake. The problem is the thing that needs solving.

Once people feel threatened or criticized, their energy goes into defending their self-esteem, not into solving the problem. Keep the focus on the problem, even if you feel another person is at fault.

Remember, the other person may be constructing the situation in a totally different way. Ask yourself, "How does the other party see the situation?" A good way to find out is to ask questions and then lean forward and really listen. Don't assume anything. Talk to the other person about his or her perceptions, and then feed them back to be certain you have heard correctly. "If I understand what you're saying, you feel my request for attending this conference is unreasonable because of the current increase in our case loads. You also seem to feel that I have already received more support from the department than anyone else on the team. Am I on track?" Parroting back what someone has already clearly stated is a ridiculous strategy; however, the message is often clearly stated and needs to be brought out in the open: "Estella, you've mentioned quality problems several times, but I'm not sure what those problems really are. Could you give us an example?"

Another key is to establish rapport. We'll talk about rapport in the section on effective oral presentations, but rapport is important in any approach to negotiation. Take the time to be in touch with the person you're dealing with before you begin dealing with the issue. As we study behavior in organizations, we often see people moving to the task before gaining rapport. For example, we often see doctors treating patients without first establishing rapport. In medicine it's called "bedside manner," and there is enough research and common sense to prove that bedside manner is vital to the healing process. Gerald Goodman, an expert on interpersonal communication, has studied the serious problems created when physicians fail to establish rapport with their patients. Patients need to feel that their doctor has empathy for their them or they will often not ask important questions, and they will often resist following the physician's counsel.

> *I'd bet the majority of problems between physicians and their patients comes from communication maladies. My former student, Professor William Stiles of the University of Miami, Ohio, found serious gaps in the ways typical patients gather factual information from physicians. Often, patients fail to cooperate because certain courtesies or modesty, or minor intimidation keeps them from driving a hard bargain for the specific, detailed guidance wanted. Scientists are recognizing this "noncompliance" as a major health problem. My UCLA colleague, Professor Bertram Raven. . .found that patients who felt empathy from their physicians ("I took the same thing when I had your illness") were able to cooperate better. They were less cooperative when doctors used their usual hard commands: "Take this twice a day and don't use any dairy products." (Goodman and Esterly, 1985, p. 275)*

We see teachers begin their classes before connecting with their students. We see managers giving directions and pronouncing policies, but not relating to the people they are talking to. These leaders don't seem to understand that people are saying, "I'd care a lot more about what you care about if I thought you cared more about me."

When you focus on problems and not personalities, you are better able to let people blow off steam without your taking it personally. There's an old German proverb that says, "Let anger fly out the windows." It's good advice because it saves both parties from that chain reaction of one person's anger feeding off another. The next time someone at work or at home unloads on you, do yourself a favor and imagine yourself opening a window and letting the heat of that anger out. In the meantime, collect yourself to deal with the problem behind the anger. All professional negotiators seem to agree: *Don't react too quickly to emotional outbursts.*

FOCUS ON INTERESTS, NOT POSITIONS

When we negotiate, we often begin by taking a "position." We believe that in the final outcome we can feel good if we have defended that position. But positions can be traps. For years, during the cold war, the Soviets and Americans argued from different positions on limiting strategic weapons. The U.S. team was committed to a position of allowing for at least six missile base inspections per year by each side. The Soviets dug in for a maximum of three. Negotiations were stalemated for weeks over the magic numbers six and three.

The problem was that no one had really thought through the needs and concerns behind the positions they had taken. Both parties had hunkered into their positions. Someone needed to ask, "What is an inspection? One person walking around a missile site for one day, or a team of eight people spending a week?" The United States was apparently concerned about sufficient frequency and thoroughness in inspections, and the Soviet Union was anxious about how intrusive the inspections would be. But on reflection, it became obvious that the number of inspections was not the major issue (Fisher, Kopelman and Kupfer-Scheider, 1994, p 37).

When we coach executives we challenge them to put their purpose before their initial position. You are not your position, we tell them, so don't become too invested in that position. Focus on the goals and principles behind your position, and separate those goals from your own ego (as best you can). There may be other ways of reaching your goal than those offered by the first position you develop. Thus, the next rule of thumb: Generate other possibilities.

GENERATE OTHER POSSIBILITIES: MAKE THE PIE BIGGER

When people are arguing over how to divide a pie, most of them never consider the possibility that the pie could be made bigger. Often it can. Good negotiators try to think of options that are of low cost to them but of high benefit to the other party. This strategy is often called "dovetailing" or collaborating. In order to dovetail your needs with the needs of the other party, you have to probe what those needs are, and not take the other party's position at face value. When a fellow manager says that he or she must have control of the training rooms in your facility every Friday afternoon, his or her position may be based more on a need for power and control than a practical need for those rooms at that time. It may also be that he or she needs guaranteed space over time, but not necessarily every Friday afternoon. The trap is in reacting to that manager's position before uncovering his or her real needs. That act of questioning and probing will usually enable you to come up with alternatives.

For example, in negotiating over price with a box supplier, a purchasing agent from a small company saw an opportunity. The agent learned from the discussion that the supplier was in a cash-flow squeeze after purchasing a very expensive fabrication machine. The supplier had taken a rigid position on price, and now the purchasing agent knew why. Seizing the opportunity, the agent offered to prepay the supplier for the entire job in exchange for a faster turnaround time *and a major price reduction* (Calano and Salzman, 1988, p. 76). These opportunities for win–win agreements are too often overlooked because negotiators fail to solve the other side's problems first. Dovetailing your needs with those of the other party requires you to separate your needs from your position, but also to separate the other party's needs from its position.

If alternatives don't come to mind right away, don't panic. Take some time. Huddle with a few associates and friends you trust and do some brainstorming. Come up with creative alternatives based on everything you know about your needs, the needs of the other party, and the facts of the situation at hand.

As a manager, you may need to use your negotiating skills in helping others resolve problems or reach compromises. This process is called *mediation*. Expert brokers think twice before intervening in a dispute or disagreement between colleagues or subordinates. It's usually best to wait to be invited, but this is not always possible. For example, if two people have to work together, and a disagreement is making it impossible for them to work effectively, their manager may need to become involved. As their manager, you would have to decide if you want to deal with the people individually or together, and determine how willing they are to solve the problem. For cases in which you decide it's necessary to function as mediator, here are some principles to help you develop a strategy:

1. Acknowledge to your people that you know a conflict exists, and propose an approach for resolving it.

2. In studying the positions of both parties, maintain a neutral position regarding the disputants—if not the issues.

3. Keep the discussion issue oriented, not personality oriented. Focus on the impact the conflict is having on performance.

4. Help your people put things in perspective by focusing first on areas where they might agree. Try to deal with one issue at a time.

5. Remember, you are a facilitator, not a judge. If you assume the role of judge, each person will focus his or her energy on trying to persuade you,

rather than on solving the problem and learning something about negotiation. Judges deal with problems; facilitators deal with solutions.

6. Make sure your people fully support the solution they've agreed upon. Don't stop until both parties have a specific plan, and if you sense hesitancy on anyone's part, push for clarification: "Tom, I sense you're less enthusiastic than Carol about this approach. Is there something about it that bothers you?"

GIVE ME A REASON: INSIST ON USING OBJECTIVE CRITERIA

Fisher and Ury (1986) advise us to make negotiated decisions based on principles, not pressure. Often negotiators make the process a contest of wills: It's my stubbornness and assertiveness against yours. Some people call this "yes we will, no we won't" cycle "inefficient disagreement." A way around this trap is to find some objective standards or criteria that will help the parties test the reasonableness of a position. For example, your car is totaled in an accident and you refuse to argue with the insurance adjuster over a price based upon sentimental value: "My father gave me that car!" or "I've owned that care since I was in high school!" You would have to refer to some standard, like market value as indicated in the "blue book," or some other objective that both parties could consider reasonable.

It's smart to look for the theories and assumptions behind the position. If your bureau chief unveils a plan for deciding how to award release time for training, you may want to know more about the criteria behind the procedures. It's not a matter of trust or professionalism; it's a matter of knowing what criteria are behind the position the person is taking. Fisher and Ury use the following example from a colleague whose parked car was totaled by a dump truck. It was time to settle with the insurance company through an adjuster (Fisher and Ury, 1986, pp. 96–98).

Adjuster: We have studied your case and have decided the policy applies. That means you are entitled to a settlement of $3,300.

Tom: I see. How did you reach that figure?

Adjuster: That was how much we decided the car was worth.

Tom.: I understand, but what standard did you use to determine that amount? Do you know where I can buy a comparable care for that amount?

Adjuster: How much are you asking?

Tom: Whatever I'm entitled to under that policy. I found a second-hand car just like mine for about $3,850. Adding sales and excise tax it would come to about $4,000.

Adjuster: $4,000! That's too much!

Tom: I'm not asking for $4,000, or 3 or 5; I'm asking for fair compensation. Do you agree it's only fair I get enough to replace the car?

Adjuster: Okay, I'll offer you $3,500. That's the highest I can go. Company policy.

Tom: How does the company figure that?
Adjuster: Look, $3,500 is all you get. Take it or leave it.

Tom: $3,500 may be fair. I don't know. I certainly understand your position if you're bound to company policy, but unless you can state objectively why that amount is what I'm entitled to, I think I'll do better in court. Why don't we study the matter and talk again?

Adjuster: Okay Mr. Griffith, I've got an ad here for a 1978 Fiesta for $3,400.

Tom: I see, what does it say about the mileage?

Adjuster: It says 49,000, why?

Tom: Because mine had only 25,000 miles. How much does that increase the value in your book?

Adjuster: Let me see, $150.

Tom: Assuming the $3,400 as possible base, that brings the figure to $3,550. Does the ad say anything about a radio?

Adjuster: No.

Tom: How much extra in your book?

Adjuster: That's $125.

Tom: What about air conditioning?

A half hour later, Tom walked out with a check for $4,100. Notice how unemotional Tom was? He was working from a need to ground their discussion of price on objective criteria acceptable to both parties. He didn't lose control, and he didn't cave in to personal pressure. He knew his appeal to objective criteria was fair and reasonable. Negotiating can be an emotional ordeal, but good negotiators don't lose control. They keep dragging an emotional discussion back to the issue at hand.

THE FREEDOM SCALE:
NEGOTIATING EXPECTATIONS UP AND DOWN

One of the greatest sources of stress in organizational life is caused by unclear expectations. We want the people who manage us to be more explicit about what they want, and how they want us to operate with them. And as managers we are often confused by the people we manage." Didn't I explain how I wanted her to report to me on that project? Why is she bugging me with questions on all these details?" The problem can be solved in part by negotiating your position on what Oncken calls the "freedom scale" (Oncken, 1984, p. 106). The freedom scale describes the degree of freedom or discretion you want to enjoy in your working relationships: up, down, and across the organization. You are the person who has to take the initiative to negotiate, or discuss your position on the scale with your boss and with those you manage. Your position will change over time and with various projects and assignments you work on. Here's the scale.

Level 5   Act on your own, routine reporting only.

Level 4   Act, but advise your boss at once.

Level 3   Recommend a course of action; dialogue and negotiate with your boss; then take resulting action.

Level 2   Ask what to do.

Level 1   Wait until told.

The most critical role to work out is that in which you are the managee, the person being managed. You may be operating at level 3 with your manager, but feel a need to move to level 4 on most (not all) projects. Your manager may, when presented with the idea, be delighted to give you more discretion and room in which to operate. This change would save your manager time and energy. Of course, the freedom scale is like an insurance policy. You can save your manager time and energy by taking out a very cheap policy—one that allows your manager to let you make the decisions and report routinely. The risk, however, is that if something goes wrong, your manager will be only distantly involved and may take a great deal of blame if things get out of control. That is why your position on the freedom scale will vary, depending upon your manager's anxiety level and personal interest in various projects and responsibilities in which you are involved. The most expensive policy a manager can have is to be surrounded with people who are waiting to be told what to do (level 1). This means that the manager is essentially micromanaging everything, taking very little risk, but paying too much for his insurance policy. The manager is working too hard, and the people he or she manages are probably frustrated.

Think about your future role as manager. If a consulting team talked to the people you supervise, would they be able to clearly explain where they feel they are on the freedom scale in their working relationship with you? Have you ever made your employees' role and level of discretion explicit? This is a simple but powerful tool that you can put to work immediately with your superiors, peers, and subordinates.

Directions   Now it's time for you to practice some mediating and negotiating strategies of your own. Remember, the same principles of negotiating apply to mediation, but as mediator, you're trying to help other parties resolve their differences. This three-person simulation can be used to demonstrate both ineffective and effective approaches to mediation.

Role for Tony Lodge
You manage 10 people in Production Supply. You've been with the department almost two years now and are quite pleased with your job.

Three months ago your unit was assigned to a new project. It required your people to work a lot of overtime and change vacation plans. Now the project has been expanded and another unit, headed by Billie Deore, a woman in her mid-thirties who has transferred recently from another branch office, has been brought in to help. Employees will still need to work overtime for a least two months.

The people in your unit are tired and are complaining that they haven't seen much of their families during the past three months. You feel Billie's people should assume the major portion of the overtime to give your employees a rest. Your people are burned out and morale is slipping. Billie's people, on the other hand, are fresh. You have heard, however, that Billie intends to have her unit pick up only half the overtime.

Your manager has told you that he expects you and Billie to settle the overtime issue and then inform him of your joint decision. On the way to get a cup of coffee, you meet Billie Deore. You decide to bring up the issue.

Role for Billie Deore
You manage 10 people in Production Supply. You've been with the agency just over one year and are generally happy with your job.

Your unit has been assigned to help Tony Lodge on a recently expanded project. The project has required and will continue to require people to work overtime. The project is expected to last at least two months.

Your manager has asked that you and Tony work out the distribution of overtime. You like Tony and look forward to working on the project with him. You feel the overtime should be evenly split between your two units. That way, there will be minimal disruptions in people's schedules as vacations near.

However, you have heard through the grapevine that Tony expects your unit to assume all the overtime. It is his feeling that someone else has to take up the slack because his people have done it for the past three months. You can sympathize, but you don't want your people to take on all the overtime. Your manager has told you that he expects the two of you to work out the details and inform him of your decision. On the way to get a cup of coffee, you meet Tony Lodge. You decide to bring up the issue.

Role for Leslie MacIntosh
You're a friend of Tony and Billie and a unit manager in Production Supply. You've been with the department for seven years and are quite happy in your job.

As you walk into the coffee lounge this morning, you notice the two managers, Tony and Billie, seemingly engaged in some kind of argument.

This disturbs you because you depend on their cooperation to meet production demands. If they fail to reach an agreement on the staffing for the special project, the entire department will be disrupted.

You decide to sit down with them and see if you can help them. You want to do whatever you can to help Tony and Billie work through the problem.

Instructions for "Failure" Third Party (Leslie)
Your instructor has assigned you to demonstrate how to fail as a mediator. You're going to play the part of a person who has the best of intentions but the worst possible approach to mediating. Please follow the instructions as closely as possible. In real life, of course, you would not do as badly as in this demonstration. Remember, you're very serious about helping the two parties, but you're going about it in all the wrong ways.

1. Listen to the discussion for a short time.

2. Begin to communicate nonverbally your discomfort with the discussion (sit back, fidget a bit, shake your head).

3. Intervene in the discussion. Some possible actions you might take are:

   ■ Agree with one of the people but not the other—take sides.

   ■ Say that they shouldn't be talking about this kind of thing at work or where others can hear them.

   ■ Suggest that their discussion would be better held later when they've cooled off.

   ■ Talk about the fact that they're both wrong.

   ■ Say that you think the boss ought to be handling this.

   ■ See if you can get both of them to attack you.

   ■ Get up, wash your hands of the whole affair, and leave.

Instructions for "Success" Third Party (Leslie)

Your instructor has assigned you to demonstrate how one might effectively help two people who are engaged in a heated argument to listen to each other. Please follow these directions as closely as possible.

1. Listen to the discussion for a short time.

2. Begin to lean forward intently to listen to both persons. Show your interest by physical movements.

3. Intervene in the discussion, attempting to use the following process.

   ■ Say something like, "It may be we're not clear on what either of you is saying. I'd like to ask you to try something with me."

   ■ Do some checking with one of the people, asking that person to feed back what he or she thinks the other person has said. The other can then comment on it—a check to see if communication has been clear.

   ■ Quickly, before the first person starts the check, tell the second that you want him or her to do the same thing when the first person has finished. This should convey to both of them that you are not taking sides, but only trying to facilitate communication.

   ■ If they have trouble during the process, help them; continue to be active and be positive about what you want them to do.

PRACTICE   The Copy Machine Problem

Directions   In this activity you will have the chance to practice some negotiation on a work-unit level. Work in pairs. Each of you will seek a compromise using some of the strategies and principles discussed in the course material. Note: If you are unable to solve your problem, you may call upon another mediator from the class.

The Situation

There is a problem with the use of the copying machine. In the last two weeks, members of two work units have been fighting for use of the machine they share. Yesterday the conflict erupted into an argument with yelling and name calling between workers from each unit. Managers, Doyle Buchanan and Mary Caputo, have decided to meet and try to solve the problem.

Doyle Buchanan

Your unit has extensive contact with the public. You have 10 workers who need to use the machine for routine documentation of their work. Most of the copies are photocopies of signed documents that must be returned to the signer. The original is filed.

Your unit's workflow is regular, not sporadic, and in the past workers made their single copies throughout the day and returned to their workstation. Your workers need access to the machine throughout the day.

Mary Caputo

Although your unit has less direct contact with the public, your unit is responsible for periodically mailing important documents to citizens throughout the state. You have three workers who use the machine for larger work orders. They need one to two hours at a time to complete the copying. Your unit's workflow is sporadic and not predictable, but you have tight deadlines when you do get work.

APPLICATION Negotiating Positions on the Freedom Scale

Choose one of the following exercises to work on over the next two weeks. Write the results of your work in a memo to your instructor.

1. Take an issue in your life—buying a VCR or some other expensive item, scheduling shifts in a summer or part-time job, or solving a problem in a personal or family relationship. Describe the issue in terms of the negotiating techniques you have learned in this chapter.

2. Describe your efforts at working with William Oncken's freedom scale. You may choose to focus on the levels of initiative you pursue with your own manager, the levels you have negotiated with those whom you manage, or both. The freedom scale is a powerful concept. You may wish to talk explicitly about it with your staff, or your manager. If you feel that approach would be inappropriate, you may want to take a more casual approach and focus on a particular task you have been assigned (if you're dealing with your manager), or one you have recently assigned to someone on your staff.

The idea behind this assignment is to come to a clear and supportive agreement with the other party on what level of initiative the two of you can expect. What level are you now on? Do you agree about the current level? If not, why? Where do each of you want to be? If you want to work on level 4 and your manager wants you on level 3, what do you do?

Write a two-page discussion of your experiences in negotiating positions on the degree of freedom scale. Address such questions as:

1. What were your biggest challenges in implementing this principle?

2. Were your manager or your co-workers threatened by this idea, or encouraged by it?

3. Were your discussions about mutual expectations positive and productive, or awkward?

4. Did you feel comfortable with the process?

5. What do you need help with, and how can you get that help?

Competency 3 Presenting Ideas: Effective Oral Presentations

ASSESSMENT The Presenter's Touch: You May Have It and Not Know It

Directions Teachers are constantly discovering students who are superb oral presenters, but who have little idea of how good they are. They also find students who can dramatically improve their presenting ability with minor adjustments in their approach. Many of us have the presenter's touch and don't even know it. Answer the following questions.[1]

Yes   No

____ ____ 1. Do you get a kick out of helping other people solve their problems?

____ ____ 2. Do you use the word "you" more than "I"?

____ ____ 3. While watching TV panel shows, do you sometimes answer the questions before the experts do?

____ ____ 4. Can you cut through a rambling, foggy conversation—dig out the main point—and say it so that everybody understands and agrees?

____ ____ 5. Do you have a high energy level? Do other people seem to you to be talking slowly?

____ ____ 6. Is there a bit of the cheerleader in you? Do you usually lead the applause?

____ ____ 7. Do you like to tell people what you've learned? Would you make a good teacher?

____ ____ 8. Are you a good editor? Can you digest lots of material into simple, clear language?

____ ____ 9. Do you like the feeling of being "in control"?

____ ____ 10. Can you handle pressure without blowing your top? Can you deal with provocative questions without flaring up?

____ ____ 11. Do you like to demonstrate what you're talking about? Do you tend to "act out" what you're describing?

____ ____ 12. Do you look people in the eye when you talk to them, and when they talk to you?

____ ____ 13. Do people turn to you when it's time for the meeting to be summed up?

[1]These questions are adapted from *I Can See You Naked* by Ron Hoff. Copyright © 1988 by Andrew & McMeel.

*Scoring and
Interpretation* If you answered "yes" to half of these questions, you are probably a very strong presenter right now. If you scored less than that, don't be discouraged. Your honesty will be a great asset in improving your ability to communicate. You need to believe you really can improve, which is possible by applying some of the principles presented in this third competency.

LEARNING Presenting Ideas: Effective Oral Presentations

Public speaking is the number-one phobia of people in this country. In surveys asking people what they most dread, giving a speech is invariably first on the list. For most of us, there is no way around the requirement, because our jobs bring us in front of people regularly. In organizational life we do most of our work in groups. This is why communication is vital to every role you play as a manager.

In this final section, we will discuss presentations, and give you some practice on giving them and evaluating them. However, everything discussed will also apply to all communication tasks: writing, interviewing, negotiating, mediating, coaching, and so on.

For this brief discussion of effective presentations, we will use Al Switzler's (Praxis Group, 1994, p. 8) framework for effective communication. Switzler says that our strategies and choices for how to communicate with a group should be driven by three considerations:

1. Our purpose.

2. Our audience.

3. Our resources.

We have to know our purpose and not assume our audience will automatically share that purpose. We also have to know as much as possible about our audience. We can learn a lot about an audience just by looking at them and listening to them talk among themselves. We can ask lots of questions about a group if we're invited to speak to them. This information will guide our choices. Do these people know a lot about this topic, or very little? Are they likely to agree with the position or advice or approach we plan to use?

Finally, resources are time, money, energy, and information. All are finite and in limited supply, but we often have more than we think. What resources do you have available in making a presentation? Can you get some additional advice on a topic or some help with graphics? How much is the presentation "worth" to you? How much time can you spare for preparation? What kind of presentations is this audience accustomed to hearing? Do they like detail or very broad outlines? How much time will you really have to present? What does the situation require?

SSSAP

The other elements of Switzler's framework are known as **SSSAP**: Set, Support, Sequence, Access, and Polish.

SET

Set deals with an audience's initial impressions and expectations. When competitive sprinters step up to the starting blocks, the starter says, "On your mark, get set . . . ." "Set" is the perfect position for starting quickly. When you set your audience, you help them get into the right position, psychologically, physically and intellectually. Good communicators connect with their audiences early to prepare them for the journey they are about to take. Good presentations are audience centered, not speaker centered. Most poor presentations are built on weak set. Set does three things: (1) It creates a mood and tone favorable to listening and acceptance; (2) it assures the listener that you are worth listening to; and (3) it maps the journey you are asking the listener to take with you. Switzler calls these three functions of set the credibility set, climate set, and content set.

Climate Set

Climate set is the effort you make to establish rapport with the audience and cue them to a mood or style appropriate to the presentation. Climate set is frequently neglected, and at great cost. First, consider the speaker's task: establishing rapport. *Rapport* is a French word meaning to bring back or refer. In English it has come to mean having an accord or harmony with another person. We tend to feel a rapport, or lack of it, when we speak to people individually, but rapport is equally important in speaking to groups. Without rapport, you will not be allowed to communicate.

As a way of improving your ability at gaining rapport, try to apply some of the following principles at the next meeting you are required to conduct.

1. Be in the room first and greet each person.

2. Make eye contact. Notice the facial expressions and energy level of the people coming in. Does Kay look tired or distracted? Is Craig irritable or bored before the meeting even begins? Don't ignore these cues. Use them to establish rapport by helping you key in on the group's mood and energy.

3. As you begin the meeting, make eye contact with every person present. In larger groups, scan sections of the audience. People will feel that you are connecting with them, even though you can't make eye contact with many individuals.

4. Be positive and pleasant, but don't press too much energy onto a resistant group, especially at first. Try to mirror their energy level close enough so as not to turn them off. You can show more energy and enthusiasm as you go.

Most groups will resist abrupt jumps between their energy level and that of a speaker.

5. Be positive and supportive. Improve your "climate set" by being positive, even if you have unpleasant or difficult business to conduct. If you aren't positive, what is your justification for being in charge? When this advice is given to people, some react, "But this is just another dumb meeting. Everybody knows that. I'd feel like a jerk trying to get people to enjoy it." That's the point. Even perfunctory, routine meetings are much more bearable when the person in charge is positive and professional. Grand occasions are often less challenging to our skills than routine ones. We enjoy working with people who are professional and upbeat. Try it and see. Don't be dramatically different, but push up your level of energy and optimism, and you'll be pleased to see how contagious those qualities are.

Credibility Set
Credibility set is the assurance you provide the audience that you are informed and legitimate as a speaker—that you know what you're talking about because of your experience, credentials, interest, special expertise, and so on. Often the credibility set is offered by the person who introduces you, but, in less formal settings, you may need to provide the credibility set yourself. Obviously, when speaking to a group you know very well, you may not need to provide a credibility set at all. Sometimes the briefest comment will suffice: "I had the opportunity last summer to spend three weeks at the FBI's National Training Academy in Virginia. Susan Grace , our bureau chief, asked me to share some of the things I learned at their forensic sciences lab." Another example is, "You know, change is something we can count on. I remember how hard I worked to understand the 1986 Tax Code when I studied accounting at Penn State, and I remember how hard I worked to master the 1991 Tax Code as a junior partner with Deloitte and Touche. Now, we all face another challenge. . . ."

Don't assume people know why you are qualified to take their time. Without boasting, you need to think about your credibility set every time you address a group that doesn't know you well. Your credibility set may be very specific. "For the past two months I've been visiting all the branch offices in our company, interviewing customers and suppliers about how they feel about the services we provide. I've learned a lot from the hundreds of people I've listened to, and I hope I've learned some things that can help us move the business ahead. . . ."

Content Set
Content set is the roadmap you provide your audience. Most of us are uncomfortable with ambiguity. We want to know what's going on, what we're getting into. When you talk to a group let them know where you're about to take them and do it early in your presentation. "I want to talk for 10 minutes about why I think our record in work-related accidents is deteriorating, and make some suggestions on how to turn the corner on the problem. When I've done that, I

would like your questions and suggestions." With that "set" the audience can understand what is coming because you've given them a map to follow. A good communicator remembers what it's like not to know much about the topic in question (Wurman, 1989, p. 130). The more we know about a topic, the more inclined we are to overestimate how much our audience knows about it. Define terms and avoid jargon as much as possible. People appreciate a clear and candid style in speaking as well as writing. William Zinsser, a gifted writer and engaging speaker, shares an example of how not to do it:

> A few years ago, I was shanghaied on to an advisory panel at Time Inc., and at our first meeting someone asked the chairman what our committee had been formed to do. He said, "It's an umbrella group that interacts synergistically to platform and leverage cultural human resources companywide." That pretty much ended my interest in the committee. And when it later experienced "viability deprivation" (went down the tubes) I was overjoyed. (Wurman, 1989 p. 118)

Think about what people need to know up front so that they can relax and pay attention. Will you give people a chance to ask questions? What major themes will you cover? Without the answers to these questions, people might interrupt just before you get to the point they are interested in, or stop listening because they assume you are not covering the topic about which they want to hear. The road map you give your audience will keep their understanding and attention on track.

SUPPORT

Support is the substance of your presentation: the facts, the major arguments, the reasons you argue for doing one thing rather than another. Support is the bones of your presentation. Switzler says that the support you provide in any presentation should be correct, concrete, complete, relevant, and logical, and he gives this hint about checking on the effectiveness of your support. Ask yourself these questions:

1. What do I mean? Do I define things adequately?

2. Am I specific? Do I use illustrations?

3. How do I know? Do I invoke appropriate authorities?

4. So what? Do I make my message relevant?

Try, whenever possible, to anticipate objections to your position, or points of misunderstanding, and address them as you go. For example:

> Our field tests have shown that this new compound forms a better bond for broken pipe joints than any we've used. Admittedly it's less effective in very cold temperatures, so we will be limited to three-season use, but new batches are being developed that promise to be effective year-round. Some of you pointed out in your field report

that the compound dries much slower, but most of us who have used it think the greater durability is really worth it.

Notice that this message anticipates the objections of the audience. If you are speaking to your colleagues or members of a unit attached to your organization, use your knowledge of that culture to help you support your points. How does that organization process information? What passes for a "good reason" in this culture? Laborde (1987) talks about a colleague who was told by his manager that, in the wake of a reorganization, his office would be the smallest one in the unit. After thinking for a few days, this person went to his boss and told her that the new situation would hamper his productivity, and in fact had already gotten in the way of several important negotiations. This argument struck a chord because his boss was more concerned at that point about productivity than she was about equity, or fairness, or appearance, or any other value he could think of. There were several real and honest reasons the person could have laid on the table for getting his office changed, but he felt this one would have the most impact. It correlated more closely with the values and interests of the person with whom he was dealing. In another situation, another reason would have been more effective.

In speaking, try to use the support that has the greatest relevance, validity, and impact. Don't load too many reasons into the hopper. This tactic will weaken your arguments overall.

SEQUENCE

May I Pray While I Smoke? Certain locations have more prominence in messages than others. For example, beginnings and endings are the more prominent locations. An audience is more likely to remember the opening and closing comments you make in a talk than the things that go in the middle.

If your content set gives the audience a map of the journey, the sequence you choose is more like the journey itself. Do you go to the store first or the bank? Do you talk about the new security policy from the central office, or the events that led to the policy?

Sequence is the order or flow or linear arrangement of your talk, or the agenda you are building if you're conducting a meeting. You may have superb content, but if you present it in the wrong order, you may be misunderstood or ignored. Sequence is vital, but we often pay little attention to it. Look at these two sentences.

Carol is a superb systems analyst, but she is not good at dealing with people.

Carol is not good at dealing with people, but she is a superb systems analyst.

These sentences do not mean the same thing. Each gives us a different impression of Carol. In the first sentence, the emphasis is on Carol's purported weaknesses in interpersonal relationships. The second stresses her strengths as systems analyst, allowing for her poor performance with people. Gordon Allport, a prominent social scientist, used to tell his students about two monks who argued often about the appropriateness of smoking and praying at the same time. They decided independently to ask their superior to settle the question. One monk asked, "Father, may I smoke while I pray?" "Heavens no, my son. Prayer is a serious matter,'" was the answer. Later, the second priest, knowing the power of sequencing asked, "Father, may I pray while I smoke?" He was told, "My son, it is always good to pray."

Spill the Beans. In most presentations or briefings, the best approach is to "spill the beans." Unveil your most important message first, and then support the point with elaboration and details. A good memo tells the reader up front what its main point is. A good presentation spills the beans at the beginning and provides backup later. We love suspense when we're reading a novel or watching a film, but not when we're listening to a presentation at work.

There are exceptions to this rule. If you have bad news, you usually need to "buffer" the jolt by verbally placing your arm on your listener's shoulder. In this example a manager has to give her staff some bad news about an upcoming move.

> *I think most of you know I've been meeting frequently with our director over office space. I've played all the chips I had to win a resource for what I think is the best staff in this agency. I appreciate your support and your patience. Unfortunately, we've lost this one. We won't be moving into the new wing when it's finished. We need to talk about what that means, and how best to live with it.*

The worse the news, or the tougher the topic, the more the need for a buffer. However, don't overdo putting off the bad news. People know what's going on. They don't want to be patronized; they usually just want to be treated civilly and professionally.

Deciding on Sequence. Sometimes it's hard to decide what sequence to use. Do you present things in the order in which they happened (chronologically)? Do you go from the known to the unknown, or the simple to the complex? Any of these approaches might work, but you have to decide in each particular case. Think about your purpose and the audience's needs. You may need to persuade a group that your approach to tracking inventory is most accurate, but your audience may need to be assured that it will not take more time to implement than the current system. Remember, audience-centered communication is your goal.

A very helpful strategy is to use the magic number *three*. The number three is a very important number in our culture. "People are comfortable with things that come in threes" (Hayden-Elgin, 1987, p. 181). You can capitalize on that comfort by using three elements in your presentations, particularly if you have little time to prepare and little time to make the points you wish to make. Suzette Hayden-Elgin recommends this formula:

1. State or present the problem or situation.

2. Provide three supporting items: *a, b,* and *c.*

3. Conclude with a summary.

For example:

1. I'm very pleased to introduce Fawn Ashton.

2. Because:
   - She is the person who organized the first Concerned Citizens for Clean Air chapter in the state.
   - She is recognized as one of the best authorities in the country on air pollution and its effects on children with respiratory disorders.
   - She is a friend I have known and admired for over 20 years.

3. The best thing I can offer my associates in this cause is to give them a chance to hear Fawn Ashton.

This model of three things within a framework of three will seem familiar, logical, and nonthreatening to your audience, because we deal with this kind of structure all the time. When you think about sequencing, think about the number three, and then decide the best order in which to put those three items.

ACCESS

Some presentations are interesting, but the points they make are hard to pinpoint. **Access** deals with making information accessible to the listener. When you write, you improve access by using boldface type, white space, headings, borders, numerals, and color. When you give a presentation, you can improve access by using good visual aids and making clear transitions from one point to the next. You can also make things more concise by stating them in fewer words, or summarizing them.

Words, Numbers, Pictures. Visuals are extremely important to access. We live in a visual age. We are children of the media, and we process most of our information visually. A talking head is death in the media industry. Most network programming will not keep the camera on a person talking for more than 15 seconds. They break up the "talking head" with graphics or footage illustrating what the person is talking about. We know all this from our own experience, but time and again we see people pull their captive audiences through long, tedious presentations, glutted with details, and void of visual enrichment.

Most of the visuals used in presentations are very ineffective. Typically, the more time, money, and effort spent on visuals, the worse they are. Here are some of the reasons why. Most of us prepare a lot of word/number visuals when we give presentations. These are usually overhead transparencies with lots of words and or numbers on them. The transparencies are easy to make because of computer graphics; they are striking and professional looking, but are usually too detailed and hard to follow. Here are some guidelines for using visuals.

1. Visuals are the tail. You, as presenter, are the dog. Don't let visuals control your presentation.

2. Visuals do enhance audience comprehension and improve your credibility. Most speakers need to think more visually. When you have to talk to a group, try to translate from words into pictures. Even if you choose not to use visuals, your talk will be more vivid.

3. Visuals help you by providing a reason for moving, pausing, and pointing. This movement gives your audience the variety they need, and makes you easier to listen to.

4. Visuals need to be simpler than we usually make them. We should use line drawings, sketches, and photographs more, and be careful about flashing columns of numbers on the screen. Sometimes you have to use lots of numbers. If so, highlight the most significant ones with a colored marker, or bracket the figures in some distinct way.

5. Visuals are primarily for the audience, not the speaker. Make every choice based upon their need to understand, not your need to dwell on fine points or impress them with how much homework you've done.

6. Visuals can make a fool of you if you don't rehearse with them. Practice the pacing and sequence of your visuals, and become comfortable with handling them.

7. Visuals made from reports or other "page size" documents are usually unreadable. If your audience is 18 feet away, the lettering on your charts or overheads must be one-half inch (as the audience sees it on the chart or screen); from 32 feet they should be at least one inch.

8. Visuals need lots of white space. For word visuals, use no more than five items per visual, and no more than six words per item.

The overhead projector is now a fixture in most conference and board rooms across the world, but people are sometimes too eager to use it. Transparencies are easy to carry and very easy to produce, but the projector is noisy, and in small groups, covers too much of your audience's field of vision. Don't underestimate the effectiveness of the flip chart. You can draw lists and simple charts on them, and prepare them ahead of time and flip to them as you present. Now, electronic boards enable you to write notes or simple graphs, and then copy them with a push of a button. Flip charts and electronic boards are ideal in groups of not more than 15 people. Flip chart paper is fragile, and doesn't travel well, so for repeat presentations have your visuals mounted on poster board and placed on an easel.

POLISH

Polish is the finish you put on anything that represents you or carries your reputation with it. It is the added and extra attention to details and little things. It is having your notes in order, having good visuals arranged at the overhead projector, dressing in such a way that you do not draw too much attention to yourself, but need not worry about your appearance. Polish is arranging the environment for maximum effectiveness. People can hear you. They can see the screen. The room isn't stifling or chilly. You can't control all the aspects of the environment, but you can do some things, and these make a huge difference. Polish is the extra attention to detail that tells the audience that the topic is important, they are worth the effort, and they are not wasting their time. Polish is giving a presentation you want to have your name on.

ANALYSIS Applying SSSAP

Directions Within the next week, take special note of a presentation in which you are part of the audience. A live presentation would be better than a televised one. Use the SSSAP principles and your own experience and expertise as a communicator to evaluate the presentation. Consider these questions:

1. Was it effective? Why or why not?

2. How could the presenter have improved his or her performance?

3. What do you think the presenter's main purpose was? Was that purpose clear?

4 Did the presenter prepare the audience with climate, credibility, and content sets?

5. Was there a good summary?

6. Was the presentation vivid? Were visuals used? If not, should they have been used?

PRACTICE You Be the Speaker

Directions Prepare a six-minute presentation on a topic of your choice. It may involve a problem or project at work, but it may also be taken from another class or your personal experience. Think carefully about the SSSAP principles, and tailor your presentation to your audience. You will share your presentations in groups of eight to ten and give each other feedback and recommendations on things that worked well, and things that could be improved.

APPLICATION   You Be the Critic

Write an assessment of a presentation you have given recently at work, in a class, or in any organization or group with which you are affiliated. Ideally, this presentation should be one given since you've been exposed to the principles we've discussed in this chapter. Talk about the context of the presentation.

Discuss in writing how successful and effective you think your presentation was and why. Did your exposure to the SSSAP principles help you as a communicator? What do you need more work on in oral communication? Write your evaluation and give it to your instructor by the assigned date.

REFERENCES

Adizes, Ichak. *Corporate Lifecycles: How and Why Corporations Grow and Die and What to Do About It.* Englewood Cliffs, N.J.: Prentice-Hall, 1988.

Bazerman Max H., and Margaret Neale. *Negotiating Rationally.* New York: The Free Press, 1992.

Calano, Jimmy, and Jeff Slazman. "Tough Deals, Tender Tactics." *Working Woman* (July 1988).

Cohen, Allan R., and David L. Bradford. *Influence Without Authority.* New York: John Wiley & Sons, 1990.

Covey, Stephen R. *The Seven Habits of Highly Effective People.* New York: Simon and Schuster, 1990.

Ekman, Paul. *Telling Lies: Clues to Deceit in the Marketplace, Politics and Marriage.* New York: Berkley Books, 1985.

Fisher, Kimball. *Leading Self-Directed Work Teams: A Guide to Developing New Team Leadership Skills.* New York: McGraw-Hill, 1993.

Fisher, Roger, and William Ury. *Getting to Yes: Negotiating Agreement Without Giving In.* New York: Penguin, 1986.

Fisher, Roger, Elizabeth Kopelman and Andrea Kupfer Schneider. *Beyond Machiavelli: Tools for Coping With Conflict.* Cambridge, Mass.: Harvard University Press, 1994.

Goodman, Gerald, and Glenn Esterly. *The Talk Book: The Intimate Science of Communicating in Close Relationships.* Emmaus, Penn.: Rodale Press, 1985.

Hamel, Gary, and C.K. Prahalad. *Competing for the Future: Breakthrough Strategies for Seizing Control of Your Industry and Creating The Markets of Tomorrow.* Boston: Harvard Business School Press, 1994.

Hamlin, Sonya. *How to Talk So People Listen.* New York: Harper & Row, 1988.

Handy, Charles. *Understanding Organizations.* New York: Oxford University Press, 1993.

Harding, Ford. *Rain Making: A Professional's Guide to Attracting New Clients.* Holbrook, Mass.: Bob Adams, 1994.

Hayden-Elgin, Suzette. *More on the Gentle Art of Verbal Self-Defense.* New York: Prentice-Hall, 1983.

———. *The Last Word on the Gentle Art of Verbal Self-Defense.* New York: Prentice-Hall, 1987.

Hoff, Ron. *I Can See You Naked. A Fearless Guide to Making Great Presentations.* Kansas City: Andrews and McMeel, 1988.

Humes, James C. *The Sir Winston Method: Five Secrets of Speaking the Language of Leadership.* New York: William Morrow, 1991.

Kanter, Rosabeth Moss. *The Change Masters: Innovation for Productivity in the American Corporation.* New York: Simon and Schuster, 1983.

Kirkpatrick, Donald K. *How to Plan and Conduct Productive Business Meetings.* New York: McGraw-Hill, 1987.

Laborde, Genie. *Influencing with Integrity.* Palo Alto, Calif.: Syntony Publishing, 1987.

Larson, Charles V. *Persuasion: Reception and Responsibility* (6th ed.). Belmont, Calif.: Wadsworth, 1992.

Maccoby, Michael. *Why Work: Motivating and Leading the New Generation.* New York: Simon & Shuster Inc. 1988.

Mitroff, Dan I. and Ralph H. Kilmann. *Corporate Tragedies: Product Tampering, Sabotage, and Other Catastrophes.* New York: Praeger, 1984.

Oncken, William, Jr. *Managing Management Time: Who's Got the Monkey?* Englewood Cliffs, N.J.: Prentice-Hall, 1984.

Orsborn, Carol. *How Would Confucius Ask for a Raise? One Hundred Enlightened Solutions for Tough Business Problems.* New York: William Morrow, 1994.

Peace, William H. "The Hard Work of Being a Soft Manager," *Harvard Business Review* (November–December 1991), pp. 40–47.

Praxis Group. *Presenting with Power: A Guidebook* (training manual published by Praxis Group), Provo, Ut.: 1994.

Raiffa, Howard. *The Art and Science of Negotiation.* Cambridge, Mass.: Belknap Press of Harvard University, 1982.

Schendler, Brenton R. "How Steve Jobs Linked Up with IBM," *Fortune* (October 9, 1989): 48–61.

Senge, Peter, Richard Ross, Bryan Smith, Charlotte Roberts, and Art Kleiner. *The Fifth Discipline Fieldbook.* New York: Doubleday, 1994.

Silva, Karen. *Meetings That Work.* Burr Ridge, Ill.: Business One Irwin/Mirror Press, 1994.

Tannen, Deborah. *That's Not What I Meant: How Conversation Style Makes or Breaks Relationships.* New York: Ballantine Books, 1986.

Tannen, Deborah. *Talking from 9 to 5: How Women's and Men's Conversational Styles Affect Who Gets Heard, Who Gets Credit, and What Gets Done at Work.* New York: William Morrow, 1995.

3M Management Group. *How to Run Better Business Meetings.* New York: McGraw-Hill, 1987.

Ury, William. *Getting Past No: Negotiating Your Way from Confrontation to Cooperation.* New York: Bantam Books, 1993.

William, I. *The Practical Negotiator.* New Haven: Yale University Press, 1982.

Whetten, David A., and Kim S. Cameron. *Developing Management Skills.* New York: Harper Collins, 1995.

Woodall, Marian K. *14 Reasons Corporate Speeches Don't Get the Job Done.* Lake Oswego: Professional Business Communications, 1993.

Wurman, Richard Saul. *Communication Anxiety.* New York: Doubleday, 1989.

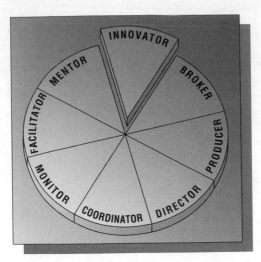

THE
INNOVATOR
ROLE

9

■ COMPETENCIES

Living with Change

Thinking Creatively

Managing Change

The **innovator role** is one of the most compelling, yet least understood, of the eight leadership roles. As one of the two roles of the open systems model, it focuses on adaptability and responsiveness to the external environment. The innovator role involves the use of creativity and the management of organizational changes and transitions, and provides a unique opportunity for managers to affirm the value of individual employees within the organizational setting.

When people think of the words *innovator* and *innovation,* they tend not to think in terms of large established organizations. Rather, they associate the terms with new entrepreneurial business endeavors or with specific corporate divisions related to such things as new product development, new design, or new advertising lingo. In fact, given the many rules and procedures that must be followed in large organizations, they often assume that managers in these organizations have little opportunity to be innovative or to create flexible, risk-taking environments.

You should be aware, however, that change is inevitable in all aspects of organizational life today. Moreover, in many cases change and innovation are desirable. They are indispensable to the function, growth, and survival of organizations. The issue today is not whether organizations will experience change, but how they will manage that change (Quinn, Kahn and Mandl, 1994).

Innovation and managed change make readiness and adaptability possible in society's increasingly changing conditions and accompanying demands. Today,

336

managers play an important role both in the initiation and the implementation of organizational change. In this chapter the three key competencies of the innovator are:

Competency 1 Living with Change
Competency 2 Thinking Creatively
Competency 3 Managing Change

Each of these competencies requires the manager to be flexible and open to new ideas, new ways of thinking, and new challenges that the managerial role presents.

Competency 1 Living with Change

ASSESSMENT Personal Acceptance of Change

Directions   The following questionnaire will help you assess your personal acceptance of change. Consider carefully the following list of changes. List any others that are applicable. Which of these changes have occurred in your life in the past five years? As you consider each change, recall your resistance to change when it happened.

In column A, place a number reflecting your resistance at the time of the change. Next, in column B, place a number reflecting your current level of acceptance of that change. If you did not experience the change, place a "0" in both blanks.

Scale A

No resistance				Strong resistance
1	2	3	4	5

Scale B

No acceptance				Strong acceptance
1	2	3	4	5

A B

_____ _____ 1. You were married or engaged.

_____ _____ 2. There was a death in your immediate family.

_____ _____ 3. You moved to a new location.

_____ _____ 4. You enrolled in a college or university.

_____ _____ 5. You had a personal health problem.

_____ _____ 6. You began work at a new job.

_____ _____ 7. An important relationship in your life changed.

_____ _____ 8. Your income level changed by over $10,000 a year.

_____ _____ 9. You were divorced or separated.

_____ _____ 10. A close friend or relative was divorced or separated.

_____ _____ 11. Other (List):

Interpretation   What do your responses reveal about how you deal with change? As you look at each item, note the difference between the number you placed in column A (resistance to change) and the number in column B (acceptance of change). A large difference (4 is the maximum possible) indicates that your ability to accept change is strong.

1. Which changes did you strongly resist at first, but now accept? Think of as many reasons as possible why you now accept these changes. Identifying these reasons may help you identify your strengths in acceptance of change.

2. Based on your responses, do you consider yourself to be open to change, or do you find change difficult to deal with?

3. Are there any events which you strongly resisted, and which you now have difficulty accepting? Seek to identify the reasons for your nonacceptance. As you compare strongly resisted events which you accept with those you do not, you may find valuable clues to your ability to cope with change in your life.

LEARNING   Living with Change

One of the greatest challenges to the manager in the innovator role is that of living with changes that are unplanned and sometimes unwelcome. As a manager you must often deal with a difficult dilemma when experiencing such change: On the one hand, you need personally to adjust to an unplanned change that you may not welcome, and at the same time you must present the change to your employees in a manner that helps them to make the adjustment as well. Both cases may require a shift in attitude toward change and a conscious effort to eliminate psychological resistance to change.

In studying change in organizations, it is helpful to recognize that people do not just work in organizations—people live in organizations. In fact, people who work full time generally spend more time at work than they do engaged in any other activity, with the possible exception of sleep.

We recognize that changes take place in life, and although we may resist, we also know that we must adjust to these changes. The same is true of changes in the workplace. What can we learn about change in our lives in general that will help us respond to changes in the organization? Let's consider several differences between planned and unplanned change in life, and relate those findings to the workplace.

PLANNED AND UNPLANNED CHANGE

In our lives we frequently experience planned changes. Generally we plan beneficial changes, and thus we welcome those changes. Some planned changes have only minor impacts on our lives, such as planning a change in hairstyle or wardrobe. Other planned changes are major and can potentially change the course of our lives, such as plans to go to college, plans to have children, and plans to buy a home. Our plans may not always have the intended results, but we usually plan changes with the intent of benefiting ourselves.

From time to time, though, we may find ourselves resisting changes that we have planned for ourselves. Why? We may resist change when we have ambivalent feelings toward those changes. For example, although we work toward graduating, we may still wonder if we can make it on our first job. We also resist changes that involve a lot of work. Moving to a new house can be exciting, but it can also be very stressful and difficult. Likewise, we resist changes that involve unknowns. Many people plan their retirement years in advance, but when the time draws close, they resist because they do not know what it will be like.

The fact that we plan change reflects the needs we have to exercise control over our lives and to know, with some certainty, what the future holds. Sometimes the need to feel in control is stronger than the reaction to the actual change. Even changes that are beneficial to you may be resisted if someone else has planned them. For example, if someone else planned what courses you should take or for what new job you should apply, you would probably find yourself resisting those plans—even if the plans exactly matched your own.

In addition, people have a need to know what will happen next. All of us are more comfortable when we can predict what will happen and how others will respond to us. Anxiety and stress increase when we find ourselves in situations where we do not know how to behave or what to expect from others. For example, if you were invited to attend religious services for a religion with which you are totally unfamiliar, you might try to contact someone who knows more about the religion to find out what to expect. With that information, your ability to predict the behavior of others, and your ability to behave appropriately, increases and you are more comfortable.

Let's turn now to unplanned change, or changes that are not anticipated changes that are sudden, imposed upon us, and largely unwelcome—and compare these to planned changes. Five important differences between planned change and unplanned change are presented here. Table 9.1 summarizes these differences.

TABLE 9.1 Differences Between Planned and Unplanned Change

1. Planned change carries a more positive connotation than unplanned change.
2. Planned change tends to involve a sense of gain; unplanned change tends to involve a sense of loss.
3. Planned changes can be anticipated; unplanned changes are sudden.
4. We are active participants in planned changes; we see ourselves as passive receivers of unplanned changes.
5. Planned changes are usually less stressful than unplanned changes.

First, planned change usually carries a more positive connotation than does unplanned change. We plan changes in our lives that are intended to benefit us.

Unplanned changes, however, are painful, difficult, or present us with personal crises. Examples of painful unplanned changes include the death of a loved one, the loss of a friend, the loss of a job, and divorce. Although unplanned changes sometimes bring long-term benefits, the short-term pain of unplanned changes is often difficult to cope with.

Second, planned change tends to involve a sense of gain, whereas unplanned change tends to involve a sense of loss. Sometimes we do lose something. For example, we may lose contact with co-workers whose promotions take them to a new location, or there may be a loss of flexibility in the organization after a reorganization. We may experience the loss of a sense of security, a sense of control, our ability to anticipate what is going to happen to us, or a sense that everything is fine.

Third, planned change can be anticipated; unplanned change is sudden. With planned change, we have time to adjust and to think about alterations that will accompany the change. Time to adjust translates into assistance with coping and adaptation. In dealing with unplanned change, however, we do not have the benefit of time. Adaptation is more difficult, and the suddenness comes as a stark reminder of how little control we actually have over our lives.

Fourth, we usually welcome planned change, but see unplanned change as imposed upon us. When we welcome change, we are active participants in the event; when change is imposed, we are passive receivers of others' actions. Within organizations, change may happen by chance, or as a result of forces beyond our control, but we usually perceive unplanned change as imposed by an organizational hierarchy. This sense of imposition is not pleasant and understandably people generally resist. Once again, unplanned change reminds us that we have little control over our lives.

Finally, planned change is usually less stressful than unplanned change. Although both types of changes may require coping and adaptation, the positive aspects of planned changes can enhance the coping process. Unplanned events are often stressful because they disturb our equilibrium, our sense of comfort with the predictable nature of life, and our sense of control over our existence.

HELPING OURSELVES AND OTHERS TO DEAL WITH UNPLANNED CHANGE

The first step in living with change is to learn about individual response to change. The more we know, the better we will be able to manage it—both at work and in our personal lives.

Understanding the roots of resistance to unplanned change in yourself and in others is most important for the manager. As a manager your challenge is twofold:

Challenge 1   To assist yourself in adapting to unplanned changes which you may not welcome and with which you may, in fact, strongly disagree.

Challenge 2   To assist your employees to do the same.

To deal with these changes you need to ask yourself, "What can I do to adjust? How can I deal productively with change, while at the same time assisting employees in doing the same? Are there things that I can initiate before a change occurs that will help my work unit adjust to unplanned changes when they occur?" The strategies that help you to cope with unplanned change can also assist others in doing the same, because you are able to offer these same strategies to your employees. Any strategy will need to be directed at reducing resistance, both yours and that of your employees. The ability to redirect resisting energy to positive work energy is an important skill of the innovator.

Here are three general guidelines for coping with unplanned change in the innovator role. These steps should be taken concurrently.

1. Recognize that you experience additional stress during times of adjustment to unplanned changes. Study the recommendations in the section on stress management in Chapter 7 and incorporate them into your life.

2. Identify strategies that have helped you deal with the stress of unplanned changes in the past. Ask yourself, "When I have been faced with unplanned changes in my life, in or out of the workplace setting, what has been helpful to me?" Here are three frequently reported sources of strength for individuals facing unplanned change in their lives.

   - A supportive environment where people around you understood your difficulties and provided a setting where you did not have to defend or justify your feelings. Adjustment to unplanned change involves emotions. Some people are very uncomfortable with dealing with their emotions, especially in the workplace. The relief and positive energy that is given to individuals when they realize that it is acceptable to express their emotional responses without being negatively evaluated should not be underestimated.

   - A feeling from others that you are accepted and respected for your strengths. People often feel vulnerable during times of unplanned change. Concern for how others view you may prevent you from expressing emotions about unplanned change. At these times it is important to be the recipient of respect from other people.

   - A hopeful belief in the potential benefit, or gain, from successfully dealing with the change. An attitude of optimism about the future and its improvement over today can give you impetus to face changes with renewed vigor.

3. Seek ways to replicate the conditions in step 2, and any others which you can identify, when you need the assistance. In your managerial position, you need to encourage the expression of these conditions in your work unit as well.

Once you have met the challenge of establishing your personal coping strategy, your second challenge is to assist your employees in adjusting to unplanned changes. Consider the situations that you experience outside the workplace when helping friends and others deal with unplanned changes in their lives. What do you usually do to be helpful to others during trying circumstances? Most likely, you may try to do for others what you have identified as helpful for you. Within the organization, can you help your employees to deal with unplanned changes? In this situation you have two major tools at your disposal: (1) the organizational culture and (2) your leadership style.

USING THE ORGANIZATIONAL CULTURE TO DEAL WITH UNPLANNED CHANGE

In many ways, organizations mirror society. One striking way in which this takes place is that, like societies, organizations have cultures. An organizational **culture** is a collection of meanings, values, beliefs, expectations, and attitudes that are shared by members of the organization. It is seen in the taken-for-granted assumptions about how individuals behave and how the work is to be done. Organizational cultures are powerful entities that influence the members of the organization.

An organization's culture reflects its philosophy and mission. It influences the way organizational members perceive events and situations. Cultures also influence the way in which members of the organization interact with one another and with outsiders in job-related responsibilities. For example, at each of the Disney theme parks, the culture reflects a strong emphasis on customer service; employees are expected to "go the extra mile" to ensure that the customer is satisfied. Similarly, an organization's culture may reflect a strong emphasis on human resources, individual development, and training. In addition, how an organization deals with planned change is reflected in its culture. Note, however, that organizational cultures are not engraved in stone; they change and interact with the values and beliefs of members, as well as with the society from which the members come (Walton, 1995).

How can your organizational culture help you in your efforts to assist employees in dealing with unplanned change? If the culture is one which embraces values of inflexibility and resistance to change, or if the culture promotes the belief that the way things have always been done in the past is the only way to do things in the future, then the culture may be a hindrance. IBM had such a culture, and it led to the disintegration of the company into many smaller companies. As you examine your organizational culture, identify those elements of the organizational culture that reinforce resistance to change, and try to reduce their strength. Also identify those elements of the organizational culture that are consistent with a supportive environment, and seek to strengthen those elements. As a member of the organization, and as a manager, you have a great deal of influence over the organizational culture, especially within your work unit.

Moreover, *before* the crisis of an unplanned change occurs, begin now to reduce the strength of the resistant forces and strengthen the supportive elements of your organizational culture so that you are more prepared for change as it occurs. Three ways for using your organizational culture to deal with unplanned change are as follows.

First, support an organizational (work unit) culture that values flexibility and adaptability. If necessary, take opportunities to raise the issue of change for discussion in your work unit. Advance the notion that change is in the nature of things, and that change should be expected. Let your employees know that opportunities for change are opportunities for learning and growth, and that these can be welcomed. Reflect this belief in your reactions to change as it occurs.

Second, encourage employee participation in work unit changes. Wherever possible, when implementing change, allow employees to suggest alternative methods of implementation that are respectful of their attitudes, values, and concerns. Again, by encouraging employee involvement, you are reducing resistance to change and thus engaging in cultural change. At American West, chairman of the board Edward Beauvais and president Michael Conway have created a culture that strongly encourages employee participation by maintaining an open-door policy for all employees.

Finally, think of employees as creative resources. Tapping employees' creativity helps them see their value and unique strengths. Such encouragement will undoubtedly assist them when coping with unplanned changes.

USING YOUR LEADERSHIP STYLE TO DEAL WITH UNPLANNED CHANGE

The second tool available to you in helping employees to deal with unplanned change is your own leadership style. The phrase *leadership style* refers to the way managers treat and interact with employees. How one treats and interacts with employees is likely to affect whether employees resist unplanned change, or are open and flexible to suggestions.

There are two types of leadership styles: the manager as conductor and the manager as developer (Bradford and Cohen, 1984). In the manager-as-conductor style, the manager is boss and gives instructions to employees, who are simply expected to carry out the instructions. The second leadership style is the manager-as-developer style. This is also known as the "empowerment" leadership style because managers take the posture of supporting employees in the performance of their responsibilities.

The manager-as-conductor style is perhaps the most familiar, and it is what we tend to think of when we consider management in hierarchical organizations. In this model, there is a formal hierarchy of authority, which also describes approved lines of communication. The manager using this style figures out how best to coordinate the work efforts, and how to get subordinates to do things properly. Using the orchestra as a metaphor, the manager-as-conductor literally

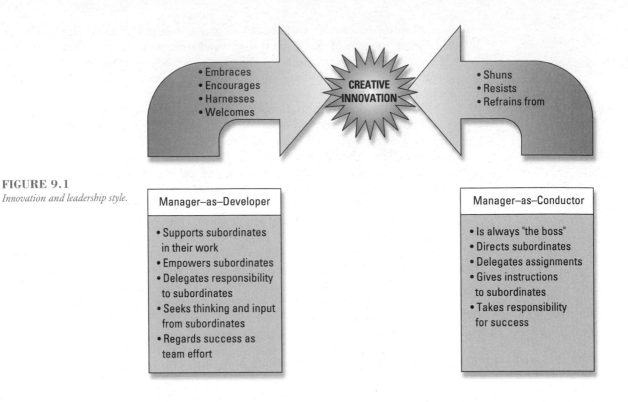

FIGURE 9.1

Innovation and leadership style.

orchestrates the situations being faced in the most productive way possible. The manager-as-conductor style, however, potentially can lead to resistance because employees feel no sense of control and see no credit or reward for successful implementation of change. They feel that although they have performed well in getting the work accomplished, the manager-as-conductor takes total responsibility for the success; after all, without someone there to coordinate and motivate, the work would not be done.

In contrast, the manager-as-developer seeks ways to "empower" subordinates, helping them to realize their potential. The manager-as-developer engages employees in the decision-making process and delegates responsibilities without necessarily telling individuals how to do it. The manager-as-developer focuses on the unit's work as a joint venture, a team effort. Under this leadership style, employees often feel that "their brains are being tapped" and that their views and creative ability are welcomed and valued. Employees of the manager-as-developer learn and grow from the work experience.

To be successful, the manager-as-developer gives credit to employees for their accomplishments, rather than taking credit for the work done in the unit. The manager-as-developer is not threatened by the talent and success of employees, but rather welcomes employees' abilities and seeks ways to use their strengths. Figure 9.1 summarizes the characteristics of both leadership styles.

One advantage of using your own leadership style as a tool for helping to deal with unplanned change is that it is within your control. Although it may be the case that others around you engage in the manager-as-conductor leadership style, you can still embrace the manager-as-developer style for yourself and your work unit. Moreover, managers who adopt the manager-as-developer leadership style can expect to experience less resistance to change from employees than those who adopt the manager-as-conductor leadership style.

ANALYSIS   Resistance to Change

Directions

Read the following paragraph, and think of yourself as the manager in this organization. In the questions that follow, analyze how you would react to these changes. Try to be as honest as possible in considering your reactions.

You are a manager in a relatively small division of a large corporation. The division employs approximately 600 people. You have been with this organization for 12 years. You have come up through the ranks and consider yourself well regarded by your boss and others in upper management. You are responsible for a work unit of 35 employees. Suddenly and with no warning you find that major organizational changes are about to occur: Your division will be structurally reorganized and moved to a larger and more spacious building. You will maintain your same title and salary, but other things will change: You will now be responsible for managing 25 people. The office space for your unit will be more desirable (higher floor, more windows), but the space is smaller in proportion to the decrease of the staff. Because of the larger parking lot, you and a number of other managers will now have your own assigned parking space. Currently there is no assigned parking owing to space limitations. You will report to another manager, who in turn reports to your current boss. Although you have nothing against this newly hired manager, this change does require an unexpected adjustment; you have come to regard your current boss as a good friend.

Discussion Questions

How would you describe your feelings? Check all that apply:

_____ I feel hurt.

_____ I feel angry.

_____ I feel less valued by the organization.

_____ I feel demoted even though the salary and title remain the same.

_____ I feel like getting another job somewhere, if personal circumstances permit.

_____ I feel like I would like to talk this out with someone in higher levels of management, but I feel powerless to do so.

_____ I feel that others in the organization are looking on me and my work unit differently, and that they may be regarding my work unit as less important to the organization's purpose.

_____ I feel less pride in my work.

_____ I feel unappreciated by the division manager and others in upper management.

_____ I feel a decreasing sense of accomplishment.

_____ I feel as if I have been abandoned by my boss.

2. Do you have other feelings? Elaborate.

3. What are the sources of your resistance to this change? Analyze the situation and write down three factors that may account for your feelings.

PRACTICE   Resistance to Change Revisited

Directions   Refer to your responses to the preceding analysis activity. In that activity you analyzed your feelings with regard to a hypothetical situation of unplanned change at work. Now switch roles: Pretend that you are in upper management, and you are the change agent for these same changes. Identify how you would handle the change by responding to the following statements:

1. I expect the positive responses of my employees to this change will be
_____.

2. I expect the negative responses of my employees to this change will be
_____.

3. Sources of their resistance to the move include _____.

4. My employees' questions about the move will be _____.

5. The areas and issues I will have to address concerning the move are
_____.

6. I can help defuse some of my employees' resistance and negative responses by using the organizational culture to _____.

7. I can help defuse some of my employees' resistance and negative responses by using my leadership style to _____
_____.

8. To initiate this change, my three most important actions will be_____
_____.

APPLICATION Diagnosing Your Organizational Culture

Write a brief case study on the culture of an organization in which you are, or have been, involved. After a careful description, respond to the following questions:

1. What are some of the shared meanings, values, beliefs, expectations, and attitudes that are reflected in your organization's culture?

2. What are some unquestioned basic assumptions in the organizational culture?

3. Based on your answers to questions 1 and 2, would you describe your organizational culture as supportive or nonsupportive of employees in dealing with unplanned change? Why?

4. What specific steps would you take to enhance the way that your organization deals with unplanned change? Choose at least two of these steps, and write an action plan that indicates how you would implement these changes if you could.

Competency 2 Thinking Creatively

ASSESSMENT Are You a Creative Thinker?

Directions   Listed are a series of statements describing individual behaviors or attitudes that have been found to be related to creative thinking ability. Read each statement and place a check mark next to those items that you are surprised to see related to creativity. Then review the list, and circle the number of those statements that you think describe you.

_____ 1. In a group, voicing unconventional, but thought-provoking opinions.

_____ 2. Sticking with a problem over extended periods of time.

_____ 3. Getting overly enthusiastic about things.

_____ 4. Getting good ideas when doing nothing in particular.

_____ 5. Occasionally relying on intuitive hunches and the feeling of "rightness" or "wrongness" when moving toward the solution of a problem.

_____ 6. Having a high degree of aesthetic sensitivity.

_____ 7. Occasionally beginning work on a problem that could only dimly be sensed and not yet expressed.

_____ 8. A tendency to forget details, such as names of people, streets, highways, small towns, and so on.

_____ 9. Sometimes feeling that the trouble with many people is that they take things too seriously.

_____ 10. Feeling attracted to the mystery of life.

LEARNING Thinking Creatively

When we think about who is creative, our popular notions of creativity tend toward individuals who we regard as singularly unique, gifted, talented, and just different from the rest of us. In the arts and sciences we think of people like Bach, Handel, Einstein, and Rembrandt. In business we think of people like Steve Jobs (co-founder of Apple Computers), Jack Welch (General Electric), and Anita Rodick (The Body Shop). People rarely think of creative ability existing in the general population. More importantly, we are rarely encouraged to think or learn about being creative. It is not surprising, then, that many people underestimate their creative abilities.

In fact, a very wide range of behaviors and personality traits have been found to be associated with creative ability. More important, creative thinking is a skill that each person can develop.

Creativity is a way of thinking that involves the generation of new ideas and solutions. More specifically, it is the process of associating known things or ideas into new combinations and relationships. Illustrations of this definition of creativity are found in many diverse areas, from science to humor.

Louis Pasteur's discovery of vaccines against disease provides a good example of creative thinking. The idea of vaccination had been widespread since the mid-1700s, but it had been associated only with cow-pox and small-pox disease. It was not until 1879 that Pasteur discovered the prevention of infectious diseases by inoculation, quite by accident. Previously no one had applied the idea of vaccination to other diseases because it involved two different frames of reference: vaccination and the concept of disease being caused by microorganisms. Pasteur had knowledge of both; Pasteur brought the two together.

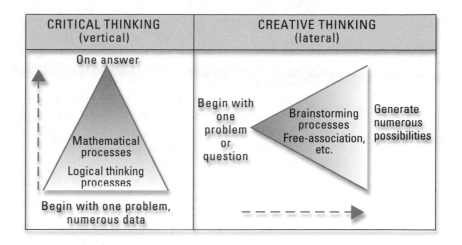

FIGURE 9.2
Critical and creative thinking.

In much the same way, researchers at 3M who know about adhesive and that people often use small pieces of paper for notes brought the two ideas together to create Post-it note pads.

These two examples illustrate how creative thinking often involves utilizing information that is already known, and discovering new associations, rather than, as many people think, generating new ideas out of nothing. In Pasteur's words, "Fortune favors the prepared mind."

How can we increase our ability to engage in creative thinking? First, we need to recognize that all of us have assumptions and thought patterns that we use, but do not question. As we learn to think more creatively, we break away from these thought patterns. In a classic and telling statement, Koestler (1964, p. 96) referred to creativity as "an act of liberation: the defeat of habit by originality." Many creative thinking skill exercises are designed to assist us in developing different ways to look at things, and specifically, to look beyond our assumptions.

Second, we need to recognize that the information used in generating new relationships among things and ideas is already in the mind. Creative thinking is the act of combining those pieces of information in new and unique ways. Thus, although there is a great deal of evidence that creative thinking is not linked to intelligence, creative ability in certain areas is often linked to knowledge and expertise in those areas. For example, one could say that any biologist could have invented penicillin, but not any person.

How does creative thinking differ from critical thinking? It would be useful to compare them briefly. Generally, critical thinking is analytical, logical, and results in few answers; creative thinking is imaginative, provocative, and generates a wide variety of ideas. Critical thinking is often described as vertical, logically moving up until you arrive at a correct answer. In contrast, creative thinking is described as lateral, spreading out to find many possible solutions (de Bono 1970). Figure 9.2 summarizes these differences.

For example, suppose that you, as a marketing specialist, have been assigned to join a special citizen's task force in your community. The task force is considering the problem of how to persuade families and tourists to take their vacations in your home state this year. Notice that there is not merely one answer to this; there are perhaps hundreds or thousands of ways to persuade people to take their vacations in your state. Notice, too, the need for imagination, and the prospect of generating many ideas.

By contrast, consider any mathematical problem whose solution has a single answer. Such a problem involves critical thinking; information is analyzed to determine the one best or correct solution. If your task force has generated a large number of suggestions, it will need to use critical thinking in order to decide which ones would be best to implement. Further, critical thinking skills will be necessary in order to arrive at a viable plan of action.

The two modes of thinking are complementary; the findings of the creative thinking process can be analyzed for usefulness by critical thinking. Although our Western culture has traditionally emphasized critical thinking skills, the value of creative thinking has become increasingly recognized, within organizations and in society as a whole. Moreover, there is a growing assumption that both creative and critical thinking skills will be needed to meet the challenges of the twenty-first century.

DEVELOPING CREATIVE THINKING SKILLS IN YOURSELF AND OTHERS

People often underestimate their own creative ability. Research indicates, however, that there is one major difference between people who exhibit creative tendencies and people who don't: personal belief in creativity. That is, those who engage in creative thinking tend to regard themselves as creative; the others see themselves as noncreative.

Since many people simply do not see themselves as creative, the manager has an opportunity to affirm employees as individuals by recognizing their creative potential and encouraging the use of creative thinking. In this way subordinates are strengthened both on the job and as individuals. By empowering employees to think creatively, managers increase the probability that new and better ways will be found to do things.

To focus on developing creative thinking skills, both in yourself and in others, consider the three dimensions of creativity: domain-relevant skills, creative-relevant skills, and task motivation (George T. Geis in Kuhn, 1987).

DOMAIN-RELEVANT SKILLS

Domain-relevant skills are associated with the basic and expert knowledge that is essential to creative thinking. Increasing your domain-relevant skills primarily involves increasing your knowledge base. Not just anyone could have discovered penicillin, but perhaps any biologist with the requisite expert knowledge could have. Remember that creative thinking is largely knowledge-based, using information already in the human mind.

Within organizations, some knowledge differs from area to area. For example, knowledge required for financial planning differs from that required for personnel management. Alternatively, knowledge of organization and management skills are relevant across various areas of an organization. In reading this textbook, you are increasing your domain-relevant skills for creativity in the managerial role. You can also increase your domain-relevant skills by learning how other organizations in the United States, in other Western cultures, and in non-Western cultures structure their work environments. For example, Japanese management differs in how manager-employee relationships are regarded, in the role of management in organizations, and in the role of organizations in society. Although the extent to which it is either possible or desirable to implement concepts of Japanese management in the United States will vary across organizations, exposure to these ideas may help you to think creatively about your own work environment and relationships with employees.

CREATIVE-RELEVANT SKILLS

Creative-relevant skills are those that enable individuals to associate previously unrelated concepts and to think differently. A vast array of techniques, often called "creativity heuristics," ranging from using analogies to mental imagery, are available to enhance your creative-relevant skills. These techniques are individual strategies that will help you as an innovator to develop your personal creative thinking skills.

One key to enhancing your creative-relevant skills is to learn to break away from commonly held assumptions regarding the relationships between ideas and things, so that you are able to consider new relationships. It is especially important to recognize cultural barriers to creativity, those commonly held assumptions that are a part of our societal or organizational culture. For example, Western culture traditionally has embraced reason and logic to the exclusion of feeling and intuition. This emphasis on reason and logic has created several barriers to creative thinking, including:

1. A negative value on fantasy and reflection as a waste of time, a sign of laziness, or even a bit crazy.

2. The belief that only children should play and that adults should be serious.

3. The assumption that problem solving is serious and, therefore, humor is out of place.

4. A negative value on feeling and intuition, which are regarded as illogical and impractical.

Although we cannot change these societal-based cultural barriers, we can guard ourselves against their influence. If we are able to diminish our cultural barriers to creative thinking, we enhance our abilities to think differently and develop skills for creativity.

In addition to the barriers presented by our societal-based cultural assumptions, individuals often make assumptions that hinder their attempts to become more creative. Like cultural barriers, individual barriers can be overcome if we consciously seek change.

Individual barriers frequently have an emotional basis. These barriers result from personal beliefs and fears associated with taking risks, trying out a new idea, or trying to convince others of the value of our new ideas. Ten of the most common individual barriers to creative thinking are:

1. *Resistance to change.* It is natural to become secure in the way things are and to resist change.

2. *Fear of making a mistake and the fear of failure.* To counter this fear, the Limited clothing stores encourage mistakes by evaluating buyers on their failures as well as on their successes. They believe that if employees do not make mistakes, then they may not be taking initiatives and trying new ideas. Somerset Maugham once said, "You'll win some. You'll lose some. . . . Only mediocre people are always at their best" (quoted in Miller, 1987, p. 17).

3. *Inability to tolerate ambiguity.* Our need for predictability nurtures our inability to tolerate ambiguity. We like to know the way things are, and to be able to categorize things, events, and people in our lives. Creativity requires flexibility in our thinking; inability to tolerate ambiguity is an inability to tolerate flexibility.

4. *The tendency to judge rather than to generate ideas.* This is an expression of the culturally based preference of critical thinking over creative thinking. Many of us are trained to be critical in our thinking, and judgmental in our approach. To some extent, we may feel better about ourselves if we are able to critique another's work or action.

5. *Inability to relax or to permit any new idea to incubate.* Many of us find a perverse comfort in having too much to do, and as a result, find relaxation uncomfortable and difficult. Some people report that they do not know how to relax. Others relax by engaging intensely in another demanding project. Research has shown, however, that freeing our conscious minds, through relaxation or repetitive activity (e.g., cutting the grass or cleaning the house) increases our ability to seek associations amidst old ideas.

6. *The tendency toward excessive self-criticism.* Many of us are taught to be excessively self-critical. In this respect, some people are kinder to people they

actively dislike than they are to themselves. Efforts to eradicate this self-defeating tendency can increase your creative abilities.

7. *Fear of looking foolish.* This is the biggest barrier of all and the hardest to remove. No one likes to appear foolish to others. We find, however, that often we think we appear foolish when we actually do not. The development of a "so what?" attitude can be helpful in these instances (Rawlinson, 1981, p. 21).

8. *Conformity, or wanting to give the expected answer.* This is very apparent in groups and organizations. Individuals may not want to rock the boat or present an unpopular argument (see the discussion of groupthink in the section on participative decision making in Chapter 3). Managers should actively encourage employees to present different ideas or perspectives (Rawlinson, 1981, p. 16).

9. *Stereotyping, or limiting the possibilities of objects and ideas to their "known" use.* The inability to see a problem from various viewpoints is a function of mental stereotyping (for example, a chair is for sitting).

10. *Lack of information, or too much incorrect or irrelevant information.* Lack of information may limit the creative handling of data.

Are you afflicted by any of these barriers? The extent to which you are is an indicator of how much your creative ability is hampered. Equally important for managers is that the encouragement of these barriers in employees will hinder employee creativity as well.

TASK MOTIVATION

Task motivation refers to the existence of a nurturing organizational environment for employee creativity. All individuals have the potential to be creative. The issues are: (1) will they and (2) what can managers/innovators do to increase the opportunities for their employees to use their creative thinking abilities.

The task of providing an environment which is conducive to creativity has many challenges. The individual and cultural barriers often decrease our abilities to create such environments. Managers must be aware of these barriers as they strive to enhance creativity in the workplace.

There are two types of organizational barriers which managers must overcome to increase employees' opportunities and abilities to use creative thinking. The first is inherent in the definition and structure of organizations; the second is associated with managerial style and attitudes and affords more of a chance to make changes.

Hierarchical, highly structured organizations inevitably create barriers to creative thinking. Set procedures, rules and regulations, specialization of work, criteria for employment evaluation, formal channels of communication, and the preference for status quo over change are inherent characteristics of large organizations. Since these organizational characteristics are unlikely to change, it is helpful for managers to recognize these barriers for what they are, and to anticipate that resistance to creative endeavors may take root in these barriers.

Other barriers, however, are within the manager's realm of influence. These barriers are attributable to managerial style, which is itself often fostered by the hierarchical highly structured organization. As discussed in the previous section, the manager-as-conductor style (Bradford and Cohen, 1984) is one that regards the manager as "boss." Inherent in this style are several characteristics that create obstacles to creativity in employees, including authoritarianism (an inflexible, closed attitude) and "functional fixedness" (the attitude that there's only one way to do things). Alternatively, the manager-as-developer style empowers employees and helps them to do their jobs better. This style is conducive to innovation and creativity.

Table 9.2 is a checklist that may help you to assist your employees to become more creative. Review this checklist monthly, and assess yourself on each item. Ask yourself: (1) To what extent is change needed to help my unit be more creative? (2) To what extent is this within my control?

TABLE 9.2 Task Motivation Checklist for Managers

1. Do not overdirect, overobserve, or overreport.
2. Recognize differences in individuals. Have a keen appreciation of each person's unique characteristics.
3. Help subordinates see problems as challenges.
4. Ask your employees regarding ways they think they are most creative or would like to be most creative, and what sort of creative contribution they would most like to make.
5. Allow more freedom for individuals to guide their own work.
6. Train yourself and others to repond to the positive parts of proposed ideas rather than react to the often easier-to-spot negative ones.
7. Develop greater frustration tolerance for mistakes and errors.
8. Provide a safe atmosphere for failures.
9. Be a resource person rather than a controller; a facilitator rather than a boss.
10. Act as a buffer between employees and outside problems or higher-up demands.
11. Enhance your own creative ability through special workshops and seminars, specialized reading, and practice of creative exercises and games. This sets an excellent example employees will want to emulate, and makes it easier for you to recognize and relate to the creative ability of others.
12. Make sure that innovative ideas are transmitted to your boss with your support and backing; then insist on a feedback mechanism. Without feedback, the flow of creative ideas dries up because innovators feel that their ideas are not given a fair hearing or taken seriously.

Adapted from Eugene Raudsepp, President, Princeton Creative Research, Inc. in R.L. Kuhn, *Handbook for Creative Managers* (New York: McGraw-Hill. 1987), pp. 173–182. Used with permission.

BRAINSTORMING AND THE
NOMINAL GROUP TECHNIQUE

One of the most effective strategies for finding and encouraging employee creativity is **brainstorming.** Marshalling the skills, thinking, and knowledge of employees, brainstorming is a technique used for generating new ideas. In brainstorming sessions, group members are encouraged to contribute ideas, without regard for quality. Evaluation of ideas is withheld until all have been expressed. Nominal group technique (Delbecq, Van de Ven and Gustafson, 1975) is a process that uses brainstorming to generate new ideas and then uses group discussion and systematic voting to choose from among the ideas generated by the group. It is often used when the problem has a large number of potential alternative solutions.

Assume that 10 professional employees who depend very heavily on secretarial and clerical support report to you. Two secretaries have just left for higher paying jobs and one clerk will be out for several weeks for surgery. As time progresses, it is apparent that conflicts are about to develop over the need for support staff time. You have several options: You may devise a plan and issue memoranda to your employees regulating the use of the available secretarial and clerical resources (and hope they are pleased enough with your solution to happily go about their work in order to finish before the deadline); you may go to your boss for direction (risking, perhaps, the judgment that you cannot handle this yourself); or you can plan a nominal group technique session during which you will get ideas from your employees and, with them, arrive at a workable solution.

Before you hold a brainstorming session, you must first settle in your own mind that you genuinely want the ideas from your employees. Brainstorming sessions can be inadvertently sabotaged by well-meaning managers who have hidden agendas and use the session as a way to manipulate employees to accept an already formulated plan. You must resolve that all ideas should be heard; you must provide a safe environment for the free flow of ideas from employees. You have to be able to accept good ideas from employees, and not feel that you have to be the one to generate all of the good ideas at work.

The following steps should be used for planning a nominal group technique session.

1. *Make sure that everyone agrees on the problem definition.* If there is not agreement on the problem definition, you may find that different members of the group are solving different problems.

2. *Have participants write down all their ideas.* Even ideas that do not seem feasible may give other people ideas. During this time no one should talk, except to ask questions about the problem definition. This step may take anywhere from 10 minutes to one-half hour.

3. *Use a round-robin procedure to allow participants to share their ideas.* Have each

participant give one idea at a time. Record the ideas on a flip chart so that all ideas are visible to all participants. Again, do not allow discussion as the ideas are being recorded.

4. *After all ideas are recorded, review each idea one at a time.* Allow participants to ask questions and share reactions regarding the feasibility and merits of the idea. Use your meeting management skills (discussed in Chapter 3, Competency 2) to ensure that you stay on track and that people are contributing appropriately.

5. *Have participants vote on their preferred alternative solution.* Generally, the voting should be secret, and a rank vote should be used. That is, have participants individually identify their top five ideas, and then assign a score of five to their first-ranked idea, four to their second-ranked idea, and so forth.

6. *Review the voting pattern.* If one alternative stands out as the obvious preferred choice, then you are ready to decide how to implement that choice. If not, choose the top 5 to 10 alternatives and return to step 4, this time rank ordering only the top three choices.

THE IMPORTANCE OF CREATIVE THINKING IN ORGANIZATIONS

The use of creative thinking in problem solving allows organizations to access human resources that often go untapped. In comparing Japanese and American organizations, Deming (1986) has argued that "the greatest waste in America is failure to use the abilities of people." Managers should recognize that employees' abilities are a free resource. Although most resources have extra cost factors involved, creative thinking does not. From this perspective, one could argue that no organization—public or private—can afford to waste this resource.

Beyond the overall organizational benefits, managers should recognize the personal benefits of encouraging creative thinking among their employees. Creative thinking can increase the effectiveness of the unit through better problem solving. In addition, creative thinking can be used as a motivational tool. In the work environment of large organizations, it is sometimes easy for employees to see themselves as a replaceable cog in the giant wheel and to become demotivated. When individuals are encouraged to be creative in their thinking and problem solving, they are more likely to feel unique, valued, and affirmed as important employees of the organization. Thus, not only are there benefits from the employees' good ideas, but individuals feel better about themselves as employees. In sum, the encouragement of employees' creative thinking can result in substantial benefits to the organization, to the work unit, and to the individuals who exercise their creative skills.

ANALYSIS   Creativity and Mangerial Style

Directions   Creative problem-solving skills are not always tied only to your own thought processes. Often creativity involves knowing how to work with other people who are creative, and using techniques that will maximize the probability that those people will generate creative solutions.

As a manager, you can either encourage or discourage employee creativity. To examine your own managerial style, first reflect on the managers with whom you have worked. If you have not yet been employed, use this exercise to reflect on the skills of a parent, teacher, or anyone else who has evaluated your work. Choose one person for this exercise and analyze whether that person's style helped or hindered the tapping of your creativity. Check any of the following which applied to your situation:

_____ 1. Were you instructed to do things according to a set pattern?

_____ 2. Did this person seek your opinion regarding matters that affected you?

_____ 3. Did this person ever reconsider a decision in light of your input?

_____ 4. Did you have a tendency to fear that you may appear foolish to this person?

_____ 5. Did this person value your ideas and your thinking?

_____ 6. Did you ever feel that there was a better way to do something, but did not bring it to the attention of this person?

_____ 7. Did you feel that it was important for this person to like you?

_____ 8. Did you feel that this person would like you more if you tended to agree with him or her?

_____ 9. Did you feel as if this person was always evaluating you?

Discussion Questions   1. How did you feel about yourself in that situation?

2. From your responses, identify specific behaviors that helped you feel affirmed as a valued person, and those that did not.

3. How would you answer question 2 focusing on two other persons: one with whom you had a very positive experience, and one with whom you had a negative experience?

4. From your responses to the preceding items, which areas do you need to give special attention as you develop in your role as a manager?

5. What specific strategies would you use in order to encourage more creativity in a work unit?

PRACTICE   Creative-Relevant Skills

Breaking Established Thinking Barriers

1. *The Paper Clip.* To assist in thinking differently about objects and concepts, list on a separate piece of paper as many uses as you can think of for a paper clip.

2. *The Restaurant.* A new restaurant is opening adjacent to your campus. It will feature vegetarian food. Think of as many possible names for this restaurant as you can.

Developing Mental Imagery

One of the skills in developing one's creativity is to practice mental imagery. The following exercises are designed to assist you in improving your imagination. Translate each of the following descriptions into a mental image. As you do, rate its clarity according to the following scale:

Scale | C = Clear | V = Vague | N = No image at all

Can you visually imagine:

_____ 1. A familiar face.

_____ 2. A rosebud.

_____ 3. A body of water at sunset.

_____ 4. The characteristic walk of a friend.

_____ 5. A newspaper headline.

The following descriptions are intended to evoke other modes of sensory imagery. Can you imagine:

_____ 1. A bird twittering.

_____ 2. Children laughing at play.

_____ 3. The prick of a pin.

_____ 4. The taste of toothpaste.

_____ 5. An itch.

Don't be discouraged if you were not able to create clear images. This was a skill-developing exercise designed to fine-tune your mental imagery processes. Test yourself again in several months and note the improvement.

Using Analogies

Identify three pressing problems which you currently have at school or work. Describe each one briefly in writing. Then review the following list of analogies. Try to apply an analogy from this list, or from your own thinking, to each problem.

1. A snowball rolling downhill, gathering speed, and growing rapidly.

2. Finding your way in the fog.

3. Trying to start a car on a cold winter morning.

4. Having a bath.

5. Frying potatoes.

6. Sending a letter.

7. Trying to untangle a ball of string.

8. Cutting the grass with a pair of scissors.

9. A child playing with a new toy.

10. A fish out of water.

Identify the feelings you have associated with each problem, and describe them with an analogy. The use of analogies should help you to see the problems differently. Describe the different perspectives which you now have on each problem. Use the perspectives to generate possible solutions to the problems.

APPLICATION   New Approaches to the Same Old Problem

Write a three- to five-page paper describing your plans to approach an old problem in a new way.

1. Start by writing a description of the problem.

2. Restate the problem in several ways.

3. Write down as many facts related to the problem as possible.

4. Identify advantages to this problem.

5. Identify as many new ways as possible to approach this problem.

6. Identify people who might be able to help you with this problem.

7. Determine which action you will take first in arriving at a solution to this problem, and write down on your calendar the date and time that you will take that action.

8. Identify a strategy to help you increase your use of creative thinking skills whenever you face a problem that you always approach in the same way.

Competency 3 Managing Change

ASSESSMENT Changes in My Organization

Directions   Think about two changes that have taken place in an organization with which you have been involved. The organization may be a work organization, a school-related organization, or a community group. On a separate piece of paper, carefully describe the following:

1. An implemented change which in your view was needed, implemented, and was successful long after implementation.

2. An unsuccessfully implemented change.

3. From what you have observed, why was the first change implemented successfully and not the second one? If you can distinguish the content of the idea from the methods for implementation, identify the extent to which the success (or lack of success) of the proposed changes was due to content versus the implementation strategies.

4. Write down one change that you would like to make in that organization. If you received approval to make that change, what is the most important thing you would do in your efforts to implement that change? Why?

LEARNING Managing Change

Our society is currently experiencing change at an exponential rate. Each day, the potential exists for advancements in technology and knowledge that could change the way we live. In addition, national and global social, political, and economic changes affect both our personal and organizational lives.

Changes are necessary in order to accomplish goals and objectives, such as improving efficiency, improving cost effectiveness, competing for money and resources, advancing technologically, meeting government regulations, enhancing services to clients, and addressing public pressure. Although we make these changes to respond to societal changes, these are not necessarily unplanned or imposed changes. Rather, these are changes and adjustments we choose to make in order to fulfill the mission of the organization more effectively as it functions in a dynamic, changing world. In the sidebox, we present a brief case study of the changes that were made at the New York State Department of Motor Vehicles during the early 1990s, under the leadership of Patricia Adduci. This case is particularly striking because it shows how a large, established bureaucratic organization used technology and employee involvement to turn itself around to become a customer-oriented, efficient government agency that received high praise from local press and citizens across New York State.

PATRICIA ADDUCI AND THE REINVENTION OF THE NEW YORK STATE DEPARTMENT OF MOTOR VEHICLES

Up until the early 1990s, the New York State Department of Motor Vehicles (DMV), like its counterparts in most states, had the reputation of being "the agency that people loved to hate." It was seen as the epitome of bureaucratic red tape, complete with confusing forms and a maze of endless lines. Many viewed the process of obtaining or renewing a driver's license or car registration as a potentially major ordeal and, at best, a generally unpleasant experience. Today, the agency's image has changed dramatically as a result of major efforts to change the way in which the agency does its business. Today, the agency can be proud of its service record and its customer satisfaction ratings. As one journalist put it, "The DMV just ain't what it used to be." And although she herself will argue differently, most people who have watched the change occur give much of the credit for the change to Commissioner Patricia Adduci.

In 1985, when Pat Adduci decided to accept Governor Cuomo's invitation to serve as Commissioner, she also decided that she was going to change the agency's image. Indeed, when the Governor asked her why she would want such a job, she answered that she wanted the job in large part because she wanted the challenge of changing the public's perception of the agency they most frequently encounter. And while many of the dramatic changes occurred during the last three years of Commissioner Adduci's 10 years with the DMV, there is no doubt that she was a major force in transforming the agency from an organization that was characterized in the press as having a "reputation so poor it (could) apply for federal reputation-disaster aid" (*New York Daily News,* January 1993) to an organization that could be characterized as customer-friendly with new offices, new technologies, and "a whole new outlook" (*Staten Island Advance,* December 8, 1993).

The story of the DMV's transformation is fascinating and could fill an entire book. It is a story that can be appreciated by almost anyone who has ever worked in or dealt with a large, bureaucratic organization and sensed that there must be a better way. Here we present a brief synopsis of the changes, as well as some of Pat Adduci's thoughts on what factors contributed to the transformation. While only a brief summary, you will likely find in this story some important insights on how change can be successfully managed.

PATRICIA ADDUCI . . . CONTINUED

As indicated above, Pat Adduci came to the DMV with the goal of making a change in the agency's image. After several attempts were made to change the organizational culture, using a variety of different approaches, the real changes began to occur after the agency was given a $4 million appropriation in FY 93–94 based on a proposal to Governor Cuomo to "dramatically change systems and business processes to improve customer service and public perception of the agency [using] additional resources and new technology." The proposal included five major goals:

- To restructure several customer contact programs and increase customer convenience by relying on phones as a contact point for information and transactions; by creating more flexible payment options, including credit cards; by creating more service outlets that are accessible, convenient, and pleasant; and by simplifying procedures in order to minimize frustration and maximize customer satisfaction.

- To adopt technology (like customer queuing devices, bar coding, and photo and document imaging) to streamline business procedures, expedite customer service, and increase productivity.

- To enlist external "business partners" (like County Clerks, dealers, rental companies, driving schools, and others) to provide DMV services.

- To invest in quality through the active and visible participation of the DMV's staff and customers.

- To reinvent the DMV's relationship with County Clerks to provide better service to customers, eliminate costly duplication of services, and develop improved funding arrangements that will stabilize their operations.

One year later, the Department issued a report showing the progress it had made toward achieving each of the goals and identifying the work that still needed to be done. The agency had expanded service delivery by opening new offices, renovating others, installing new sitting areas in some of the most congested offices, and providing new local outlets for some of the services that had previously been handled only in district offices. It had adopted new digital imaging technology to produce driver licenses and installed computer-based queuing systems in 16 of the most congested offices. The agency began to develop new types of relationships with external business partners, enhancing both the agency's and the businesses' operations. It also made considerable progress toward its goal of reinventing its relationship with County Clerks, whose offices provide the motor vehicle services in many areas of the state.

Perhaps the most dramatic changes were in the area of employee involvement and employee empowerment. As implied above, Pat Adduci prefers not to take credit for the organizational changes, and is quick to indicate that the changes were "a team effort, with every employee contributing in important ways." She believes strongly that "when you empower those who are doing the job, they will tell you how they can do the job more efficiently and effectively. When you give people the opportunities, they will seize them."

Encouraging employees to think about how to do their jobs more effectively requires that they understand the big picture. They need to see how organizational processes are connected and be given information that in the past was "owned" by management. During 1993, every agency employee received "quality awareness training," and many received additional training to prepare them for specific assignments. Adduci argues that training is absolutely critical to the success of organizational change. People need to know what the organization is doing and what is expected of them; they need to know how their job relates to others' work.

PATRICIA ADDUCI . . . CONTINUED

Employees also need to know that finding ways to do their jobs more effectively will not put them out of a job. Adduci recognizes that it is natural for employees to be concerned about their jobs. But technology and other organizational changes will inevitably lead to shifts in organizational structures and priorities. If employees are expected to work for the good of the organization, they need to feel that the organization supports them. Under a Union Partnership Agreement, employees were promised that there would be no layoffs as a result of any quality project. They were told that there was no guarantee that they would have the same job, but they knew they would have a job. Adduci argues that you have to deal with this issue up front, or employees will resist the change process.

Beyond knowing that their good ideas will not put them out of a job, employees need to know that they will not be punished for "bad ideas." They need to be encouraged to take risks and to try new things; "they need to be free to 'think outside the box'. Adduci admits that risk taking is difficult in government because the press is always there. But she also argues that you "can't be afraid to fail," and that rather than punish employees who make mistakes, managers should treat mistakes as learning experiences.

Adduci also recognizes the importance of management's open and active support of the change at all levels. She argues "top management support is essential but not enough; everyone needs to walk the talk." Moreover, she says that you cannot expect employees to act as team players if management is not doing the same. Nor can you expect lower-level managers to encourage participation from their employees if they themselves are not encouraged to bring new ideas to the change process. Her open-door policy and her belief in management-by-walking-around set an example for other managers and allowed employees to feel that they were partners in the change process.

Pat Adduci talks with great pride about the changes that took place at DMV during her tenure as commissioner. When she left the position in January 1995, she knew that the agency was a different place than when she arrived. Her enthusiasm for changing the organization's image had spread throughout the organization and long-term employees had a new outlook on their jobs. Adduci admits that change can be scary and frustrating, as well as exciting and stimulating—a bit of a rollercoaster ride. But she says, "You must understand that this is the right thing to do."

COMMON PROCESSES ASSOCIATED WITH ORGANIZATIONAL CHANGE

In reviewing the research on innovation in organizations, Van de Ven (1993) identifies six of the most common processes associated with organizational change. As can be seen in the following list, the processes are complex and require many of the management skills discussed in this book. Even with the mastery of such skills, the author notes, "management cannot control innovation success; only its odds." Clearly the management of change is a significant challenge.

1. Innovation and change are facilitated when organizations create a stage that enables and motivates innovation. It was found that stage-setting initially involves an extended gestation period lasting several years and involving many organizational participants (not on the spur of the moment, nor by a single dramatic incident, nor by a single entrepreneur). However, once the innovation process begins, repeated efforts at restructuring the organizational and environmental settings are necessary to transform innovative ideas into practical realities for adoption and diffusion.

2. "Shocks" (not mere persuasion), produced by exposing individuals to direct personal confrontations with needs or problems, are necessary to trigger attention and action for innovation. When people reach a threshold of sufficient dissatisfaction with existing conditions, they initiate action to resolve their dissatisfaction. Managing the attention of innovation participants is critical to initiate innovation development, and it is an ongoing challenge for linking technical possibilities with market or end-user needs throughout the innovation process.

3. Once innovation activities begin, the process does not unfold in a simple linear sequence of stages and substages; instead, it proliferates into complex bundles of innovation ideas and divergent paths of activities by different organizational units. Organizations that manage change successfully find ways to keep the innovation process relatively simple in the face of constant pressures to proliferate into related and unrelated paths to the core innovation idea.

4. Setbacks and mistakes are frequently encountered during the innovation process, either rejection of the innovation or opportunities for learning though reinvention. Learning fails when events are caused and consequences are felt by different individuals. Through reinvention, organization participants learn by reconnecting the causes and consequences of innovation invention, development, and adoption activities to changing organizational and environmental circumstances.

5. Innovation adoption is facilitated by modifying the innovations to fit the local organizational situations, through extensive involvement in and commitment to the innovation by top management, and by use of various techniques that maintain task completion and momentum throughout the adoption process.

6. Organizational change processes vary with the novelty, size, and temporal duration of the innovations being developed and adopted. The greater the novelty, size, and temporal duration of an innovation, the more the above process elements are prevalent and the more complex the innovation process (Van de Ven, 1993).

UNDERSTANDING RESISTANCE TO PLANNED CHANGE

Resistance to change occurs frequently. Even changes that are necessary and desirable are resisted. For example, if everyone in your work unit enthusiastically agrees that there needs to be more communication with other work units, and you introduce a change that would increase this communication, you might still expect to encounter some resistance to that change simply because it involves changing the status quo.

In addition to resistance from people, you are also likely to meet resistance from the organization. Just as hierarchical organizations present barriers to creative thinking and innovation, they also offer many of the same characteristics as barriers to change. Organizational barriers include the power of existing organizational routines and organizational structure, resource limitations, an organizational cultural value that tradition is preferable to change, and so on.

Five types of organizationally related change are likely to provoke employee resistance. These changes cause resistance because employees perceive them as negatively affecting their expected job behaviors. As in the case of planned change, understanding these sources of resistance to change will better equip you to make appropriate changes and to implement them in such a way as to ensure their success.

1. *Changes that affect knowledge and skill requirements.* Employees will resist changes (such as automation) that make their skills seem outdated or unnecessary.

2. *Changes associated with economic or status loss.* Employees will resist changes that result in a demotion or loss of employment. The resisting employee does not have to be the person directly affected by the job changes. Resistance may also come from employees who perceive that the change may somehow negatively affect them. For example, when Kodak's CEO, Colby Chandler, cut 11,000 jobs in his first year, many of the remaining employees were demoralized, fearing that they would be the next to be fired.

3. *Changes suggested by others.* Sometimes good ideas are resisted because they are not our ideas. For example, when one employee is jealous of the success of another employee, or there is the perception that one employee's success diminishes the esteem the manager has for the other employees, or when there is intense competition within a work unit, employees are unlikely to accept others' ideas.

4. *Changes involving risks.* Risk taking sometimes results in mistakes. When an organization's culture does not value risk taking, individuals will not want to take the chance of making a mistake, and will probably be reluctant to suggest or embrace changes that involve risks.

5. *Changes that involve disruption of social relationships.* Although organizations have public missions and purposes, they also provide a social environment in which people associate and form friendships. For many people, their work organization is a primary source of social interaction. When these patterns of interaction are disrupted, people often resist.

Resistance to change reminds us that change must be carefully planned. Resistance often forces us to consider carefully the impact of the change so that ill-advised changes may be avoided.

DESIGNING CHANGE AND DESIGNING HOW TO CHANGE

Once the decision has been made that a change in the work processes, procedures, or structure should occur, the manager must focus on two issues: (1) the design of the change, and determining what change needs to occur, and (2) the process of implementing the change.

DESIGNING CHANGE

Designing change involves considering various alternative courses of action, anticipating consequences of such actions, and choosing what specific course of action is appropriate.

The design of the change is the first issue that faces the manager. The manager must ask whether a change is necessary, and if so, what specifically should be changed. Kurt Lewin (1951) proposed a model called **force field analysis.** This model is based on laws of physics: An object at rest will remain at rest unless the forces on the object to move are greater than the forces for it to remain stable. For example, when your car is parked in the driveway with the emergency brake engaged, it will remain there, in a stable condition, even if your neighbor's nine-year-old son decides to push on the car to move it. The emergency brake is a stronger stabilizing force than is the boy's force. If the car is put into the neutral gear with the emergency brake disengaged, however, the forces for its stability are diminished, and it becomes more possible that the young boy could disrupt the equilibrium.

Similarly, there are forces within organizations that are pressures for change and forces that are resistances to change. When the forces for change are stronger than the resistant forces, change will occur; likewise, when the forces against change are stronger than the pressures for change, change will not occur.

Let's set up a force field analysis list to examine some of the pressures for organizational change, known as **driving forces**, and the pressures against organizational change, known as **resisting forces**.

Force Field Analysis of Change in Organizations

Pressures for Change (Driving Forces)	*Pressures Against Change* (Resisting Forces)
Social change in society	Perceived threats to power
Economic change in society	Routine and structure
Improved efficiency	Resource limitations
Improved cost effectiveness	Preference for tradition
Competition for money and resources	Changes in skill requirements
Technological advances	Economic or status loss
Compliance with government regulations	Nonsupport of others' ideas
Public pressure	Reluctance to take risks
Expansion	Disruption of social relationships
Improved effectiveness	
Administrative changes	
Availability of new products	

It is necessary to consider more than the length of the list; you must also look at the importance or relative force of the individual items. Some items may have more impact on a situation than others. To make the list more useful, you would need to assign weights or values to each item.

The following steps are necessary to set up a force field analysis:

1. List the driving forces and the resisting forces.

2. Examine each force and assess its strengths. Note the possible consequences of each force and its value. You may wish to assign a numerical value to each force.

3. Identify those forces over which you have some influence or control.

4. Analyze the list to determine how to implement the change. Your analysis will reveal several natural choices for action:

   - Increase the strength of driving forces.

   - Add new driving forces.

   - Decrease the strength of resisting forces.

   - Remove some of the resisting forces.

   - Determine whether any of the resisting forces can be changed into driving forces.

Research has shown that the last three strategies, which involve diminishing the effect of resisting forces, are more effective than the first two strategies. Increasing the effect of the driving forces often serves only to increase the resistance.

Once you have worked through this process, you have a chart of the driving and resisting forces to the proposed change, the relative weight of each force, and an assessment of which forces you can influence. Identifying the items over which you have some influence should tell you where to direct your efforts and planning when implementing your changes.

IMPLEMENTING CHANGE

Implementing the change—designing how the change should occur—is just as critical for innovators as the process of designing what change should occur. Although a proposed change might objectively be the very best thing for the organization or for the work unit, careless implementation could potentially make the proposed change look foolish, resulting in the ultimate failure of the idea.

Unfortunately, the process of designing how to change is often given less attention than is necessary. First, we assume that once we have determined that a proposed change is necessary, appropriate, and beneficial, we are inclined to see its value as so obvious that we expect others to endorse it and work for it with vigor and enthusiasm! Since we have worked so hard at the analysis, we often assume that the hard part is over. A poorly implemented change, however, will reflect on the credibility of the proposed change, and careless attention to implementation of even the best idea will, more often than not, result in failure. Assuming that a given change is seen as desirable and beneficial to the organization, implementing the change will require the same thoughtful effort and consideration as the design of the change.

THREE APPROACHES TO MANAGING CHANGE

In attempting to manage change within organizations, as well as in their personal lives, individuals tend to use one of three general approaches: rational-empirical approaches, normative-reeducative approaches, and power-coercive approaches (Chin and Benne, 1976).

RATIONAL-EMPIRICAL APPROACHES

Rational-empirical strategies for change are based on two assumptions: (1) people are rational, and (2) once a proposal has been clearly explained, individuals see that it is in their best interest and subscribe to the change. This approach encourages the acquisition of knowledge and data to better understand the substantive aspects of change. An important strength of this strategy is that it requires you to examine the pros and cons of a situation carefully and to present the logic of the decision. Generally people respond more positively to change when the process and details are explained to them.

A major weakness of this strategy, however, stems from a flaw in the logic of the basic assumptions. It is incorrect to assume that if we explain to people the logic and benefits of a change, they will embrace it. Even when individuals understand that a change is in their best interest, we cannot assume that they will comply. How many times have we known, for example, that it is in our best interest to lose weight, to exercise, or to stop smoking? Quick reflection reveals that it is a rare individual who complies with a needed change simply because of the realization that it is needed.

Further, no matter how well we think we have explained something to an individual, we cannot assume that the individual understands it in the way we intend. If we want people to comply with a change, we need to also consider their perceptions of what we have said to them.

NORMATIVE-REEDUCATIVE APPROACHES

Normative-reeducative approaches to change consider the values, attitudes, meanings, and habits of individuals in the change process. This approach assumes that individuals are affected emotionally and personally by their work experiences. Normative-reeducative strategies for change also recognize the impact of the organizational culture as forces for or against change.

A strength of this approach is its usefulness in both the design and implementation of change. The normative-reeducative approach requires us to focus on the change in terms of how people will react, what the change means to them, and whether their needs are adequately met by the change. Normative-reeducative strategies tend to be most effective in overcoming individual resistances to change.

The major weakness with this approach is that it is slow; its effects are often detected only after considerable time has passed. One reason for this slowness is that sometimes people do not want to change. Furthermore, organizations often want change to occur faster than it does. Managers must exercise considerable patience and farsightedness in order to plan change utilizing normative-reeducative strategies.

However, the normative-reeducative approach is the most respectful of the individuals involved in the change process, and as such it is highly successful in the long term.

POWER-COERCIVE APPROACHES

Power-coercive approaches to change are based on the assumption that the individual desiring the change has more power than the individual who is expected to comply with the change. The latter individual will change because of fear of punishment or the withholding of some valued reward. In organizations, we tend to think of those higher up in the hierarchy as having the power to create a negative situation (e.g., by giving poor performance evaluations or demotions, or by making the work environment more difficult). Employees, however, can use power-coercive strategies as well. For example, employees may slow down their work efforts in order to get managers to comply with their wishes.

Strategies associated with the power-coercive approach focus on two types of power. First is power which accompanies the hierarchical position of the individual, along with the implicit threat of economic sanctions against individuals who do not comply. Second is the use of moral power, where guilt and shame are used in order to initiate compliance to change.

A strength of this approach for organizational change is its recognition of the importance of legitimacy of the upper administrative levels. Sometimes, when individuals are resistant, rules are required to implement mandated changes. For example, laws against sexual harassment may be required to change the behaviors of individuals who do not see such behavior as negative.

The major weakness of this approach is that the use of threats, guilt, and shame are not, in the long term, effective strategies of change. These are manipulative techniques which often work only in the short run. In the long run, they build resentment. Further, this strategy may provoke the sabotage of future proposed changes.

EFFECTIVE MANAGEMENT OF CHANGE

The three approaches to managing change in organizations provide helpful strategies for the design and implementation of proposed changes. With the recognition of the strengths and limitations of each strategy, managers can be more cognizant of the potential consequences of their efforts at change. Table 9.3 presents guidelines for effective management of change. Note that these steps incorporate elements from the empirical-rational approach, as well as from the normative-reeducative approach.

TABLE 9.3 Guidelines for Effective Management of Change

1. During the planning of the change, encourage participation of those affected by it. Encourage use of creative thinking by employees in problem solving.
2. Let employees experience the need for change.
3. Maintain open and frequent communication with employees.
4. Avoid a "we-they" mentality.
5. Consider needs of individual employees.

ANALYSIS   Reorganizing the Legal Division

Directions   Read the following case study and answer the questions that follow each section.

The Relocation and Reorganization Begins. As part of a new relocation and reorganization plan for the legal division of a large corporation, the director, Paul Lindford, decided to set up a central paralegal pool. This pool would handle all of the research reports for the entire office, which consisted of 20 attorneys. In the old location, the paralegals had been located in offices adjoining those occupied by the attorneys for whom they worked. Several paralegals even had their own small private offices.

The nature of the office was such that many of the attorneys traveled a considerable amount and consequently were away from their offices for extended periods. During these absences the paralegal assistants had little to do.

Stop Reading   Respond to the following questions.

1. Based on the limited information, what advantages of the change approved by Paul Lindford can you identify?

2. What might be the response of the paralegal assistants to this change?

3. What might be the response of the attorneys to this change?

4. If you were Paul, what problems would you anticipate at this point?

The Case Continues   For some time, Paul had felt that establishing a central paralegal pool would result in a saving of personnel, as well as more efficient use of the paralegal staff. Paul had been reluctant to make this change in the old location, where the attorneys and paralegal assistants were accustomed to working in adjoining offices. But now, with the new office, he felt the time was right to try out the new arrangement.

Two weeks before the move, Paul asked Ashley Ricci to coordinate the move for the paralegal assistants, even though she was not the most senior paralegal. There were two others at higher ranks, with more experience than Ashley, but Paul felt good about his choice. Ashley had a lot of energy and was well liked by her co-workers. She seemed to best fulfill the requirements for the job as he saw it. She had worked on some special projects for Paul in the past, and she had been exceptional. At this point, Paul had not really given any thought to who would be directing the paralegal assistants when the move was complete.

Stop Reading   Respond to the following questions.

1. Paul has chosen to implement this change when the general office moves into a new location. Why does he see this timing as advantageous? Do you agree?

2. If you were Paul, would you have chosen Ashley to coordinate the move? Why or why not?

3. What mistakes do you believe Paul has made so far in the implementation process?

The Case Continues Paul announced his plans for the new central paralegal pool one week before the move. It was received with little enthusiasm. Several assistants objected and threatened to leave rather than accept the change. Some insisted they could not work for more than one person; others complained they would be unable to work in a small cubicle office in a large room. Many of the attorneys affected by the new policy were resentful as well. They believed that a personal paralegal assistant was essential for efficient conduct of their respective offices.

Although Paul knew this change was unpopular, he believed the feelings of the attorneys would change as the benefits of the more efficient service became apparent. Although many of the attorneys probably felt the loss of a personal paralegal assistant as something in the nature of a "demotion," Paul felt they should understand and help make the new plan work. He felt that the few diehards should not be pampered.

During the first few weeks after the move, Ashley did everything she could to maintain the workload at a high level and hoped that, as a result, the complaints from the attorneys would decrease. Their complaints centered around: (1) errors made by paralegal assistants who were unfamiliar with the attorneys' caseloads; (2) the slowness of the paralegal staff in bringing back final drafts of the reports that had been assigned to them; and (3) the excessive time they themselves had to spend in minor research efforts that had previously been handled by their personal paralegal assistants.

Stop Reading Respond to the following questions.

1. What are the specific sources of resistance from the paralegal assistants and the attorneys? Do you see these resisting forces as unreasonable or legitimate?

2. Do you think that Paul is correct in his prediction that the complaints will decrease after the change has been in operation for a while and its benefits are noted? Why or why not?

3. What type of change strategy is Paul using? How well is it working? What should Paul do at this time?

The Case Continues Ashley also listened to complaints from the paralegals. They felt very strongly that: (1) the work they were getting was neither challenging nor generally very interesting; (2) they were not able to consistently work on a particular caseload, and, therefore, the quality of their work was decreasing; and (3) they were tired of taking abuse for the changes they themselves had not instituted.

After the new system had been in operation for six months, Ashley suggested to Paul that perhaps some of these complaints might be eliminated if each attorney were allowed to have priority claim on the time of one paralegal assistant. This arrangement would allow the paralegal to become familiar with the particular work of one attorney, including the issues and current caseload of that attorney.

The paralegal could then be asked to work elsewhere when not busy with the work of the attorney. Paul, however, felt that such a move would defeat the very purpose for which the central paralegal pool had been established.

Stop Reading   Respond to the following questions.

1. What are Paul's sources of resistance? Are they legitimate?

2. If you were Paul, what would you do at this point? Why?

The Case Continues   After much prodding by Ashley, Paul finally agreed that something had to be done to make things run more smoothly. Paul admitted that he shared some of her doubts about the success of the new arrangement and wondered if perhaps the change had not been managed well. More important, he wondered if something could be done to regain the full support and cooperation of the attorneys and paralegals. He even considered returning the office to its old method of operation, allowing each attorney to work solely with one paralegal assistant.

Discussion Questions

1. What do you think Paul may have learned about this experience regarding implementation of change?

2. Do you think the change was well designed? Why or why not?

3. What strategies could Paul have used in the beginning to help him sort out the aspects of the proposed change, and to help him plan?

4. If you were a consultant and Paul commissioned your professional expertise, what advice would you give him about what he should do now and how to do it?

PRACTICE   Force Field Analysis

Directions   Examine the preceding case study, "Reorganizing the Legal Division," and pretend that you are Paul. Do a force field analysis, listing the driving forces and the resisting forces of the case. Weigh the value of each force with a number from 1 (least forceful) to 10 (most forceful). Also, identify your level of influence over those forces using the following scale:

Scale   IS = able to influence strongly   IM = able to influence moderately
NI = unable to influence

Discussion Questions

1. What forces for change did you identify? What are the forces against change?

2. Which are the strongest forces over which you have the most control?

3. How could each force be altered?

4. Which actions are most feasible?

5. What should be the plan of action?

Directions   In the assessment activity at the beginning of this third competency, you were asked to write down one change that you would make in an organization in which you had been involved. Do a force field analysis for this situation, listing the driving forces and the resisting forces of the change. Again, weigh the value of each force with a number from 1 to 10 and identify your level of influence over those forces using the scale on page 373. Also answer questions 1 to 5 (p. 373) for this situation.

In the assessment activity, you were also asked to identify the most important thing you would do in your efforts to implement that change. Do you agree with your earlier thinking? If not, why? Write down any changes to your original assessment and the reasons you have for your views.

APPLICATION   Planning a Change

On a separate sheet of paper, write today's date. Then describe a change which you wish to make—either at work or in your personal life. Determine when you would like to begin implementing the change. The format should be as follows:

Today, write:	Today's date. Description of a change you wish to make. Implementation target date. Design of the change. Strategies for implementing the change.
On the implementation target date, write:	Description of your experience to date and an evaluation of your plans. Target completion date.
On the target completion date, write:	Description of your experience, evaluating the strategies you used.

Now, answer the following questions.

1. How did you feel once you identified the change and the implementation date? Many people feel vaguely dissatisfied with themselves when they want to change something and often think the dissatisfaction will remain until the change is completed. However, as you probably experienced in this activity, when we take action toward change, the dissatisfaction with ourselves often diminishes, and we are thereby encouraged to continue our plans.

2. What difference do you note in writing down your proposed change, with its accompanying dates, rather than merely having these ideas in your head? Writing down the proposed change is a clarifying effort, and by so doing you tend to increase your belief that it will happen.

REFERENCES

Bradford, David L., and Allan R. Cohen. *Managing for Excellence.* New York: John Wiley & Sons, 1984.

Chin, Robert, and Kenneth D. Benne. "General Strategies for Effecting Changes in Human Systems," in *The Planning of Change* (3rd ed.), Warren G. Bennis, Kenneth D. Benne, Robert Chin, and Kenneth E. Corey (eds.). New York: Holt, Rinehart and Winston, 1976.

De Bono, Edward. *Lateral Thinking: Creativity Step-by-Step.* New York: Harper & Row, 1970.

Delbecq, Andre L., Andrew H. Van de Ven, and David H. Gustafson. *Group Techniques for Program Planning.* Glenview, Ill.: Scott, Foresman, 1975.

Deming, W. Edwards. *Out of the Crisis.* Boston: Massachusetts Institute of Technology Center for Advanced Engineering Study, 1986.

Kiel, John M. *The Creative Mystique: How to Manage It, Nurture It, and Make It Pay.* New York: John Wiley & Sons, 1985.

Kimberly, John R., and Robert E. Quinn. *Managing Organizational Transitions.* Homewood, Ill.: Richard D. Irwin, 1984.

Koestler, Arthur. *The Act of Creation.* New York: Macmillan, 1964.

Kuhn, Robert Lawrence (ed. in chief). *Handbook for Creative Managers.* New York: McGraw-Hill, 1987.

Lewin, Kurt. *Field Theory in Social Science.* New York: Harper and Row, 1951.

McKim, Robert H. *Experiences in Visual Thinking.* Monterey, Calif.: Brooks/Cole, 1972.

Miller, William C. *The Creative Edge: Fostering Innovation Where You Work.* Reading, Mass.: Addison-Wesley, 1987.

Nierenberg, Gerald I. *The Art of Creative Thinking.* New York: Cornerstone Library, 1982.

Pascale, Richard T., and Anthony G. Athos. *The Art of Japanese Management.* New York: Simon and Schuster, 1981.

Peters, Tom. *Thriving on Chaos.* New York: Harper & Row, 1987.

Quinn, R.E., Joel Kahn, and Michael J. Mandl. "Perspectives on Organizational Change: Exploring Movement at the Interface," in *Organizational Behavior: The State of the Science,* Jerald Greendberg (ed.). Hillsdale, N.J.: Lawrence Erlbaum Associates, 1994.

Rawlinson, J. Geoffrey. *Creative Thinking and Brainstorming.* New York: John Wiley & Sons, 1981.

Van de Ven, Andrew. "Managing the Process of Organizational Innovation," in *Organizational Change and Redesign: Ideas and Insights for Improving Performance,* George P. Huber and William H. Glick (eds.). Oxford, England: Oxford University Press, 1993.

Walton, A. Elise. "Transformative Culture: Shaping the Informal Organization," in *Discontinuous Change,* David A. Nadler, Robert B. Shaw, A. Elise Walton and Associates (eds.). San Francisco: Jossey-Bass, 1995.

Whetten, David A., and Kim S. Cameron. *Developing Management Skills.* Glenview, Ill.: Scott, Foresman, 1983.

The Broker and Innovator Roles

We have now completed the last two of the managerial leadership roles—the broker and the innovator. Once again, let us put these roles in the context of the competing values framework. By now it should be well understood that you will find these roles are more appropriate in some situations and less appropriate in others. Having now seen all eight roles, you may even recognize that some situations do not require you to choose between roles, but rather suggest that you use multiple roles simultaneously. Indeed, one of the challenges that you need to think about now is when to call upon specific competencies associated with specific roles and when to try to blend the different perspectives in a multidimensional whole. This issue will be discussed in greater depth in the last chapter, but we note it here as we put these last two roles into the larger context.

A BRIEF REVIEW

The broker and innovator roles are part of the open systems model. In this model the desired ends include external support, resource acquisitions, and growth; and the assumed means to these ends have to do with insight, innovation, and adaption. In this quadrant we are most concerned with developing innovative approaches to deal with an ever-changing environment. This model sees change as a challenging opportunity for positive growth and development, both for the organization and for employees. To facilitate growth and development, the manager performs in the broker and innovator roles, looking to the future and identifying ways to move away from the status quo.

WHEN THE BROKER AND INNOVATOR ROLES ARE APPROPRIATE

Once again, to understand when this model is appropriate, let's review the two axes that define the model. Like the director and producer roles, on the horizontal axis the model is defined by an external focus and thus a greater sensitivity to action. Like the mentor and facilitator roles, on the vertical axis the model is defined by high flexibility, which is needed when situations are not well defined or have ambiguous elements. When a situation is defined by high pressure to act and high ambiguity, action is often based on intuition and creative responses. Managers in these situations often act on hunches, before they are certain of the "correct" answer, and take intelligent risks. In deciding to take a risk, however, the managerial leader must be certain that he or she will have necessary support to do something out of the ordinary. Thus, to be seen as effective in the roles of broker and innovator, a manager must acquire the complementary abilities of making educated guesses and then convincing others that this is the correct path to follow.

COMPLEMENTARY ROLES

Given the current emphasis on the global economy and changes in computing and related technologies, there is a tendency to believe that the open systems model is the correct model for our times. In direct response to concerns that we have created organizations that are too controlled, there is a tremendous emphasis on creating flexibility through ad hoc organizational structures through which decisions can be made and action taken more quickly. There is an overriding sense in many organizations that they need to reinvent, reengineer, and restructure. In opposition to the age-old maxim of "If it ain't broke, don't fix it," organizational consultants are suggesting "If it ain't broke, break it." But like the other roles, there are times when acting as a broker or innovator is not the best course that a manager can take. As with the roles in the other three quadrants, failure to balance and blend these roles with other roles, particularly the monitor and coordinator in the internal process model, can lead to problems. As indicated in Integration 2, if you want the "trains to run on time," you need to value stability and continuity as much as, if not more than, innovation and change.

People who excel in the broker and innovator roles are often entrepreneurial and may start a new organization around their vision of a new product or service. Within organizations, these people are sometimes referred to as *intrapreneurs* and are generally seen as powerful change agents. Whether creating a new organization or creating a power base within an existing organization, these leaders are generally very successful at acquiring resources to support their ideas, allowing their organizations to grow very rapidly, both in terms of fiscal and human resources. Interestingly, the ever-increasing number of people causes a problem. As the organization becomes larger and more complex, the need for predictability and control increases. People begin to ask about policies and procedures, lines of authority, formal information systems, and other structures that standardize and routinize. Often, people who excel in the broker and innovator roles resist these trappings of the internal process model. They believe that they have reached success by avoiding the values associated with the monitor and coordinator roles and so conclude that these approaches are antithetical to good management. As a result, some organizational founders are forced to leave their own organization. One famous example is Steve Jobs, who was forced to leave Apple

Computers. Alternatively, some founders stay and lead their unit to organizational death. Such was the case with Don Burr, the founder of People Express Airlines. Burr used creative genius to build a spectacular company in a very short period of time, but was not able to let the organization go through some critical processes of formalization as the company expanded to become the fifth largest airline in the United States between 1980 and 1986.

Clearly the roles in the open systems quadrant must be seen in context and must be used appropriately. Growth and innovation are important values in an organization, but there is also value in having structures and procedures that create certainty and continuity. When managerial leaders become too focused on expansion and change, they lose awareness of the need for stability and create an atmosphere of chaotic anarchy, where there is great uncertainty and confusion. Alternatively, there are times when a leader must create change because the current path leads to certain organizational death. It is the managerial leader's job, in the roles of the broker, innovator, monitor, and coordinator, to see to it that these orientations are appropriately balanced.

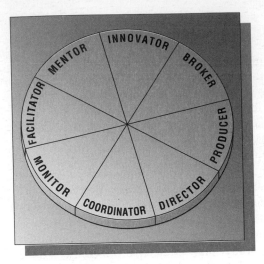

10

INTEGRATION AND THE ROAD TO MASTERY

Understanding the Developmental Process[1]

W e have now presented all eight roles in the competing values framework. You have had the opportunity to work on many of the 24 competencies, and you may have experienced some significant change. If you completed the competing values self-assessment instrument at the outset of the course (the assignment at the end of Chapter 1), it may now be useful to return to the instrument and assess yourself again.

ASSESSMENT Reexamining Your Profile

Complete the competing values self-assessment instrument and again examine your profile. Comparing the two profiles, respond to the following questions. (If you did not complete the self-assessment at the outset of the course, answer the questions based on your own understandings of how you have changed.)

1. What were my greatest strengths and weaknesses at the outset?

2. How do I see myself differently at this time?

[1]Portions of this chapter are adapted from *Beyond Rational Management: Mastering the Paradoxes and Competing Demands of High Performance* (Quinn, 1988). Used with permission.

3. In which areas do I feel I still need to enhance my skills?

4. To what extent do I feel comfortable in choosing from among the roles to approach group or organizational problems or issues?

5. To what extent do I feel comfortable using several roles in complementary or supplementary ways to approach group or organizational problems or issues?

LEARNING   Integration and the Road to Mastery

Using this book you have had the opportunity to develop skills associated with eight different roles of managerial leadership. The mastery of management, however, requires more than just the development of skills alone. It requires the ability to enter a situation, to see it from contrasting perspectives, and to call upon contrasting competencies. It often requires the blending of contrasting competencies. This is not easy. Consider, for example, the following story that might have been told by the instructor of your own class.

This week in class the topic was building teams. The students were assigned to engage in several group activities outside of class; we also did several in-class exercises. I began the class with a lecture, discussing the differences between groups and teams. I emphasized that when the team is performing at an optimal level, people get inspired and work productively without much need for intervention or control on the part of the boss. I also pointed out that groups evolve through predictable stages before becoming a team and that if this evolutionary process is managed correctly, the team can become one of the manager's most powerful tools.. After presenting several concrete examples, I noted that few managers ever experience the phenomenon because managers have a hard time letting go of their control and so the evolutionary process is hindered in its early stages. I presented a list of task functions and a list of process functions that must occur in order for the group to evolve.

As we discussed task functions such as initiating structure, giving information, clarifying, summarizing, and evaluating, they had little difficulty understanding. When we turned to process functions such as processing observations, empathizing, participating, surfacing rather than smothering conflict, and managing interpersonal tension in positive way, they seemed more challenged. Then we did the exercises.

After class, one of the students wanted to talk. He said he had noticed during the first exercise that one of the members was not involved. He decided that he would try to include that student. This is what he told me. "I totally failed. When you assigned the second exercise, I noticed that this guy was again sitting around and not saying anything. But I decided that I could not do anything about it. We had only so much time and the work had to get done. I do not think it is possible to get the work done and also do those other things you were talking about. You cannot worry about doing both at the same time."

Many managers are like the student in the preceding story. They perform well in some situations, but they have difficulty or feel uncomfortable in others. Or they excel in several of the competencies or roles, but they find that integrating them with other competencies or roles is difficult. The objective of this chapter is to put all the competencies into a dynamic perspective and to show how they are interrelated. Understanding this aspect of the model may help you to avoid some pitfalls and to move, with practice, toward mastery. We should note, however, that when we talk about moving toward mastery, we are just as concerned with the journey as with the destination. The notion of *becoming* a master manager recognizes that there are always more things to learn and new ideas that will challenge you to enhance your abilities. Moreover, as discussed in Chapter 1, you will find that as you move up the organizational hierarchy, you will need to learn new skills and abilities, as well as unlearn others, to perform well in each of the managerial leadership roles presented in this book. Thus, as you near mastery at one level, you will likely be promoted or moved into a new area where you will be faced with new responsibilities and new challenges, and therefore return to the process of becoming. You will see that as you go through the different stages of your career, you will always need to develop new competencies. The earlier you understand the need for continuous learning, the earlier you learn to value the process of becoming, the more effective you will be as a manager.

THE ROAD TO MASTERY

The road to mastery of an activity is essentially a learning process that takes place over time. Although this learning can take place at times when you are not consciously aware that you are learning, it generally requires a focused effort at understanding new concepts and practicing new skills. Here is an example to clarify what we mean.

> *Recently, one of our colleagues told us a story about a conversation she had with another faculty member in her department. The faculty member was complaining that despite his best efforts to give students group projects so that they could improve their group skills, students were still raising objections to doing these projects because they had trouble coordinating their efforts and found some of their student colleagues to be less willing to pull their weight. When our colleague asked what group management skills he had taught, he looked at her bewildered and said, "I didn't think that I had to teach group skills; I just assumed that they would figure it out by doing it."*

Just as you cannot become an expert swimmer by jumping in the deep end of the pool, you are unlikely to become a master manager by taking charge of a large organization. You need to start at a level at which you are comfortable and consciously work at developing your competencies, always challenging yourself to perform at a higher level. Dreyfus and Dreyfus (1986) provide a five-stage model that describes the journey from novice to expert (see Figure 10.1).

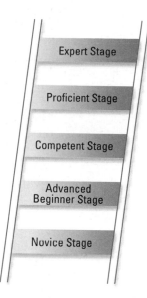

FIGURE 10.1
Five steps to mastery.

Stage 1: The Novice. As a novice, you learn facts and rules. The rules are learned as absolutes, which are never to be violated. For example, a beginning chess player learns the names of the pieces, how they are moved, and their value. He or she is told to exchange pieces of lower value for pieces of higher value. In management this might be the equivalent of learning the various task and group maintenance functions and being told that team performance requires attention to both sets of functions. The student in the story was still at the novice stage in trying to perform the maintenance functions in a group.

Stage 2: The Advanced Beginner. In this stage, experience becomes critical. As real situations are encountered, performance improves and you are able to put into practice the stated facts and rules. As you observe certain basic patterns, you begin to recognize factors that were not stated in the rules. A chess player, for example, begins to recognize certain basic board positions that should be pursued. The new manager discovers the importance of understanding basic norms, values, and culture of the organization. Technical procedures, types of relationships, appropriate dress, and typical career paths are among the things that may vary dramatically from what the novice learned in textbooks. The student in the story was just beginning to experience real-world challenges as he tried to apply the rules to the specific situation he encountered.

Stage 3: Competence. As you gain competence, you gain a better appreciation of the complexity of the task and recognize a much larger set of cues. You develop the ability to select and concentrate on the most important cues. You are no longer aware of the absolute rules; they are assumed. With this your competence increases and you develop some personal "rules of thumb" that guide, but do not direct, your actions. You engage calculated risks and complex trade-offs. A chess player may, for example, weaken board position in order to attack the opposing king. This plan may or may not follow any rules that the person was ever taught. The manager may experiment with going beyond the basic tools and techniques taught in school as he or she experiments with new behaviors. Here the manager is more willing to trust his or her intuition and take risks or suggest new approaches. This may occasionally result in successful outcomes; many times it will not. Here the trial-and-error process is critical to continued development. If the student in the original illustration had continued with his group, he might have begun to experiment with stopping the group process to check what quiet members were feeling, or he might have tried to surface conflicts that were being avoided. In this stage we learn when and how to best make such interventions.

Stage 4: Proficiency. Here, calculation and rational analysis seem to disappear. Unconscious, fluid, and effortless performance begins to emerge, and no one plan is held sacred. You learn to unconsciously "read" the evolving situation. You notice and respond to new cues as the importance of the old ones recedes. New plans are triggered as emerging patterns call to mind plans that worked previously. Your grasp of the situation is holistic and intuitive. Probably only professional chess players achieve the level of play where they have the ability to recognize and respond to change in board positions intuitively. Managers who reach this stage are seen as highly effective because they are capable of performing in a wide variety of situations and dealing with seemingly contradictory demands.

In the proficiency stage our student would be able to manage the various task and maintenance functions in a seemingly effortless way. But, the effort is hidden; proficiency does not come easily. Consider, for example, John Sculley of Apple Computer. When he arrived at Apple in 1983, after leaving PepsiCo as a marketer, he knew nothing about personal computers. He knew he had to immediately set about the task of learning a new business from the ground up. Although Sculley sees himself essentially as an intuitive leader, he regularly points out that a person can only be intuitive about something he or she fully understands. Sculley's intuitive decisions have made Apple a highly successful company. He is proficient, perhaps expert, because he consciously made the effort to move through the first three stages and into the fourth.

Stage 5: Expertise. At this level optimal performance becomes second nature. People at this stage are not consciously aware of the details, rather they use a holistic perspective that gives them a deep understanding of the situation. They have programmed into their heads multidimensional maps of the territory of which the rest of us are not aware. They see and know things intuitively that the rest of us do not know or see. They frame and reframe strategies as they read changing cues. This ability facilitates their engagement of the natural flow of events. Here the manager fully transcends any natural blind spots and is able to shift roles as needed. The expert seems to effortlessly meet the contradictions of organizational life.

THE PROFILE OF A MASTER MANAGER

Is it appropriate to apply the notion of mastery to the tasks of management? Certainly managerial leaders progress through stages where we expect them to become increasingly effective in their performance. In the first chapter we discussed three challenges that are associated with effective management. We review them here:

Challenge 1. To appreciate both the values and the weaknesses of the four models of the competing values framework.

Challenge 2. To acquire and use the competencies associated with each of the roles in the framework.

Challenge 3. To dynamically integrate the competencies from each of the roles within the managerial situations that we encounter.

Thus, becoming a master manager requires not only ability to play all eight roles (at least at a competent level), it also requires that the manager have the ability to blend and balance the competing roles in an appropriate way. Recall from Chapter 1 the notion of behavioral complexity, "the ability to act out a cognitively complex strategy by playing multiple, even competing, roles in a highly integrated and complementary way" (Hooijberg and Quinn, 1992, p. 164). Becoming a master manager requires that the individual attain a level of behavioral complexity, where he or she is able to play more of the roles, play them to a greater extent, and even play several roles simultaneously, as appropriate.

As you consider the eight roles and 24 competencies in the competing values framework, you may question whether it is possible to perform all of these well. During this course, you may have found that you felt very comfortable performing in some of the roles and uncomfortable in others and you may ask whether it is possible to link the demands of one role with the demands of a role in an opposite area of the framework. In order to approach this issue, we will briefly review a study of ineffective and effective managers.

Using the competing values model, Quinn, Faerman, and Dixit (1987) found that ineffective organizational leaders tended to have profiles that were badly out of balance. Those leaders might be above average on the top four roles (mentor, facilitator, innovator, broker) and then be well below average on the bottom four (monitor, coordinator, director, producer). Such managers were seen by associates as impulsive and chaotic, spreading disorder everywhere. Some had the opposite profile. They were seen as narrowly focused on control and abrasive toward people. Among the ineffective, there were several other profiles as well, but all were badly out of balance. Four of the ineffective profiles are shown in Figure 10.2.

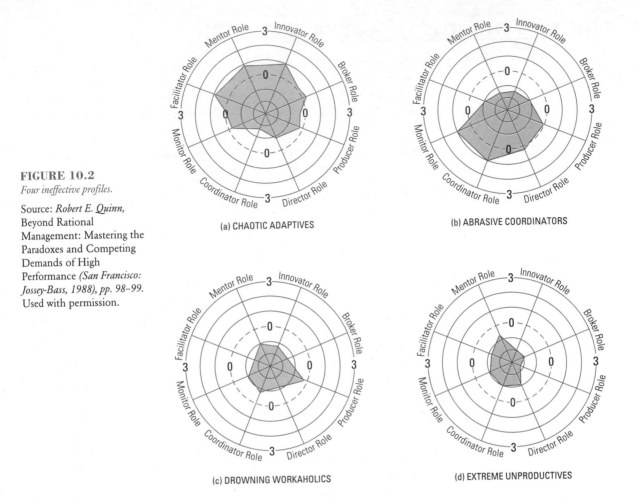

FIGURE 10.2
Four ineffective profiles.

Source: *Robert E. Quinn,* Beyond Rational Management: Mastering the Paradoxes and Competing Demands of High Performance *(San Francisco: Jossey-Bass, 1988), pp. 98–99.* Used with permission.

Interestingly, most of the effective profiles also had some imbalance in them. But here there was a difference. In the effective profiles, people tended to have high scores on more than half of the roles. In addition, the scores on their weaker roles tended to fall near the average. In other words, they did not neglect any of the roles. Nevertheless, they were not free of style. Most tended to emphasize some areas more than others.

Figure 10.3 shows four types of effective profiles, labeled aggressive achievers, conceptual producers, peaceful team builders, and masters. The aggressive achievers tend not to excel in the human relations quadrant. The conceptual producers tend not to excel in the internal process quadrant, and the peaceful team builders are near the average on the two roles on the right side of the framework. Although each of these three clearly reflects a style, all are seen as effective profiles of managerial leadership.

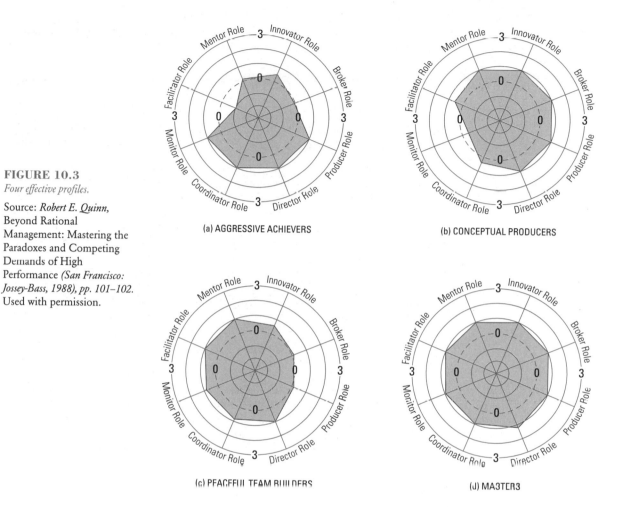

FIGURE 10.3
Four effective profiles.

Source: *Robert E. Quinn,*
Beyond Rational
Management: Mastering the
Paradoxes and Competing
Demands of High
Performance *(San Francisco:
Jossey-Bass, 1988), pp. 101–102.*
Used with permission.

(a) AGGRESSIVE ACHIEVERS

(b) CONCEPTUAL PRODUCERS

(c) PEACEFUL TEAM BUILDERS

(d) MASTERS

The fourth profile is different from the others—it is big and round. This profile was labeled "masters" because these managerial leaders seem to have transcended style; they seem to appreciate the underlying values in each quadrant and can also employ the behaviors that are represented in each one. What cannot be seen in the profile, however, is that these individuals are not only capable of playing each of the roles, they are able to integrate the roles and to use the competencies in complementary ways.

How do these individuals come to "round out" their profiles? Part of the answer lies in experience. Masters tend to be in upper-middle and top-level positions. It is reasonable to suggest that these managers did not begin their careers as masters. Although some people have years of experience and are still not effective in all eight roles, masters tend to focus on personal and professional development. They recognize the need to constantly grow; they welcome transitions that are the most challenging and come out of these transitions with a wider array of competencies, less tied to a particular style. To understand this change process, we now turn to a case illustration.

ONE JOURNEY TOWARD MASTERY

Consider the case of a truly successful organizational leader whose journey toward mastery pivoted around a crucial crisis and transformation (Quinn, 1988).

He had graduated from a five-year engineering program in four years and had taken a job with his current organization. Starting out in a brilliant fashion, he was promoted rapidly. He had an ability to take a complex technical problem and come up with a better answer than anyone else. He was also a hard-driving person who pushed his people to accomplish some impressive tasks. Initially he was seen as an action-oriented person with a bright future. His profile was that of an aggressive achiever (see Figure 10.3).

After his last promotion, however, everything started to change. He went through several very difficult years. For the first time he received serious negative feedback about his performance. His ideas and proposals were regularly rejected, and for the first time he was passed over for a promotion. In reflecting on those days, he said:

"It was awful. Everything was always changing and nothing ever seemed to happen. They would sit around forever and talk about things. The technically right answer didn't matter. They were always making what I thought were wrong decisions, and when I insisted on doing what was right, they got angry and would ignore what I was saying. Everything was suddenly political. They would worry about what everyone was going to think about every issue. Your appearance, attending cocktail parties, that stuff, to me was unreal and unimportant.

"I went through five and a half terrible years. I occasionally thought I had reached my level of incompetence, but I refused to give up."

Finally, a critical incident occurred. Like many critical incidents in the transformational process, it may seem comical to an outside observer. On several occasions, the engineer's boss commented that he was very impressed with one of the engineer's subordinates. Finding the comment somewhat curious, the engineer asked for an explanation. The boss indicated that no matter how early he, himself, arrived at work, the subordinate's car was always there.

The engineer then went to visit the subordinate and indicated that he had noticed that no matter what time he came in, the subordinate's car was already in the lot. The subordinate nodded his head and explained,

"I have four teenagers who wake up at dawn. The mornings at my house are chaotic. So I come in early. I read for a while, then I write in my personal journal, read the paper, have some coffee, and then I start work at eight."

When the engineer left his subordinate's office, he was at first furious. After a couple of minutes, though, he sat down and started to laugh. He later explained, "That is when I discovered perception." He went on to say that from that moment everything started to change. He was more patient. He began to experiment with participative decision making. His relationships with superiors gradually improved.

Eventually he actually came to appreciate the need to think and operate in more complex ways at the higher levels of the organization.

This story represents a learning process. The engineer was very adept in using the skills in the two lower quadrants. Here he was in the proficient or expert stages. Rapid promotions, however, put him into a new and more complex situation. At the higher organizational levels, skills in the top two quadrants, skills that he had not learned as an engineer, were much more important than they had been previously. With respect to the skills in these top two quadrants, he was in the novice or advanced beginner stage. He applied his old assumptions and governing rules only to see them fail. The resulting frustration and panic led him to try even harder and intensify his use of his old skills. This, in turn, resulted in more failure and frustration.

Peter Senge (1990) refers to this phenomenon as "fixes that fail." It is a common occurrence in organizations and stems from the inability to see that short-term successes may have unintended consequences that create new problems. By being successful as an engineer, our protagonist was promoted into a situation where the rules of engineering did not apply. Fortunately for the engineer, he did not quit. With a greater understanding of the power of perception, he was able to examine other assumptions about what it meant to be a truly effective manager. The one event gave him the critical, creative insight that he needed, an insight that led to a reframing about what it means to be successful. As the human and political domains (human relations and open systems models) began to become a part of his world view, he began to explore and experiment with new skills. This was eventually followed by a marked improvement in performance.

As a manager this man was not now perfect. Clearly he had his share of bad days. There were occasions when he got discouraged and there were times when his subordinates felt he was too harsh. Nevertheless, he had widened his range of capacities and most of the time displayed an ability to call upon them in successful ways. Moreover, he had opened himself up to learning about new management approaches and was committed to trying new ideas. For the most part, he had achieved, with considerable effort, a profile resembling those we label as "masters," managers with the capacity to both play and integrate competing roles.

HOW MASTERS SEE THE WORLD

Having examined part of the journey of one master manager, we turn to the broader issue of why some individuals are more successful in their journey to become a master manager than others. What other characteristics differentiate these managers from other managers? Why are some people better able to integrate seemingly opposite modes of behavior? Although we cannot say for certain, our experience has suggested that the answer begins with an understanding of how master managers see (think about) the world. People who become masters of management do not see their work environment only in structured, analytic ways. Instead, they also have the capacity to see it as a complex, dynamic system that is constantly evolving. In order to interact effectively with their work environment, they employ a variety of different, sometimes contradictory, perspectives or modes. In other words, they employ different modes of thinking. Here we will briefly discuss two modes of thinking that appear to be related to behavioral complexity: systems (dynamic) thinking and paradoxical thinking.

Peter Senge describes *systems thinking* as "a discipline for seeing wholes. It is a framework for seeing interrelationships rather than things, for seeing patterns of change rather than static 'snapshots.'. . . [It is] a discipline for seeing the 'structures' that underlie complex situations, and for discerning high from low leverage change" (1990, pp. 68-69). One of the key elements of systems thinking is the concept of *feedback*, or the "reciprocal flow of influence" (1990, p. 75). In a situation where there is feedback behavior, if A influences B, and B influences C, C (or something that is influenced by C), will ultimately influence A. Often, when C and A are separated in time, it is difficult to recognize the feedback.

Recall that the engineer's initial superior performance resulted in his promotion into a position for which he was not prepared, a situation where his performance was poorly evaluated. Thus, as a result of a reciprocal flow of influence, superior performance led to inferior performance. This is an example of negative, or balancing, feedback. Alternatively, positive, or reinforcing, feedback will occur when actions lead to ever-increasing (or -decreasing) levels of behavior. When the engineer intensified his use of his old skills, he received poorer and poorer performance reviews. And the more he failed, the more he tried to return to the old tried-and-true approach.

Most of us, like the engineer in the preceding story, learn to think about organizations in a very static and purposeful way. We see the world in terms of simple one-way cause-and-effect reasoning, where we believe that events will cause (or are caused by) other events—if you cut expenditures, profits will rise; if you send employees to training, their performance will improve; if you get good grades, you will (at least you should) get a good job. We tend not to notice that actions taken today can result in new problems that we will need to deal with several months (or years) down the line; we tend to believe that a problem addressed in one area of the organization has no consequences for other areas. As noted by Senge, this type of cause-and-effect thinking "distract[s] us from seeing the longer-term patterns of change that lie behind the events and from understanding the causes of those patterns" (1990, p. 21). When organizations exist in stable, predictable environments, this cause-and-effect thinking is acceptable and there is no need to concern ourselves with the larger patterns of action. But few, if any, organizations exist in stable, predictable environments. Instead, organizations exist in dynamic, changing environments, where small changes in the social, political, economic, and technological environment can have a major impact on the organization's future.

Margaret Wheatley (1992) suggests that one reason why we tend to use simple, linear cause-and-effect thinking is that much of our thinking is influenced by seventeenth-century Newtonian physics. "Each of us lives and works in organizations designed from Newtonian images of the universe. We manage by separating things into parts, we believe that influence occurs as a direct result of force exerted from one person to another, we engage in complex planning for a world that we keep expecting to be predictable, and we search for continually better methods of objectively perceiving the world" (1992, p. 6). But, as Wheatley notes, science has changed, and so should our images of organizations. We need to be far more aware of interrelationships. "In a quantum world, relationships are not just interesting; to many physicists, they are *all* there is to reality" (1992, p. 32, emphasis in the original). Recall that master managers use holistic recognition in a way that allows them to deeply understand the situation. The ability to see the underlying structures, to see the interrelationships, and to understand that actions have long-term impact is essentially the basis of systems thinking.

Paradoxical thinking is somewhat related to systems thinking in that both help us deal with apparent contradictions. In Chapter 1 we introduced the notion that organizational leaders spend much of their time living in fields of perceived tensions. They are constantly forced to make trade-offs; there are often no right answers. Moreover, the higher one goes in an organization, the more exaggerated these tensions become. One-dimensional guidelines (care for people; work harder; get control; be innovative) are simply half-truths representing single domains of action. What exists are contradictory pressures. Much of the time the choice is not between good and bad, but between good and good—or bad and bad. In such cases there is sometimes a need for paradoxical thinking, thinking that transcends the contradictions and recognizes that two seemingly opposite conditions can simultaneously be true.

In order to engage in paradoxical thinking, one must be willing to engage in contradiction. This does not simply mean that managers are willing or able to perform different roles at different times. It means that they must be willing to try to resolve the contradiction, and to integrate seemingly opposite ideas or behaviors. It means trying to be a mentor at the same time you are being a director, being an innovator at the same time you are being a coordinator, and so on. To do this, managers must be willing to move outside their current level of thinking and attempt to see things from a new perspective. Albert Einstein is quoted as saying "No problem can be solved from the same consciousness that produced it" (quoted in Wheatley, 1992, p. 5).

The competing values framework is built around the notion of paradox. It assumes that organizations need to be simultaneously adaptable/flexible and stable/controlled; that in order to perform effectively they need to focus simultaneously on their external environments and competitive position and on their internal environments and the people and work processes. As a conceptual model, the framework itself suggests that we tend to think of roles on opposite sides of the axes as antithetical. In addition, throughout this book, we have mentioned paradoxes that occur within roles, such as the need for individuals to take energy breaks in order to be more productive (producer) and the strategy of creating conflict in order to reduce conflict (facilitator). In a similar vein, toward the end of Chapter 1, we presented the notion of negative zones, where strength in any one role can turn into a weakness; this notion was also borne out in the study of effective and ineffective managers. Implicitly the model suggests that managers who are most capable of thinking paradoxically would also be most capable of performing in seemingly opposite roles.

One of the most effective ways to increase your ability to engage in paradoxical thinking is to challenge yourself to see the value in areas that are not your strength, to seek out that which is outside of your comfort zone. McGee-Cooper argues that *"We need most what we find most threatening"* (1992, p. 260, emphasis in original). Recall from Chapter 7 (the producer role) the concept of brain hemisphericity, that the two sides of the brain have different functions and two different ways of processing information. In that chapter we discussed the idea that people tend to rely primarily on either convergent or divergent thinking, and that this influences their work style. Having a dominant style does not, however, mean that the other mode does not exist inside us. Indeed, McGee-Cooper argues that one of the biggest energy drains we face results from the "battle" between the two sides of the brain. She suggests that you become more effective in your actions by learning to integrate the two sides of your brain, by listening to both sides and managing the conflict, as you would manage a conflict between two people with two opposing views, by trying to fully understand both sides of the story and then finding a mutually agreeable solution. Finally, as a way of reinforcing the synergy of whole-brained thinking, McGee-Cooper suggests that "we need not only to make friends with our opposites but also to become interdependent team players, both with our own shadow side and with those around us who see what we can't and who think in ways that we find threatening" (1992, p. 260). In the next section we will see how these ideas can be incorporated into a strategy for improvement.

THE POSSIBILITY OF SELF-IMPROVEMENT

The engineer in the earlier case "stumbled" into a new paradigm. He was both determined and lucky. Many people who encounter his problem are defeated by it; they are not willing to open themselves up to seeing the world in a different way. Although you are also likely to encounter problems in your development, you have some major advantages. First, you have a framework to help you appreciate the necessity of performing in the areas that do not come naturally. Second, you have had the opportunity to practice using different competencies and so should have greater self-confidence in your ability to perform the various roles. Building on the foundation of competencies developed in this course and related experiences, you should be able to continue developing as a managerial leader. Finally, your experiences in this course should have given you an understanding of the necessity to think complexly and to integrate diverse competencies. Thus you have both cognitive and behavioral (performance) tools to help you improve yourself.

One of the enduring questions asked in the field of leadership is "Are leaders born or made?" While we do not know "the answer" to this question, or even if there is a simple answer, we are convinced that conscious self-improvement is possible. When a person is willing to put forth the effort required to make a change, and is determined to make a change, that person is likely to succeed. Many managers, however, excuse themselves from this responsibility. There is an unlimited number of excuses for not trying:

- "I am simply not creative, and there is no way to change that."

- "I hate details, and I will never be a good monitor."

- "Being a hard-driving producer is fine, but it is not worth the effort—life is simply too short."

- "Different people have different talents, and working with people is not my thing."

In each case the statement is an excuse for not making changes. In each case the statement is untrue. It is always possible for someone to make improvements in his or her weak area. He or she may legitimately choose not to, since, as we learned in a previous section, it is possible to somewhat neglect certain roles and still be effective. However, it is inaccurate to say, "I have a particular style and I am not capable of performing in a different manner." Although sometimes difficult, it is in fact always possible to make improvements in one's weak areas. Here we will outline a procedure for doing so.

AGENDA FOR SELF-IMPROVEMENT

Table 10.1 provides an agenda for self-improvement that involves three general steps: learn about yourself, develop a change strategy, and implement the strategy. Within each of these steps are some key subpoints. This process has been used with many practicing managers and graduate students. In the beginning of the process, many participants are cynical, and some make only half-hearted efforts. Needless to say, they show little achievement. But others attack the process with zeal, and they naturally achieve considerably more. The interesting thing is that the people who make progress do so in whatever quadrant they choose. It is possible to learn and to improve in any area.

TABLE 10.1 Agenda for Self-Improvement

1. Learn About Yourself
   - Complete the competing values self-assessment instrument.
   - Do a written self-evaluation of each role.
   - Have others evaluate you.
   - Discuss your skills with people who will be honest.
   - Keep a journal.

TABLE 10.1 Agenda for Self-Improvement continued

2. Develop a Change Strategy
   - Identify specific areas in need of improvement and set specific goals.
   - Identify positive role models for your weak areas.
   - Read relevant books.

3. Implement the Change Strategy
   - Be honest about the costs of improvement.
   - Develop a social support system.
   - Evaluate your progress on a regular basis and modify your strategy, if necessary.

Learn About Yourself. There are many ways by which you can learn about yourself. Some focus on looking within; others involve reaching outside to learn about how others see us. You can start by doing a self-assessment. This involves filling out the competing values self-assessment instrument, analyzing your skills in each role, and doing a written assessment of yourself in each role. In the written assessment, you should explain why you believe you are strong or weak in each area. Completing the self-assessment can be a relatively simple task, but it can also be misleading. Often people assess themselves differently, either more positively or more negatively, than do their subordinates, peers, and superiors. This is why it is important to obtain honest feedback from others.

Although many people claim that they want to receive honest feedback from those around them, they in fact behave in ways that prevent such feedback. In one class students were assigned to not only improve themselves in the course of a semester but also to go out and improve a manager. They arranged to act as consultants to a practicing manager. Over the semester they analyzed the manager's behavior and worked with the person to improve weak areas. This provided an important mirror that allowed the student to see the flaws and the resistances in themselves by seeing them first in another person. The following is a typical statement about feedback, written by one of our students.

> *Perhaps one of the most amazing things to me is that, not only the manager we worked with, but virtually every manager that was helped by one of the teams in the class, was so deeply interested in feedback from subordinates and others. They were simply unsure about what others thought about them. In every case, it was the first time in their careers that they received such feedback. As I think about it now, it seems incredible that such a simple thing could be so powerful.*

Feedback from others is indeed powerful. Sometimes, however, it can be too powerful. Occasionally a person receives feedback that suggests that other people see him or her as less effective in a given area than the person sees himself or herself. Although most people can handle this negative message, some cannot, and this can be a cause of crisis. Some people get depressed and withdraw; others get angry and want to punish those who gave the feedback. Neither response is healthy.

When you get feedback that comes as a surprise, use it as a springboard for honest exploration and discussion. First, wait long enough to get in the proper frame of mind so that you are indeed ready to hear what people have to say. This may take some time and preparation. Go to those who know you best, ask questions, and then listen carefully to what they have to say. This strategy takes a certain level of maturity and self-esteem. If you feel unsure of yourself, you should wait until some future time to seek feedback. Be careful not to behave in ways that would lead people to say only those things that you will find acceptable.

You may feel unable, for whatever reason, to approach particular people for feedback, but that should not be a cause for concern. In fact, it is a common occurrence. People should talk to those few others with whom they have a trusting and caring relationship, but who will nevertheless be honest in their feedback.

Finally, we suggest that you keep a journal. Often people have difficulty remembering experiences that occur over a period of time. As you develop a particular skill, you may not be able to accurately recall what your skill level was when you began, what were some of the milestones that signaled progress, or what issues you encountered along the way. Keeping a journal allows you to learn about yourself by providing written record of your behaviors and thoughts over the time period. If you had been keeping a journal during this course, you would now be able to review your accomplishments and this might give you a better sense of how you have progressed.

Develop a Change Strategy. Once you have sought feedback from others, you might then make a final assessment of what you think are your strong and weak areas. As you write a final assessment of your strengths and weaknesses in each role of the competing values framework, pinpoint the ones on which you most need to work. In doing so you should also identify someone who does very well in your weak role. This will help to make concrete the kinds of behaviors that are appropriate in this role. When you are in situations that call for behavior in the role, you can ask yourself: "What would the person do in this situation?"

This step sometimes makes you uncomfortable because you may not like the people who do well in your weak areas. For example, one of our students had a colleague who, in terms of the competing values framework, was an exact opposite in outlook, strategy, and behavior. Working with him was very difficult. There was conflict over nearly every decision they had to reach together. But the student learned to embrace what he found threatening. In a final paper the student wrote:

> *Although the costs of working with him have been high, I have also learned a great deal from him. In many situations I have watched him do the exact opposite of what I would have done. It sometimes has been shocking to see his strategies work far better than my own. Over time I have come to recognize certain situations in which his thinking might be better than mine. I am now able to stop before implementing my natural strategy and ask myself what he would do in this case. Often I am dissatisfied with the answer and proceed with my own approach. There are, however, times when I go against my instincts and follow his lead. Thinking about him as a role model in my weak areas enlarges my pool of possible strategies. Sometimes, following uncomfortable strategies results in the development of a wider array of behaviors and skills.*

Another key activity is to read literature that is related to your weak roles. At the end of this chapter you will find "A Competing Values Reading List." It is organized according to the eight roles in the competing values framework and lists approximately 12 to 15 books under each role. Some are self-improvement books; others are professional management books. Most are very basic. Many managers have used the list as a source of ideas on how to enhance their performance in a particular role. You should not, however, be limited by the list. Take time to browse through the books in the management section in your library or favorite bookstore.

In some cases you should select the most relevant books and read them very rapidly. Then briefly record any useful ideas in your notebook, and on a regular basis consolidate these ideas into strategies that you would like to try. In other cases you may find that you want to read more slowly, taking time to self-reflect. This may suggest important modifications to your change strategy. In still other cases you may just want to skim some books to see if you want to include reading them in their entirety as part of your change strategy.

Implement the Strategy. After you finish analyzing your strengths and weaknesses, considering role models, reading for ideas, and consolidating insights into possible action strategies, it is time to implement your strategy. The first step is to be honest with yourself about the personal costs of improvement. Some people are simply not interested in changing; others want to change but are so impatient that they quickly become disillusioned by the setbacks and failures that they encounter. Just as you would not expect to become a master chess player, a master musician, or a master athlete after taking one course, you should not expect to become a master manager too quickly. The improvement process involves a great deal of practice, as well as a fair amount of patience.

Because it is not always easy to engage in this process, it is important to develop a social support system. The key is to find someone to talk to—perhaps a friend, a close relative, or colleague—who will be able to provide encouragement and creative insights. Many managers choose their immediate superiors to play this role. When this is a comfortable arrangement, it can turn into a more long-term mentoring relationship. Others feel uncomfortable with their superiors and prefer to select some other person at work or rely on a spouse or significant other. Regardless of whom you select, arrange a schedule that will allow you to regularly meet with that person to discuss your successes and failures.

As you begin to experiment with new strategies, remember that leaving the status quo usually involves some risk. It sometimes means moving into a situation that requires assumptions very different from those with which you are familiar. Instead of trying to avoid failure, you may need to embrace failure and to see it as an indispensable part of the learning process.

As you implement your strategy, try to be aware of your progress. Keep your notebook close at hand. Use it to record and analyze successes and setbacks, and to record insights. On a regular basis, review your notes, evaluate your progress, and modify your strategies if necessary. You will be impressed with what you will learn if you consistently monitor your own behaviors, as well as your reactions to others' behaviors. One manager with whom we worked scored low on the broker role and was very concerned about his inability to make persuasive presentations. He worked through all the steps described here and reported a dramatic improvement in performance. Here is what he wrote about how he monitored his progress:

> *I had never before kept a journal. It was very hard for me to get used to the idea. But I was intense about trying to improve, and it was clear that a journal was going to be important. I read everything I could get my hands on, and I made lots of notes. Whenever anyone made a presentation of any kind—a salesperson, a politician, a young kid in my Sunday School class—I would analyze what was effective and what was not. Each time I drew lessons for myself. Whenever I made a presentation, I would immediately find some time to do a self-analysis. I was a tough self-critic.*
>
> *Every so often, I would make notes of my notes. That is, I would reduce them to a list of those principles that seemed to be most important for me. I was, without knowing it, building my own personal theory of persuasive speaking. The important thing is that it was an applied theory. It told me "how to." After four months or so, I really started to show signs of progress. People told me they were amazed at how much better I was doing.*

THE RESULTS

The improvement process is sometimes easier than one thinks it is going to be. While change takes time and perseverance, if you have the patience and the will, you can be successful. Recall from Chapter 7 (the producer role) that the number-one strategy for time and stress management was "clarify your values." If this is an important item on your agenda, if you truly want to improve, you will need to devote the necessary time. We offer here one final example. The competing values profile of one manager suggested that she was very strong in all the roles except that of monitor. She saw herself as a visionary, and she thought that being a monitor was simply "not her style." Hence, it was with some dread that she undertook the implementation of the steps outlined earlier. Here is her report:

> *I picked a role model, read some books, made some notes, and designed a change program. It was really very simple. Basically it boiled down to setting times to do a whole raft of tasks that I normally ignored. That was all there was to it. I was amazed. It was not a matter of ability; it was actually quite easy. It is now hard to believe that I once thought I was incapable of doing the things in the monitor role.*

We close this section by encouraging you to believe in yourself. It is possible to become a better manager, particularly to improve in those areas that seem far from your natural style. If you are willing to follow the steps outlined herein, they can be very helpful in moving you forward along the road to mastery.

ANALYSIS   The Transcendence of Paradox

Directions   In this chapter we discussed the transcendence of paradox in terms of the ability to integrate seemingly opposite approaches to management. Much of the discussion focused on the need to blend several roles (and their associated competencies) when faced with a complex managerial situation. We also mentioned that paradox is evident *within* each of the roles. Here are a few examples:

Broker   —When we empower others, we increase our own power.

Producer —We become most effective in our use of time when we learn the value of taking breaks.

Facilitator—In a team, when every person fully understands each individual's role, team members are more willing (and able) to act outside their own role.

Director —Planning increases your flexibility.

1. Think about each of the eight roles. Try to find the paradoxes within each role.

2. Examine the four pairs of seemingly opposite roles (facilitator-producer, mentor-director, innovator-coordinator, broker-monitor) and try to find similarities between the two roles.

3. Think about the implications of these paradoxes and similarities for increasing your behavioral complexity.

PRACTICE   The Evaluation Matrix

Directions   Based on all you have learned from Chapters 1 to 9, and from the assessment exercise at the outset of this chapter, complete the matrix shown in Table 10.2.

TABLE 10.2 Evaluation Matrix

	Mentor	*Facilitator*	*Monitor*	*Coordinator*	*Director*	*Producer*	*Broker*	*Innovator*
1. In regard to this role, what do I know about myself?								
2. How could I more effectively play this role?								
3. Who are some people I could observe?								

TABLE 10.2 Evaluation Matrix continued

	Mentor	Facilitator	Monitor	Coordinator	Director	Producer	Broker	Innovator
4. What books should I read?								
5. What objectives and deadlines should I set?								
6. With whom should I share my objectives?								
7. How will I evaluate my efforts?								

APPLICATION   Your Strategy for Mastery

Review the material in the chapters focusing on the individual managerial leadership roles (Chapters 2 to 9), as well as your personal work (e.g., assessment exercises, application exercises, etc.). Based on this material, and the material in this chapter, write a long-term development plan that focuses on enhancing your behavioral complexity. Discuss what specific things you can do to enhance your ability to integrate the various roles.

REFERENCES

Dreyfus, Hubert. L., Stuart E. Dreyfus, with Tom Athanasiou. *Mind Over Machine: The Power of Human Intuition and Expertise in the Era of the Computer.* New York: Free Press, 1986.

Hooijberg, Robert, and Robert E. Quinn. "Behavioral Complexity and the Development of Effective Managers," in *Strategic Leadership: A Multiorganizational Perspective,* Robert L. Phillips and James G. Hunt (eds.). Westport, Conn.: Quorum Books, 1992.

McGee-Cooper, Ann, with Duane Trammell and Barbara Lau. *You Don't Have to Go Home From Work Exhausted.* New York: Bantam Books, 1992.

Quinn, Robert E. *Beyond Rational Management: Mastering the Paradoxes and Competing Demands of High Performance.* San Francisco: Jossey-Bass, 1988.

Quinn, Robert E., Sue R. Faerman, and Narendra Dixit. "Perceived Performance: Some Archetypes of Managerial Effectiveness and Ineffectiveness." Working paper, Institute for Government and Policy Studies, Department of Public Administration, State University of New York at Albany, 1987.

Senge, Peter. *The Fifth Discipline: The Art & Practice of The Learning Organization.* New York: Currency Doubleday, 1990.

Wheatley, Margaret J. *Leadership and the New Science.* San Francisco: Berrett-Koehler, 1992.

A COMPETING VALUES READING LIST

This resource contains a reading list organized according to the completing values framework and designed to help you identify books that address areas in which you need improvement. It is meant to suggest a few of the many readings that can expand your knowledge in each area. Readers are encouraged to send the authors additional suggestions of books for inclusion.

Mentor Role

Bolman, Lee G., and Terrence E. Deal. *Leading with Soul: An Uncommon Journey of Spirit,* San Francisco: Jossey-Bass, 1995.

Bolton, Robert. *People Skills: How to Assert Yourself, Listen to Others, and Resolve Conflicts.* Englewood Cliffs, N.J.: Prentice-Hall, 1979.

Covey, Stephen R. *The Seven Habits of Highly Effective People: Powerful Lessons in Personal Change,* New York: Simon & Schuster, 1989.

DePree, Max. *Leadership Is an Art.* New York: Currency-Doubleday, 1990.

Kouzes, James M., and Barry Z. Posner. *Credibility: How Leaders Gain and Lose It, Why People Demand It.* San Francisco: Jossey-Bass, 1995.

McGregor, Douglas. *The Human Side of Enterprise.* New York: McGraw-Hill, 1960.

Richards, Dick. *Awakening Joy, Meaning and Commitment in the Workplace.* San Francisco: Berrett-Koehler, 1995.

Rogers, Carl R. *On Becoming a Person.* Boston: Houghton Mifflin, 1961.

Sashkin, Marshall. *Assessing Performance Appraisal.* San Diego: University Associates, 1981.

Schein, Edgar H. *Career Dynamics: Matching Individual and Organizational Needs.* Reading, Mass.: Addison-Wesley, 1978.

Facilitator Role

Buchholz, Steve, and Thomas Roth. *Creating the High-Performance Team.* New York: John Wiley & Sons, 1987.

Cox, Taylor, Jr. *Cultural Diversity in Organizations: Theory, Research and Practice.* San Francisco: Berrett-Koehler, 1993.

Dyer, William G. *Team Building* (3rd ed.). Reading, Mass.: Addison-Wesley, 1995.

Harrington-Mackin, Deborah. *The Team Building Tool Kit: Tips, Tactics and Rules for Effective Workplace Teams.* New York: AMACOM, 1994.

Johansen, Robert, David Sibbet, Suzyn Benson, Alexia Martin, Robert Mittman, and Paul Saffo. *Leading Business Teams: How Teams Can Use Technology and Group Process Tools to Enhance Performance.* Reading, Mass.: Addison-Wesley, 1991.

Katzenbach, Jon R., and Douglas K. Smith. *The Wisdom of Teams.* New York: HarperCollins, 1993.

Larson, Carl E., and Frank M. J. LaFasto. *TeamWork: What Must Go Right/What Can Go Wrong.* Newbury Park, Calif.: Sage Publications, 1989.

Loden, Marilyn, and Judy B. Rosener. *Workforce America! Managing Employee Diversity as a*

Vital Resource. Homewood, Ill: Business One Irwin, 1991.

Martin, Don. *TeamThink: Using the Sports Connection to Develop, Motivate, and Manage a Winning Business Team.* New York: Penguin Books, 1993.

Opper, Susanna, and Henry Fersko-Weiss. *Technology for Teams: Enhancing Productivity in Networked Organizations.* New York: Van Nostrand Reinhold, 1992.

Ray, Darrel, and Howard Bronstein. *Teaming Up: Making the Transition to a Self-Directed Team-Based Organization,* New York: McGraw-Hill, 1994.

Tjosvold, Dean. *Learning to Manage Conflict: Getting People to Work Together,* New York: Lexington Books, 1993.

Weisbord, Marvin R. *Productive Workplaces: Organizing and Managing for Dignity, Meaning, and Community.* San Francisco: Jossey-Bass, 1987.

Wilson, Jeanne M., and Jill A. George. *Team Leader's Survival Guide.* Bridgeville, Penn.: Development Dimensions International, 1994.

Monitor Role

Bounds, Gregory, M., Gregory H. Dobbins, and Oscar S. Fowler. *Management: A Total Quality Perspective.* Cincinnati, Ohio: Southwestern, 1995.

Currid, Cheryl. *Reengineering Toolkit: Fifteen Tools and Technologies for Reorganizing Your Organization.* Rocklin, Calif.: Prima, 1994.

Davenport, Thomas H., *Process Innovation: Reengineering Work Through Information Technology.* Boston: Harvard University Press, 1993.

Flood, Robert. *Beyond TQM.* West Sussex: John Wiley & Sons, 1993.

Frame, Davidson J. *The New Project Management: Corporate Reengineering and Other Business Realities.* San Francisco: Jossey-Bass, 1994.

Gabor, Andrea. *The Man Who Discovered Quality: How W. Edwards Deming Brought the Quality Revolution to America: The Stories of Ford, Xerox and GM.* New York: Penguin Press, 1990.

Goldratt, Eliyahu. *The Haystack Syndrome: Sifting Information Out of the Data Ocean.* Croton-on-Hudson, N.Y. North River Press, 1990.

Handy, Charles. *Understanding Organizations: How Understanding the Ways Organizations Actually Work Can Be Used to Manage Them Better.* Oxford: Oxford University Press, 1993.

Harrington, James S. *Total Quality Improvement: The Next Generation in Performance Improvement.* New York: McGraw-Hill, 1995.

Roberts, Harry V., and Bernard F. Sergesketter. *Quality Is Personal: A Foundation for Total Quality Management.* New York: Free Press, 1993.

Silver, Susan. *Organized to Be the Best: New Timesaving Ways to Simplify and Improve How You Work.* Los Angeles: Adams-Hall, 1991.

Coordinator Role

Frame, Davidson J. *The New Project Management: Corporate Reengineering and Other Business Realities.* San Francisco: Jossey-Bass, 1994.

Galbraith, Jay R., Edward E. Lawler, III & Associates. *Organizing for the Future.* San Francisco: Jossey-Bass, 1993.

Hammer, Michael, and James Champy. *Reengineering the Corporation: A Manifesto for Business Revolution.* New York: HarperBusiness, 1993.

House, Ruth Sizemore. *The Human Side of Project Management.* Reading, Mass.: Addison-Wesley, 1988.

Kerzner, Harold. *Project Management: A Systems Approach to Planning, Scheduling, and Controlling* (3rd ed.). New York: Van Nostrand Reinhold, 1989.

Kimmons, Robert L. *Project Management Basics: A Step by Step Approach.* New York: Marcel Dekker, 1990.

Lawler, Edward E., III. *The Ultimate Advantage: Creating the High-Involvement Organization.* San Francisco: Jossey-Bass, 1992.

Meyer, Christopher. *Fast Cycle Time.* New York: Free Press, 1993.

Parker, Glenn M. *Cross-Functional Teams: Working with Allies, Enemies, and Other Strangers.* San Francisco: Jossey-Bass, 1994.

Roman, Daniel D. *Managing Projects: A Systems Approach.* New York: Elsevier Science Publishing, 1986.

Rummler, Geary A., and Alan P. Brache. *Improving Performance: How to Manage the White Space on the Organization Chart.* San Francisco: Jossey-Bass, 1990.

Spinner, M. Pete. *Improving Project Management Skills and Techniques.* Englewood Cliffs, N. J.: Prentice-Hall, 1989.

Director Role

Collins, James C., and Jerry I. Porras. *Built to Last.* New York: Harper Collins, 1994.

Galbraith, Jay, Edward E. Lawler, III & Associates. *Organizing for the Future.* San Francisco: Jossey-Bass, 1993.

Goldratt, Eliyahu, and Jeff Cox. *The Goal* (2nd rev. ed.). Croton-on-Hudson, N.Y.: North River Press, 1992.

Hammer, Michael, and James Champy. *Reengineering the Corporation: A Manifesto for Business Revolution.* New York: HarperBusiness, 1993.

Kaufman, Roger. *Strategic Planning Plus: An Organizational Guide.* Newbury Park, Calif.: Sage Publications, 1992.

Keidel, Robert W. *Corporate Players: Design for Working and Winning Together.* New York: John Wiley & Sons, 1988.

Lawler, Edward E., III. *The Ultimate Advantage: Creating the High-Involvement Organization.* San Francisco: Jossey-Bass, 1992.

Meyer, Christopher. *Fast Cycle Time.* New York: Free Press, 1993.

Mintzberg, Henry. *Mintzberg on Management: Inside our Strange World of Organizations.* New York: Free Press, 1989.

Nanus, Burt. *Visionary Leadership: Creating a Compelling Sense of Direction for Your Organization.* San Francisco: Jossey-Bass, 1992.

Schwartz, Andrew E. *Delegating Authority.* Hauppauge, New York: Barron's Educational Series, 1992.

Treacy, Michael, and Fred Wiersma. *The Discipline of Market Leaders: Choose Your Customers, Narrow Your Focus, Dominate Your Market.* Reading, Mass.: Addison-Wesley, 1995.

Tregoe, Benjamin B., J. W. Zimmerman, R.A. Smith, and P.M. Tobia. *Vision in Action: How to Integrate Your Company's Strategic Goals into Day-to-Day Management Decisions.* New York: Simon and Schuster, 1990.

United States Marine Corps Book of Strategy. *Warfighting: Tactics for Managing Confrontation.* New York: Currency Doubleday, 1994.

Producer Role

Alesandrini, Kathryn. *Survive Information Overload: The 7 Best Ways to Manage Your Workload by Seeing the Big Picture.* Homewood, Ill: Business One Irwin, 1992.

Campbell, John P., Richard J. Campbell and Associates. *Productivity in Organizations: New Perspectives from Industrial and Organizational Psychology.* San Francisco: Jossey-Bass, 1988.

Covey, Stephen R., A. Roger Merrill, and Rebecca R. Merrill. *First Things First: To Live, to Love, to Learn, to Leave a Legacy.* New York: Simon and Schuster, 1994.

Grove, Andrew S. *High-Output Management.* New York: Random House, 1985.

Grover, Ron. *The Disney Touch.* Homewood, Ill.: Business One-Irwin, 1991.

Latham, Gary P., and Kenneth N. Wexley. *Increasing Productivity Through Performance Appraisal* (2nd ed.). Reading, Mass.: Addison-Wesley, 1994.

McCall, Morgan W., Jr., Michael M. Lombardo, and Ann M. Morrison. *The Lessons of Experience: How Successful Executives Develop on the Job.* Lexington, Mass.: Lexington Books, 1989.

McGee-Cooper, Ann, with Duane Trammell. *Time Management for Unmanageable People.* New York: Bantam Books, 1994.

McGee-Cooper, Ann, with Duane Trammell and Barbara Lau. *You Don't Have to Go Home From Work Exhausted.* New York: Bantam Books, 1992.

Oncken, William. *Managing Management Time.* Englewood Cliffs, N.J.: Prentice-Hall. 1984.

Stalk, George, Jr., and Thomas M. Hout. *Competing Against Time: How Time-based Competition Is Reshaping Global Markets.* New York: Free Press. 1990.

Tichy, Noel M., and Stratford Sherman. *Control Your Destiny or Someone Else Will.* New York: Doubleday, 1993.

Broker Role

Baker, Wayne E. *Networking Smart: How to Build Relationships for Personal and Organizational Success.* New York: McGraw-Hill, 1994.

Bolton, Robert. *People Skills: How to Assert Yourself, Listen to Others, and Resolve Conflicts.*

DeBono, Edward. *Six Thinking Hats.* Boston: Little, Brown, 1985.

Deep, Sam, and Lyle Sussman. *What to Ask When You Don't Know What to Say: 555 Powerful Questions to Use for Getting Your Way at Work.* Englewood Cliffs, N.J.: Prentice Hall, 1993.

Fisher, Roger, and William Ury. *Getting to Yes: Negotiating Agreement Without Giving In.* New York: Penguin, 1986.

Gillette, Jonathon, and Marion McCollom. *Groups in Context: A New Perspective on Group Dynamics.* Menlo Park: Addison-Wesley, 1990.

Lipnack, Jessica, and Jeffrey Stamps. *The TeamNet Factor: Bringing the Power of Boundary Crossing into the Heart of Your Business.* Essex Junction, Vt.: Oliver Wight Publications, 1993.

McKay, Matthew, Martha Davis, and Patrick Fanning. *How to Communicate: The Ultimate Guide to Improving Your Personal and Professional Relationships.* New York: MJF Books, 1983.

Mooney, William, and Donald Noone. *ASAP: The Fastest Way to Make a Memorable Speech.* Hauppauge, N.J.: Barrons, 1992.

Wiener, Valerie. *Power Communications: Positioning Yourself for High Visibility.* New York: New York University Press, 1994.

Zucker, Elaina. *The Seven Secrets of Influence.* New York: McGraw-Hill, 1991.

Innovator Role

DeBono, E. *Lateral Thinking: Creativity Step-by-Step.* New York: Harper & Row, 1970.

Goldratt, Eliyahu. *Theory of Constraints.* Croton-on-Hudson, N.Y.: North River Press, 1990.

Kanter, Rosabeth Moss. *The Change Masters: Innovation for Productivity in the American Corporation.* New York: Simon & Schuster, 1983.

Kelly, James N., and Francis J. Gouillart. *Transforming the Organization.* New York: McGraw-Hill, 1995.

McCarthy, J. Allan. *The Transition Equation: A Proven Strategy for Organizational Change.* New York: Free Press, 1994.

Ogilvy, James. *Living Without a Goal: Finding the Freedom to Live a Creative and Innovative Life.* New York: Currency-Doubleday, 1995.

O'Toole, James. *Leading Change: Overcoming the Ideology of Comfort and the Tyranny of Custom.* San Francisco: Jossey-Bass, 1995.

Price Waterhouse Change Integration Team. *Better Change: Best Practices for Transforming Your Organization.* Homewood, Ill.: Irwin Professional Publishing, 1994.

Senge, Peter M. *The Fifth Discipline: The Art and Practice of the Learning Organization.* New York: Currency-Doubleday, 1990.

Shefsky, Lloyd E. *Entrepreneurs Are Made: Secrets From 200 Successful Entrepreneurs.* New York: McGraw-Hill, 1994.

Whyte, David. *The Heart Aroused.* New York: Currency-Doubleday, 1994.